DATE DUE

MY 21 '97			
AP 16 '97			
DE 2 '97			
DE 7 '98			
NV 24 '99			
OC 18 '99			
JE 6 '00			
NO			
AP 17 '01			
OC 5 '01			
FE 11 '03			
FE 15 '03			
FE 3 '04			
OC 18 '04			

DEMCO 38-296

THE CLINTON PRESIDENCY

THE CLINTON PRESIDENCY
First Appraisals

Edited by

Colin Campbell
and
Bert A. Rockman

Chatham House Publishers
Chatham, New Jersey

THE CLINTON PRESIDENCY
First Appraisals

Chatham House Publishers, Inc.
Box One, Chatham, New Jersey 07928

Publisher: Edward Artinian
Editor: Christopher J. Kelaher
Production supervisor: Katharine F. Miller
Jacket and cover design: Lawrence Ratzkin
Composition: Bang, Motley, Olufsen
Printing and binding: R.R. Donnelley and Sons Company

LIBRARY OF CONGRESS CATALOGING-IN-PUBLICATION DATA

The Clinton presidency : first appraisals / edited by Colin Campbell and Bert A. Rockman.
    p.   cm.
Includes bibliographical references and index.
ISBN 1-56643-013-5 (cloth). — ISBN 1-56643-014-3 (paper)
   1. United States—Politics and government—1993– . 2. Clinton, Bill, 1946– . I. Campbell, Colin, 1943– . II. Rockman, Bert A.
E885.C55   1996
973.929′092—dc20

95-22611
CIP

Manufactured in the United States of America
10 9 8 7 6 5 4 3 2 1

Contents

Tables and Figures

Tables

Figures

Introduction

COLIN CAMPBELL AND BERT A. ROCKMAN

This volume follows on one we published in 1991 assessing the Bush presidency at midterm. A great deal has happened in the intervening four years,
the most surprising being that George Bush is no longer president. Bush's
failure to win reelection seemed unlikely at the time and so should sober
anyone inclined to write off Bill Clinton in 1996. When our volume on his
presidency was going to press, Bush was reaping the benefits of a huge rally
effect based on the ousting of Saddam Hussein's forces from Kuwait through
Operation Desert Storm. Although he had given a lackluster performance in
domestic policy, the public seemed to expect not much more than this. It
seemed that Bush had called it right. In an age of fiscal constraint, the public
would excuse the president for focusing on his commander-in-chief role at
the expense of his chief legislator role. In fact, the ink had hardly dried on
the Bush volume when the public mood soured in the midst of an economic
downturn and began to view Bush less charitably for his lack of attention to
domestic matters. Among other issues that he was especially criticized for
neglecting was the future of health care. Public opinion and political fate can
both be fickle.

Rivaling the demise of the Bush administration for surprise value was
the ascendancy of Bill Clinton to the Oval Office. When Clinton announced
his candidacy in the fall of 1991, Campbell was approached by his university's student newspaper to offer his views. Throwing caution to the winds,
he proclaimed that "most Democrats will view Bill Clinton as a Republican
in Democrat's clothing, so he doesn't stand a snowball's chance in hell in the
[Democratic Party] primaries." There was a kernel of truth in this assessment; we are still, after all, debating Clinton's true political colors. Nevertheless, Bill Clinton is very much president. Chastened by experience, neither of us wants to count him out before the final bell in November 1996.

When comparing this volume with the earlier one assessing Bush, the reader will be struck by the extent to which Bush's goals and the context in which he was operating were relatively harmonious in comparison with the disharmony between Clinton's aspirations and his context. The Bush book mostly saw the Bush presidency as a limited presidency in a rather unusual time of limited expectations. It argued that Bush generally was performing in a way the public saw as appropriate given his circumstances. (The public, of course, would change its assessment soon thereafter.) The authors high-lighted especially the constricting legacy left by Ronald Reagan. Bush had a hard act to follow in Ronald Reagan, who cut a compelling figure. The Rea-gan era's legacy of limits accorded well with Bush's limited aspirations, but it would have its downside for a president with an ambitious policy agenda, such as Bill Clinton. The budget deficit that played havoc with Bush's cam-paign promise of no new taxes would limit even more a president disposed to policy entrepreneurship and activist government. Clinton, the policy wonk, entered the candy store just as its shelves had been emptied.

While Bush was seen in the earlier volume as a figure limited by his times and by his own desires to leave well enough alone, this volume clearly takes note of the discrepancy between Clinton's policy ambitions and the constraints of his policy and political environment. Clinton, too, is often seen to contribute to his problems. Many authors believe that Clinton has not adequately defined who he is. A number of contributors think that he ran as a "New Democrat" but, as president, failed to adhere to this centrist view of the future of his own party. He flirted instead with policies and per-sonnel choices that failed to expand on his core Democratic base and there-fore put in danger his New Democratic identity. A few authors think that his flirtation with the center has itself been problematic and is the main source of his political identity problems.

Many authors also cite difficulties involving Clinton's character and style of leadership. While such factors may be less influential than ones in-volving political resources, such as the power bases provided by the presi-dent's electoral mandate and the makeup of Congress, this volume tries to connect such political considerations with an equally full examination of Clinton's personal character and leadership style. How, above all, has his personal character added to or detracted from his political resources? How, furthermore, has he managed his political resources?

Every contributor, as well, gives some attention to core questions about the viability of presidential leadership in the current era, recognizing that the potential for gridlock between the president and Congress stems from an integral part of the Constitution, namely, the separation of powers. Realisti-cally, a vast institutional overhaul is not in the cards, and what it would pro-duce is in fact uncertain. The contributors to this volume, though, have con-cluded that the dynamics of the separation of powers have changed in substantial ways.

Presidents face a very different art of the possible today than they did in the middle part of this century when many of our images of executive leadership became imprinted. Ronald Reagan obviously enjoyed his experience with the presidency. And most Americans seemed to approve of his stewardship. But Reagan's presidency was a harrowing joy ride for some Americans, and it exacerbated some already difficult problems. In their own ways, Bush and Clinton have served more responsibly and diligently. For their efforts, Bush received the ignominy of defeat in 1992 and Clinton suffered the loss of both chambers of Congress in 1994 and the risk of his remaining years in office becoming an irrelevancy. Does this tell us that the presidency has become viable only for someone prepared to carry out an ideological mission undisturbed and unperplexed by annoying facts? If it makes any sense to work at being president, how ought an incumbent work at it?

How This Book Is Organized

This book includes eleven separate assessments of the Clinton administration, followed by Walter Dean Burnham's chapter, which projects the political force likely to affect the 1996 elections. Chapter 1, by Charles O. Jones, sets the stage by locating the performance to date of the Clinton administration within the wider context of American democracy, especially the operation of the separation of powers. In chapter 2, Colin Campbell focuses on changes in the institutional leverage of the presidency and associated problems with the organization and operation of the Clinton White House.

Three chapters examine the Clinton administration from the perspective of the different branches of government. Barbara Sinclair analyzes the relations between Clinton and Congress (chapter 3); David O'Brien (chapter 4) provides an inventory of Clinton's effect on the judiciary; and Joel D. Aberbach (chapter 5) assesses Clinton's impact on the executive branch through both selection and placement of political appointees and the use of permanent officials.

The next three chapters look into other elements of the political system impinging on the operation of the Clinton administration. In chapter 6, Harold Stanley takes stock of changes in the U.S. party system, as revealed in the 1992 and 1994 elections, and their implications for Bill Clinton's policy and political possibilities. In chapter 7, Graham K. Wilson offers an overview of Clinton's experience with efforts to mobilize interest-group support for his various initiatives. In chapter 8, George Edwards ponders what went wrong with Clinton's ability—manifest during the primaries and the 1992 election campaign—to rally public opinion.

Next, two chapters bring us to the question of what difference the Clinton administration, with all the strengths and weaknesses identified in the preceding chapters, has made in policy terms. Paul Quirk and Joseph Hinchliffe (chapter 9) assess the administration's performance in the broad sweep of domestic policy, while Larry Berman and Emily O. Goldman (chapter 10) take on a similar task in foreign policy.

Chapter 11 by Bert A. Rockman distills the results of looking at Clinton from all of the above perspectives. He then draws a number of conclusions about what the experience of the Clinton administration is telling us about the current state of executive leadership in the United States. Chapter 12 by Walter Dean Burnham closes out this volume with provocative reflections on whether Clinton's difficulties and the stunning results of the 1994 congressional elections indicate that the U.S. political system has gone through a major transformation, perhaps even a partisan realignment.

Some Things to Look For

All the chapters in this book register, in varying magnitude and kind, reservations about the performance of the Clinton administration to date. None of them is likely to bring much cheer to those inside the administration, nor do they augur especially well for Clinton's reelection prospects in 1996. More fundamentally, many of the chapters worry about what the experience of the Clinton administration tells us about the health of the American political system. Under current circumstances, what is the likelihood that politics as it has evolved recently will serve up incumbents who can actually be effective in the presidency?

In this regard, Jones helps bring us back to the fundamental institutional arrangement that structures American politics, namely, the separation of powers. No other functioning democratic system has enshrined the principle of separation of powers between the executive, legislative, and judicial branches of government to the degree that the United States has. Institutional traditions have embellished and, for the most part, further complicated the ways in which the separation of powers works. In addition, the American people have helped sustain the separation of powers through an enduring preference for, but sporadic frustration at, institutional checks on political power. Clinton's failure to eliminate gridlock, contrary to the hopes of sympathetic observers and his supporters, stems, in Jones's view, from a failure to understand that each administration must forge partnerships with Congress in order to govern. Clinton's political strategy, from this perspective, never got past the campaign, where the maxim is to maximize.

Clinton thus assumed a majoritarian strategy, without having a majority. He accepted more or less exclusively his party's congressional leadership, believing that it could deliver majorities on his behalf. But Clinton's party majority in the first half of his term did not necessarily translate into policy majorities. To achieve these, he would need help across party lines—a political tactic that he avoided until it was too late.

Jones accepts that certain presidents must employ compensatory approaches to help them gradually close the gap between high expectations and weak electoral mandates. An important compensatory strategy employed by Clinton was to go public.[1] Far too often, he took his appeals on the road or to the airwaves, perhaps cheapening the presidential currency and serving ultimately to confuse, rather than clarify, the presidential message. By going to the bank too often, Clinton may have left too little in his political account.

What is Jones's advice to Clinton for the remainder of the term? Stop aggressive agenda setting and engage Congress in bargaining of the kind that ultimately can lead to compromise.

Campbell likewise sees Clinton's problems, to a degree, as rooted in the nature of the Constitution. Divided government, where one party controls the presidency and another controls one or both chambers of Congress, makes us especially aware of the significance of the separation of powers. Yet the separation of powers also influences, if to a lesser degree, unified government, when the same party controls both the presidency and Congress. This result is produced by the distinctive electoral dynamics of the separate campaigns waged for the presidency, the House of Representatives, and the Senate.

A situation has emerged in which presidents seem hobbled by the institutional constraints associated with the separation of powers. In an era of confused and even intemperate politics, the public sends garbled messages —if in an angry voice. The confusion and distemper make it very difficult for presidents to identify the core themes, amplify them, and lead the nation in new directions, as Clinton presumably has wanted to do. Campbell expresses a concern that these formidable conditions have lulled us into a minimalist view of what a president can do. He notes that a "let's deal" approach, similar to Jones's bargaining approach, probably serves as the most realistic objective for incumbents under the current circumstances. Lowering presidential sights, however, cannot serve as a justification for inattention to and underengagement of the apparatus available for the president to do his job.

Here Campbell's analysis focuses on Bill Clinton's organization and operation of the White House. It asserts that from the outset Clinton failed to pay careful attention to these aspects of his presidency. The usual scenario has played itself out. More experienced hands have come in to replace older ones, but can Clinton still get a grip on his administration? This remains to be seen over the next two years, but so far this administration's operations and those of the principal himself tempt Campbell to conclude that Clinton is so pathologically a-institutional that no manner of reorganization of his team would have any lasting effects.

Consistent with her contribution to the previous volume on George

Bush, Barbara Sinclair assesses Clinton's relationship with Congress by reiterating a crucial point about factors determining presidential performance. Structural and contextual effects, Sinclair claims, are more important than the skill of the president and his team, notwithstanding some possible lack thereof in President Clinton.

Sinclair notes that the public's desire to end gridlock provided exceptionally strong incentives for Clinton and congressional Democrats to work together. The lack of experience of the two, however—the former in Washington and the latter in unified government—meant that the potential institutional synergy failed to come to full fruition. On the basis of extensive interviews, Sinclair argues that Clinton set up an effective congressional liaison staff in the White House. Yet Clinton could not reap the full benefits of this staff. He overloaded it by imposing too many initiatives without attention to proper sequencing. Nor did he know how to bargain to greatest effect—compromising too early in some instances and too late in others. Perhaps too often he let his former campaign aides, who came to occupy key positions in the White House, override the liaison office's strategic and tactical advice.

In the end, however, the Republicans came together in both chambers in massive solidarity against the administration's initiatives. Where they could not work their will through majorities in the House, they utilized the filibuster in the Senate to block Clinton's proposals. The seeming reimposition of gridlock toward the end of the second session of the 103rd Congress apparently worked to jeopardize the Democratic majority and with it any prospects that Clinton had for advancing his legislative agenda in the now Republican-dominated 104th Congress.

David M. O'Brien's chapter assesses Clinton's effects on legal policy and the courts. These appear to be mixed. On the one hand, Clinton has not succeeded at two fundamental elements of presidential leadership: the communication of a clear and convincing political vision and the installation of a strong and loyal staff to help bring that vision to fruition. On the other hand, O'Brien credits Clinton with making a commendable series of appointments to the federal courts. His appointments have been strong both on professional criteria, as judged by the American Bar Association, and in promoting diversity on the federal bench. Clinton seems to have followed a New Democratic approach in this area, eschewing an ideological missionary one. Clinton also has brought Congress back into the process by restoring the custom of senatorial courtesy, abandoned by Jimmy Carter and his successors, whereby on federal district court vacancies the president defers to nominations from the homestate senators.

O'Brien's real concerns about Clinton's management of legal policy and judicial appointments stem from his confusing signals and his difficulties in managing appointments. These difficulties manifested themselves during the search for an attorney general and in the filling of other key positions in the Justice Department. It extended even to his two Supreme Court nominations, the first of which took an unprecedented three months. In the 1992 election campaign Clinton said that he would appoint a pro-choice justice. When a position became vacant, Clinton indicated that he wanted a person with elective experience who had a feel for the impact that the law had on people's lives. He did not want a legal technician as such. His first nominee, Ruth Bader Ginsburg, was, among other things, a superb legal technician. But she had no political experience and had expressed reservations as to whether the Supreme Court's 1973 *Roe* v. *Wade* decision was an appropriate one. (Her argument was not anti-choice, of course, but concluded instead that political means were opening up for pro-choice forces and that the political route would have provided a more legitimate path to a similar outcome.) Before making his second nomination, Clinton indicated that he wanted someone "with a big heart," preferably again a political figure. He ended up with Stephen Breyer, a highly regarded jurist and superb legal technician, who in these respects was scarcely distinguishable from Justice Ginsburg.

O'Brien is most critical of Clinton's inconsistencies in legal policy. While advocating gay rights in the military, for example, Clinton allowed the Defense Department to pursue a hard line against gays and lesbians in cases concerning the military. On a different matter, that of child pornography, the Justice Department in the case of *Knox* v. *United States* twice reversed its position under pressure from the right and the left, thereby adding fuel to an already volatile controversy.

Joel D. Aberbach examines the executive branch under Clinton from two perspectives, that of career civil servants and that of political appointees. Aberbach traces developments in the career ranks over the past twenty-five years. He notes that the extant assumption that the permanent officials represent a bastion of Democratic, or at least anti-Republican, sentiment no longer obtains. A potential for symbiosis therefore existed between the more centrist career civil service and Bill Clinton's aspirations to pursue a New Democrat's agenda. In fact, though, Clinton seemed to provide little discernible direction, or otherwise pay much attention, to the bureaucracy. Seemingly, Clinton's main emphasis was to achieve diversity in his political appointments. The most significant impact of the president's approach became the appearance of disorganization associated with delays in getting credible appointees nominated and confirmed because the appointees so often had to meet criteria that would enable Clinton to point to the diversity of his administration. Despite these obstacles, Aberbach finds that Clinton has adhered to strong meritocratic norms in his appointees.

Aberbach pays substantial attention to the National Performance Review (NPR) that has taken place under the Clinton administration's banner of reinventing government—a vintage New Democratic theme. He echoes concerns registered elsewhere that the NPR has promoted simplistic views of how red tape might be reduced and how agency clients might be transformed into "customers." While not wholly unsympathetic with the objectives of NPR, Aberbach also notes that the NPR is insufficiently anchored to either the political system or the administrative system. It frequently overrides or remains blissfully unaware of statutory mandates. It also tends to ignore the potential role of the Senior Executive Service (top-level civil servants) in managing change. In view of past efforts at administrative reform, Aberbach remarks that the launching of the NPR has about it "an eerie ahistoricity" as to how to build on reform efforts over the past twenty years.

Harold W. Stanley's chapter is the first of three that turn our attention outside the formal governmental compass to the wider political environment. Stanley first lays the groundwork by showing us how changes in the party system, manifest in the 1992 election, impinged on the art of the possible for Bill Clinton as president. In a sense, Clinton found himself a hostage of gridlock even though he won the election by successfully selling himself as the candidate best able to dispel it. Clinton could not deliver on this promise, and Stanley holds that this failure is at the core of the public indictment of Clinton's performance as manifested in the 1994 midterm elections.

What did Clinton do wrong from this standpoint? In Stanley's view, Clinton failed to fulfill his pledge to function as a New Democrat. With the exception of his promotion of the North American Free Trade Agreement (NAFTA), Clinton was perceived to govern as a traditional Democrat, staking out opening positions on the left and then trying to buy votes by easing himself to the center. The cumulative effect of this approach and its associated partisan struggles and concessions to special interests apparently reignited rather than dispelled public concerns about gridlock.

Graham K. Wilson's chapter closely examines the role of interest groups during the Clinton administration. He notes how much the interest-group universe has expanded and how much more complicated this makes a president's political and governing problems. Wilson concludes also that interest-group political strategies have become increasingly sophisticated in their tactics. In some respects, especially on matters that seemed most central to his own policy agenda, Clinton was outflanked by interests he needed either to bring along or to outmaneuver. He was unable to do either (at least often enough), and the question is, why? Some of the answer is that maneuvering in this game is now inherently more difficult, especially for Democrats. Some of it, however, is that Clinton lacked Washington experience and bargaining and mobilizing strategies. He may have antagonized some groups by confrontation. With others, he lost the struggle because their message came to dominate his. Clinton's own personal amiability and flexibility often worked to his disadvantage. He thought a good president should listen to different claimants. His tendencies, however, were to agree with them at the end, therefore leaving them and him uncertain. Clinton's somewhat plastic political identity and his perceived need to position himself in the center often led him to beat up on friends, such as labor in the NAFTA debate, as well as foes, such as pharmaceutical manufacturers and insurance companies.

George C. Edwards III analyzes Clinton's effectiveness in rallying public support. Charles Jones's chapter noted Clinton's pursuit of a compensatory strategy for his administration to try to close the gap between his weak electoral mandate and relatively ambitious policy aspirations. Edwards probes how this approach has worked out in practice.

Edwards stresses the degree to which the administration displayed both an exceptional interest in polls and a high degree of confidence that it could modulate its tactics and priorities so as to maximize returns in the form of public support. He notes that Clinton's pollster, Stan Greenberg, boasted at the outset of the administration that it would prove to be "a presidency that integrates its policy goals and its communications abilities." The Clinton administration then proceeded to spend almost ten times as much on polls in 1993 alone as George Bush spent in his first two years in office.

Yet all these resources did not finally achieve Greenberg's aspiration to mesh policy and communication. The Clinton administration came into office more like a wounded duck than a soaring eagle. Its political mandate was considerably less than compelling, but like most administrations of policy ambition, it took what it had been given and tried to make more of it —more than it really could. Exit polls from the 1992 election, for example, suggested the degree to which the election was an anti-Bush rather than a pro-Clinton result. Edwards observes, for instance, that 54 percent of exit poll respondents wanted lower taxes and were willing to tolerate fewer services. Edwards ticks off a bill of particulars highlighting the degree to which the administration failed either to accommodate this reality or reverse it. A key here is the drag provided by Clinton's character problems. A president whom the public does not trust may be one it will not follow. In addition, the harrowing and ugly nature of many of the administration's legislative victories contributed to the president's difficulties. Clinton was less often seen as pulling rabbits out of hats than as being picked apart by legislators from his own party. Finally, Clinton was unable to derive any sustained rally effect from those instances where he performed decisively in foreign affairs.

Paul J. Quirk and Joseph Hinchliffe provide the first of two chapters focusing on Clinton's performance in advancing his policy agenda. Quirk and Hinchliffe look at domestic issues. They set the stage by underscoring the difficulty of pursuing New Democrat policies given the atmospherics of American politics. Such an approach would rely on coalitions of moderate Democrats and Republicans that would likely face endless assaults from the right and the left. Both extremes could mobilize to fan opposition within their respective parties. At the outset, the fact that congressional Democrats, especially in the House, did not fit the centrist mold that Bill Clinton campaigned on meant that he would have to buck his own party if he promoted New Democrat positions without some accommodation to the left, a point made subsequently in Bert Rockman's chapter.

Perhaps a stronger and more savvy leader could have coped with the ambiguities served up by these political realities. Quirk and Hinchliffe identify in Clinton's case a process whereby the president never effectively staked out or consistently defended New Democrat or, for that matter, old Democrat positions. The Republicans were consistently able to paint Clinton as a tax-and-spend liberal. From this perspective Clinton's victories, at least in retrospect, were both narrow and shallow. The 1993 budget victory rested exclusively on Democratic votes. And perhaps because of that, it failed to launch other legislative successes. Again from this perspective, the administration seemed unable to identify when flexibility might accomplish more than rigidity. Clinton's dare to Congress on universal health-care coverage boomeranged, just as Bush's "no new taxes" pledge had done. Each wound up looking like a case of unsustainable posturing.

Consistent with a number of other contributors, Quirk and Hinchliffe point to Clinton's character problems and his ineffective management of decision-making processes as factors exacerbating his difficulties in delivering on the domestic policy side—difficulties that, for the most part, were hardly in need of being further exacerbated.

Larry Berman and Emily O. Goldman cover Bill Clinton's performance in the field of foreign policy. They begin by presenting a picture of how radically global politics has changed since the end of the Cold War. They emphasize that the new world circumstances present the United States with no central organizing principle for its foreign policy. In addition, the United States faces a situation in which alliances, most significantly NATO, no longer as sharply define its relationships with and commitments to other countries.

The circumstances probably call for more, rather than less, presidential attention to international affairs. Clinton, however, has displayed neither a strong interest in nor a clear aptitude for foreign affairs. Berman and Goldman argue that the current situation calls for reconceptualizing the dangers faced by the United States and an ability to communicate these to the public. Instead, they see in Clinton a president easily swayed by political exigencies and seemingly incapable of identifying for the public the core issues faced by the United States in a changed world. While the authors point to several cases to illustrate their contentions, they direct their most severe criticism to Clinton's handling of most favored nation (MFN) trade status for China and his treatment of North Korea's development of nuclear arms. In both instances they see him backing away from the opportunity to define and clarify the American position in the post–Cold War world.

Bert Rockman provides the final chapter assessing Bill Clinton by taking stock of what Clinton's presidency tells us about the current state and foreseeable future of executive leadership in the national political arena. He notes that in the aftermath of the 1992 election there were high expectations that Clinton and the Democratic Congress would cooperate. As matters turned out, they both did and did not. Cooperation proved to be possible on some things but less so on others. Yet cooperation between the White House and the Democratic majority in Congress was made more difficult, rather than less, by the solid phalanx of Republican opposition. Republican opposition gave pivotal members of the Democratic majority extra incentive to hold out. The fact is that there was incentive to hold out, for even Clinton's victories turned into disasters for members of his congressional party in the 1994 election. Tax increases, gun restrictions, and liberal social policies all galvanized opposition to him and to his party.

Rockman raises the issue of the viability of the Democrats as a presidential party. He ponders whether the Clinton presidency was doomed to failure by virtue of what his party demanded but neither the system nor the party could supply, namely, sufficient cohesion for expansion of the programmatic role of government. As a political leader frequently torn between alternatives, Clinton had difficulties coping with the internal dilemma of leadership in the Democratic Party. How does one move a fragmented party to positions of greater viability in the general atmosphere of contemporary American politics and still retain the loyalty of core constituencies whose views about the role of government provide the adhesive for the party's agenda? Clinton's dilemma in the end, as it is with the rare successful Democratic presidential candidate these days, is the need to avoid being pegged programmatically in order to win the presidency. Then, having won, the candidate lacks clear identity and comes under attack from all sides.

Walter Dean Burnham's chapter places the experiences of the Clinton presidency and the 1994 election results in a broader historical perspective. Burnham finds that the 1994 outcome flies in the face of conventional wisdom in political science. Especially during the 1980s, it became clear that partisan loyalty was playing a substantially reduced role in voting behavior in the United States and other advanced democracies. Thus, analysts developed the view that "dealignment" had brought about the most change in electoral outcomes. For instance, the shift of Reagan Democrats to the Republicans in 1980, 1984, and 1988 did not mark a permanent realignment. These voters simply were keeping their options open in presidential elections while voting Democratic in others. In fact, a large proportion of them supported Ross Perot in 1992.

If we can think of presidential Democrats and congressional Democrats, dealignment was bad for the former but not necessarily for the latter. Burnham's analysis presents a bleaker picture for the Democrats. The proportions of the swing toward the Republicans—at state levels as well as on the federal level—suggest that the dam has broken and the Republicans may become the natural party of government for perhaps a generation. If the 1994 election marks a true realignment, then we might expect the Democrats to come back into hegemony during the next generational swing, which will probably be in twenty-five to thirty years.

Despite the depth of the swing to the Republicans in the 1994 election, however, the imputed realignment did not take classic form in every respect. It occurred relatively soon after the last realignment, it did not take root in a major triggering event such as a war or depression, and it did not generate a substantial increase in voter turnout.

Burnham identifies white middle-class males, 30–44 years old—the Great Protestant White Middle (GPWM)—as the group that propelled so many Republicans to victory in 1994. These voters, Burnham maintains, feel especially the consequences of the U.S.'s economic decline over the past two decades and the growing realities of increased violence in society. It is too early to tell whether the Republicans can respond sufficiently to the GPWM's demands to convince them to vote for the Republican nominee in the 1996 presidential election.

If Bill Clinton wins reelection, we could imagine major prospects for gridlock and deepened GPWM disaffection. The GPWM could be highly susceptible to appeals by a third-party candidate. The opposite situation, one in which Republicans controlled the White House, the Senate, and the House of Representatives, might result in policies so focused on the GPWM that other segments of society become militant about their own protection. Burnham cites Andrew Kohut, the pollster who said in March 1995 that the Democrats seemed to be "asleep out there." What happens if they awaken? Such an occurrence would certainly quicken the rejuvenation of the Democratic Party. It remains to be seen, however, whether the aggrieved in aggregate would constitute the nucleus of the next realignment. Clearly, the United States is going through a major political convulsion. Burnham's chapter gives us a sense of just how uncertain the future is.

Systems and Skills

The authors of this volume seek to connect elements of Clinton's leadership style and ability to a political system that is always difficult to maneuver and a set of political circumstances that had been interpreted as being open to new possibilities but was in fact constrained by its narrow political leeway. Bill Clinton brought singularly large assets and liabilities to his job, but he certainly brought with him little clear mandate. How he should have reacted to this condition remains debatable. There are hunches as to what he might have done better but no definitive conclusions that better results would have been forthcoming had he done things differently.

Whatever differences of emphasis exist between the various contributors to this volume are likely to rest on the issue of how much was within Clinton's capacity to control. Another difference, we suspect, is what it might mean to do it better. Some say New Democrat, others say old Democrat; some say accommodate, others say anchor yourself; some say compromise, others say stiffen resolve; and so on and on. Examining Clinton's presidency after his party has suffered shattering losses of its congressional majorities is not likely to be kind to an assessment of his leadership skills or his political prospects. At the same time, the galvanizing of opposition to Clinton's party during the 1994 elections may have had more to do with his successes—particularly the banning of assault weapons, the Brady bill, and the overturning of Reagan-Bush executive orders such as the gag rule on abortion counseling and the fetal tissue ban—than with his failures. Supporters of the National Rifle Association (NRA) and the Christian Coalition were highly mobilized and disproportionately represented in the 1994 electorate. One must inevitably wonder, moreover, what we would have been saying were we writing about Truman's leadership skills and political prospects in 1947. Thinking such thoughts is inevitably humbling. And that exercise leads us to conclude that there is much of Clinton's tenure in office ahead of him. We are only a bit past the first half.

Half-Time Is Still Half-Time

In our midterm assessment of George Bush, there were scarcely any signs pointing to his failure to win reelection. By contrast, the current volume underscores the many respects in which the Clinton administration's bright promise appears to have been doused. Such an assessment does not necessarily translate into assertions on the part of our authors that Clinton will be defeated in 1996. The Republicans must do at least three things to give themselves a chance for that to happen. First, they must demonstrate that they can break the appearance that gridlock still holds the system in its grip. Second, if they are able to do so, they will need to ensure that their initiatives resonate with public concerns. Third, they must come up with a viable candidate for the presidency. None of these tasks will be easy to carry out.

Some observers might be tempted to interpret the 1994 election results as something akin to Clinton's going into the locker room well behind his opponent at half-time. The game is really much closer than that—perhaps a tie or a slight half-time edge in favor of the Republicans. Whatever the expectations in the stands that the Clinton team could turn things around, the initial plays in the third quarter will be crucial. The few that have taken place do not yet seem to provide a clear trend to what lies ahead. The Republicans, in contrast, especially those in the House, have shown the promise that derives from clarity of conviction. It may help them, at least initially, that they have a game plan—their "Contract with America." Sooner or later, however, the system is likely to slow the progress of their bold initiatives. If so, that is American politics as it normally is—Newt Gingrich and his hordes will be subject to the conditions that have influenced the prospects of Bill Clinton's presidency. If not, and we may know in 1996, this could prove to be a rare moment of unambiguous political signals and thus a rare moment of distinctive partisan victory on behalf of an equally clear policy agenda. We recommend watching but not betting.

Note

1. Samuel Kernell, *Going Public: New Strategies for Presidential Leadership* (Washington, D.C.: CQ Press, 1986).

I

Campaigning to Govern:
The Clinton Style

CHARLES O. JONES

As reported in Bob Woodward's *The Agenda*, "Mandy Grunwald [media adviser to President Clinton] ... repeated her belief that the president's popularity first had to be improved, and then Congress could be moved by a popular president." "It's a bank shot, ... What you say to the American people bounces back to the Congress."[1] By this one-track plebiscitary theory, the president engages in a continuous campaign to close the gap in the separated system between the presidency, the House, and the Senate. Yet each of the three institutions is independently elected and intentionally disconnected by the design of the constituencies and term length for each. By the Grunwald theory, however, the purpose of active presidential campaigning is to create a dependency—Congress on the presidency—that is at odds with the separationist government designed by the Founders.

The "bank shot" is a version of the "going public" strategy that Samuel Kernell identifies as characteristic of contemporary presidential politics. Kernell asserts that campaigning for policies "is a strategic choice grounded as much in contemporary political relations as in available technology."[2] Perhaps the Clinton presidency completes the transition to a campaign style of governing, Clinton being the first of the so-called baby boomers to move into the White House, the first president to have grown up with television. If true, then it is important to study this presidency for the lessons to be learned about governing the nation in the twenty-first century.

This chapter reviews the presidency in the post–World War II period so as to place Clinton in comparative perspective, identifies President Clinton's political resources on entering office, discusses the problems associated with organizing his presidency, reviews the Clinton priorities and the style relied on to achieve them, analyzes his domestic and foreign policy record during the first two years in office, and examines the 1994 midterm election results. A final assessment includes a forecast of what the future might hold for this new-generation president.

The Presidency in a Separated System

In August 1993 I presented a paper on the American presidency at a conference in Taegu, South Korea. My presentation was followed by one on the South Korean presidency. In this second paper no mention was made of the National Assembly, South Korea's legislature. I cannot conceive of a credible analysis of presidential power in the United States that failed to mention Congress. The difference is, of course, that South Korea has a strong presidential system, the United States has a separated system. Ours is not a separation of powers into well-delineated cubicles. As Richard E. Neustadt has observed, what we have instead is "separated institutions *sharing* powers."[3] It is apparent that these institutions, particularly the House, Senate, and the presidency, often *compete* for shared powers. Thus a first postulate in understanding the role of any one president is that *the presidency was never intended to be the whole government.* The principal challenge for a new president is in designing a strategy for competing in the separated system.

A second postulate is simply that *presidents are not created equal.* As shown in table 1.1, they come to the White House under a variety of circumstances. Some are *elected*—that is, they win an initial term outright. In the post–World War II era, this group includes two who won by landslides, Dwight D. Eisenhower and Ronald W. Reagan, and four who won by narrow or modest margins, John F. Kennedy, Richard M. Nixon, Jimmy Carter, and Bill Clinton. Others are *reelected* to a second term. This group includes three Republicans in the modern era, Eisenhower, Nixon, and Reagan, each of whom won by a landslide. There have been three *nonelected* presidents since 1944, that is, vice-presidents serving out the terms of their predecessors: Harry S Truman, Lyndon B. Johnson, and Gerald R. Ford. Two of these, Truman and Johnson, were subsequently elected—yet another variation in entering the White House, since neither would likely have been elected otherwise.[4] Truman won unexpectedly and narrowly, Johnson won in a landslide. And occasionally an *heir apparent* wins the office, as with George Bush in 1988.[5]

A further distinction among presidents is whether their party was successful in winning majorities in the House and Senate, and by what margin. Table 1.1 shows the results for the types of presidents identified above. Note that in seven of the fifteen full or partial presidential terms, the president's

TABLE 1.1
PRESIDENTS ARE NOT CREATED EQUAL

	Presidential vote (%)			Party majority	
	Popular	Two-party	Electoral	House	Senate
Elected/landslide					
Eisenhower	55	55	83	Yes*	Yes*
Reagan	51	55	91	No	Yes
Elected/other					
Kennedy	50	50	56	Yes	Yes
Nixon	43**	50	56	No	No
Carter	50	51	55	Yes	Yes
Clinton	43**	53	69	Yes*	Yes*
Reelected					
Eisenhower	57	58	86	No	No
Nixon	61	62	97	No	No
Reagan	59	59	98	No	Yes*
Nonelected					
Truman	–	–	–	Yes*	Yes*
Johnson	–	–	–	Yes	Yes
Ford	–	–	–	No	No
Elected vice-presidents					
Truman	50**	53	57	Yes	Yes
Johnson	61	61	90	Yes	Yes
Heir apparent					
Bush	53	53	79	No	No

SOURCE: Calculated from data in Harold W. Stanley and Richard G. Niemi, *Vital Statistics on American Politics,* 3d ed. (Washington, D.C.: CQ Press, 1992), tables 3–14; 3–17; pp. 111–15, 122–25.

* The president's party lost its majority in the subsequent midterm election.

** There was a third major candidate in each of these elections: George Wallace, Ross Perot, and Strom Thurmond, respectively.

party lacked majorities in one or both houses of Congress. In three other cases, majorities on entering office were lost in subsequent midterm elections.

These variations in the circumstances and margin of victory direct attention to differences in the political resources and institutional status of presidents. They are the measures of their inequality on entering office. The continuum extends from the landslide winner with substantial majorities in the House and Senate (e.g., Lyndon Johnson following the 1964 election) to the nonelected president facing substantial opposition majorities in the House and Senate (e.g., Ford following the 1974 midterm elections). Note that most presidents are somewhere in the middle, each with strengths and weaknesses for placing themselves into the permanent government.

The third postulate follows directly from the first two: *presidents must design strategies for governing that account for their political resources and governmental status.* Those few with impressive resources and high status, such as Johnson and Reagan, are free to pursue an aggressive strategy. In fact, since their influence is likely to wane, they are well advised to "hit the ground running," as the phrase has it.[6] Reelected presidents often are encouraged to adopt a guardian strategy designed to protect the achievements that won them reelection. Nonelected presidents who have taken over for their popular predecessors may have to employ a custodial strategy, essentially taking custody of the existing record of accomplishments. Those presidents who win narrowly and enter having to establish their status within the government are encouraged to develop a compensatory strategy. This latter group is the largest in the post–World War II period. It includes Truman, Kennedy, Nixon (1968), Carter, and Clinton, each of whom faced the daunting task of meeting the high expectations of the office, yet having to bolster a modest showing at the polls and a poor case for a coattail effect. A first task for these presidents is to create additional sources of power for meeting their obligations in the separated system.

The Clinton Presidency: Status and Resources

An overriding dilemma has characterized the Clinton presidency from the start. On the one hand, the election was advertised as being about *change* —in people, in style, and, mostly, in policy. For many it was time to let the "baby boomers" take over, to modernize leadership, to represent the tortured Vietnam generation. It was time to appoint more women and minorities to positions of influence in the government. It was time to be much more aggressive in reforming major policy programs, as well as the organization and operation of the government. And it was time to concentrate on the home front, giving foreign and national security policy a lower priority than in the recent past.

On the other hand, the separated system is not well designed to produce major changes in a short time. Dividing power across institutions and between levels of government results in protracted decision making. Many persons have the legitimate right to participate in such a system. Various forms of representation are permitted, with the result that the best laid plans are subjected to lengthy consideration through an elaborate lawmaking process.

How is it that we ever get policy breakthroughs in such a system? Mostly it requires a crisis or tragedy so serious as to interrupt the usual tedious and incremental workings of our government. The New Deal was enacted in response to the Great Depression, the Great Society was put in place following the assassination of President Kennedy, and the dramatic multiyear tax cuts were approved in the wake of the serious recession at the end of the Carter presidency (the attempted assassination of President Reagan also played a role). In each of these periods, the president (Roosevelt, Johnson, and Reagan, respectively) entered the White House with a so-called mandate. Each won an overwhelming victory, and each winner's party realized substantial gains in Congress. It was believed in each case that there was reason to bypass the normal lawmaking process.

Do the Clinton circumstances meet these criteria for effecting large change? They do not. There was no crisis or national tragedy. The recession was judged to be mild, though stubborn. Economists were divided on what or whether action should be taken. There was no dramatic event that could be interpreted as providing carte blanche for change by a new administration. And whereas "change" was a dominant theme in the 1992 campaign, the election results did not produce a clear mandate for the winner. The principal change desired by the voters appeared to be that of removing George Bush from the White House. Of those wishing for this outcome, two-thirds voted for Bill Clinton and one-third voted for a sure loser, Ross Perot—hardly a ringing endorsement for the new president.

While no two elections are alike, the Clinton victory in 1992 bears some resemblance to that of Nixon in 1968, when third-party candidate George Wallace ran. Nixon and Hubert H. Humphrey each received 43 percent of the popular vote, Wallace got the rest. Perot received no electoral vote in 1992, however, whereas Wallace garnered 46 votes in 1968. Thus, the two-party electoral count between Clinton (69 percent) and Bush (31 percent) was not very different from that between Nixon (61 percent) and Humphrey (39 percent). Certainly no one judged that Nixon had a strong mandate in 1968, and, in fact, the new president proceeded very cautiously on most policy fronts.[7]

Also relevant to defining the strength of a new president is how his party fared in congressional elections and whether a favorable outcome in those contests displays evidence of coattails. Table 1.2 identifies those cases in this century when the president's party experienced a net loss of seats in the House and/or Senate. Among Republican presidents, George Bush entered office in the least advantageous position. His party was already in a minority in each house and suffered further small net losses. Among Democratic presidents, Woodrow Wilson had the barest of majorities in the House and Senate following the 1916 election, but this was his second term. Bill Clinton had the least advantages among the first-term Democratic presidents. Kennedy had about the same Democratic Party margin in the House but a substantially greater number of Senate Democrats.

A minority vote win akin to that of Nixon in 1968, combined with a net loss of House seats and no gain in the Senate, does not justify declaring a mandate for large change. Lacking a strong showing at the polls, Bill Clinton had to develop a strategy for enhancing his influence, a strategy that

TABLE 1.2

CASES OF THE PRESIDENT'S PARTY EXPERIENCING A NET
LOSS OF SEATS, HOUSE AND/OR SENATE,
1900–92

	House			Senate		
	Net loss	Num-ber left	Percent-age left	Net loss	Num-ber left	Percent-age left
First Term						
Taft, Republican (1908)	−3	219	56	−2	59	64
Kennedy, Democrat (1960)	−20	263	60	−2	64	64
Bush, Republican (1988)	−3	175	40	−1	45	45
Clinton, Democrat (1992)	−10	258	59	0	56	56
Second Term						
Wilson, Democrat (1916)	−21	210	48	−3	53	55
Eisenhower, Republican (1956)	−2	201	46	0	47	49
Reagan, Republican (1984)	*			−2	53	53
Third Term						
Roosevelt, Democrat (1940)	*			−3	66	69

SOURCE: Calculated from data in Harold W. Stanley and Richard G. Niemi, *Vital Statistics on American Politics,* 3d ed. (Washington, D.C.: CQ Press, 1992), table 3-17, pp. 122–25.
* The president's party in these cases experienced a net gain in House seats: +14 in 1984, +5 in 1940.

would moderate the high expectations typically accompanying a change in party control of the White House. Illustrative of these expectations was the judgment by some that the 1992 election produced unified and therefore effective government. By this view, a Democrat in the White House and congressional Democratic majorities in both houses of Congress automatically meant the end of gridlock. As James L. Sundquist explained early into the new administration:

> If the government cannot succeed in the present configuration [a Democratic president and Congress], when can it possibly ever succeed? As Joan Quigley, the former official astrologer, might have said, the stars are really aligned right for the next four years.
>
> The country has finally gotten back to unified government. For the first time in twelve years, somebody is going to be responsible. In the last three election campaigns, the Republican president has been able to say, "Don't blame me, blame those Democrats in control of Congress." And Democrats have been able to say, "Don't blame us, blame the president." Now the day of buck passing and blame shifting is over.[8]

Alas, unified government did not end blame shifting. For example, when Senate Majority Leader George Mitchell (D-Me.) declared in late September 1994 that health-care reform, the president's principal domestic priority, could not be achieved in the 103rd Congress, he blamed "the insurance industry on the outside and a majority of Republicans on the inside...." The Senate Republican leader, Robert J. Dole (R-Kans.), scoffed at this analysis: "Senator Mitchell blames Republicans for everything except the plane that crashed into the White House."[9] As it happens, focused responsibility is not an obvious consequence of the workings of a separated system.

A former Reagan administration official, Kenneth Duberstein, predicted some such outcome at the same meeting in which Sundquist offered his sanguine analysis. Duberstein's view in February 1993 was much more accepting of the separationist politics that characterizes the American system:

> I hope the American people will not be disappointed, but I am concerned that the end of gridlock is unlikely. The system is biased toward gridlock, not toward action....
>
> The American people are rooting for Bill Clinton and rooting for our system of government to work. Yet in spite of both ends of Pennsylvania Avenue being controlled by the same political party, we still will have two competing governments—one on the Hill, one at the White House.... The challenge for Bill Clinton is to find a way to preside over both. And I think the odds, at least institutionally, are against him.[10]

To say that the new president lacked the political standing of a Lyndon Johnson or a Ronald Reagan is not to suggest that he lacked resources. Bill Clinton was of a new generation—the first president born in the post–World War II period. During the long campaign he demonstrated an impressive capacity to identify an agenda of major issues requiring action by government, thereby seemingly connecting with the large majority of Americans also born since 1945. And if the Democrats did not fare that well in the congressional elections, many new-generation representatives and senators were elected, including record numbers of women, blacks, and Hispanics. Though nearly all elected congressional Democrats ran ahead of President Clinton in their states and districts, there was an enthusiasm for showing that Democrats could govern in exactly the manner suggested by Sundquist. Then there was the sheer energy of the Clinton-Gore campaign, demonstrated by the youth and vitality of the candidates themselves and their young staffs. Whether or not there was a mandate, the new team was prepared to propose change by reason of its campaign experience and the excitement of a win over an incumbent president identified with the past.

Getting Organized—The Transition

At least two major transitions occur as a consequence of a presidential election. The first is from candidate to president-elect, the second from president-elect to president. The first is, perhaps, the more dramatic, since it involves a striking shift from a self-centered, intense, collective activity aimed toward a day certain, to a much less focused period in which the winner begins to organize his presidency. No doubt many in this position repeat to themselves, if not to others, the last line from the movie *The Candidate*, as Robert Redford, playing the candidate, pondered what was in store for him once the campaign was over. The line was reportedly used by Bill Clinton's campaign manager at the victory announcement by the president-elect:

> David Wilhelm was walking away, threading his way through the kissing couples and the conga lines on the lawn of the Old State House [in Little Rock]. Turning to the reporters trailing him, he smiled and quoted one of the great and famous questions of politics, "What do we do now?" he said. "Right?"
> . . . .
>
> Mr. Clinton is not Mr. Redford, and Mr. Wilhelm meant the line as a joke, but the question is nevertheless the one of the hour here. After 13 months of life in the tightly wound, sharply focused atmosphere of a presidential campaign, Bill Clinton and the people who helped get him elected got up this morning to find themselves facing the heart of the matter: the framing of a structure of governance.[11]

In making this move from being candidate to serving as president-elect, one imposing task is that of withdrawing from the campaign organization so as to ease into the new and different role as president. This conversion may require breaking ties with loyal aides. And, in fact, it may demand an unnatural act on the part of these aides, that is, to release their candidate so that he may prepare to govern. Having just experienced an intense and emotional commitment to this person, it is difficult to decompress and depart. Yet many may serve the president-elect best by doing so. James Carville, Clinton's campaign strategist, understood these matters as well as anybody in that position ever has. In regard to the campaign itself, he explained that "the cause has to be the candidate." And after it is over? Carville likened it to the stillness following a battle:

> Anyone who's been on a battlefield, whether it's a real battlefield or a political battlefield or a game will know this: There's the smell, the odor, the feel that draws you back after it's done. They say in war it's the smell of cordite, of gunpowder. It stays in the air.
> Same exact thing the morning after an election. All of that emotion and hollering, the shouting, the hugging. It stops and it don't ever come back. It doesn't peter out, it doesn't fade away. It's there; then it's gone. And no one needs you.[12]

Candidate Clinton designated a transition advisory board several weeks before the election. It included former Deputy Secretary of State Warren M. Christopher, former National Urban League President Vernon Jordan, Campaign Chairman Mickey Kantor, former San Antonio Mayor Henry Cisneros, former Vermont Governor Madeleine Kunin, and a long-time Clinton friend from Arkansas, Thomas F. McLarty III.[13] There was the expected infighting and jockeying among staff in the immediate postelection period as aides sought to gain an advantage in the transition. "It's a bloody, ugly mess," one staff member was reported to have said.[14] A part of the problem seemingly developed from animosity toward Mickey Kantor as campaign chairman, with some staff concerned that Kantor might head the transition team. Clinton quickly resolved the matter by appointing Christopher and Jordan to lead the transition operation. He later appointed former Governor Richard Riley (South Carolina) as director of personnel for the transition with the responsibility "to coordinate sub-Cabinet appointments with Mr. Clinton's Cabinet choices."[15] An effort was made to ensure that the White House influenced the selection of those appointed at lower levels so as not to repeat the mistake made in the Carter administration of losing control of these appointments.

Like all transitions, that of President-elect Clinton included both policy and organizational aspects. Since he had promised to "focus like a laser on the economy," Clinton announced an economic conference to be held in Little Rock in mid-December. The purpose was to draw attention to the broad issue and hear from various interests as well as professional economic analysts. Coincidentally, it also provided a stage for the president-elect to display his own knowledge of and concern for the issue, as well as to build public awareness of and support for his efforts. It was an early sign of Clinton's campaigning or outside-in style of governing.

Accomplishing the organizational goals of a transition is an intricate endeavor, requiring the careful screening of potential appointees as well as the establishment of an executive tone for the new administration. Clinton "pledged to the American people that [his] Cabinet will look more like America than previous administrations."[16] In this spirit, the transition team itself reflected racial, ethnic, and gender diversity. The president-elect chose to work with his close campaign aides and the transition group during much of November and December rather than appoint a chief of staff and other White House staff personnel. Thus many aides and advisers were uncertain during this time as to what positions they might eventually assume (though Clinton may well have personally reassured them). Meanwhile, in late November, coordinators were appointed for nine "clusters" of issues, with instructions to report back to the president-elect regarding problems and personnel needs by late December.[17] Coordinators were told not to expect top appointments in the departments and agencies they were reviewing, though

TABLE 1.3
SEQUENCE OF CABINET SECRETARIAL AND
MAJOR WHITE HOUSE APPOINTMENTS,
CLINTON TRANSITION

Cabinet

Department	Appointee (date)	Previous position
Treasury	Lloyd Bentsen (12/10/92)[a]	Senator (Texas)
Labor	Robert Reich (12/11)	Professor (Harvard)
Health and Human Services	Donna Shalala (12/11)	Chancellor (University of Wisconsin)
Environmental Protection Agency	Carol Browner (12/11)[b]	State administrator (Florida)
Commerce	Ronald Brown (12/12)	Democratic Party chairman
Housing and Urban Development	Henry Cisneros (12/17)	Former mayor, San Antonio, Texas
Veterans Affairs	Jesse Brown (12/17)	Executive director, Disabled American Veterans
Education	Richard Riley (12/21)	Former governor, South Carolina
Energy	Hazel O'Leary (12/21)	Executive, power company (Minnesota)
Defense	Les Aspin (12/22)[c]	Representative (Wisconsin)
State	Warren Christopher (12/22)	Former deputy secretary of state
Interior	Bruce Babbitt (12/24)	Former governor, Arizona
Justice	Zoë Baird (12/24)[d]	Executive, insurance company (Connecticut)
Agriculture	Mike Espy (12/24)[e]	Representative (Mississippi)
Transportation	Federico Peña (12/24)	Former mayor, Denver

a. Bentsen was replaced by Robert Rubin.
b. Browner was given cabinet status because the president intended to propose legislation to make EPA a department.
c. Les Aspin was replaced by William Perry.
d. Baird withdrew her name from consideration; Janet Reno was appointed and approved.
e. Espy was replaced by Dan Glickman.

an exception was made for Federico Peña, who headed the transportation cluster and was then appointed secretary of transportation.[18]

Interviews with prospective cabinet secretaries began in November, with the first appointments announced on 10 December, just prior to the economic summit in Little Rock. In keeping with his campaign priorities, the president-elect first appointed an economic team. Senator Lloyd Bentsen (D-Tex.) was the designee as secretary of the treasury and Representative Leon Panetta (D-Calif.) would direct the Office of Management and Budget, with Alice Rivlin, formerly the director of the Congressional Budget Office, as his

TABLE 1.3 — CONTINUED

White House Staff

Position	Appointee (date)
Chief of staff	Thomas F. McLarty III (12/12/92)[f]
Communications director	George Stephanopoulos (1/14/93)[g]
Press secretary	Dee Dee Myers (1/14)[h]
Domestic policy adviser	Carol Rasco (1/14)
Counsel	Bernard Nussbaum (1/14)[i]
Legislative affairs	Howard Paster (1/14)[j]
Political affairs	Joan Baggett (1/14)
Cabinet secretary	Christine Varney (1/14)[k]
Staff secretary	John Podesta (1/14)

f. McLarty was replaced by Leon Panetta.
g. Stephanopoulos was replaced by David Gergen.
h. Myers was replaced by Michael McCurry.
i. Nussbaum was replaced by Lloyd Cutler, who was replaced by Abner Mikva.
j. Paster was replaced by Patrick Griffin.
k. Varney was replaced by Kathryn Higgins.

deputy. Roger Altman and Robert Rubin, both from Wall Street, were appointed deputy secretary of the treasury and director of a new Economic Council, respectively.

As shown in table 1.3, the other cabinet secretaries were appointed during the next two weeks, completing the task just before Christmas. The first to be appointed were the major domestic departmental secretaries. Often the secretaries of state and defense are appointed early in order to send signals to the international community. That Clinton did not adopt this sequence may reflect the changes that occurred with the end of the Cold War as well as his own preferences for domestic policy. Also playing a role, perhaps, was the fact that Warren Christopher was serving as transition director.

The president was true to his word in being attentive to diversity. He appointed more women (four),[19] African Americans (four), and Hispanics (two) than any other president to that time. All but the nominee for attorney general were confirmed on 20 or 21 January. Zoë Baird's nomination as attorney general was withdrawn following revelations concerning the hiring of undocumented illegal aliens as household workers. After a second unsuccessful try to appoint an attorney general (Kimba Wood), Clinton appointed Janet Reno, who won approval.

White House Chief of Staff Thomas F. McLarty III was appointed on 12 December, with the remainder of the staff announced in mid-January 1993. This timing was similar to that of Carter, though Carter did not initially appoint a chief of staff. The other two recent presidencies representing a change in parties, Nixon and Reagan, each designated a chief of staff and other principal White House staff starting in mid-November. Thus the White House staff in those cases was in a position to aid in cabinet and subcabinet selection. Clinton was himself very involved in these decisions, while accepting advice from a coterie of advisers that included his wife and Vice-President-elect Gore.

Hillary Clinton played a very active role in the transition, an indication of her strong influence within the new administration. She interviewed prospective cabinet appointees, "was vested by her husband with selecting an attorney general," would have an office in the West Wing, and had important officials reporting to her. It was understood that she would be in charge of the domestic issues that interested her. "The title Domestic Policy Adviser was seriously considered, but it was decided that Mrs. Clinton would essentially have the role without the title—it would be less threatening."[20]

McLarty was unsure about his new post. And, in fact, there is no job description for the chief of staff, apart from knowing how it is that the president wants to define the position. Howard H. Baker, Jr., who served President Reagan in this capacity, stated that "the office of chief of staff has veered all over the lot in its brief history. Sometimes he is very powerful. Sometimes he is purely an administrative person. Sometimes he is deeply involved in policy formulation. Sometimes he simply effects policy."[21] McLarty judged that "he would not serve as a terribly aggressive gatekeeper."[22] It seemed that Clinton's freewheeling style did not invite a chief of staff system of organization. The description of Presidents Kennedy and Johnson by former Johnson aide Harry McPherson appeared to suit Clinton as well: "Johnson and Kennedy didn't need chiefs. They were very bright men with enormous appetites for information, and what they really wanted was that all things came to them."[23] Still, having a chief of staff in name only came to be a liability for Clinton, and he appointed a Washington-wise Leon Panetta to take over for McLarty in mid-July 1994. As one account had it: "Panetta is ... known for his ability to find the nexus between policy and politics, a credit to his detailed knowledge of both."[24]

There were clear signals from the transition period as to what to expect from the new administration. First was the fidelity to the campaign priority of improving the economy. The president appointed his economic team first and held a much-heralded economic summit. Second was the attention given to diversity in making key appointments. Clinton aggressively pursued affirmative action in building his government. Third were the indications of how personalized would be the organization of the White House. The president-elect did not judge it important to appoint staff early because he and his wife would be intimately involved in making the cabinet and other key appointments. However the final organization might look on paper, it became apparent that it would be a system operating around the president as the main star. Finally, there were strong hints that as president, Bill Clinton would continue to play to the outside, to reach beyond the White House press corps in communicating with the American people.

The Clinton Priorities and How They Changed

During the campaign, James Carville, the political director for the Clinton campaign, placed these reminders on a post near his desk:

> Change vs. more of the same
> The economy, stupid
> Don't forget health care[25]

Loss of the central message was a particular problem for the Clinton campaign because the candidate loved to talk about policy issues and to explore the dimensions of public problems and the range of potential solutions. Clear signals were sent during the transition that stimulating the economy would be the first priority. But the failure to create an organization before the inauguration meant that "beyond the president-elect, there was no central authority, just a lot of people doing a lot of separate work, much of it seemingly unconnected to any concrete plan."[26] According to Woodward's account, the new economic team, led by Rubin, insisted on meeting with Clinton in early January. A meeting was arranged, with Rubin serving as the "master of ceremonies" so as to avoid having it "degenerate into one of the endless, rambling policy seminars that Clinton loved."[27] It was a meeting that lasted for six hours and resulted in educating the president-elect on topics ranging from the importance of reducing the deficit to the future prospects of fulfilling other campaign promises.

Before this meeting, the Office of Management and Budget (OMB) issued significantly larger deficit projections, thus creating the context for the economic team to propose a reordering of priorities. Clinton had promised in the campaign to cut the deficit in half in four years. With the new projections, he backed off that pledge.[28] The revised priority of cutting the deficit was made evident on Capitol Hill with the confirmation hearings for Leon Panetta, the newly appointed director of the OMB. "Our first priority is to develop that deficit reduction plan," then to "lay out the investment path we want to follow." The promised tax cut for the middle class came next, "dependent" on what happens in meeting the first two priorities.[29]

The reordering of priorities even before the inauguration had special significance for the Clinton administration. It raised the fundamental question whether the changes promised during the campaign could be achieved. How free was the new president to promote his program? He was being told very early of the constraints of a deficit generated over two decades by the Great Society programs of Lyndon Johnson and the Great Tax Cut of Ronald Reagan. He was also advised on the extent to which the huge deficit made the Federal Reserve Board, chaired by a Republican, Alan Greenspan, and the bond market critical to the future economic health of the nation. Woodward quotes the president as saying: "You mean to tell me that the success of the program and my reelection hinges on the Federal Reserve and a bunch of . . . bond traders?" His economic advisers nodded in agreement.[30]

Such a revelation was bound to result in a clash between such Washington insiders as Panetta, Bentsen, and Rivlin and the outsiders, primarily the campaign consultants Paul Begala, James Carville, and Mandy Grunwald. For the latter it was as though they had won the presidency only to be captured by the government. The campaign theme had been about change, yet they were being told that government had mortgaged its capacity to make change for some time to come. The only gear left was reverse, and not even Republican presidents had been able to move effectively in that direction.

The new president was understandably distressed by these circumstances. An outsider himself, he was anxious to effect change. Yet as an avid policy analyst, he comprehended the dilemma. And as an adroit campaigner, he resorted to a "going public" strategy as the political option most suited to his talents. He appeared to accept the importance of concentrating on a limited number of priorities. But he also wanted to be a president of achievement. Therefore he was attracted to new initiatives, working constantly to find the means for legislative achievement within the constraints of the budget realities. There are few problems that Bill Clinton does not want to solve, and yet there are few solutions that do not add to the deficit.

It was precisely this conflict between the promise of change and the reality of its cost that motivated the political consultants to advise going to the people. The consultants were concerned that their candidate was becoming captive to Washington insiders. Woodward reports on a conversation between Paul Begala and Alice Rivlin that illustrates the diverse perspectives:

> "We have to walk people through the journey the president has gone from November to February. We have to explain why the deficit got worse and how it got worse," Begala said, focusing on The Story.
> "That's nonsense," Rivlin said bluntly, her voice cold with assured professionalism. "Bill Clinton knew where this deficit was going," she said, adding that they had to face the fact that the campaign fundamentally misrepresented the situation. There was no need to revisit that journey, she said.
> Begala was steaming.[31]

The consultants were bound to lose this battle for influence on policy priorities. In a reported conversation, Begala questioned: "Mr. President, why are you listening to these people? They did not support you. It's not what you're about." "We need them," Clinton said, his temper rising. "We can't do anything for people unless we reduce the deficit."[32]

The president sought to manage these conflicting pressures in a well-received speech, first to the American people on 15 February, then to Congress on 17 February. Essentially the message was that before "investments" could be made in the future, it would be necessary to raise, not lower, taxes.

I had hoped to invest in your future by creating jobs, expanding education, reforming health care and reducing the debt without asking more of you. . . .

But I can't—because the deficit has increased so much beyond my earlier estimates and beyond even the worst official Government estimates from last year. We just have to face the fact that to make the changes our country needs, more Americans must contribute today so that all Americans can do better tomorrow. . . .

As we make deep cuts in the existing Government programs, we'll make new investments where they'll do the most good. . . .[33]

The package was crafted to satisfy Democratic constituencies. As reported in the *Wall Street Journal*, "President Clinton has staked his fortunes on party discipline and reduced his margin for error. . . . While shoring up the president's partisan base, that approach has drawn scathing criticism from Republicans. . . ." Representative Steny Hoyer (D-Md.) predicted that "he's got to count on getting 218 Democrats."[34] As it happened, that is precisely the number of votes his budget proposal received in the House.

The shift in priorities from investments to deficit reduction did not go unnoticed in the press, in spite of the president's artful rhetoric. Typical was the analysis by Jeffrey Birnbaum: "The crash you may have heard last night was the sound of campaign promises breaking."

For Mr. Clinton, the big question is how mad people will be about his broken promises. He has spent the past several weeks preparing the American people for disappointment about them, citing what he calls a surprising surge in the projected size of the deficit since the election. Many experts, though, doubt that he could really have been that surprised, because much of the bad news about the deficit was publicly understood long before Election Day.[35]

A national lobbying effort was launched following the speech to sell the proposals. "Clinton led the way in a St. Louis campaign-style rally. . . ."[36] It was a pattern that would be repeated often. In this case it provided some satisfaction for both camps in the Clinton White House. The insiders won the battle for revising the priorities, the outsiders were offered something to sell to the American people, to perfect their "bank shot." There was no escaping the effect of what had happened in that first month in office, however. The president had accepted the policy box created for him by the growth in entitlement programs and tax cuts. His other priorities, in particular health care and welfare reform, would be evaluated for their effects on the deficit.

The Campaign Style of Policymaking

Presidents vary dramatically in their governing styles. Among recent presidents, Lyndon Johnson was very much the lawmaker as president. He knew the Congress well and was his own most effective lobbyist. Richard Nixon was more aloof, preferring to concentrate on foreign and defense policy as a means for building public and congressional support. Like Johnson, Gerald Ford capitalized on his congressional experience but relied heavily on a veto strategy. Jimmy Carter stressed the correctness of his proposals, believing that they should get support because they were right for America. Ronald Reagan emphasized goals more than programs, relied heavily on staff, and capitalized on his public persona. George Bush employed a management style that suited his limited agenda.

Like Reagan, President Clinton preferred a public strategy in working for his agenda. Unlike Reagan, he was very involved in the details of policy and thus found it more difficult to delegate. Further, he worked the country much harder than did Reagan. How much did he travel? How did his travel compare to that of his immediate predecessors? And did this travel build support for him and his programs? These are the questions to consider in this section.

Table 1.4 shows Clinton's domestic travel by region, place visited, and number of appearances. Also included is the regional contribution to his electoral vote. Not included are personal trips to Arkansas (8), visits to Camp David (7), and vacation trips (4). Also excluded are the foreign visits —5 trips, 25 places, 48 appearances. It should also be noted that this compilation records only the travel as officially recorded in the *Weekly Compilation of Presidential Documents* and thus does not include unscheduled stops or brief remarks made along the way in any one city.

The travel by region shows heaviest concentration in the East, South, and West (primarily California). It is interesting to note the source of Clinton's electoral vote as an indicator of his travel. The proportion of travel to the East conforms exactly to his electoral vote count. Travel to the South (though not the Southwest) is somewhat greater than would appear to be merited based on the electoral count, though surely the region is judged to be important for a southern governor. The Midwest is slighted and California is favored. Nearly 80 percent of the appearances in the West and 15 percent of all appearances were in California. Judging the travel only in reelection terms, the strategy appears to be: hold the eastern base, work the South, and invest substantially to win again in California.

Table 1.5 shows the issues discussed by President Clinton, either as a principal topic or along with other issues. There are no surprises in this table for those who have been attentive to the Clinton priorities. The economy and health-care reform were major agenda items for the president through the election and into his presidency. Crime came to be more important with

TABLE 1.4

PRESIDENT CLINTON'S POSTINAUGURAL TRAVEL:
FEBRUARY 1993 THROUGH AUGUST 1994

Region	Places[a]		Appearances[b]		Electoral vote	
	Number	*%*	*Number*	*%*	*Number*	*%*
East	51	34	65	32[c]	122	33
South	41	27	51	25[d]	63	17
Southwest	6	4	11	5	5	1
Midwest	22	15	36	18	89	24
West	30	20	40	20[e]	91	25
Totals	150		203		370	

SOURCE: Compiled from data in the *Weekly Compilation of Presidential Documents,* Office of the Federal Register 29, nos. 1–52, and 30, nos. 1–9 (Washington, D.C.: Government Printing Office, 1993, 1994).
a. Refers to the places he visited at different times. The same city may have been visited more than once, and he may have visited several cities on any one trip.
b. Refers to the total number of appearances. He may have made two or three appearances in any one visit.
c. Includes 13 appearances in Maryland.
d. Includes 11 appearances in Virginia.
e. Includes 31 appearances in California.

rising public concern about this issue. The president was criticized for failing to emphasize the environment and campaign finance reform. The data in table 1.5 suggest that this reproach is justified, since neither was a frequently discussed topic on the road.

It is revealing of presidential styles and priorities to compare Clinton's travel during the first seven quarters with that of his immediate predecessors, Bush and Reagan. President Bush was known to be a frequent traveler, yet he did not match Clinton, and his travel was different in several respects. In the comparable period, Bush traveled domestically to 136 places, with 178 appearances. But many more of these appearances were political or partisan in nature—41 (23 percent) as compared to 17 (just 8 percent) for Clinton. Many of Bush's political appearances were for fund raising. Not surprisingly, Bush had more foreign travel than Clinton—10 trips to 26 places and 58 appearances (contrasted with 5 trips to 25 places and 48 appearances for Clinton). Bush also went to Camp David, the presidential retreat in Maryland, much more frequently, as well as to his home at Kennebunkport, Maine. It was his practice often to meet foreign leaders at one or the other of these retreats. Finally, his appearances were less policy campaign oriented in style, primarily because he had a much less ambitious legislative program to sell.

The contrast between the Clinton and Reagan travel schedules is even more striking. In the comparable period, Reagan traveled to 45 places and

TABLE 1.5
ISSUE TOPICS FOR APPEARANCES
BY PRESIDENT CLINTON:
FEBRUARY 1993 THROUGH AUGUST 1994

Topic	As major issue	With other issues	Totals
Health care	32	29	61
Economy/budget/taxes	21	40	61
Crime/gun control	11	20	31
Foreign affairs/defense	16	11	27
Education/national service	6	10	16
Trade	5	7	12
Defense conversion/technology	3	5	8
Reinventing government	4	3	7
National disasters	7	–	7
Welfare	2	3	5
Campaign finance	–	2	2
Environment	1	–	1
Other topics	1	10	11

SOURCE: Compiled from data in the *Weekly Compilation of Presidential Documents,* Office of the Federal Register 29, nos. 1–52, and 30, nos. 1–9 (Washington, D.C.: Government Printing Office, 1993, 1994).

made 58 appearances. Like Bush, many of these appearances (16 of them, or 28 percent) were political or partisan in nature (again, mostly for fund raising). Reagan's travel schedule was severely limited in the month following the assassination attempt. Yet prior to the wounding he had just 4 appearances outside Washington, compared with 20 for Bush and 13 for Clinton. Further, Reagan's appearances were not primarily designed as "bank shots" for specific policy proposals. They were often ceremonial in nature. His foreign travel was more restricted than that of Bush. In fact, of his five trips, just one was outside this hemisphere.

Has Clinton's travel outside Washington enhanced his public approval ratings? There is no obvious connection. Table 1.6 shows his Gallup poll approval and disapproval quarterly averages for the first seven quarters of his presidency. His highest approval average was during the first quarter; the second-highest one year later (though his disapproval average increased substantially during that time). Apart from the first months in office, his highest single ratings occurred following his economic message, 17 February 1993 (an increase of eight points to 59 percent); his health-care message, 22 September 1993 (an increase of ten points to 56 percent); and his State of the Union message, 25 January 1994 (an increase of four points to 58 percent). These three messages were delivered not on the road but in Washington, before Congress.

TABLE 1.6
APPROVAL AND DISAPPROVAL RATINGS
FOR PRESIDENT CLINTON,
QUARTERLY AVERAGES

Quarter	Approval	Disapproval	No opinion
First	54.5	30.6	14.8
Second	44.3	45.4	10.2
Third	46.1	44.7	9.1
Fourth	49.6	42.5	7.9
Fifth	53.0	39.4	7.6
Sixth	48.2	44.2	7.7
Seventh	41.3	50.0	8.7

SOURCE: Calculated from Gallup poll data reported in *American Enterprise,* various issues.

Figure 1.1 displays the first seven quarterly averages for nine elected presidents in the post–World War II period (the averages for Truman and Johnson are those following their election, not their assumption of office). Note that there are two groups, with Nixon falling in between. The first group of Eisenhower, Kennedy, Johnson, and Bush maintained relatively high averages within a limited range. Clinton is in the second group, which also includes Truman, Carter, and Reagan. These presidents have substantially less impressive average ratings. Note that Clinton lags among those in this weaker group, exceeding their quarterly averages in just two of the quarters (the fifth and sixth). His range of scores was narrow—41 to 55. Among these presidents, Truman and Carter never did recover. Truman's subsequent quarterly averages were in the twenties and thirties; Carter's reached 51 percent in the thirteenth quarter, but the final three quarters of his presidency were in the thirties. Only Reagan was successful in substantially bettering his performance after the initial twenty months in office. He was the only president in the postwar period to leave with a higher quarterly average than that with which he entered.

Another indicator of the success of Clinton's travel is the extent to which his principal priorities were backed by the public. Most closely tracked was the public's view of his health-care proposal following the president's speech, 22 September 1993. Support peaked immediately after his initial speech. It remained relatively high during the fall months, then peaked again with the State of the Union message.[37] Support then faltered as the proposal came to be considered in Congress. The president's campaigning seemingly had little positive effect. The plan itself failed to be enacted and, contrary to most predictions, was not then a major issue in the midterm elections.[38]

The public view of Clinton's management of the economy essentially

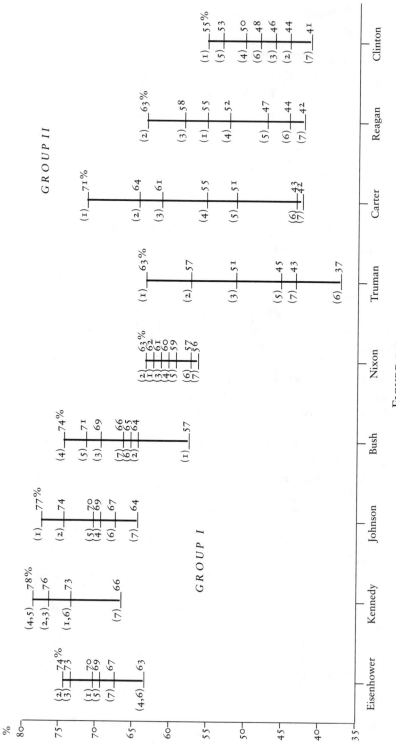

FIGURE 1.1

PRESIDENTIAL APPROVAL SCORES, GALLUP POLL, FIRST SEVEN QUARTERLY AVERAGES

SOURCE: Calculated from Gallup poll data reported in *American Enterprise*, various volumes. No data for Truman, fourth quarter, and Johnson, third quarter. (1): Numbers in parentheses indicate the quarter(s) in which the average approval percentage was recorded.

tracked his approval ratings, though it was somewhat lower most of the time. His travel failed to overcome public doubts about his accomplishments. His ratings on handling of the economy remained mostly in the forties in spite of a substantial increase in the respondents' perceptions of the state of the economy (see figure 1.2). As shown, the quarterly average approval of the president's handling of the economy broke the 50 percent mark for just one quarter, with the seventh quarter falling below 40 percent. Yet the respondents' estimates of the state of the economy steadily increased during the seven quarters. These data are the basis of the frustration felt by White House staff, who believed that the president was not getting the credit he deserved for an improved economy.

Bill Clinton vigorously employed the traveling salesman approach to building support for his proposals, as was consistent with the advice given to him by his political counselors. The superficial evidence suggests, how-

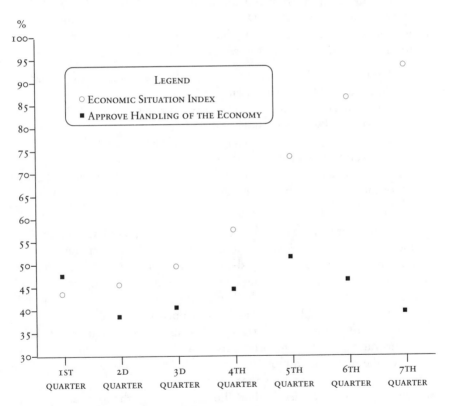

FIGURE 1.2

CLINTON AND THE ECONOMY: QUARTERLY AVERAGES

SOURCE: Calculated from data in *American Enterprise* (September/October 1994): 112.

ever, that the "shot" did not "bank." The president's approval ratings either remained steady or declined during his first twenty months in office.[39] There is little or no evidence to suggest that the president's frequent travel was having the desired effect on the public, let alone Congress. Further, even where he could legitimately claim success, as with the steady improvement in the economy, the public was not moved to credit the president.

The Domestic Record — Clinton's Role in the Separated System

Presidents enter an ongoing system of government and are therefore challenged to find their place so as to have influence. An important facet of any working government is the pipeline of issues and policy proposals. Given the competition in the 102nd Congress between congressional Democrats and a Republican president, there was a substantial backlog of legislation likely to find favor with a newly elected Democratic president. Thus in evaluating the domestic lawmaking record during the first two years of the Clinton administration, the following points are relevant:

1. Presidents don't pass laws; they work with, alongside of, or against the House and Senate in lawmaking.
2. An agenda of working issues is always present and affects lawmaking regardless of who is president.
3. Certain issues will be designated as priorities; the president plays an important role as a designator.
4. The president's special policy initiatives will be treated in the context of the set of working issues and alternative proposals already in the pipeline.

These realities advise one to take the whole system into account in judging the record of any particular period. What, then, did the separated system produce by way of domestic legislation in 1993 and 1994, and what explains this productivity? It is both convenient and rational to consider each of the two years because they look very different and what happened in 1993 helps immeasurably to explain what happened in 1994.

"The first session of the 103rd Congress produced a spate of new laws, as Democratic policies and programs flowed freely down the legislative sluice for the first time in more than a decade."[40] The product was of three types. First were those matters that carried over from the 102nd Congress. Some bills had been passed by both houses but were then vetoed by President Bush; other proposals were in the pipeline but had not as yet reached the president's desk. President Clinton was Congress's willing partner in signing several such pieces of legislation, including family and medical leave, the so-called motor voter bill to ease restrictions on voting registration, the

Brady bill requiring a waiting period for the purchase of a handgun, and revision of the Hatch Act limitations on political activities of federal employees. The pipeline was not emptied, however. Campaign finance reform was put off until 1994 (see below), abortion rights progress was less than had been expected by some, and revisions of the Mining Law and western land grazing fees were once again postponed.

Second were the big ticket items—those highly visible issues either so designated by the president or the result of events or both. The president wanted health-care reform to be one such priority in 1993, but circumstances prevented that from happening. The two major priorities were Clinton's economic plan as incorporated in the budget reconciliation package and the North American Free Trade Agreement (NAFTA). Both were highly controversial. Both illustrate the hazards in assuming that single-party government represents a model for the American system. In regard to the Clinton economic plan, an early effort to enact a stimulus spending package so as to soften the blow of subsequent budget cuts displayed the problems of gaining support within the president's own party as well as the complexities of congressional rules in enacting legislation. Many deals had to be made in order to get House Democratic approval, and even more were needed to keep Senate Democrats in line. In the end it was not possible to muster the sixty votes necessary to kill a filibuster in the Senate, and the stimulus package was defeated.

Building a winning coalition for the rest of the economic plan was no less problematic. After intense negotiation and substantial revision along the way (which made the bill very much a congressional as well as presidential piece of legislation), the plan was approved in the Senate with Vice-President Gore's tie-breaking vote and in the House by a two-vote margin, 218–216 (41 Democrats voting with all 175 Republicans in opposition). Fortunately for the president, a budget reconciliation measure is not subject to a filibuster, or it, too, would have been defeated.

The other major priority was a treaty negotiated during the Bush administration. Candidate Clinton was critical of NAFTA, insisting that side agreements be negotiated (as they were when he became president). Once he announced his support of the agreement, President Clinton campaigned hard for its approval. In the meantime, however, certain congressional Democratic leaders (notably the House majority leader, Richard Gephardt of Missouri, and the House majority whip, David Bonior of Michigan), had not only announced their opposition but, in the case of Bonior, expressed an intention actively to work for the defeat of the agreement. The legislation to implement the agreement could pass only with Republican support. Here was a case in a single-party government of the Democratic president working with the House and Senate Republican leaders to build majority support. A majority of Democrats in each house opposed the agreement.

The third class of lawmaking activities during the first session of the 103rd Congress were the Clinton initiatives. The economic plan falls into this category, though the budget reconciliation measure was a standard vehicle for the consideration of Clinton's proposals. The president had a mixed record in regard to other initiatives. His preference for lifting the ban on homosexuals serving in the military was substantially modified in congressional action, with provisions added to the Defense Authorization bill that essentially confirmed the ban (though new recruits would no longer be asked about their sexual preference). The "reinventing government" initiative was carried forward by Vice-President Gore. Much of this plan could be put into effect without congressional approval. Where budget cuts were called for, however, the president not only had broad support but many Republicans and some Democrats were prepared to go beyond the president's recommendations. Timothy Penny (D-Minn.) and John Kasich (R-Ohio) prepared such cuts to be put in place over a five-year period. Clinton was forced to oppose their bill and it was defeated narrowly, 213–219. A third Clinton initiative was directed to young people, exchanging community service for financial credit to attend college. The National Service Act eventually passed both houses in a pared-down version, giving the president his most clear-cut win among new initiatives in the first session.

Many contentious issues carried over to the second session, thus making 1994 a substantially more challenging year for the president. Clearly the most important of these issues was that of health-care reform. The president promised swift and dramatic action in 1993 but was not able to deliver. Rather than act in one hundred days, he introduced his plan in a speech to Congress on 22 September 1993, to rave reviews. Even his political adversaries were admiring. Newt Gingrich (R-Ga.) exclaimed that "it reminds me a lot of *The Music Man*—I have that same sense of excitement."[41] The legislation was not yet forthcoming, however. And in fact one senior White House aide was quoted as stating: "We really didn't think we would be asked, 'Where is the legislation?' when we thought everybody knew we were working as fast as we could to get the legislation up there."[42]

The process by which the health-care plan was developed may have contributed to its downfall. Essentially, the White House, under the direction of Hillary Rodham Clinton and Ira Magaziner, created a new organization to produce the plan, rather than relying on the existing structure of the Department of Health and Human Services and the relevant congressional committees. A 500-member task force was put in place, one that drew on those within and outside government. The awkwardness of this arrangement was compounded by the unusual role played by the First Lady.

> Another source of discomfort at the health care meetings was Mrs. Clinton's presence. Some of those who attended found her intimidating—hard to argue

with and uninterested in the points they made. Mrs. Clinton's style was very direct. She told people straight out what she thought.... One person said, "There was a little feeling on her part of 'You're not in my caste, and I'm not going to debate you'—even when she'd said, 'Great, let's debate this.' You can't debate across caste lines."[43]

At the early stages of congressional consideration, it was also difficult for members of Congress to be critical as long as Mrs. Clinton was so identified with the plan. After she testified before the House Committee on Ways and Means, Robert T. Matsui (D-Calif.) said: "We were not going to bring up the details and concerns before the First Lady, we just weren't going to do it. The issue is one of her stature."[44] Instead they saved the criticism for Secretary of Health and Human Services Donna Shalala.

Postponing serious consideration of health-care reform until 1994 meant that it would be considered in the political context of the forthcoming midterm elections. Media attention was naturally directed to the popularity of the president's plan, associating the results with his approval rating. Both Democrats and Republicans could be expected to monitor these tests as barometers of the public mood. Thus the longer it took to consider the plan, the more it would be judged in an electoral rather than a policy context.[45] Enacting a program of any kind came to involve more of a political risk than further postponing the issue.

Other difficult issues were also saved for the second session of the 103rd Congress. A comprehensive crime bill came to be a priority with the increase in public concern about crime as an national issue. Crime bills have traditionally been contentious because the issues set off strongly held views about punishment, gun control, and the federal role in relationship to the states and local communities. Republicans have typically held a political advantage on the crime issue. The president, however, assumed a tough stance and was successful in blunting the Republican advantage. After an embarrassing loss on a procedural vote in the House (the rule to debate the conference report was defeated), the White House agreed to further compromises and a revised conference report, which then passed both houses when a sufficient number of Senate Republicans broke ranks to support the revisions. Of the remaining major issues on the agenda—the General Agreement on Tariffs and Trade (GATT), elevation of the Environmental Protection Agency (EPA) to cabinet status, telecommunications competition, campaign finance reform, and lobbying disclosure—not one of them was enacted during the regular session. GATT was voted on and approved in a special session after the election.

As has been typical of lawmaking in recent years, most of the major bills were still pending late in the session. The "bank shot" or campaigning strategy is not well designed for this kind of lawmaking schedule. If support has not already been garnered, then the president is left, in an election year, with little influence in the frenzied pace of a Congress anxious to leave Washington. The advantage is with those united enough to obstruct. There simply is not enough time for the president to launch public campaigns for several pieces of legislation. Moreover, in President Clinton's case, his principal priority, health-care reform, was already dead, leaving him to select among several second choices, all of which received substantially less attention in his travels (see table 1.5).

Most of the legislation in the end-of-session logjam was blocked or delayed by Republican filibustering, real or threatened. But enough of it was blocked by Democratic Party divisions to diffuse the criticism of the opposition party. For example, House and Senate Democrats were divided on campaign finance, and Senator Ernest Hollings (D-S.C.) singlehandedly forced a delay in the consideration of the GATT. Evaluations of the Congress were scathing, and spared neither party.

Washington Post

This will go into the record books as perhaps the worst Congress—least effective, most destructive, nastiest—in 50 years. The wisdom at the moment is that the dismal record represents a victory for the Republicans. They succeeded in blocking much of the Clinton agenda, and a government in which the Democrats controlled both elected branches was made to look like a caricature of itself.... The theory is that the Republicans will somehow pay less of a price for having been obstructionists than the Democrats will for not having made the system work.

The Republicans will richly deserve what they get if that isn't true. But it's also a myth to claim that they bear the entire responsibility for the failure that has occurred. The Democrats brought a major part of the wreckage on themselves.[46]

New York Times

The Republicans must shoulder the ... burden imposed on them by Mr. Gingrich [Republican House whip] and Senator Bob Dole [Republican Senate leader], whose ugly behavior in the waning days of Congress helped kill campaign finance and lobbying reform.

But Republicans cannot be held responsible for whatever harm the Democrats suffer in November because their participation was never part of the original promise. If the voters are sour, and they are, it has more to do with Mr. Clinton's failure to consolidate the majority they handed him and the failure of the party to unify itself.[47]

In summary, Clinton's record with Congress during the first two years was mixed. Major bills were enacted during the first year, several of which were carried over from the previous Congress. The two wins most identified with his presidency were the economic reform package and the National Service Act. Still, he favored many of the bills that did pass and therefore received a high support score from the *Congressional Quarterly* (among the highest for a post–World War II president).[48] By measure of what was produced, the second session was much less successful. Whereas seven major bills were enacted in 1993, just three passed in 1994 (with GATT postponed and to be dealt with in a special session). By comparison with other administrations, 1994 was the least productive second year for any newly elected president, as shown in table 1.7.[49]

Foreign Policy

In an interview for *Time* magazine in fall 1994, President Clinton discussed his record in foreign policy:

> We're doing it better; we're making few mistakes. Part of that is, I think, just learning. . . .
>
> I came here as a governor. I'd never served in the Congress. My exposure to foreign policy, as an adult at least, was largely through international economic measures. I also think, in fairness to our whole team, we were confronting a very different world than had previously been the case. . . .
>
> When I came in, I knew there was a limit to how much I could get done. I wanted to have as much time as I could to get my economic program going, because I was afraid that unless we reversed our economic course, nothing I did in foreign policy would permit the U.S. to really succeed. . . .[50]

TABLE 1.7

MAJOR LEGISLATION ENACTED, POSTWAR ELECTED
PRESIDENTS (FIRST TWO YEARS)

President[a]	Number in first year	Number in second year
Truman	5	7
Eisenhower	1	8
Kennedy	9	6
Johnson	15	7
Nixon	6	16
Carter	7	5
Reagan	2	7
Bush	2	7
Clinton	7	3

SOURCE: David R. Mayhew, *Divided We Govern* (New Haven: Yale University Press, 1991), table 4.1.
a. Ford not included because he was never elected.

This candid analysis identifies President Clinton's perspective on international issues, as well as his limitations. The 1992 election was primarily about domestic issues. George Bush was the foreign policy president, and he lost. Bill Clinton entered office intending to concentrate on improving the economy and reforming health care.[51] He explained:

> You know, the country will not permit a president to engage in foreign policy to the exclusion of dealing with the domestic problems. But the country might permit a president to engage in domestic problems to the exclusion of foreign policy, until some wheel runs off somewhere, and then it'll be obvious that that was an error as well.[52]

Clinton's emphasis on the economy justified an interest and participation in international economic issues. Thus he was actively engaged early in his administration in economic reform in Russia, holding a meeting with President Boris Yeltsin in Vancouver, Canada, in early April 1993. He received high marks for his participation in the G-7 economic summit in Tokyo in July 1993. By the fall of his first year in office, however, there were serious criticisms of the administration's handling of U.S. involvement in Somalia, Bosnia, and Haiti. The loss of American lives in Somalia and ordering a troopship to return in the face of threats from a group of armed Haitians led to uniformly scathing criticism. A sampling of headlines during October 1993 tells the story: "Foreign Policy, Left Unclear," "President Strives Mightily to Shift from Trouble Abroad to Goals at Home," "Running from Foreign Policy," "Foreign Policy Morass," "Wobbling Dangerously," "Clinton Reexamines a Foreign Policy under Siege," "The Road to Panic."[53]

The first eight months of the new year did little to reduce the criticism. The president appeared indecisive on renewing most-favored-nation status for China before agreeing to extend the trade advantage. He was heavily criticized for reversals in his Haitian policy, as well as for a failure quickly to resolve the flood of refugees coming by boat from Cuba. Further, his handling of the failure of North Korea to allow inspection of nuclear production facilities was complicated by the intervention of former President Carter, who went to North Korea to meet with President Kim Il Sung. Questions were raised about who, exactly, was managing foreign policy. Clinton's foreign policy approval rating dropped to 34 percent in one poll taken in August 1994.[54]

With the end of the congressional session and the failure to enact his health-care proposal, however, the president turned his attention to foreign policy. In late September he announced that the United States was poised to invade Haiti. At the very last minute former President Carter led a delegation to meet with the Haitian military leaders, coming away with an agreement by which they would step down and permit President Aristide to return. Earlier an agreement had been reached with Cuba to stop the flow of refugees coming by boats to Florida. Then in October Saddam Hussein appeared ready to launch an invasion of his own, massing troops on the border with Kuwait. Clinton acted swiftly to move forces into the region, and Hussein withdrew his troops. Meanwhile, negotiations with the North Koreans in Geneva resulted in an agreement that averted a confrontation for the time being. Buoyed by these successes, the president took the unusual step of canceling his midterm campaign schedule two weeks before the election to travel to the Mideast to witness the signing of a peace treaty between Israel and Jordan. While there, the president also met with leaders of Egypt, Syria, Saudia Arabia, and the Palestine Liberation Organization, as well as visiting the troops in Kuwait.

Not surprisingly, these events resulted in a substantial increase in the president's foreign policy approval ratings, and thus a positive effect on his overall score. One poll showed his approval rating in foreign policy at 50 percent, exceeding his disapproval rating for the first time in six months.[55] Thus encouraged, the president of change ended his second year following a standard practice, that is, turning to foreign policy in the face of serious problems in building support for his domestic program. As he explained it:

> When you're dealing with these domestic problems, the president is one of a zillion decision makers; not just Congress, but you've got people in the private sector and individuals in their own lives. . . .
>
> So foreign policy has a certain satisfaction when you can be active and you can achieve a result, and sometimes it's easier to see a beginning, a middle and an end . . . in foreign policy your actions are more self-contained.[56]

The Midterm Upheaval: Fall Elections

In a memorandum entitled "Strategic Guide to the 1994 Election," Stanley Greenberg, President Clinton's pollster, advised Democrats to run for reelection on their own record of accomplishments. "There is no reason to highlight these as Clinton or Democratic proposals. Voters want to know that you are fighting to get things done for them, not that you are advancing some national agenda." Greenberg also suggested emphasizing the crime bill rather than health-care reform.[57]

A midterm election is a particularly effective reminder that we have a separated, not a presidential, political system. The president is, at best, an awkward participant in 435 local House races and 33 state Senate races (35 in 1994). That fact does not prevent analysts from evaluating the results as a test of presidential success or failure. But in structural terms, the election is justified as a means for maintaining citizen access to and control over representatives. Members of Congress are elected separately from the president, a feature that contributes to their independence as a branch of government.

Therefore, a president who wishes to participate obviously does so on the invitation of those from his party who judge that his involvement will be helpful. Most of the time presidential campaigning in midterm elections will have only a marginal effect.

A campaigning president like Bill Clinton naturally found it difficult to sit out an election, especially one in which he was said to be a major issue. Yet he was forced to be quite selective in his travel schedule in the fall of 1994. Democratic candidates did not welcome him in several states; in others, they did not all appear with him when he showed up. The signing of a peace treaty between Israel and Jordan provided an opportunity for the president to travel to the Mideast just days before the election. Buoyed by improved public approval ratings on his return, Clinton barnstormed through the upper Midwest, the Northeast, and the Pacific coastal states, primarily to encourage Democratic turnout in a number of tight races. One of the effects of his highly publicized campaign swing was to reinforce Republican claims that his record was an issue, as well as to ensure that the results would be interpreted as a test of his record.

The election outcome was stunning. The Republicans won a majority in the House of Representatives for the first time since 1952 and garnered the most members since the 1946 election. They also recaptured control of the Senate and won 24 of 36 governor races (Democrats won 11, independents 1). No Republican incumbent was defeated—representative, senator, or governor. One Democratic senator, Richard Shelby from Alabama, even switched parties the day after the election.

The Republicans, in effect, took charge of the lawmaking branch. Two events provided them with a postelection policy advantage. First was Clinton's active involvement in the latter days of the campaign, thus contributing to the view that the huge win for the Republicans represented a rejection of the president's program. Second was the issuance of a "Contract with America," designed under the direction of House Minority Whip Newt Gingrich of Georgia and Republican Conference Chairman Dick Armey of Texas. The "Contract" was signed by most of the Republican candidates for the House in a media event at the Capitol on 27 September.

Gingrich, scheduled to be the new Speaker of the House of Representatives, exclaimed that the victory for Republicans constituted an endorsement of the "Contract" and that he was honor-bound to fulfill his pledge to ensure a vote on each item during the first one hundred days of the 104th Congress. The consequence of these developments was that Clinton lost control of the agenda and was therefore in the unenviable position for a president of having to reclaim that function while being responsive to Republican initiatives. On 15 December the president took the first step in that direction with a brief speech to the nation outlining a plan to cut taxes and spending.

Ironically, the 1994 elections produced a virtual mirror image of the split-party government during the last two years of the Bush administration—against which Bill Clinton campaigned. Bush employed a veto strategy so as to influence the shaping of legislation and prevent the passage of bills to which he was opposed. He was heavily criticized as contributing to gridlock. It remains to be seen how Bill Clinton will manage. The immediate postelection rhetoric was conciliatory on both sides. And there are numerous examples from the Eisenhower, Nixon, and Reagan presidencies that split-party government can produce major legislation. On the other hand, relations between the last Democratic president to face a Republican Congress, Harry Truman and the 80th Congress, would not lead one to predict smooth sailing.

Summing Up and Looking Ahead

President Clinton's troubled first two years in office ended in a disaster for the Democrats at the polls. He had an ambitious agenda, but lacked a mandate. His freewheeling and personalized style did not facilitate an effective White House organization. His penchant for travel and campaigning induced his political consultants to participate in devising policy strategy to a greater extent than normal. Approval ratings are typically the test of a "going public" strategy, and Clinton's scores were low. Concentration on difficult domestic issues was often at the cost of ignoring or delaying consideration of foreign and national security issues. Organizational adjustments were made along the way, often poorly handled until Leon Panetta was appointed chief of staff.[58] And the cloud of scandal hung over the Clintons throughout, involving a sexual harassment suit and an investigation into the Whitewater real estate venture. Interestingly, the president and the First Lady achieved celebrity status as a result of his "going public" strategy and the attention given to their personal lives, yet that stardom did not carry with it high approval of either their style or performance in the White House. Celebrity status does not necessarily correspond with presidential stature.

In his evaluation of the president's first year in office, Fred I. Greenstein concluded that "the presidential style of William Jefferson Clinton remained very much a work in progress.... The jury remains out on Bill Clinton's presidential leadership...."[59] Little has changed to alter that summation. The president continued to engage in a campaign style of governance through 1994, with decidedly mixed results. His major domestic priority of health-care reform was not enacted, nor was there time to act on welfare reform. Then, not having fully formed his presidency during the first twenty-one months in office, President Clinton was faced with dramatically different political conditions—loss of Democratic majorities in both houses of Congress.

At the close of the second year, Elizabeth Drew spotted a "stature problem" for the president. Often by his own hand, the president eroded "the moral authority and the stature of the office he holds." One consequence was to make the president more than ordinarily vulnerable in the face of a defeat for his party in the midterm elections:

> Clinton has been too much with us; in his efforts to show his accessibility to the people, he overdid it. He was on television too often and he talked too much....
>
> Through his excessive accessibility, Clinton became, as one White House staff member put it, "an undifferentiated president...."
>
> Without the office itself as protection, Clinton is out there all alone, exposed—just another pol, to be given no benefit of the doubt and no particular respect. To the extent that the people sense that he himself has undermined the dignity of the office, they resent him for it.[60]

On balance, and in spite of the president's problems, the separated system could be said to have worked very much as expected during the 103rd Congress. That is to say, a president with limited political resources identified the major issues and expressed a willingness to compromise, and an unloved Congress, one almost supersensitive to its public, passed important bills until it became politically risky to act further. Most legislation bore the imprint of both the executive and Congress. The 103rd Congress was in no sense "Clinton's Congress," as, say, was the 89th "Johnson's Congress," or the 97th "Reagan's Congress," making the 103rd Congress much more typical than the 89th or 97th.

The 1994 elections transformed Washington politics. The president had to cope with aggressive and ambitious Republican leaders. Senate Majority Leader Robert Dole of Kansas was a prospective presidential candidate in 1996; the new Speaker of the House, Newt Gingrich, was determined to seize the policy initiative from the White House. Meanwhile, House and Senate Democrats had to elect new leaders. Speaker Thomas Foley of Washington was defeated for reelection, and Senate Majority Leader George Mitchell of Maine retired. In the House, Richard A. Gephardt (Missouri) and David E. Bonior (Michigan) beat back challenges to their leadership as Democratic floor leader and whip, respectively. In the Senate, Tom Daschle of South Dakota narrowly defeated Christopher J. Dodd of Connecticut for Democratic floor leader. Therefore the Republican advantage in achieving majority status in Congress was amplified by a comparative edge in momentum in the House and leadership experience in the Senate.

Campaigning to govern will be an even less effective strategy for the president in the 104th Congress than it was in the 103rd. If the president continues to press for an ambitious domestic agenda, he will need to attract Republican support. Going public is, typically, going partisan, and going partisan is unlikely to be welcomed by House and Senate Republican leaders buoyed by their electoral boost in 1994. President Clinton may prefer position taking rather than a more aggressive agenda-setting and policy strategy.

The president will also have to respond to policy initiatives from Capitol Hill, as outlined initially in the "Contract with America." Conditions are right, then, for copartisan politics in which the president and Republican leaders offer counterproposals, potentially resulting in cross-partisan bargaining. This pattern of presidential-congressional interaction was familiar during the split-party eras of Republican presidents and Democratic Congresses. It need not produce gridlock. In fact, recent history suggests that it can be a productive mode of national policymaking and be reaffirmed by the voters. After all, three of the largest landslide elections in the post–World War II period (1956, 1972, 1984) returned opposite parties to the White House and Capitol Hill. That fact may discourage an aggressive "give 'em hell" strategy by President Clinton as he looks forward to the 1996 election. On the other hand, copartisan politics works best when both sides are roughly equal in resources. In this regard, the president entered the new year at a distinct disadvantage.

Acknowledgments

I wish to acknowledge the assistance of Corey Cook, David Howat, Laurel Imig, and Andrew Shaw in the preparation of this chapter, as well as the continuing support of the Hawkins Chair in Political Science, University of Wisconsin–Madison; and the Douglas Dillon Chair in Governmental Studies, Brookings Institution.

Notes

1. Bob Woodward, *The Agenda: Inside the Clinton White House* (New York: Simon and Schuster, 1994), 248, 141.

2. Samuel Kernell, *Going Public: New Strategies of Presidential Leadership,* 2d ed. (Washington, D.C.: CQ Press, 1993), 109.

3. Richard E. Neustadt, *Presidential Power among the Modern Presidents* (New York: Free Press, 1990), 29.

4. Ford also ran and was defeated.

5. Other heirs apparent were nominees: Nixon in 1960, Humphrey in 1968, and in a less direct example since it was four years hence, Mondale in 1984.

6. See Paul C. Light, *The President's Agenda: Domestic Policy Choice from Kennedy to Reagan* (Baltimore: Johns Hopkins University Press, 1991); and James Pfiffner, *The Strategic Presidency: Hitting the Ground Running* (Chicago: Dorsey Press, 1988).

7. See Light, *President's Agenda,* 45. In his first three months in office, Nixon proposed just 12 percent of his total legislative requests, compared to Johnson (94 percent) and Kennedy (76 percent).

8. James L. Sundquist, ed., *Beyond Gridlock? Prospects for the Clinton Years —and After* (Washington, D.C.: Brookings Institution, 1993), 25.

9. Quoted in Adam Clymer, "National Health Program, President's Greatest Goal, Declared Dead in Congress," *New York Times,* 27 September 1994, A1.

10. Ibid., 18, 20.

11. Michael Kelly, "The Winners Shift Gears: What Now?" *New York Times,* 5 November 1992, B3.

12. Mary Matalin and James Carville (with Peter Knobler), *All's Fair: Love, War, and Running for President* (New York: Random House, 1994), 429, 471.

13. Reported in Pamela Fessler, "Clinton Plans for Smooth Start with Focus on the Economy," *Congressional Quarterly Weekly Report,* 7 November 1994, 3555–56.

14. Quoted in Gwen Ifill, "Clinton May Quickly Name Transition Chief in Effort to End Dispute within Staff," *New York Times,* 6 November 1992, A19.

15. Thomas L. Friedman, "Clinton Is Taking Big Role in Picking Cabinet Deputies," *New York Times,* 18 November 1992, A22.

16. News Conference, *Congressional Quarterly Weekly Report,* 14 November 1992, 3643.

17. Michael Kelly, "Clinton Names Team to Probe U.S. Agencies," *New York Times,* 16 November 1992, A16.

18. Elizabeth Drew, *On The Edge: The Clinton Presidency* (New York: Simon and Schuster, 1994), 30. In an interview with the author, one Clinton official explained that several coordinators expected to be appointed, notwithstanding the warning in advance.

19. His nominee for ambassador to the United Nations was also a woman, Madeleine Albright. Despite these many appointments, Clinton was still criticized by some women's groups, prompting the president-elect to refer to his critics as "bean counters." Gwen Ifill, "Clinton Chooses Two and Deplores Idea of Cabinet Quotas," *New York Times,* 22 December 1992, A1.

20. See Drew, *On the Edge,* 22–24. Mrs. Clinton's chief of staff, Margaret Williams, also served as an assistant to the president, thus formally linking her organization to that of the president.

21. Quoted in Michael Kelly, "Clinton's Chief of Staff Ponders Undefined Post," *New York Times,* 14 December 1992, B6.

22. Ibid.

23. Ibid.

24. Beth Donovan, "Calling Dr. Panetta," *Congressional Quarterly Weekly Report,* 2 July 1994, 1794. The task of reorganizing took a long time, however, and was barely accomplished when the Republicans won a huge victory in the midterm election.

25. Matalin and Carville, *All's Fair,* 244. It was a problem that Clinton himself recognized. Very early in the campaign, he was reported to have told Carville and Paul Begala: "What I need most of all from you guys is focus, is clarity. I don't know how to bring it down, to condense it." Ibid., 84.

26. Woodward, *The Agenda,* 80.

27. Ibid., 81.

28. Robert Pear, "Clinton Backs Off His Pledge to Cut the Deficit in Half," *New York Times,* 7 January 1993, A1.

29. David E. Rosenbaum, "Budget Nominee Testifies Clinton May Set Aside

Tax-Cut Pledge," *New York Times*, 12 January 1993, A1. It is interesting to note that Panetta had not altered his view of the Clinton priorities from the time of the Democratic convention to the meeting on 7 January. He was quoted following the convention as stating that "the tough choices are still there. In my view, the new president [would] have to target very limited investments and put the major effort into cutting the deficit. Clinton is concerned about the deficit, but he's also concerned about all those constituencies whose support he needs in this election." Quoted in Daniel Southerland, "Clinton's Manifesto vs. Reality," *Washington Post*, 19 July 1992, H1.

30. Woodward, *The Agenda*, 84.

31. Ibid., 114.

32. Ibid., 126.

33. "Transcript of President's Address on the Economy," *New York Times*, 16 February 1993, A14.

34. Both quotations from John Harwood and David Rogers, "A Plan That's Tailored to Suit the Democrats," *Wall Street Journal*, 18 February 1993, A11.

35. Jeffrey H. Birnbaum, "Important Campaign Promises Are Left in Dust by President," *Wall Street Journal*, 18 February 1993, A11.

36. Ann Devroy and Dan Balz, "Clinton Team Deploys to See Economic Plan," *Washington Post*, 19 February 1993, A1.

37. As reported in "Health Care Update," *American Enterprise*, July/August 1994, 94. However, there was skepticism about the effects of health-care reform early in the process. A CBS News/*New York Times* poll in September 1993 showed that only 17 percent of the respondents believed that the quality of health care would improve with the adoption of the Clinton plan. Meanwhile, 80 percent thought that their taxes would increase with the adoption of the plan, though 61 percent said they would be willing to pay higher taxes. Robin Toner, "Poll on Changes in Health Care Finds Support amid Skepticism," *New York Times*, 22 September 1993, A1, A19.

38. Adam Clymer, "Defying Omens, Health Care Drops from Campaign Stage," *New York Times*, 22 October 1994, A1.

39. Though there was evidence of improvement in the eighth quarter, mostly due to a series of foreign policy successes.

40. "Fresh Faces Transform Agenda as 103rd Congress Begins," *Congressional Quarterly Almanac* 49 (Washington, D.C.: Congressional Quarterly, 1994), 3.

41. Quoted in Alissa J. Rubin and Janet Hook, "Clinton Sets Health Agenda: Security for Everyone," *Congressional Quarterly Weekly Report*, 25 September 1993, 2552.

42. Quoted in Gwen Ifill, "Events Steal Health Plan's Thunder," *New York Times*, 18 October 1993, C10.

43. Drew, *On the Edge*, 194.

44. Quoted in Dana Priest, "Shalala's Health Plan Testimony Is Given Bruising Reception on Hill," *Washington Post*, 6 October 1993, A4.

45. One administration official observed that a change occurred among Republicans when they captured the seat of William Natcher (D-Ky.) in a special election held 24 May 1994. By this view, Republicans were emboldened to oppose the president more vigorously than before.

46. "Perhaps the Worst Congress," *Washington Post*, 7 October 1994, A24.

47. "Gridlock's Political Price," *New York Times,* 9 October 1994, 14.

48. See "When Congress Had to Choose, It Voted to Back Clinton," *Congressional Quarterly Almanac,* 44, 3C. Clinton's score was 86.4 percent.

49. See David R. Mayhew, *Divided We Govern: Party Control, Lawmaking, and Investigations, 1946–1990* (New Haven: Yale University Press, 1991), table 4.1. It should be noted that the count for 1993–94 is based on Mayhew's initial estimations. He judged that six or seven laws would meet his criteria in 1993 and three or four for 1994. See Stephen Gettinger, "View from the Ivory Tower More Rosy Than Media's," *Congressional Quarterly Weekly Report,* 8 October 1994, 2851.

50. "Blending Force with Diplomacy," *Time,* 31 October 1994, 35.

51. Jim Hoagland, a columnist for the *Washington Post,* reported on a conversation he had with an official "who attended many of this administration's most important meetings about foreign policy and national security." The official identified two surprises: "How much of the meeting was not about the meeting.... And how much Bill Clinton hates making decisions on foreign policy. The only thing he would hate more would be letting someone else make the decisions. That he won't do." Jim Hoagland, "Image Isn't Everything," *Washington Post,* 31 May 1994, A17.

52. Ibid., 36.

53. This sampling includes news stories, editorials, and op-ed pieces. The sources are, respectively: *New York Times,* 3 October 1993, A14; 11 October 1993, A9; 11 October 1993, A11; *Washington Post,* 12 October 1993, A19; 13 October 1993, A21; 17 October 1993, A1; *New York Times,* 22 October 1993, A29.

54. The CBS News/*New York Times* poll, as reported in *American Enterprise,* September/October 1994, 104–5.

55. Richard Morin, "Poll Shows Clinton with Higher Rating," *Washington Post,* 25 October 1994, A6. The *Washington Post*/ABC poll also showed Clinton's overall approval rating to have exceeded his disapproval rating, 49 percent to 48 percent. On the other hand, his approval rating on handling the economy improved only slightly.

56. "Blending Force," 36.

57. As reported in Richard L. Berke, "Advice for Democrats in Fall: Don't Be Too Close to Clinton," *New York Times,* 5 August 1994, A1.

58. Panetta also received criticism in the aftermath of the election, primarily for failing to move swiftly enough to make changes in the White House staff. In a postelection memo reportedly directed to Panetta from White House aides, it was stated that among the reasons for the repudiation of the Democrats "was the jarring picture of a White House that never got its act together, fed by recurring images of utter haplessness." Ann Devroy, "Reasserting Presidency Means Rethinking Almost Everything," *Washington Post,* 14 November 1994, A1, A6.

59. Fred I. Greenstein, "The Presidential Leadership Style of Bill Clinton: An Early Appraisal," *Political Science Quarterly* 108, no. 4 (1993–94): 598–99.

60. Elizabeth Drew, "Desperately Seeking Stature," *Washington Post,* 11 December 1994, C1.

2

Management in a Sandbox: Why the Clinton White House Failed to Cope with Gridlock

COLIN CAMPBELL

This chapter focuses on the role of the White House in what we might call the gridlock era of the U.S. presidency. Its analysis concentrates on Bill Clinton's experience by the midpoint of his term. But it lays the groundwork for this analysis by underscoring the antecedents of gridlock in the Reagan/Bush years.

The disarray of the current administration prompts us to ask what difference might organization of the White House have made? The White House was neither completely amorphous nor porous when Clinton assumed office. Further, the administration has made several efforts—some of which have achieved good results—at improving the structure and operation of the White House. Nevertheless, things have gone badly wrong. Thus we have to entertain two possibilities: either Bill Clinton pathologically lacks the ability to connect with organizational structure or the magnitude of gridlock has reached the point where any incumbent, independent of personal style and the organization of his White House, would encounter frustrations of the degree currently experienced by the president.

What do we mean by gridlock? If years from now historians go back and look at the 1992 presidential election, they are going to be tempted to call it the gridlock election. Continued frustrations with spasmodic governance in Washington have now led to the chastisement of the president—the first time that a Democratic president has had to deal with a Republican-dominated Congress since 1947–49. Ironically, this probably means that voters have just bought into two years of the most horrific gridlock conceivable.

During the 1992 election, there were those who faulted the Democratic Congress for gridlock. George Bush pushed this interpretation. If voters would only elect a Republican Congress, all the problems would go away. Then there were people who said that George Bush had caused gridlock. If the election produced a Democratic president, finally the nation could address its ills. The actual 1992 election results produced a 43 percent plurality behind this view—a technical victory for the Democrats that Bill Clinton construed as a mandate.

More significantly, a fairly substantial segment of the population—19 percent if we read directly across from the side of the vote for Ross Perot —had abandoned hope in either the Republicans or the Democrats. This mood swing proved almost unique to the 1992 election. The degree to which people had become concerned about general paralysis within the system gave an unprecedented profile to the dysfunctions of divided government.

Many Americans had become greatly concerned about the constant struggles between the president and Congress.[1] Their anxieties focused on the incapacity of the system—as dominated by the two conventional parties—to handle many of the key problems that America faces today. From fears about gridlock there emerged what many observers viewed as a fanciful and dangerous idea. Many ordinary voters began to see the way around gridlock as going directly to the people—through the type of electronic "town-hall" democracy that Ross Perot utilized so effectively.[2]

We might ask, "Why not go to electronic voter participation in specific decisions?" Presidency scholars have written about a postmodern presidency —less reliant on links to institutional power bases among interest groups and Congress—for at least a decade.[3] And incumbents increasingly "go public" with direct appeals to voters—going over the heads of traditional loci of power.[4] Modern technology brings radically different modes of governance into the realm of the possible.

Yet the Perot approach sent chills down the spines of those concerned with the integrity of the American democratic system. Perhaps Perot himself was too successful by half in executing his campaign. His appeal, based as it was on oversimplification of issues, populist meanderings, and a seemingly unlimited supply of cash, flew in the face of a constitutional heritage that for more than 200 years had deliberately eschewed majoritarianism and populism.

More germane to this chapter, the Perot candidacy raised the specter of yet another iteration in the seemingly relentless drift of presidential leadership to personalized, a-institutional formats. When this tendency first appeared incarnate in Ronald Reagan, political scientists tended to view it benignly. Aloofness from the ongoing state apparatus and highly selective and sporadic engagement of the permanent civil service became the hallmarks of the Reagan administration. The conventional wisdom in political science saw this approach as consistent with the institutionalization of the presidency against the resisting forces within the executive branch.[5] It chose as its core instruments strengthening the shadow bureaucracy in the White House and fine-tuning subcabinet appointments to reflect the ideology of the president. And these clearly fit within an apparent trend since Kennedy, whereby presidents had become increasingly focused on "responsive competence"—that is, maintaining their electoral viability—and decreasingly enamored of "neutral competence"—that is, the utility of tapping the expertise and sagacity of the standing bureaucracy.

The first Reagan term will perhaps stand in history as representing the salad days of the institutionalized presidency. In the second term, the dysfunctions of detachment from and disengagement of the state apparatus came home to roost.[6] The Iran-*contra* affair, an instance in which the National Security Council staff free-lanced even from the president, serves as the clearest instance of how error-prone an administration can become when it eventually crafts and implements its policies with virtually no reference to the standing bureaucracy.

More fundamentally, detachment and disengagement had begun to characterize the relationship between the president and the administration itself. Reagan played little part in the process whereby his chief of staff, James Baker, switched jobs with his treasury secretary, Don Regan. Reagan then delegated day-to-day direction of the White House to Regan as if he were prime minister and Reagan were monarch. Ironically, Regan—a former chief executive officer of Merrill Lynch—tried to run the White House like the headquarters of a major corporation. He had neither the sensitivity to politics nor the acuity for Washington gamesmanship to contribute to the maintenance of the president's responsive competence.

George Bush continued this pattern. He essentially delegated responsibility for domestic policy to his chief of staff, John Sununu.[7] Sununu, ever the ideologue and enamored of his intellectual brilliance, used his position to confound even the most reasonable efforts at accommodating the Democratic Congress. This preordained that even a rudimentary domestic legislative agenda would become ensnarled in petty disputes between Republican moderates and conservatives.

This chapter takes the view that institutionalization of the presidency in fact involves two gearboxes.[8] The first, dwelt on by Terry Moe and others, concerns the connection between a president and his administration, and the standing bureaucracy. The second, which has received much less scholarly attention, structures the relationship between the president and his advisers and key officials, both within the White House and in the cabinet. Over the past decade, observers have tended to focus on the strengthening of the presidency vis-à-vis the first gearbox. But a review of the same period suggests that the president's control derived from the effective operation of the second gearbox has actually declined. As a result, institutional development has at best produced mixed results.

The emergence of gridlock as a core issue in the operation of the U.S. presidency has not helped matters. Being president has clearly become more difficult. Optimists (regardless of partisan allegiance) might see the outcome of the November 1994 congressional elections as an opportunity to resolve gridlock by electing a Republican president in 1996. But we might reasonably ask whether the Republicans would actually achieve greater coherence between the executive and legislative branches if they had the presidency and majorities in each house of Congress? Probably not. Recent research, most notably by David Mayhew and Charles O. Jones, has not lent much support to arguments that majorities in both houses actually improve the president's ability to press forward coherent and consistent programs.[9]

In fact, Jones argues that we should dramatically downsize our expectations of presidents. He maintains that we misinterpret the intent of the Founding Fathers if we ascribe to them the desire to make presidents progenitors of responsible party government. In this regard, no one who has observed the diversity of views warring within the Republican Party—as, for instance, at the 1992 National Convention—would remain unguardedly optimistic about its ability to sustain unified governance.

This takes us back to basics. Divided government links to the separation of powers. It is an old and recurrent theme in American politics. It might not loom large in every election, but we should not view it as an aberration. Much of the political science discipline in the United States would go out of business if it lacked the division of powers and its consequences. For instance, congressional studies would become a sleepy backwater, much like parliamentary studies has always been in the United Kingdom, Canada, and Australia.

Neoinstitutionalism and Its Consequences

So far, this chapter has introduced two issues. First, analysts mistakenly assumed that the presidency has been strengthened over the past two decades. Their assessment was based on an emphasis of development concerning the first gearbox—that between an administration and the standing bureaucracy. It overlooked weaknesses in the second gearbox—that between a president and his team. Second, as gridlock has become a persistent trait characterizing the dynamics between the executive branch and Congress, observers have tended to discount the salience of presidential style and gearbox issues on the grounds that the presidency has become institutionally straitjacketed.

Over the years, various groups of political scientists have promoted developments that would streamline the operation of the system. During the expansion of the welfare state, the most dramatic intervention occurred in 1950. In that year, the American Political Science Association Committee Report on Political Parties called for a responsible two-party system in the United States.[10] Such a system, the authors believed, would allow parties to set out their programmatic goals and then maintain sufficient cohesion —while in government—actually to deliver on them.

Similarly, the 1980s ushered in a period in which neoliberals began to look longingly across the Atlantic at Margaret Thatcher. Here a chief executive could actually implement the top-down, command-oriented leadership deemed necessary for the staunching of deficits' depletion of national wealth and turn the state apparatus into an agent of enterprise. Ronald Reagan had talked very much like Mrs. Thatcher. In his first term, he identified goals similar to hers: easing the tax burdens of the wealthy, cutting social programs, and re-enshrining the military as an expenditure sacred cow. Yet, notwithstanding a strong start, he eventually found himself thwarted by dissension in his administration and the resistance of Congress.[11]

Within political science, neoliberalism has become associated with public choice theory and neoinstitutional analysis. This approach traces its lineage to such scholars as James Buchanan and Gordon Tullock,[12] and William Niskanen,[13] who led the way toward studying politics as an economic phenomenon. Their work focused on what they called principal–agent relationships. In democracy, they argued, the principal is the citizen. He or she engages the services of an agent, that is, the politician. Elections serve as the core mechanism that sustains principal–agent relationships.

Consistent with the centrality of the principal–agent relationship, the view emerged that, in fact, party discipline short-circuits the connection between the citizen and the politician. Individual politicians find their accountability diminished if they feel themselves beholden to an entity beyond their ultimate principals. This view laid the groundwork for views of leadership that stress individual mandates for change. Notions such as responsive competence clearly place the onus on the leader to deliver notwithstanding institutional constraints such as partisan cohesion. It applied equally to issues surrounding the interface between political authorities and the state apparatus. The latter would now be expected to play an almost entirely passive role toward the former. Institutionalization of the presidency would come at the cost of a weakening of the role of parties in Congress and of the permanent public service in policy decisions.

During the 1980s, the neoliberal view informed political leadership in several advanced democracies. With varying degrees of specificity, presidents and prime ministers embraced the principal–agent theory of governance. Neoliberals ask first not "What you should do for your country?" but

"How can you move toward getting it off your back by eliminating functions—especially social ones?" Such an emphasis shifts the focus of accountability onto the clearly transactional dimensions of political leadership. Through its strong association with fiscal conservatism, public choice also packages itself as a means to controlling the aggregate size of government, although its actual follow-through has proven patchy at best, certainly in the United States and Canada and now—under John Major—in Britain too.[14] It has failed most clearly at the connecting points in political leadership, where macro meets micro, where policy and administration become intertwined.

An irony emerges if we compare the actual effects of public choice in the United States to those in other liberal democracies. The two strategies, disaggregated governance and automatized budgeting, have encountered various degrees of success in some Anglo-American systems—New Zealand, Australia, and the United Kingdom in descending order.[15] They have achieved virtually nothing in Canada. Canada labors under a larger deficit problem than that of the United States. It has made relatively little progress in the areas of privatization, commercialization, and contracting out.

What explains the different experiences of New Zealand, Australia, and the United Kingdom, on the one hand, and Canada and the United States on the other? One possible answer comes to mind immediately. Both Canada and the United States function within the context of divided government. In each case, the ambivalence of the respective founding fathers has carried over to our present epoch. For Canada, this concerns fears of an overpowerful federal government vis-à-vis provincial, ethnic, religious, and regional interests. For the United States, it relates to deep suspicions of executive authority. In each instance, divided government has impeded the pursuit of public choice options as much as it impaired the process of expanding the welfare state during the candy-store phase of politics. Separation of powers, parties as brokers and restrainers of power, states and provinces with some level of autonomy, and specialized, client-oriented (as opposed to customer-oriented) bureaucracies are means by which the various elements of fragmented societies protect themselves from arbitrary rule.

Yet, in the age of constraint, U.S. presidents still had to deal with essentially the same fractious political arena that hobbled their predecessors during the era of expansive governance. They have achieved virtually nothing to make the bureaucracy in the United States more managerial. They lack a coherent government to reinvent.[16] It has become a banality to say that gridlock stands at the root of the intractable deficit. And through it all, presidents must bravely assert that America competes with economies that have spurted ahead of the United States precisely because of their mode of governance. That is, they plan. They have not disaggregated governance; they maintain a structured coherence, a capacity to relate all of the parts to the whole.[17]

The rise of gridlock as the motif of governance in the United States has not placed in question neoinstitutionalism. If anything, the mounting evidence that the presidency in fact has weakened rather than gained strength has tended to draw attention further from management style and the gearbox issues. The persona of an incumbent increasingly takes a back seat to the institutional straitjacket of divided government. There has been a tendency, as well, to excuse presidential nonperformance on the grounds of institutional constraints. Obeisance to the view that presidents can do little has limited attention to the relationship between personality, management style, and presidential performance during the past fifteen years.

By way of illustration, the standard assessment of George Bush that prevailed among political scientists until about twelve months before his defeat in the 1992 election was that voters did not see him as capable, institutionally, of advancing a domestic agenda. Allegedly, the public did not expect Bush to be addressing domestic problems. They perceived him as someone whose strong suit was foreign policy. Is it problematic, though, to give so much credence to institutional factors? Did this obscure from analysts two very serious dysfunctions in the administration that, ultimately, would lead to trouble?

In the early 1970s James David Barber's work raised a debate in the United States about the role of personality in the presidency.[18] Barber introduced a paradigm that most American political scientists and many of their students can recite by heart. It postulates four types of presidents: active-positive, active-negative, passive-positive, and passive-negative. All of this makes for an iffy theoretical framework. It is very difficult to establish who fits into which of the quadrants. Yet the paradigm is strongly evocative. What can be done with it to enhance its salience for presidential studies?

Let us assume that all presidents start off being pretty active and pretty positive about their job. The question remains, "Active and positive about what?" History certainly serves up "new order" presidents who wanted to do great things; we conventionally put the acronym presidents here: FDR, JFK, and LBJ. Then we find exceedingly active and positive presidents who view themselves as gifted at running things and making them more efficient. They have an appetite for detail and a passion for finding how things actually run. Jimmy Carter stands as a perfect illustration of this kind of president. Because of his résumé, many analysts expected George Bush to fit this mold. He did not.

We also have had "being there" presidents. What these presidents are active and positive about is massive engagement of themselves in the symbolic dimensions of office. Ronald Reagan serves as a very strong illustration, if not the archetype, of this sort of president. Finally, there is the "let's deal" president, a pragmatic leader who is very finicky about tackling seemingly intractable problems. If he takes on an issue, he will want fairly rapid outcomes. He will deploy his energy and concentration within a very short time frame.

George Bush was this type of president. His approach achieved what was deemed success in foreign affairs; it failed on the domestic front. Clinton, too, is a "let's deal" president. The emergence of two leaders of this type in immediate succession should prompt us to ask, has something happened to the system to promote such forms of leadership?

The rest of this chapter examines precisely this point. It probes two issues. Did the Reagan presidency function as a harbinger for dysfunctions in two gearboxes—that between an administration and the standing bureaucracy and that between the president and his administration? If so, is the "let's deal" presidency a symptom of these dysfunctions, an art-of-the-possible method for addressing them, or both? The analysis, of course, focuses on Bill Clinton. But it first examines how Reagan and Bush coped under pressures that might have transformed the presidency. These pressures include not only acute fiscal constraint but, more fundamentally, exacerbation of the intractable gridlock characterizing the system.

Preparing the Way for Clinton's Failure? Ronald Reagan and George Bush

It would appear that instead of heralding an age of presidential ascendancy, the Reagan presidency was a harbinger for dysfunctions in two gearboxes—that between an administration and the standing bureaucracy and that between the president and his administration. The success of the Reagan administration in its first term prompted some analysts to assert that the presidency had assumed a wholly new trajectory as central manager of the federal government. Such assessments fit with Reagan administration stratagems, such as centralization of political appointments and trimming of the policy agenda.

To be sure, the new regime spelled the decline of bureaucratic power. In a democracy, however, only the ability to win elections really counts. The enshrinement of this norm was leading to a gradual institutionalization of the presidency—the condition whereby an administration would stop chasing the right decision at the end of the analytic rainbow and start placing political viability at the heart of its leadership approach.

This neoinstitutional view of the presidency certainly struck a chord. It came on the heels of an administration—Carter's—that time and again overrode considerations of political responsiveness in favor of prolonging the quest for the "right" option. Yet the neoinstitutional analysis failed to capture the distinctive character of the Reagan administration. The mood of the times had made working the gearbox between an administration and the bureaucracy less complicated. A simple agenda characterized by the imperatives of making America profligately defended, getting the federal government off people's backs, and eliminating or sharply curtailing do-gooder programs hardly constituted the statecraft equivalent of rocket science.

From the beginning of the second term, it became clear that Reagan had lost the Midas touch with regard to coordinating his administration team. Virtually all the features that had lent such force to Reagan's direction of his administration in the first term went by the boards in the second term. In the White House, hierarchy supplanted teamwork. The much-vaunted cabinet councils stopped functioning. As the administration's handling of arms sales to Iran and aid to the *contras* made clear, relatively low-level White House aides counted more than cabinet secretaries. None of the resulting disarray and dysfunction would do much to lend credence to the view that the presidency had re-institutionalized and turned the corner in its capacity for executive leadership.

The second term demonstrated an important point about the presidency under the conditions of divided government in the age of constraint. Even incumbents who have chosen to build down government must maintain a high level of engagement and pay close attention to the design of the decision-making process. In this regard, Reagan in the first term served practically as a model. His administration did great damage, not through executive incompetence, but through the defects of the highly ideological policies it pursued.

In the second term, the administration proved inadequate in both regards. The result: an exacerbation of the malaise and distrust. The stage was set for George Bush.

During the 1988 campaign, George Bush emerged as potentially an "executive president," someone who would uphold the core commitments of the Republicans under Reagan and at the same time give greater attention to detail.[19] Things would run more smoothly. In addition, a Bush administration would engage in some fine-tuning. The argument that it would provide a "kinder, gentler" form of leadership rested on the assertion that the president and his team would know how to modulate policies according to fundamental fairness and humanity. It would not navigate so much on the automatic pilot of ideological presuppositions.

Much of the appeal of Bush as an executive president derived from his résumé. We find ourselves in an age in which political outsiders have risen to power in advanced democracies in unprecedented proportions.[20] Bush recalled an earlier era in which chief executives had proven themselves in high office within the national government they ultimately led. Further, unlike Carter and Reagan, Bush did not run against Washington.

Much of Bush's campaign rhetoric and earlier pronouncements once elected lent support to the notion that the permanent public service performed a necessary function within the policy arena.[21] This seemed to restore a modicum of standing to "neutral competence" as a component of governance.

Notwithstanding these auspicious signs, George Bush failed to connect as an executive president. Instead, he adopted a "let's deal" style. Throughout his administration, he remained highly selective, even in foreign affairs,[22] about the issues in which he would engage himself. Once he locked into a matter, he betrayed an impatience for results that tended to undermine dispassionate management.

This pattern emerged even in Bush's most acclaimed accomplishments, Desert Shield and Desert Storm. Here the "let's deal" approach consistently overwhelmed whatever aptitude Bush might have had for executive-style leadership. The evidence suggests that Bush could have prevented the Iraqi invasion of Kuwait had he paid more attention to Saddam Hussein's various threats.[23] Even after the invasion, it required prodding by Margaret Thatcher before Bush took ownership of the crisis as something that concerned the vital interests of the United States. To be sure, he became deal maker *extraordinaire* in gaining international ascent to Desert Shield. Yet, apart from participation from the United Kingdom, the non-U.S. contributions to the venture were largely symbolic.

The actual combat, which occurred under the banner "Desert Storm," so shocked the world that the allies chose to cease hostilities rather than pursue the enemy deep into Iraq. This raised questions about whether assembling a force of 500,000 had amounted to using a howitzer to knock out a mosquito.[24] As well, the nature and size of the allied force introduced huge distortions to the usual character of UN responses to such incidents. (These elements even left their signature in Bush's committing U.S. troops to the UN action in Somalia.) At precisely the time when Europe should have been focusing on the dangerous refragmentation of the Balkan states, Bush's leadership approach forced commitments that left little time or resources for attention to Yugoslavia. And, at the end of the day, the approach proved less than surgical regarding the key criterion for success—removing Saddam Hussein from power. In fact, it seems not even to have taught Hussein a lesson.

Regarding the two gearboxes under Bush, the first—that between the administration and the bureaucracy—functioned reasonably well. This owed partially to a fair amount of continuity between Reagan and Bush administrations, both in objectives and political appointees. The new administration's leadership style remained relatively control oriented and directive. What Bush had added was a supportive public rhetoric about the bureaucracy. This lent an aura of comity to what, in many respects, still involved a great deal of top-down discipline.

Unlike the first gearbox, the second—that involving the relationship between the president and his administration—operated very poorly. The use of consultative mechanisms declined notably from the outset of the Bush administration. Thus, teamwork within the administration became spasmodic. Even the National Security Council—a statutorily buttressed body that normally functions fairly systematically—rarely met at the principals' level. The deputies of the various council members kept in regular contact; however, they normally held their meetings through video conference calls. This served as a stricture on candor. Members of the deputies' group became chary of those not in view of the cameras who might, nonetheless, be listening in on meetings. As one traces through the administration's handling of events in the buildup to Iraq's invasion of Kuwait, one can see how the irregularity of principals' meetings and constraints on candor among deputies contributed to the failure of Bush to perceive and address the obvious danger.

On the domestic side, the administration developed into a dysfunctional family writ large. Certain flaws in Bush's leadership style seemed to set him up for his immense problems in this area. He saw domestic affairs as a field that could pretty much run on its own or at least function under the direction of a surrogate. He enforced no round-tabling norm for resolving intra-administration disputes. And he certainly found scant occasion to meet with cabinet secretaries over domestic issues. Even considering these factors, Bush might have performed reasonably well on the domestic side had he not chosen John Sununu as his chief of staff.

Anyone who knew Sununu as well as Bush did should have been able to anticipate difficulties. The previous unfavorable Republican experiences with strong chiefs of staff—Sherman Adams under Eisenhower, H.R. "Bob" Haldeman under Nixon, and Donald Regan under Reagan—should have given the president further pause. There are limits to the "good-cop, bad-cop" act in any administration. That is, there is a fine line between a strong chief of staff serving as a lightning rod for the president and his arrogation of the president's power.[25]

Sununu set out to suck even the most tangential domestic issues into the vortex of the conservative social agenda. He manifested much more interest in scoring ideological points than in keeping presidential trains—like efforts to reduce the deficit—running on time. On tax increases, he freely contradicted the president and infuriated even the leadership of his own party in Congress. On a host of issues, he made Bush into more of a nonconciliatory ideologue than Reagan. Witness his machinations concerning the Clean Air Act and the gag rule against abortion counseling.

Sununu left the administration in December 1991—too late to allow Bush to reverse the damage already incurred. What he had done was raise in the public mind the image of the intractable presidency. Voters quickly put this together with their already profound feelings that Congress could not resolve the key issues facing the nation. They developed anxieties about the governability of the United States that perhaps had never before emerged to such a strong degree. This provided rich soil for the paranoid politics of Perotism and, more recently, Gingrichism, whose impacts have hovered over the Clinton administration like an albatross.

Bill Clinton

In his more focused moments, Bill Clinton has struck observers as a "new order" president. Certainly, scenes of the newly inaugurated president boarding his Marine helicopter with a biography of FDR would support the view that he harbors hopes in this direction. In fact, Clinton operates much more as a "let's deal" president. This is a viable form of leadership. Indeed, it may be the most appropriate to this particular age.

The issue of the appropriateness of "let's deal" leadership to the current age arises in part because recent presidents have found themselves so constricted by fiscal pressures. But it may owe more fundamentally to the mandates that emerge from election campaigns waged through electronic media. Electronic appeals, especially those on television, work much more on emotions than did earlier approaches dependent on the print media. Electronic appeals tend to highlight personal attacks rather than differentiate the policy approaches of candidates. In the process, they often exacerbate divisions among the electorate. They also obscure the potential common ground for resolution of the core issues that would serve as the focus of more constructive campaigns.

Under the circumstances, deeply committed "new order" types would find it difficult to gain election. Even if they did, they would not easily rally support for dramatic policy changes. The public, on the other hand, will wink at candidates who give lip service to the importance of fundamental change, just as long as these aspirants' track records and "vibes" telegraph the fact that their fervor falls short of zeal.

Incumbents who mouth bromides about the bold steps required to heal what ails the country can rest assured. Most of the populace will not hold them to account for not pursuing this order of action. Still, to maintain their credibility, they must rise to the occasion in those circumstances that do indeed require at least middle-range government action. In those cases, they must prove to be heat-seeking missiles. They must quickly arrive at negotiated positions and deals that will at least provide them cover from the accusation that not only have they not acted boldly, they have failed to do anything.

Early in Clinton's term, it became apparent how he likely would perform as a "let's deal" president. First, in keeping with the age, he incurred a weak and diffuse mandate. To be sure, he became the beneficiary of a fair amount of good feeling immediately after his election victory. But this hardly translated into concrete support for specific actions, even if Clinton had made a host of explicit commitments. Of course, he had not: even the incantations for health-care reform remained distinctly vague and tentative.

It should not have surprised many people, then, that Clinton experienced such a truncated honeymoon—by some accounts scarcely 100 hours, much less 100 days. Insofar as his difficulties related to the times, Clinton enjoyed an advantage over Bush. In an epoch in which domestic politics have assumed greater significance than foreign affairs, Clinton's strengths fit the times. Bush's had clashed with the shift in circumstances and with popular expectations that the president should spend more time on domestic affairs.

Clinton brought another quality to the presidency that might have given him an advantage over his predecessor: an upbeat personality. This gave the public different signals from those transmitted by Bush. Normally, they could sense when the likes of Saddam Hussein or recalcitrant congressional Democrats had gotten to Bush. Such incidents would induce Bush to reveal his dark side—his tendency to personalize conflict and couch his reasoning in harsh and vindictive terms.

During his frustrating first few months, Clinton looked very much like the rookie coach who realizes that he will lose a few games before he gets the hang of his job. The election campaign—involving as it did roller-coaster reversals, including intimate probes of the candidate's draft record and marital fidelity—revealed a Bill Clinton with a hugely resilient ego. Clinton's past behavior might in various ways have revealed character defects. Yet these did not seem to touch on his fundamental aptitude for the rough-and-tumble of the modern presidency. This president does fly into temper tantrums regularly—one of the alleged roles of Al Gore is to defuse these with humor.[26] Only occasionally do stories appear suggesting that he has become bitter, however, nor does he often reveal his anger publicly.[27]

Two problems present themselves in evaluating how well suited Bill Clinton is to the "let's deal" mode of leadership. The first of these relates to the art of the possible in the age of constricting views of what the government should do. When asked during the campaign what his favorite Scripture passage was, Clinton cited Galatians 6:9: "Let us not grow weary while doing good for in due season we shall reap, but do not lose heart."[28] When Bill Clinton lost his first reelection bid in Arkansas, he recognized that insofar as "doing good" meant pursuing the liberal agenda, discretion was the better part of valor. Some profiles of the president's past indeed suggest that the exigencies of Arkansas politics have given him an exceptionally high tolerance for compromise and even moral and ethical ambiguity while professing to pursue noble objectives.[29]

Yet, at his core, Clinton wants to change the circumstances of the average American for the good. He therefore has found building down government or embracing economic policies that cater to the bond markets extremely frustrating.[30] Bob Woodward has Clinton railing at his staff after it became clear that his first budget would contain no major stimulus programs and tax breaks for the middle class: "We're Eisenhower Republicans here, and we are fighting Reagan Republicans. We stand for lower deficits and free trade and the bond market. Isn't that great."[31] If Clinton actually uttered these words, we have an instance of one side of his brain berating the other.

The other difficulty that presents itself in Bill Clinton's pursuit of a "let's deal" style relates to the complexity of governance in our age. Even if the president chooses to base leadership on his bargaining ability, he must negotiate from the basis of well-worked-out principles. Paul Quirk has called on Dean Pruitt's notion of "flexible rigidity" in negotiations to underscore the need for presidents, especially under the current political circumstances, to maintain flexibility about means and rigidity about goals.[32]

While this objective seems to be quintessential Clinton, the preponderance of analysis suggests that the president has never defined his goals sufficiently to enshrine his rigidities. Nor has he known when to be flexible. At several important turning points in the administration, observers have noted that the president has failed to devise fundamental strategies,[33] revealed a tendency to store up ideas and let them gush out without any thematic coherence,[34] and put his team through a seemingly endless succession of relaunches.[35] Asked to comment on yet another downturn in his approval levels, Clinton himself acknowledged his lack of a core strategy: "I think in a way it may be my fault. I keep, I go from one thing to another."[36]

In his analysis of George Bush, Quirk asserted that Bush displayed a tendency to get the principles of negotiation turned around—betraying a flexibility about goals and rigidity about means.[37] Clinton seems to have rigidity about nothing. In the case of NAFTA, he embraced a Republican proposal that stood as an anathema to much of his party's core constituency, as even his pollster Stanley Greenberg recognized.[38] He then proceeded to cut deals for its passage that would impinge hugely on the utility of NAFTA actually to serve as a vehicle for free trade, often without delivering a number of votes proportionate to the cost of compromise.[39]

Similarly, some observers have noted that Clinton's effort to co-opt insurance companies by pushing "managed competition" in health-care reform rather than a single-payer system created such needless complexity that the status quo in the health-care sector subsequently became more acceptable than the Clinton alternative.[40] Clinton ultimately lost the support even of congressional reformers when he began in July 1994 to suggest that he would be flexible about universal coverage and employer mandates to pay insurance premiums.[41] In May of Clinton's first year, one aide voiced the fear that Clinton "is getting defined by his compromises, not his principles."[42] Even his later successes seemed to result more from expediency than from principle. One aide noted in February 1994 that the White House knew that the president was running the risk of becoming "negotiator-in-chief instead of commander-in-chief."[43] He has yet to get himself off this slippery slope.

Clinton's problems with identifying and pursuing key goals has plagued the administration in the national security field at least as much as it has on the domestic side. While it did not reflect on the resilience that he brought to office, Clinton's draft record would have made it difficult for him to gain credibility in the national security community under the best of circumstances. Scholars conventionally argue that the United States is nonstatist— that it accords no special status to the permanent custodians of the governmental apparatus.[44] This is not at all the case with national security. Militarism, especially since the creation of the army and naval academies at West Point and Annapolis during the first half of the nineteenth century, has prospered in the United States. From that time, the armed services played a decisive socializing role for many of the nation's elite. The Civil War, which brought mankind's capacity for mass mobilization and horrific destruction of life and property to previously inconceivable heights, ran on the military aptitude amassed through the process of putting some of the most able young men in the nation through the academies.

The nation has placed three former military leaders—Ulysses Grant, Theodore Roosevelt, and Dwight Eisenhower—in the presidency since the Civil War. Indeed, Theodore Roosevelt took an interval from his political career during the Spanish-American War. He had seized the opportunity to prove his mettle. As he observed to a friend: "If I am to be of any use in politics it is because I am supposed to be a man who does not preach what I fear to practice, and who will carry out himself what he advocates others carrying out."[45] Franklin Delano Roosevelt served as assistant secretary of the navy.

Bill Clinton, by his own admission, evaded his commitment to serve. He did this in the midst of perhaps the most trying period ever faced by the U.S. military. We might expect, under the best of circumstances, that the military establishment would resent Clinton as commander-in-chief. Nevertheless, two factors exacerbated the potential for misunderstanding between Clinton and the Pentagon.

First, candidate Clinton temporized throughout his campaign over the exact circumstances whereby he avoided military service and the motives behind his actions. This simply drew public attention to his lack of credentials in this dimension of the national security field. Second, Clinton embraced the objective of equality for gays in the armed services.

The conventional wisdom has it that this second element of Clinton's problems with the military emerged unnecessarily from his desire to clinch the gay vote. That is, observers have noted that the gay vote would have gone to Clinton whatever. They have argued further that Clinton needlessly threatened the Pentagon by pressing a policy that, in its eyes, would undermine the integrity of the military culture.

In fact, this interpretation misses an essential component of Clinton's problems. During the 1992 campaign, General Colin Powell, then chairman of the Joint Chiefs of Staff, publicly criticized Clinton's plans for gays in the military. Forging a coalition with Senator Sam Nunn and other friends of the Pentagon in Congress, he subsequently assumed the toughest possible negotiating positions in resisting the new administration's efforts to implement Clinton's pledges. These included threats to resign and abandon a secret deal struck with Nunn on cutting redundant programs in the services.[46] At one point, the president even blinked and suggested that gays might be excluded for certain kinds of duty—a clear instance of bending over backward to appear conciliatory.[47] Ultimately, a "compromise" emerged that might actually make things worse for gays in the military. The Pentagon agreed to a situation whereby it would not ask either recruits or actual members of the military their sexual preference. But it also imposed a requirement that individuals not declare their orientation. More important, it won from the administration strict sanctions against those who involve themselves in homosexual or lesbian sexual acts on or off military bases.

One might argue, then, that Clinton failed to manage Colin Powell. Efforts to clarify their roles in the military responded to changes in public views about gays and fell within the compass of recent court decisions in the United States[48] and the more tolerant policies emerging from other NATO countries. These changes called out for attention from a Democratic presidential candidate. Yet Clinton ran for cover when Powell first opposed his stance during the 1992 election.

Instead, Clinton should have occupied the high ground by reminding the country that the commander-in-chief, not the chairman of the Joint Chiefs of Staff, heads the military. Without personally attacking Powell, he could then have stated that, as a potential commander-in-chief, he would not want his options foreclosed by the public utterances of the person whose job it is to serve the president.

Perhaps Clinton calculated that, given his draft record, he could not pull off such a response. Nonetheless, he paid mightily for not sitting on Powell immediately on the latter's public intervention during the campaign. He essentially vacated the commander-in-chief role to the Pentagonphiles in Congress. This has greatly weakened the national security side of Clinton's first gearbox—that between the administration and the state apparatus.

Powell's retirement in fall 1993 did not change matters. Immediately after the Republicans' November 1994 recapture of Congress, Jesse Helms, chairman-designate of the Senate Foreign Affairs Committee, impugned Clinton's credibility as commander-in-chief. Helms based his attack on the grounds that his mail suggested that the military holds Clinton in contempt.

This reduced the administration to engaging the chairman of the Joint Chiefs General John Shalikashvili, in a round of phone calls to journalists disavowing Helms's remarks. In the end, Helms's gambit backfired. And his further remarks placed in question his suitability for the chairmanship of the Foreign Affairs Committee. Nevertheless, his boldness most certainly stemmed from Clinton's continuing vulnerability in the national security field.

With the rest of the first gearbox—the Clinton administration's relation to the standing bureaucracy—we found at best mixed signals at the beginning of the administration. First, Clinton did well in tapping the great and the good to head his key departments. With Treasury going to Lloyd Bentsen, State to Warren Christopher, the Office of Management and Budget to Leon Panetta, and Defense to Les Aspin, the new president added immensely to his cachet with the Washington establishment.

Yet a certain disjunction surfaced here between the president's youthful, sweep-with-a-new-broom campaign and the people he called on to head his key departments. The president revealed an especially unimaginative approach toward staffing his national security team. Christopher; Anthony Lake, assistant to the president for national security; Samuel Berger, Lake's deputy; James Woolsey, the CIA director; and Madeleine Albright, ambassador to the United Nations, all had served in the Carter administration. They struck many observers as retreads. Indeed, Lake speculated nine months into the administration that Clinton perhaps had stressed too much building a national security team consisting of collegial, like-minded advisers: "I think there is a danger that when people work well together, you can take the edge off the options."[49]

When one considers that fully twelve years had passed between the end of Carter's administration and the beginning of Clinton's, one cannot help but wonder if Clinton could have used a bit more initiative in making his choices. Certainly, national security constitutes one area where the administration displayed at the outset an exceptional lack of inspiration. It deferred to Bush precedents in handling pressure points such as Bosnia and Somalia. Warren Christopher—too much the cautious insider—found himself marginalized in virtually every issue he tried to tackle. Even in the first clear breakthrough in the early days of the administration, the September 1993 peace accord between the Israelis and Palestinians, the administration seemed only to have bolted itself onto the process with a hastily arranged Rose Garden signing ceremony.

A few weeks into the administration, officials characterized Clinton's personal involvement in foreign policy as pedestrian.[50] One observed, "He is there to do things when asked. But that is the extent of it"; another noted, "I think that the most interesting thing is that Mr. Clinton has not been present for a lot of the discussions. My sense of it is that he does not like this stuff because he in not a master of it."

Two messages regarding foreign policy came across during the first half of the administration. First, the core issues of global instability have truly metamorphosed—the enmity between the United States and the former communist states has almost completely dissipated, and mortal tribal enemies in the Middle East have decided to set aside their swords. Second, several nettlesome trouble areas, most notably civil and ethnic struggles in Bosnia, Somalia, and Rwanda, the Cuban and Haitian refugee problems, and North Korea's development of nuclear arms, have served up problems that call for a delicate balance between diplomatic maneuvering and military intervention.

For the most part, the administration's early handling of these intricate and sensitive problems made the United States appear peculiarly musclebound and suspect within the new framework for international relations. Clinton and his team accomplished little that assured observers that they would lead the nation into a more suitable posture for the times. And this owed significantly to the president's limited foreign affairs attention span and constant vacillation on issues that did engage him. It also derived from a seeming incapacity of his cabinet and White House advisers to organize themselves so as to compensate for the president's deficiencies in foreign policy. In this respect, Clinton was not receiving full value from his erring on the side of experience when picking his team.

As a candidate, Clinton proclaimed time and again that he would appoint a cabinet that looked like America. On the foreign policy side, this aspiration proved to be a pious hope. On the domestic side, the administration indeed paid a great deal of attention to diversity. But the administration's pledges proved difficult ones to observe. The president went through a number of agonizing decisions. Here his first efforts to appoint a woman as attorney general proved especially painful. Indeed, it, and other abortive nominations (not all at the cabinet level), proved deeply damaging to the president. By stressing diversity to the degree that he did, Clinton introduced a representational imperative to cabinetmaking much stronger than has ever prevailed in the United States.

Clinton's efforts exposed two pitfalls to such a representational approach to cabinetmaking. First, presidents who give the choice slots to white male members of the Washington establishment and the less crucial positions to minorities and/or women will encounter allegations of tokenism. Second, while minorities and women fulfill representational criteria, they may encounter difficulty in actually obtaining confirmation. Senators and the attentive groups will hold their fire rather than oppose accepted members of the great and the good. They will show less consideration for nominees with little or no standing in Washington. However much the United States has moved from "insider" to "outsider" politics,[51] those bent on embarrassing a new administration will pick at unknown nominees in search of a fatal flaw.

Regarding the second gearbox—that between the president and his own advisers—Clinton chose at the outset an eclectic approach that reflected his personality. This did not mean it suited the presidency at this stage. We discussed earlier the difficulty of striking a balance in the organization of the White House. Top-to-bottom, command-oriented White Houses with strong chiefs of staff have more than failed. They have also contributed to monocratic leadership and the abuses that seem inevitably to follow from this.

On the other hand, a loose, bottom-up organizational approach that fits the spokes-in-a-wheel format runs into two difficulties. First, the complexity of current governmental problems and the volatility of support in the electronic era make it difficult to sustain open-ended countervaillance. Prolonged examination of options in search of the best solution can make the president look ponderous and, when combined with leaks, give away hostages to the opposition. Second, especially since relative outsiders often occupy the Oval Office, not every president can call on the ringmaster skills required of the spokes-in-a-wheel arrangement.

Almost from the day that the election was over, observers began to note that Clinton, who benefited greatly from extremely hierarchical and decisive campaign organization, returned to the inclusive and deliberative governance style that had served him well in Arkansas. As a long-time friend noted soon after the election, "Very few decisions have been made. This is Bill's style: being extremely deliberate if not slow. He always wants to do things carefully and right."[52] Just before the inauguration, officials were already talking about the squandered opportunity of the transition—with advisers and senior Democrats declaring that "the old Clinton is back" and "I won't even try to spin you . . . [it's] awful."[53]

Not surprisingly, then, Clinton pursued a spokes-in-a-wheel approach. At first, his implementation of the model seemed to have fallen short of Carter's in achieving chaos, but not by much. Clinton at least appointed a chief of staff at the outset of the administration. The first incumbent to this position was Thomas "Mack" McLarty. The chairman of a natural gas conglomerate, McLarty had no previous experience in Washington. In defining how he would function as chief of staff, he stressed his management skills and loyalty to Clinton:

> As chief of staff I will do whatever I can to help him organize, manage, facilitate and carry out the duties of President of the United States. And as his friend I will always be straight with him and he knows that. Bill Clinton has my complete loyalty and trust—always has and always will.[54]

Some analysts wondered out loud whether McLarty had become simply a figurehead in a White House where more assertive aides would now find themselves free to pursue their own agendas. As one adviser had noted,

"They were all delighted with the McLarty appointment because it will allow them to do their thing."[55]

One of the key variables in determining power in the Clinton administration is one's FOB (Friend of Bill) factor. McLarty brought to the West Wing unrivaled credentials in this regard, having known the president since the two were three years old. He certainly did not give so much as a hint of letting power go to his head. Thus he did not turn into a Bob Haldeman, a Donald Regan, or a John Sununu. Indeed, he seemed to embody the "nice guy" side to Clinton's personality. Unlike the "good cop, bad cop" act that had prevailed under Bush and Sununu, the Clinton/McLarty pairing was all good cop.

The frantic efforts of the White House to reorganize itself during May 1993, after a disastrous first three months, suggested that McLarty had not gotten on top of the game. Clinton had not followed up on his original plan, which was to back up McLarty with a team of Washington-savvy deputies.[56] To his credit, his May reorganization proved relatively far-reaching, which is not to say that it brought about enduring changes in the performance of the administration.

A crucial problem with the Clinton White House was its dependence on those who had gained prominence during the campaign.[57] Here we saw a repeat of the Carter experience.[58] Just as with Carter, Clinton could not shed aides who, while effective campaigners, would not work well in the White House. As well, he was so loath to differentiate between the access of former campaign aides that he gave the run of the White House even to those not on his staff—such as Paul Begala, Stanley Greenberg, and James Carville —who gave him political advice.[59]

Clinton's attachment to George Stephanopoulos presented difficulties for the operation of the second gearbox from the beginning. During the campaign, Stephanopoulos became Clinton's most trusted and influential adviser. But he lacked the gravitas required of a chief of staff. President Clinton thus appointed Stephanopoulos White House director of communications.

This role normally goes to the person responsible for cultivating the president's image and developing an administration's overall media strategy. Stephanopoulos became the administration point man by taking daily press briefings. His combative style rankled the press. In the May reorganization, Stephanopoulos retired from the public stage to the more anonymous role of "special adviser." In a moment of candor, he recognized that the campaign technique of hopping from theme to theme in order to dominate the war of sound bites did not work for a president: "On the campaign trail, you can just change the subject. But you can't just change the subject as president."[60]

A defector from the Republicans and a true Washington pro, David Gergen, succeeded Stephanopoulos. The results were dazzling at first for

Gergen, who had earned his spurs as communications director during Ronald Reagan's first term. For instance, the administration did a marvelous job of making the relatively meager results of the July Group of Seven Tokyo Summit look like true accomplishments. One problem lurked in the background, however. Stephanopoulos, as described by himself, would remain "Clinton's personal policy and political person, to make sure ... things hang together."[61]

The administration really seemed to be on track by late summer 1993. Its tacks of focusing the fall strategy with Congress on three themes—health-care reform, passage of the North American Free Trade Agreement, and "Reinventing Government"—struck a chord for those who admired the genius of the Reagan administration at identifying a few, easy-to-remember themes and pushing them relentlessly. One could see the hand of David Gergen in all of this. But many observers feared that Clinton's themes—however easy for voters to remember—touched on goals of much greater complexity and potential divisiveness than Reagan's core commitments.

In looking through the White House and upper-level appointments elsewhere in the administration, one found an unsettling collection of Clinton mafias. He brought with him FOBs from Arkansas; Georgetown, where he received his undergraduate degree; Oxford, where he studied as a Rhodes scholar; Yale, where he took his law degree; and the Democratic Leadership Council, in which he earned his reputation as a rising centrist in his party. His wife, Hillary, added to this list by finding places for a host of left-leaning friends, some of whom had met the Clintons when they studied together at Yale. Many, such as health and human services secretary Donna Shalala, came with connections to the Children's Defense Fund.

The political proclivities of the two Clintons clashed, to say the least. And this introduced an element of schizophrenia to the administration.[62] Under the best of circumstances, Clinton would come off as indecisive. Hillary's influence at times forced him into staking out bold positions and then retreating in an unseemly manner when the political heat became too intense. And a subplot of the administration—right up to the response to the 1994 election debacle—has been competition between centrist and left-leaning prescriptions for rehabilitating the appeal of the administration. Here two figures whose prescriptions have not always been compatible—Al From, president of the Democratic Leadership Council, and Stanley Greenberg, Clinton's pollster—have pressed the need for establishment of a new Democratic governing coalition.[63]

The role of Hillary Clinton raised questions with constitutional and political overtones. When it became clear that she would assume responsibility for health care, some observers questioned how—as neither an elected or duly appointed official—she would be accountable.[64] As things began to go badly in areas where she had been especially involved—health care and the administration's response to the Whitewater episodes—officials began to speak out loud about the ambiguity of her role. As one Clinton friend put it, "It's hard to run a White House with nobody in charge.... It's especially hard to run a White House with nobody in charge and two presidents."[65] Indeed, polls began to suggest that the general public had qualms as well.[66]

Even those favorably disposed toward Hillary Clinton's role conveyed the sense that she was making up for deficiencies in Bill Clinton's presidential character by intervening to bring closure to discussions about the administration's core commitments[67] or providing it a moral compass.[68] When he seemed to be leaning overly on his wife's character as a defense against allegations concerning the Whitewater scandal, Bill Clinton provoked one of the stiffest attacks on himself yet encountered:

> Were it not because the president's own party dominates Congress and many other institutions, the assumption by Hillary Clinton of powers of an office to which she did not accede would be a constitutional crisis. It should be a constitutional crisis. But it is not. It is, instead, sublimated in scandal.[69]

In a presidential system, the chief executive knows no peers—he belongs neither to an elected legislature nor to a ministry that must maintain the support of a parliament. He gains entry to the executive–legislative arena through a constitutional mandate conveyed by a nationwide vote. No previous president has construed this mandate as shared with his wife. Clinton did. In fact, he specifically argued during the campaign that Americans would receive two leaders for the price of one, until at least it became clear that some voters found this formulation objectionable.

Those who place great stock in the Constitution heaved a sigh of relief when Ross Perot faded during the 1992 presidential campaign. His ascendancy, especially in the late spring, suggested that the United States had come to the brink of populism. It appeared in danger of becoming a disembodied democracy running on electronic appeals and bereft of institutional buttresses in the party system and the elected legislature.

Hillary Clinton's involvement in the administration threatened to run a close second to the presumption of Ross Perot. This was particularly the case with her assuming responsibility for health-care reform. Initially, the White House sold Hillary Clinton's role on the grounds that preparation of the health-reform initiative was in disarray,[70] and as Bill Clinton himself observed, "she's better at organizing and leading people from a complex beginning to a certain end."[71] In fact, she presided over a Rube Goldberg machine that by April had distilled the complexity into a whopping 1,100 page decision memo.[72] The central motif seemed to be: "if we throw enough great minds at this issue it's got to break sometime." The task force included some 500 officials working in endless meetings. In the words of a participant reflecting on progress by early March: "There's this sense of exhaustion and the real work hasn't begun yet."[73]

The sense was emerging as well that Hillary Clinton, aided by her ringmaster Ira Magaziner, was forcing Bill Clinton to embrace comprehensive and costly health-care reform proposals against the counsel of cooler heads in the White House and cabinet.[74] One White House official said that notwithstanding Hillary Clinton's giving all involved license to "speak your mind," "by virtue of her position as head of the task force and by being First Lady and by virtue of her own intellect, which is really quite impressive, she commands a lot of respect and is treated with deference."[75] By July 1994 it had become clear that Congress was not likely to pass a reform bill before the congressional elections. One senior aide noted, "We would have been in the reality zone a long time ago" had it not been for Hillary Clinton's "health care cult."[76]

Laurence Lynn, Jr., and David Whitman published in 1981 an analysis of why Jimmy Carter's welfare reform effort had failed. Key errors included Carter's indecisiveness, the incessant meddling of outsiders with the president's ear, a penchant for secrecy and group think, and the setting of unrealistic deadlines that inflated expectations and ultimately made the administration look inept and torn by dissension.

The entire edifice surrounding Hillary Clinton's health reform activities gave the effort the look of Carter's welfare reform writ large. Nobody would doubt Hillary Clinton's motives. But she and the president took an immense risk.

Carter's failure in welfare reform scarcely registered in the public's bill of particulars against him when they went to the polls in 1980. During the early months of the Clinton administration, few advisers seemed to have seen that an abortive health-care reform effort would have catastrophic effects on the administration. The issue concerned the management of 14 percent of GNP. It served as a focus of intense concern, especially in the business community. It had not just bolted itself to the president in the shape of a health reform czar. It had linked itself to the president's wife. Nobody seemed to have calculated that if the effort failed, the blame would go straight to a part of the administration's second gearbox that could not be hived off or marginalized. The resulting damage could ultimately compromise the future of the presidency itself.

Clinton and Institutionalization of the Second Gearbox

Earlier, this chapter noted that scholars made a great deal of the institutional strength of the presidency during the Reagan administration. But these assessments focused on the first gearbox, that is, the connection between the administration and the permanent bureaucracy. They assumed that all was well with the second gearbox—the relationship between the president and his cabinet officers and advisers. The events of the second term, especially those surrounding the Iran-*contra* scandal, suggested that the second gearbox had broken down. Similarly, Bush encountered problems with the second gearbox. He never really connected in domestic policy. Further, closer analysis would indicate that the occasion that led to his greatest triumph —the Persian Gulf crisis—occurred because of the administration's sloppy handling of Saddam Hussein's threats to invade Kuwait.

The United States presents a special case when it comes to the second gearbox. In cabinet systems of government, such as those that prevail in Britain, Canada, and Germany, the entire administration—as embodied in the members of cabinet—assumes joint responsibility for the policies and actions of the executive branch.[77] Thus it becomes very important that heads of government employ formal machinery—meetings of cabinet and its committees—in order to arrive at decisions that will win the acceptance of members of the entire administration. As well, such systems almost invariably vest the head of government with an office of permanent officials who shoulder responsibility for making sure that the second gearbox runs smoothly.

In the United States, the exercise of executive authority focuses very strongly on the president. Neither the Constitution nor conventions surrounding presidential leadership sustain a collective view of the executive power. Thus, only presidents who have become convinced of the instrumental utility of greater consultation with their cabinets have routinized these dynamics. Eisenhower, whose military training made him a firm believer in the need to structure decision processes, admired the British cabinet system and tried to transplant elements of it to his administration.[78] Following in the backlash to Nixon's extremely monocratic approach, Ford, Carter, and Reagan all pursued what they termed "cabinet government."[79] Bush, however, eschewed the concept both in the language used to describe the style of his administration and in practice.

Close analysis finds at best sporadic attention to routinized machinery for interdepartmental coordination.[80] The development and adaptation of strategic plans for administrations suffer a great deal under these circumstances. As well, administrations generally experience difficulty adhering to what commitments do emerge. The functioning of the process depends very much on personal factors and lacks institutional buttresses.[81] In many respects, each administration finds itself reinventing the wheel.

In the past, intellectually vigorous presidents who thrived on the cut and thrust of face-to-face exchanges with mixed groups of cabinet secretaries and advisers—typically scholars place Franklin D. Roosevelt and John F. Kennedy in this category—could keep all the policy balls in the air at once.[82] That is, they could keep a watching brief on all key issues and limit intensive attention to key points in the decision process. But the system seems no longer to serve up incumbents with the agility and the self-confidence of Roosevelt and Kennedy. More profoundly, the task of governance appears no longer to provide presidents the luxury of guiding their administrations through informal and ad hoc means. Things have simply gotten too complex and interconnected.

In structuring his White House and cabinet machinery, Bill Clinton seemed not to have gotten these two points. The evidence suggests that he in fact saw himself as another FDR or JFK. Aides reported his devouring 100-page briefings[83] and correcting advisers on points of detail.[84] When the administration went through its first efforts to reorganize in May 1993, many aides placed much of the blame on Clinton's love affair with detail[85] and tendency to staff himself in making decisions.[86]

Even if his actual abilities matched his self-assessment, Clinton would still have had to provide some evidence that he recognized that the requirements for coordination had become exponentially greater in the thirty-two years that had passed since Kennedy became president. That is, he would have focused a great deal more attention than he did on the organization of his White House and cabinet systems. And he would have rejoined the iterative process—advanced most under Eisenhower, Ford, and Reagan (first term)—whereby presidents have gradually matched tightening their hold over the standing bureaucracy (gearbox 1) with institutionalization of internal administration dynamics (gearbox 2).

Clinton did neither in any readily identifiable or consistent way. Indeed, his idea of organizing the cabinet consisted of a weekend retreat where members shared personal accounts of their lives. This included the president's own sharing "about how he was a fat kid when he was 5 and 6 and how the other kids taunted him."[87]

The argument that Clinton neglected cabinet-level structures even applies to his use of the National Security Council—a part of his coordinative apparatus that actually derives a modicum of authority by virtue of a congressional mandate given at the request of Harry Truman.[88] The NSC, along with its supporting secretariat in the Executive Office of the President, became highly institutionalized during the Eisenhower administration. Kennedy virtually ignored the NSC.[89] Johnson and Nixon built up the NSC staff as a counterbureaucracy, thereby setting up the situation in which the national security advisers became major players—along with the secretaries of state and defense—in foreign affairs. In many respects, the imperial presidency emerged from this centralization of power. Ford and Carter took pains to demonstrate greater respect for their cabinet officers in the foreign policy field. The NSC process actually came back to life under Carter. And it functioned reasonably effectively during Reagan's first term, although it again became staff-driven and centralized during the second term.[90]

As noted earlier, the full blossoming of the electronic era in the executive branch meant that the Bush administration could introduce a practice that pretty much preordained the continued ineffectiveness of the NSC. Bush rarely convened meetings of "principals"—that is, himself along with cabinet-level officials who are statutory members of the NSC or, as usually is the case with the treasury secretary, designated members. Instead, he allowed much of the business of the NSC to take place on frequent video hookups between deputy agency heads. This meant that many issues never received consideration in formal meetings of agency heads. Further, many of the discussions in the video hookups skirted around issues because the participants never knew who was looking on but remained out of view.

Bill Clinton seems to have taken the downsizing of institutional buttresses of the NSC process one step further. Formal meetings of NSC principals actually chaired by the president became rare. From the beginning of the administration, the same president who immersed himself in the details of domestic affairs tended to cut meetings of his foreign policy advisers on key issues, including Bosnia.[91] The assistant to the president for national security, Anthony Lake, did run a more systematic process than prevailed under Bush. This involved a set time for briefing the president on main developments, face-to-face meetings of deputies in the White House "situation room" several times a week, almost weekly meetings of cabinet-level principals, and a weekly lunch between the secretaries of state and defense and Lake.[92] But with only sporadic attention from the president, this machinery did not connect well to his actual consideration and handling of the major issues facing the administration.

By October 1993, Lake had diagnosed the problem—the president had not engaged himself sufficiently in the "larger contemplative discussions."[93] Lake hoped out loud that Clinton would "spend more time now having more sit-back-and-think-about-this kind of meetings." This never came to pass.

On the domestic side, Clinton stuck with the division of economic and general domestic policy first instituted during the second Reagan term. In the United States, standing cabinet committees with parallel secretariats have developed only very gradually. The Economic Policy Board under Ford did a pretty solid job of coordinating between economics agencies.[94] Carter instituted an Economic Policy Council, but the group included too many participants to operate effectively.[95] And Carter's assistant to the president for domestic policy, Stuart E. Eizenstat, operated more as a principal in meetings than a neutral broker and frequently corrected public comments by W. Michael Blumenthal, the treasury secretary.

During his first term, Reagan went further than any of his predecessors in differentiating cabinet business. He eventually created seven cabinet councils. Only two of these—Economic Affairs and Commerce and Trade—met with any regularity. The system received some credit for defusing middle-range conflicts between departments. But the White House, largely through the Legislative Strategy Group headed by James A. Baker III, tended to draw the really big issues into its vortex and limit participation to key players. The system pretty much fell apart during the second term when Reagan collapsed the seven cabinet councils into two—Economic Policy and Domestic Policy—neither of which met with any regularity. Bush continued the same structure and, similarly, did not operate it with any consistency.

Clinton has opted for a National Economic Council (NEC) and a Domestic Policy Council (DPC). Neither meets with any regularity. The NEC staff has done an excellent job of spin-doctoring its role, largely thanks to its head, Robert E. Rubin, who succeeded Lloyd Bentsen as treasury secretary after the midterm elections. In several newspapers stories that quoted him copiously, Rubin came across as the neutral broker par excellence.[96] Rubin set as his model his understanding of Brent Scowcroft's role as national security adviser, acting as "an honest broker efficiently to integrate and coordinate policy across agency lines." Rubin failed to distinguish whether he meant Scowcroft under Gerald Ford or Scowcroft under George Bush. In the latter case, working as he did at the president's constant beck and call and once removed from the video conference calls conducted by deputies, Scowcroft had little opportunity to link up with a formal integrative process, much less function as a neutral broker within it.[97]

The atmospherics of economic policymaking in the administration seem to belie the existence of neutral brokerage. From the outset, the administration proved deeply divided over key elements of economic policy.[98] Clinton appeared to have been railroaded into abandoning his proposals for a stimulus package and tax breaks for the middle class in the early days of the administration.[99] Deep rifts among cabinet officers over U.S. trade policies came to public view in April 1993.[100] In the same month, the budget director, Leon Panetta, publicly questioned the viability of the entire edifice of Clinton administration economic policy, including aid to Russia, NAFTA, and the affordability of health-care reform.[101] Before becoming ensnared in the Whitewater case, Roger Altman, the deputy treasury secretary, began so to eclipse the role of Bentsen that the latter was considering leaving the administration after his first year.[102] Altman's leverage rested in his cachet with Rubin and his management of the White House "war room" on the budget during summer 1993.

Even recent success stories related by Rubin suggest that he was more a stager than a neutral broker. He got members of the cabinet who were strongly opposed to invocation of "Super 310" against the Japanese to hold their noses and remain silent about protectionist measures pressed by the U.S. trade representative that clearly ran against the spirit of GATT.[103] The preparation of the budget for fiscal year 1995–96 actually saw Rubin function as the president's delegate, with cabinet secretaries working on an individual basis with Rubin, who would then funnel issues up to Clinton.[104]

The assistant to the president for domestic policy, Carol H. Rasco, had served as Clinton's policy coordinator during the campaign. She brought with her little experience that would have helped her ringmaster the unwieldy domain of domestic policy—especially when we consider that the administration planned to tackle both health care and welfare reform. In any case, the Domestic Policy Council, which she was supposed to support, did not operate in a coherent fashion. And the administration's major absorption, health-care reform, operated in its own separate orbit under the direction of Hillary Clinton and Ira Magaziner, with the latter nominally responsible to Rasco.

David Gergen, while assistant to the president for communications under Ronald Reagan, once noted that cabinet-level councils, though perhaps not a philosopher's stone for resolution of coordination problems in an administration, did, when operating properly, do an excellent job of encouraging cabinet secretaries to resolve mid-level disputes before they got to the Oval Office and contributed to the excessive decision load of the president.[105] The Reagan administration, of course, was aided by its stripped-down agenda, which required much less complicated management because it was not engaged in intricate efforts at positive statecraft. Still the Reagan administration's modulation of issue resolution in cabinet councils and management of the really contentious matters in the Legislative Strategy Group (discussed earlier) seemed to provide just the mix for moving its program forward expeditiously.

What we find missing in the Clinton administration is anything like a Legislative Strategy Group (LSG). The modified spokes-in-a-wheel organization of the White House in the Reagan administration actually provided the core for an LSG. Each of the permanent members had responsibility for an operational part of the White House, and each embodied a side of the president's personality. Thus, we saw arise an exceptional team, which included James Baker (the chief of staff), Ronald Reagan the pragmatist; Edwin Meese (the counselor), the ideological conservative; William Clark (the assistant to the president for national security), a foreign policy neophyte with strong views; and Michael Deaver (deputy chief of staff), the communicator par excellence.

The almost organic functioning of the group helped the president in three ways. It took major issues—due to their complexity and/or divisiveness—out of the cabinet council system so that options might be narrowed before they went to the president. As well, it helped hold commitments together once the president had made a decision. Finally, it led the process of reconciling differences between the administration's commitments and what was achievable through Congress.

It might well be that an individual such as Bill Clinton would never abide a group performing such functions on his behalf. But, as I implied earlier, this would make Clinton a president of the old school—that of FDR and JFK. That is, he would be relying on sheer intellectual acuity and a knack for ringmastering myriad issues in direct dialogue with his advisers and cabinet secretaries. Clinton might well display the first of these attributes; however, he clearly has failed to demonstrate the second one.

Clinton did not even have the individuals necessary to establish a modified-spokes-in-a-wheel format in regard to those whom he selected for his inner circle and/or the responsibilities he allotted to them. Mack McLarty lacked the familiarity with Washington and the decisiveness to fill the shoes of a James Baker; George Stephanopoulos lacked the maturity and control over the policy development process to function as an Ed Meese; Anthony Lake, although experienced in Washington and a competent expert in the foreign policy field, lacked the strong relationship to Clinton to serve as surrogate for a president who wanted to focus his major efforts on domestic policy. When David Gergen joined the administration in spring 1993, he soon performed a role similar to Mike Deaver's during the Reagan administration. But he lacked operational responsibility for any specific part of the White House apparatus and the trust of those such as Stephanopoulos, who saw running the presidency as a perpetual campaign in which possession of a very busy person's mind would provide a streetcar for advancement of pet policy ideas.

We have seen in several recent administrations the rise in the White House of the Washington insider who will serve as Mr. Fixit. During the Ford administration, in the wake of the Watergate debacle, Donald Rumsfeld, who had served three terms in the House of Representatives and as director of the Office of Economic Opportunity, and Richard Cheney, who had been a congressional aide and a deputy to Rumsfeld at OEO, both did excellent jobs as White House "staff coordinators" in a time when even the suggestion of centralization of power would have evoked the images of H.R. "Bob" Haldeman and the failed Nixon presidency. With the resignation of Donald Regan during the Iran-*contra* revelations, Howard Baker, the Senate minority leader, became chief of staff. He and his successor, Kenneth Duberstein, who had twice headed up Reagan's congressional relations office, kept Ronald Reagan's White House out of trouble for the remainder of the administration. With the departure of John Sununu late in 1991, Bush first resorted to his transportation secretary, Samuel K. Skinner, but ultimately called on James A. Baker III to leave the State Department and become his chief of staff. It was too late by then.

The question arises here whether Leon Panetta can provide the steady hand necessary to get the Clinton administration on a viable course. As a former chairman of the House Budget Committee and a Clinton budget director, Panetta certainly brings to the White House the capacity to cope more aptly with the art of the possible inside the Beltway.

A great deal of thunder was heard around the West Wing when Panetta assumed his position in June 1994. This was based on his claims of full authority from the president to make sweeping changes.[106] Yet Panetta immediately went into reviewing-the-situation mode, with promises of a thorough "look at all White House operations"—astounding words from someone who had viewed the chaos of the administration from one of the best perches available in Washington.[107]

As Panetta's study progressed—it took almost three months—much of the blame centered on the White House communications operation.[108] This proved awkward because a major target, press secretary Dee Dee Myers, had in late June been the subject of a call from the president to Panetta urging him to ease up on his criticism of Myers.[109] In the end, it was decided that Myers would leave the White House by the end of the year.

After the November election, Panetta received an in-house evaluation of his own role courtesy of disgruntled White House aides claiming that he had done nothing to reverse the campaign syndrome whereby Clinton remained "overhandled, overscheduled, overexposed" and "has suffered in stature and ability to focus."[110]

Conclusion

In the middle part of this century, critical assessments of the presidential system in the United States focused on the separation of powers. Observers saw a need for greater unity between the executive and the legislative branches of government. Frustrations with the system originated largely from the left —those hoping for quicker advancement of the welfare state.

The late 1960s and early 1970s saw a cooling of interest in greater unity between presidents and Congress. The separation of powers corresponded to the fragmented nature of the American political culture. It seemed to set a viable context for pluralistic leadership in a society prone to incremental change. Further, the abuses of power under the Nixon administration raised concerns about the imperialization of the presidency.

The Carter administration functioned so ineffectively that observers fretted for a while that the presidency had become too weak. Reagan turned things around dramatically. He brought a strong electoral mandate to office. The Republicans controlled the Senate. The taxpayer revolt had turned many congressional Democrats into fiscal conservatives.

A theory emerged in this period that the presidency had turned a corner. Through greater internal discipline and relentless control of the permanent bureaucracy, presidents could compensate for leadership deficits associated with the separation of powers.

This interpretation ultimately proved illusory. Reagan had gotten the gearbox between himself and his top advisers and that between his team and the permanent bureaucracy right at the outset of his administration. But the delicate balance was lost by the beginning of the second term. Further, the lack of countervaillance in the bureaucracy and Congress meant that the nation had overcommitted to policies that ultimately proved adverse to its long-term well-being.

The current malaise in U.S. presidential leadership relates much more to the legacy of Reaganite excesses than to the separation of powers. Indeed, adequately functioning checks and balances against the most extravagant Reagan policies would likely have mitigated the current crisis.

Two conditions have greatly circumscribed presidential leadership: the deficit, which has created ceaseless pressures to reduce spending without raising taxes, and the sour public mood reflected in anxieties about the accessibility of the American dream as the United States loses its economic dominance in the world.

The rise of electronically oriented populist campaigning has also greatly deinstitutionalized the power bases of presidents. The facileness with which Ross Perot served as spoiler in the 1992 campaign and continued—at least until his poor performance in the NAFTA debate with Al Gore—to undermine Clinton's support suggests two things. First, segments of the public have become deeply disaffected. Second, the fact that control of electronic media depends on ready cash gives carte blanche to those with populist tendencies who either have immense personal wealth or can tap unlimited resources.

We can understand why both Bush and Clinton have resorted to "let's deal" leadership approaches. Nevertheless, two difficulties have emerged from adoption of this style. First, it serves up centrist, least-common-denominator solutions to problems that now seem to exceed this order of difficulty. In other words, some of the post-Reagan problems seem to call for more than incremental solutions. Second, as Bush certainly discovered and Clinton seems to be finding, it often proves difficult for presidents successfully to implement a "let's deal" style, especially if they fail adequately to rig either or both of their gearboxes.

The prognosis suggests that the nation has not turned the corner in coping with gridlock. More worrying, the specter of noninstitutional, electronically based leadership looms ever larger, especially with the ascendancy of Newt Gingrich in the wake of the 1994 congressional elections. A vicious circle suggests itself. Presidents and Congress will blame one another for failures in leadership. The public will increasingly blame gridlock for the resulting paralysis. Efforts will be made to short-circuit the relationships between voters and their elected representatives with direct appeals. These will undermine public perceptions of the legitimacy of presidential and congressional leadership. The respective legitimacy deficits will further exacerbate gridlock.

Acknowledgments

The author, a Canadian, wishes to note that this chapter is a NAFTA product which relied heavily upon the research assistance of José Antonio Mejia Guerra, from Mexico, and Stephen Shannon, from the United States, both of whom are students in the Graduate Public Policy Program at Georgetown University.

Notes

1. Ross K. Baker, "Sorting Out and Suiting Up: The Presidential Nominations," in *The Election of 1992,* ed. Gerald M. Pomper (Chatham, N.J.: Chatham House, 1993), 57–59; Pomper, "The Presidential Election," in ibid., 142.

2. Wilson Carey McWilliams, "The Meaning of the Election," in ibid., 199.

3. Richard Rose, *The Postmodern President: The White House Meets the World* (Chatham, N.J.: Chatham House, 1988).

4. Samuel Kernell, *Going Public: New Strategies of Presidential Leadership* (Washington, D.C.: CQ Press, 1986).

5. Terry M. Moe, "The Politicized Presidency," in *The New Direction in American Politics,* ed. John E. Chubb and Paul E. Peterson (Washington, D.C.: Brookings Institution, 1985).

6. Colin Campbell, *Managing the Presidency: Carter, Reagan and the Search for Executive Harmony* (Pittsburgh: University of Pittsburgh Press, 1986).

7. Colin Campbell, "The White House and Presidency under the 'Let's Deal' President," in *The Bush Presidency: First Appraisals,* ed. Colin Campbell and Bert A. Rockman (Chatham, N.J.: Chatham House, 1991).

8. Colin Campbell, "Political Executives and Their Officials," in *The State of the Discipline,* ed. Ada Finifter (Washington, D.C.: American Political Science Association, 1993).

9. David Mayhew, *Divided We Govern: Party Control in Lawmaking and Investigations* (New Haven: Yale University Press, 1991); Charles O. Jones, *The Presidency in a Separated System* (Washington, D.C.: Brookings Institution, 1994).

10. American Political Science Association, Committee on Political Parties, *Toward a More Responsible Two-Party System* (New York: Rinehart, 1950).

11. Paul Craig Roberts, *The Supply-Side Revolution* (Cambridge, Mass.: Harvard University Press, 1984); David A. Stockman, *The Triumph of Politics: How the Reagan Revolution Failed* (New York: Harper & Row, 1986).

12. James M. Buchanan and Gordon Tullock, *The Calculus of Consent: Logical Foundations of Constitutional Democracy* (Ann Arbor: University of Michigan Press, 1962).

13. William Niskanen, *Bureaucracy and Representative Government* (New York: Aldine Atherton, 1971).

14. Donald J. Savoie, *Thatcher, Reagan, Mulroney: In Search of a New Bu-

reaucracy (Pittsburgh: University of Pittsburgh Press, 1994); Colin Campbell and Graham Wilson, *The End of Whitehall: The Death of a Paradigm?* (Oxford, England: Blackwell, 1995).

15. Peter Aucoin, "Comment: Assessing Managerial Reforms," *Governance* 3 (1990): 197–204.

16. Hugh Heclo, *A Government of Strangers: Executive Politics in Washington* (Washington, D.C.: Brookings Institution, 1977); Michael Hansen and Charles H. Levine, "The Centralization–Decentralization Tug-of-War in the New Executive Branch," in *Governing Organizations: Organizing Governance*, ed. Colin Campbell and B. Guy Peters (Pittsburgh: University of Pittsburgh Press, 1988).

17. Mancur Olson, *The Rise and Decline of Nations: Economic Growth, Stagflation, and Social Rigidities* (New Haven: Yale University Press, 1982).

18. James David Barber, *The Presidential Character: Predicting Performance in the White House* (Englewood Cliffs, N.J.: Prentice Hall, 1972).

19. Bert A. Rockman, "The Leadership Style of George Bush," in Campbell and Rockman, *Bush Presidency;* and Campbell, "The White House," in ibid.

20. Bert A. Rockman, "The Leadership Question: Is There an Answer?" in *Executive Leadership in Anglo-American Systems,* ed. Colin Campbell and Margaret Jane Wyszomirski (Pittsburgh: University of Pittsburgh Press, 1991); and B. Guy Peters, "Executive Leadership in an Age of Retrenchment," in ibid.

21. Joel D. Aberbach, "The President and the Executive Branch," in Campbell and Rockman, *Bush Presidency.*

22. Larry Berman and Bruce W. Jentleson, "Bush and the Post–Cold War World: New Challenges for American Leadership," in Campbell and Rockman, *Bush Presidency.*

23. Bruce Jentleson, *With Friends Like These: Reagan, Bush and Saddam, 1982–1990* (New York: Norton, 1994).

24. Michael R. Gordon and Bernard E. Trainor, *The Generals' War: The Inside Story of the Conflict in the Gulf* (Boston: Little, Brown, 1995), 153–54, 423, 431.

25. Richard J. Ellis, *Presidential Lightning Rods: The Politics of Blame Avoidance* (Lawrence: University Press of Kansas, 1994), 176–77.

26. Richard L. Berke, "The Good Son," *New York Times,* 20 February 1994.

27. Ann Devroy, "Post-Vacation Clinton Swims toward Mainstream," *Washington Post,* 6 September 1993; Michael Wines, "President Takes His Opponents to Task," *New York Times,* 2 August 1994.

28. Patricia Zapor, "Text Clinton," *Catholic News Service,* 27 October 1992.

29. See, for instance, Michael Kelly, "Bill Clinton: The President's Past," *New York Times,* 31 July 1994.

30. Robert J. Samuelson, ". . . And He Isn't FDR," *Washington Post,* 19 May 1993.

31. Bob Woodward, "Clinton Felt Blindsided over Slashed Initiatives," *Washington Post,* 5 June 1994.

32. Paul J. Quirk, "Domestic Policy: Divided Government and Cooperative Presidential Leadership," in Campbell and Rockman, *Bush Presidency,* 72. Quirk cites Dean Pruitt, *Negotiating Behavior* (New York: Academic Press, 1982).

33. Leslie H. Gelb, "Avoiding Carter's Mistakes," *New York Times,* 28 January 1993.

34. David S. Broder, "He Can't Go It Alone," *Washington Post,* 19 May

1993.

35. R.W. Apple, Jr., "Clinton at Work: Is Motion the Same Thing as Action?" *New York Times*, 30 October 1993.

36. Ann Devroy, "How the White House Runs and Stumbles," *Washington Post*, 9 November 1993.

37. Quirk, "Domestic Policy."

38. Thomas B. Edsall, "Split over NAFTA May Strengthen Force of Disaffected Voter," *Washington Post*, 19 November 1993. See also David S. Broder, "NAFTAmath," *Washington Post*, 19 November 1993.

39. Michael Wines, "A 'Bazaar' Method of Dealing for Votes," *New York Times*, 11 November 1993; Keith Bradsher, "Clinton's Shopping List for Votes Has Ring of Grocery Buyer's List," *New York Times*, 17 November 1993.

40. Russell Baker, "The Flexible Goodbye," *New York Times*, 26 July 1994.

41. Ann Devroy and David S. Broder, "Democrats Plan Longer Phase-in to Full Coverage," *Washington Post*, 22 July 1994.

42. Ann Devroy, "Clinton Shuffles Staff to Return to 'Basics,'" *Washington Post*, 7 May 1993.

43. Dana Priest and Ruth Marcus, "Key Clinton Health Ideas Face Major Opposition," *Washington Post*, 20 February 1994.

44. Bert A. Rockman, *The Leadership Question: The Presidency and the American System* (New York: Praeger, 1984), 49–52.

45. John Milton Cooper, Jr., *The Warrior and the Priest: Woodrow Wilson and Theodore Roosevelt* (Cambridge, Mass.: Harvard University Press, 1983), 38.

46. Barton Gellman, "Service Moving to Protect Turf, Powell to Rebuff Call to Streamline," *Washington Post*, 28 January 1993; "Pentagon Deadlock as a Deal Collapses, How Powell's Switch on Cuts Scuttled a Capitol Scenario," *International Herald Tribune*, 30–31 January 1993; and Sidney Blumenthal, "Rendezvousing with Destiny," *New Yorker*, 8 March 1993, 42.

47. Richard Cohen, "The Battle over Gays," *Washington Post*, 26 March 1993.

48. See, for instance, Thomas L. Friedman, "Judge Rules Military's Ban on Homosexuals Is Void," *New York Times*, 29 January 1993.

49. Thomas L. Friedman, "Clinton's Foreign Policy: Top Adviser Speaks Up," *New York Times*, 31 October 1993.

50. Thomas L. Friedman, "For Clinton, Foreign Policy Comes Afterward," *International Herald Tribune*, 9 February 1993.

51. Rockman, "The Leadership Question"; Peters, "Executive Leadership."

52. Thomas L. Friedman, "Change of Tone for Clinton: High Energy to Low Profile," *New York Times*, 11 November 1994.

53. Dan Balz, "For Clinton, Here Comes the Hard Part," *International Herald Tribune*, 18 January 1993.

54. Thomas L. Friedman, "Democratic Leader and Clinton Friend Gain Major Posts," *New York Times*, 13 December 1992.

55. Ann Devroy, "Undergirding McLarty, a Second-Tier Contest," *Washington Post*, 14 December 1992.

56. Ann Devroy and Ruth Marcus, "White House Needs 'Tighter Coordination,' Clinton Concedes," *Washington Post*, 5 May 1993.

57. Stephen Barr and Al Kamen, "Transition Momentum Bogs Down at Sub-Cabinet Level," *Washington Post*, 11 January 1993.

58. Campbell, *Managing the Presidency,* 84.

59. Gwen Ifill, "Off-the-Books Advisers Giving Clinton a Big Lift," *New York Times,* 1 April 1993; Robin Toner, "Clinton's Health-Care Plan," *New York Times,* 7 April 1993.

60. Thomas L. Friedman with Maureen Dowd, "Amid Setbacks, Clinton Team Seeks to Shake off the Blues," *New York Times,* 25 April 1993.

61. David Von Drehle and Ann Devroy, "White House Plans Broad Staff Shifts," *Washington Post,* 29 May 1993.

62. Michael Kelly, "Furor Appears to Doom Cabinet Contender," *New York Times,* 17 December 1992; Jason DeParle, "Clinton Social Policy Camps: Bill's vs. Hillary's," *New York Times,* 20 December 1992.

63. Richard L. Berke, "Centrists Are Wary of Clinton Tilting," *New York Times,* 3 December 1993; E.J. Dionne, Jr., "Anatomy of a Feud," *Washington Post,* 7 December 1993; Michael Wines, "In Defeat, Clinton Aides Find Their Silver Lining," *New York Times,* 12 November 1994; Michael Wines, "White House in Struggle to Take Back the Agenda," *New York Times,* 17 November 1994; Dan Balz, "Health Plan Was Albatross for Democrats: Big Government Label Hurt Party, Poll Finds," *Washington Post,* 18 November 1994.

64. David S. Broder, "The Clinton Generation Brings Its Own Scars," *International Herald Tribune,* 11 February 1993.

65. Maureen Dowd, "New Role, New Troubles," *New York Times,* 6 March 1994.

66. David S. Broder, "Clinton's Approval Ratings Weaken," *Washington Post,* 16 November 1993.

67. David S. Broder, "Dual Practice," *Washington Post,* 24 September 1993; Bob Woodward, "Memo from Consultants Rattles the White House," *Washington Post,* 7 June 1994.

68. Martha Sherrill, "Hillary Clinton's Inner Politics," *Washington Post,* 6 May 1993.

69. Mark Helprin, "School of Scandal," *Wall Street Journal,* 25 March 1994.

70. Robert Pear, "First Lady Gets Office and Job in West Wing," *New York Times,* 22 January 1993.

71. "Mrs. Clinton to Head Health Task Force," *International Herald Tribune,* 26 January 1993.

72. Dana Priest, "Putting Health Care under Microscope," *Washington Post,* 16 April 1993.

73. Robin Toner, "How Much Health-Care Reform Will the Patient Go Along With?" *New York Times,* 7 March 1993.

74. Robert Pear, "A White House Fight," *New York Times,* 25 May 1993; Robert Pear, "Health Planners at White House Consider Lid on Medicare Costs," *New York Times,* 30 August 1993.

75. Pear, "A White House Fight."

76. Michael Wines, "First Lady's Health Strategy: Accept Less or Gamble It All?" *New York Times,* 5 July 1994.

77. Renate Mayntz, "Executive Leadership in Germany: Dispersion of Power of 'Kanzlerdemokratie,'" in *Presidents and Prime Ministers,* ed. Richard Rose and Ezra N. Suleiman (Washington, D.C.: American Enterprise Institute, 1980), 139; Johan Olsen, *Organizing Democracy: Political Institutions in a Welfare State — The Case of Norway* (New York: Columbia University Press, 1983), 79; Patrick

Weller, *First among Equals: Prime Ministers in Westminster Systems* (London: Allen and Unwin, 1985), 105–7, 131–34; Thomas T. Mackie and Brian W. Hogwood, "Decision-Making in Cabinet Government," in *Unlocking the Cabinet: Cabinet Structures in Comparative Perspective,* ed. Thomas T. Mackie and Brian W. Hogwood (London: Sage, 1985), 7–12.

78. Fred I. Greenstein, *The Hidden-Hand Presidency: Eisenhower as Leader* (New York: Basic Books, 1982).

79. Campbell, *Managing the Presidency,* chap. 3.

80. Roger B. Porter, *Presidential Decision Making: The Economic Policy Board* (Cambridge, England: Cambridge University Press, 1980).

81. Alexander George, *Presidential Decision-Making in Foreign Policy: The Effective Use of Information and Advice* (Boulder, Colo.: Westview Press, 1980).

82. Richard E. Neustadt, *Presidential Power and Modern Presidents: The Politics of Leadership from Roosevelt to Reagan* (New York: Free Press, 1990).

83. Thomas L. Friedman and Elaine Sciolino, "Clinton and Foreign Issues: Spasms of Attention," *New York Times,* 22 March 1993.

84. Friedman, "For Clinton."

85. R.W. Apple, Jr., "Clinton's Refocusing," *New York Times,* 6 May 1993.

86. Ruth Marcus, "Vote Victory Was Vital Boost for Clinton's Beleaguered Chief," *Washington Post,* 29 May 1993.

87. Ann Devroy, "A Bonding Experience at Camp David," *Washington Post,* 5 February 1993.

88. Anna Kasten Nelson, "National Security I: Inventing a Process (1945–1960)," in *The Illusion of Presidential Government,* ed. Hugh Heclo and Lester Salamon (Boulder, Colo.: Westview Press, 1981).

89. I.M. Destler, "National Security II: The Rise of the Assistant (1961–1981)," in Heclo and Salamon, *Illusion of Presidential Government.*

90. Kevin V. Mulcahy and Harold F. Kendrick, "The National Security Adviser: A Presidential Perspective," in Campbell and Wyszomirski, *Executive Leadership.*

91. Friedman, "For Clinton."

92. Leslie H. Gelb, "Where's Bill," *New York Times,* 11 March 1993; Friedman and Sciolino, "Clinton and Foreign Issues."

93. Thomas L. Friedman, "Clinton's Foreign Policy: Top Adviser Speaks Up," *New York Times,* 31 October 1993.

94. Porter, *Presidential Decision Making.*

95. Campbell, *Managing the Presidency,* 137–40.

96. Gwen Ifill, "The Economic Czar Behind the Economic Czars," *New York Times,* 7 March 1993; Tom Redburn, "U.S. Aims to Inject Life into G-7," *International Herald Tribune,* 21 June 1993.

97. Campbell, "The White House and Presidency," 207–10.

98. "And Now, Paying for the Promises: Tax Rises and Spending Cuts Loom," *International Herald Tribune,* 15 January 1993; Gwen Ifill, "Economic Plan Grew Slowly out of Marathon Debate," 21 February 1993.

99. Bob Woodward, *The Agenda: Inside the Clinton White House* (New York: Simon and Schuster, 1994).

100. Keith Bradsher, "A Deep Rift in Cabinet Stalls U.S. Trade Policy," *International Herald Tribune,* 29 April 1993.

101. "A Too-Frank Aide and Balky Congress," *International Herald Tribune,*

28 April 1993.

102. Steven Greenhouse, "Resignations at Treasury Raise the Question: Is Bentsen Next?" *New York Times,* 25 August 1993.

103. Hobart Rowen, "Invitation to a Trade War," *Washington Post,* 3 March 1994; David E. Rosenbaum, "On Economics, White House Is Steering Clear of Bickering," *New York Times,* 27 May 1994.

104. Rosenbaum, "On Economics."

105. Personal interview, 1983.

106. Douglas Jehl, "Hinting at More Changes, Panetta Takes the Reins," *New York Times,* 28 June 1994.

107. Ann Devroy and Ruth Marcus, "Panetta Claims 'Authority' to Make Changes," *Washington Post,* 1 July 1994.

108. Ann Devroy, "Another Miserable White House August," *Washington Post,* 10 August 1994.

109. Douglas Jehl, "New Chief of Staff Gets a Lesson on Who's the Boss," *New York Times,* 30 June 1994.

110. Ann Devroy, "Reasserting Presidency Means Rethinking Almost Everything," *Washington Post,* 14 November 1994.

3

Trying to Govern Positively in a Negative Era: Clinton and the 103rd Congress

BARBARA SINCLAIR

On 20 February 1993, William Jefferson Clinton laid out his program in his first presidential address to a joint session of Congress. A multifaceted economic plan that included deficit reduction and an immediate stimulus package, health-care reform, ending welfare as we know it, the North American Free Trade Agreement (NAFTA), and comprehensive crime legislation were just the most prominent items on a big and ambitious agenda. All these and most of Clinton's other policy objectives required positive congressional action.

This chapter examines the relationship between Clinton and Congress, assesses the legislative record of the 103rd Congress, and attempts to explain both the successes and the failures. It also tries to explain the electorate's harsh judgment—a verdict that translated into an electoral catastrophe for Democrats in 1994. I argue that, while the skill of the participants does affect outcomes, structural and other contextual factors are much more important determinants of the character of presidential-congressional relations and of policy and electoral results.

The Contextual Determinants
of Presidential-Congressional Relations

Understanding the relationship between a particular president and Congress and the policy outputs that ensue requires understanding how incentives and behavior are shaped by the constitutional, institutional, and political context. We have come to expect the president to act as policy leader: to set the agenda and to engineer passage of legislation to deal with the country's major problems. The Constitution, however, establishes a relationship of mutual dependence between the president and Congress and in terms of policy-making puts the president in the weaker position.[1] The president depends on Congress not just for new programs but also for money to carry out existing programs, for approval of top-level personnel to staff the administration, and for acquiescence in many of the decisions he makes that Congress, through legislation or less formal means, could hinder. Of course, the more ambitious a president's legislative agenda, the more dependent he is on Congress for success.

The Constitution and the weak, decentralized party system it fostered provide the president with no basis for commanding Congress, but they do give him leverage. Through the veto, his control of the executive branch, and his access to the media, the president can advance or hinder the goals of members of Congress. Given his dependence on Congress, his inability to command yet his potential capacity to influence, every president needs a strategy for dealing with Congress—a plan or approach for getting Congress to do what he wants and needs it to do in order for him to accomplish his goals.

A president's strategies vis-à-vis Congress are shaped and constrained by his legislative goals and by the resources he commands. The extent to which a president's policy preferences and those of a congressional majority coincide or conflict influences how a president sets out to get what he wants from Congress as well as his probability of success. So too do the resources the president commands for eliciting support beyond that based purely on policy agreement.

Even within the weak party system in the United States, members of a party tend to share policy preferences; consequently, when members of the president's party make up the congressional majority, they and the president will often agree at least on the general thrust of policy, providing a basis for presidential-congressional cooperation. Furthermore, the members of his party have an interest in the president's success that transcends any specific legislative battle. Because many such members believe a strong president will be able to help them attain various of their goals in the future, they may be willing to support the president even when their policy preferences do not coincide with his. To the extent that presidential success in the legislative arena breeds a perception of strength that translates into future success, a member of the president's party may believe supporting the president today will pay off in terms of the passage of preferred legislation in the future. To the extent that presidential success has an electoral payoff—increasing the chances of holding the White House or increasing congressional representation—a fellow party member has an incentive to provide support for the president beyond that based purely on policy agreement.

Congressional leaders of the president's party are especially likely to see presidential success as in their best interest; they must concern themselves with the party's image and are likely to be judged by their success in enacting his program.[2] Thus, when the president's party is in the majority, the very considerable institutional and procedural advantages of control of the chamber are usually available to the president.

Members of the other party, in contrast, are likely to see a strong, successful president as a threat to their future goal advancement. They are less likely to share his policy preferences, so an increase in his legislative effectiveness may threaten their policy goals. Their electoral goals are diametrically opposed to his; the president wants his party to hold the White House and increase its congressional representation. To the extent that the president's legislative success advances his party's electoral success, contributing to that success is costly for members of the other party.

For the president to elicit support from members of the opposition party beyond that based purely on policy agreement, such members must be persuaded that the costs of opposing the president are higher than the costs of supporting him. The most likely basis for doing so is via a threat to the member's personal reelection chances. Circumstances that make that threat credible provide a president with significant resources for influencing Congress; their lack leaves a president with little leverage for persuading opposition party members to support him.

Under conditions of united control, cooperation is the dominant strategy for the president and the congressional majority. Presidential success furthers the policy goals of members of his party directly (when they agree with him on the policy at issue) and indirectly (because they expect in the future to agree with him more frequently than they expect to disagree). Presidential success may indirectly further members' electoral goals by convincing the public that the party can govern effectively.

Nevertheless, while the incentives to support the president are ordinarily considerable for members of his party, incentives to defect may also be present and may, for a portion of the membership, outweigh those dictating support. Neither of the major parties is monolithic; on any given issue, some members will disagree with the president. Policy priorities will certainly differ. Furthermore, electoral priorities differ. Members want to see their party do well in congressional and presidential elections, but their own reelection is their first priority. If the vote required to bring about the president's success would hurt a member's reelection chances, this direct cost may well outweigh the benefits to the member of presidential success. A member's best reelection strategy may dictate voting against a president of his own party on some major issues. The political context determines whether incentives to defect dominate and for how many members.

Consequently, although close cooperation with and reliance on the members of his own party is almost always the best strategy for a president whose party controls Congress, the strategy does not assure success. In the American political system, numerical majorities in Congress do not automatically translate into policy majorities. Winning coalitions must be constructed.

The Political and Institutional Context of the Early Clinton Years

Elections strongly influence the context within which a president attempts to govern. Of course, they determine who is president and the makeup of Congress; but how election campaigns are waged and how election results are interpreted also make a difference. The 1992 elections returned a Congress with substantial Democratic majorities in both chambers; in the House, Democrats outnumbered Republicans 258 to 176. The Senate margin was narrower: 57 Democrats to 43 Republicans. If, in fact, fellow partisans are more inclined than opposition party members to support the president's program, Clinton began his term much better situated than did Bush, who faced substantial opposition party majorities in both chambers, and better than Reagan, who confronted a Democratic House with a narrower margin but had a Republican Senate.

The 1992 presidential campaign was, by American standards, an issue-oriented campaign. Clinton advocated changing the direction of the country in a host of areas and doing so via government action. In contrast to Bush's issueless 1988 campaign, Clinton's winning campaign provided a possible basis for voters to send a policy message. But two factors muddied the message voters seemed to be sending in November 1992: the complexity and nonstandard character of Clinton's "New Democrat" appeal and the surprisingly large Perot vote. In contrast, the thrust of Reagan's issue-oriented 1980 campaign was simpler and therefore clearer, and its impact was not diluted by the third candidate.

How an election campaign is waged is important because it influences how the political community interprets the election. An issueless campaign will not be seen as carrying a popular mandate, even if, as in 1984, the result is a landslide. By contrast, combine an issue-oriented campaign with a big and preferably surprising winning margin, and the political community is likely to interpret the election as carrying a mandate for the president's program, an interpretation that brings great advantages to the president. Thus the issue-oriented thrust of the 1980 campaign, Reagan's ten-point margin over an incumbent president, and the surprising Republican takeover of the Senate resulted in that election's being widely viewed as carrying a mandate for Reagan's program of tax and domestic spending cuts and defense spending increases. Having seen significant numbers of their fellow

Democrats defeated, many congressional Democrats believed their constituents wanted them to support Reagan's policy departures and that they risked defeat if they opposed him, providing Reagan with a key resource for eliciting from opposition party members support beyond that based purely on policy agreement.[3]

Bill Clinton won 43 percent of the vote in a three-way race; he ran behind most winning congressional Democrats; and his party lost a few seats in Congress. With such figures, the political community is unlikely to perceive a mandate. To be sure, polls showed that had Perot not reentered the race, Clinton would have won with a healthy majority, and Democratic congressional losses were largely the result of redistricting and the House bank scandal. Such fine points, however, are irrelevant. Perot's 19 percent showing, because it was surprising, became the big story of the election results and made more credible Republican claims that the voters' message concerned deficit reduction, not an endorsement of Clinton's ambitious and much more complex program. Consequently, Clinton did not benefit from any widespread perception of a public mandate.

Although not perceiving Clinton to have a clear-cut policy mandate, congressional Democrats did read a message in the election results. They believed the public wanted them to act responsibly and expeditiously to handle the myriad significant problems facing the nation. Most believed that to counter the pervasive public cynicism about politics and government, Democrats had to break the gridlock and produce. Almost all believed that, given united control, the public would hold them collectively responsible if they failed. "Bill Clinton's success is our success, his failure is our failure," said Representative Bob Matsui (D-Calif.). "The public wants the elimination of gridlock."[4]

Furthermore, after twelve years of Republican presidents, Democrats were eager to legislate; many had high hopes that policy goals long stymied would now come to fruition.

The huge House freshman class of 110 members did believe themselves to be mandated to change the way Congress works; but Democrats and Republicans interpreted what that entailed differently. The Democratic freshman class of 65 advocated a variety of proposals to reform congressional elections and congressional functioning, but like their senior party colleagues, most gave a higher priority to producing policy to deal with the problems facing their constituents.

The congressional Democratic Party of the early 1990s was different from the party that Carter, the last Democratic president, confronted—in ways mostly favorable to Clinton. The badly splintered party of the 1970s had become much more ideologically homogeneous. After the 1982 elections, the voting cohesion of House Democrats began to increase, and in the late 1980s and early 1990s reached levels unprecedented in the post–World

War II era. From 1951 through 1970, House Democrats' average party unity score was 78 percent; this fell to 74 percent for the period from 1971 to 1982. After the 1982 election, the scores began rising and averaged 86 percent for 1983–92. During this same period, the proportion of roll calls on which a majority of Democrats voted against a majority of Republicans also increased, averaging 56 percent compared with 37 percent during the 1971–82 period.[5]

Much of the increase in Democratic cohesion was the result of increased party support by southern Democrats. From 1985 through 1992, southern Democrats supported the party position on 78 percent of partisan roll calls, while the average support of northern Democrats was 90 percent. Compare that modest 12-point difference with an average difference between the two groups of about 38 points for the 1965–76 period and 24 points for 1977 through 1984.[6]

Since the late 1960s, the constituencies of southern Democrats have become more like those of their northern colleagues.[7] In part, the convergence is the result of processes such as the urbanization of the South. More important, with the passage of the Voting Rights Act and growing Republican strength in the South, African Americans have become a critical element of many southern Democrats' election support. As a result, the policy views of the electoral coalitions supporting many of the southern Democrats are not drastically different from those of the average northern Democrat.

As southern electoral coalitions changed, incumbent southern Democrats began to modify their voting behavior, and newly elected southerners tended to be national Democrats.[8] Thus the House Democratic Party became considerably less ideologically heterogeneous. The big budget deficits of the 1980s and 1990s, which constricted the feasible issue space by making expensive new social programs impossible, also made intraparty agreement easier to reach.

Party cohesion increased in the Senate as well, though not to the same levels as in the House. The percentage of all roll calls evoking a partisan division increased modestly from 41.6 for the 1969–80 period to 46.2 for 1981–92, but important votes were much more frequently partisan.[9] On party votes during the 1980s and early 1990s, the Senate's majority party maintained high party cohesion. Republicans voted with their party 81.2 percent of the time on average from 1981 through 1986, the years in which they controlled the Senate, compared with 71.9 during the 1969–80 period. From 1987 through 1992, Senate Democrats supported their party's position on 83 percent of the roll calls on average, compared with 74.3 percent for 1969–80 and 76.2 percent for 1981–86.[10] In the Senate, as in the House, the heterogeneity of Democrats' election constituencies has declined. Most of the southern Democrats whose election in 1986 returned control of the chamber to the Democratic Party depended on black votes.

In the House of Representatives, which Democrats controlled throughout the 1980s, the decline in the ideological heterogeneity of the Democratic
membership made increasingly strong party leadership possible.[11] The congressional reforms of the 1970s had enhanced the leadership's resources.
Thus when the Speaker was given the power to nominate all Democratic
members of the Rules Committee, the leadership attained true control of the
legislative floor schedule and an invaluable tool for structuring the choices
members face on the floor. Consequently the leadership can control what
legislation gets to the floor and when and what amendments will be allowed. In the 1980s, under pressure from a conservative confrontational
president who threatened their policy and election goals, Democrats became
willing to allow and even came to demand that their leadership make aggressive use of such resources. In response, the House Democratic leadership
became increasingly active and central in the legislative process, often bro-
kering intraparty agreements at the prefloor stage, then using the Rules
Committee to structure members' floor choices advantageously and the
party's large and increasingly effective whip system to mobilize votes. Thus,
when Clinton became president, he was blessed with a more cohesive Democratic Party and a House Democratic Party leadership better equipped and
more experienced at building winning coalitions than Carter had. Clinton
could expect considerable help from the Democratic leadership in the House
in enacting his program.

The Senate Democratic Party was led by George Mitchell, an adept and respected leader. Nevertheless, the Senate is much less amenable to leadership
than the House.[12] Institutional rules give the majority-party leadership few special resources, yet they bestow great powers on rank-and-file senators. In most
cases, any senator can offer an unlimited number of amendments to a piece
of legislation on the Senate floor, and those amendments need not even be
germane. A senator can hold the Senate floor indefinitely unless cloture is in-
voked, requiring an extraordinary majority of sixty votes.

Norms dictating specialization and a highly restrained use of the great
powers the Senate rules confer on the individual lost their hold during the
1960s and early 1970s. Senators now typically become involved in a broad
range of issues, including ones that do not fall within the jurisdiction of their
committees. They are highly active both in the committee room and on the
Senate floor.[13]

Extended debate has became more frequent, and increasingly senators
are willing to use that power on issues of lesser importance. In the 1950s
and earlier, filibusters were rare; the years 1951 to 1960 saw an average of 1
per Congress. In the 1960s, the average per Congress was 4.6; in the 1970s
it rose to 11.2. From 1981 through 1986, the average per Congress was
16.7, and for 1987 through 1992 it was 26.7.[14] Full-blown filibusters are
vastly outnumbered by implicit or explicit threats to filibuster. When floor

time is tight—before a recess or near the end of the session—a single senator's threat to engage in extended debate is often sufficient to prevent the leadership from bringing up any bill that is not "must" legislation.

Institutional rules make a hyperindividualistic style possible for senators; the political system and especially the media reward it. Activism pays off in media coverage and so does high-profile opposition to a president of one's own party.

In the Senate, unlike the House, rule and norm changes that increased rank-and-file members' opportunities to participate were not accompanied by leadership-strengthening changes. The Senate majority-party leader, always institutionally weaker than the Speaker of the House, was given no significant new powers for coping with the more active, assertive, and consequently less predictable membership.

The majority leader's control over the floor schedule is tenuous, and he lacks tools for structuring choices on the floor. A single senator can disrupt the work of the Senate by, for example, exercising his or her right of unlimited debate or objecting to the unanimous consent requests through which the Senate does most of its work. Clearly, a partisan minority of any size can bring legislative activity to a standstill.

The Senate is not a majority-rule chamber. Large minorities can block action that majorities support. Even when they cannot stop legislation entirely, a determined minority can often extract substantive concessions; sometimes even a single adamant or disgruntled senator can do so.

Since in the American political system parties are never perfectly homogeneous ideologically and party leaders have a limited capacity to induce party members to vote against their self-defined electoral interests or policy goals, even presidents with partisan majorities in both chambers will sometimes need opposition-party support, and, of course, presidents would prefer the broadest possible support. Certainly the likelihood and the cost of getting opposition-party votes will influence a president's strategy.

From the beginning, the likelihood of getting House Republican support for most controversial Clinton initiatives was nil. The House Republican Party has become increasingly conservative since the mid-1970s; the 1992 elections brought in a large and almost uniformly far-right Republican freshman class. Although nominally led by Bob Michel, a pragmatist from another era, the House Republicans' real leader was Minority Whip Newt Gingrich, an aggressive, far-right conservative who believed that confrontation, not cooperation, is the best strategy for winning a House majority.[15] On most issues, Clinton's policy preferences and those of most House Republicans were much too far apart to make cooperation a reasonable strategy for either. Clearly, their electoral goals were in conflict; and Clinton's lack of a mandate meant that few individual Republicans would feel constituency pressure to support the president's proposals.

The prospects for cooperating with Senate Republicans were less clear. The Republican membership in the Senate, although predominately conservative, included a greater proportion of moderates than in the House. Since senators tend to pursue individualistic strategies, the moderates might be willing to cooperate. The Senate Republican leader, Bob Dole, is more flexible than his House counterpart. But Dole is a hard-edged and crafty leader who wants to be president. Since Democrats were short of the sixty votes needed to shut off debate, Senate rules gave Republicans considerable leverage—making it likely the necessary votes would seldom come cheap.

Working Together

As the 103rd Congress and Clinton's term began, the political and institutional context provided strong incentives for Clinton and congressional Democrats to work together, but at best weak incentives for Republicans to cooperate. Congressional Democrats, especially members of the House, who must run for reelection every two years, perceived their fate as tied to Clinton's legislative success. Democrats were eager to legislate, and most supported in broad terms Clinton's legislative agenda, many elements of which stemmed from congressional Democratic initiatives. Inevitably, however, different constituencies and different institutional vantage points give a president and the members of his party in Congress different perspectives and, often, different priorities. Moreover, in this case, both lacked the experience of such a working relationship. Clinton had no extensive Washington experience; most congressional Democrats had never served with a Democratic president.

Congressional Democrats began the 103rd with high expectations about policy and good intentions about working closely with the new Democratic administration. "The climate feels like when JFK was elected," House Majority Leader Richard Gephardt was reported to have told the freshmen. "There's now a real opportunity to have a real impact on the future of the country," a highly respected Democrat said and added that, had Bush been reelected, he probably would have left Congress. Right after the election, all the returning House committee chairmen pledged cooperation with Clinton, saying in a joint letter that "Americans have sent us all a clear message. We hear them loud and clear."[16] Aware of the problems Carter had encountered with Congress, the Clinton administration set out to avoid at least those that were self-inflicted. For the top positions in the White House liaison office, people with considerable Hill experience and thus ties to members of Congress were chosen. Many cabinet and subcabinet positions were filled by respected members of Congress or senior staff, thus creating ties between the branches. And Clinton himself worked assiduously at maintaining contact with members of Congress.

"It's a whole new world," said a senior congressional aide about relations with the administration. Democrats agreed that access to and contact with the administration was "infinitely" greater. "We spend lots more time dealing with the White House. When the other party controls the presidency, you go up there twice a year for the picnic and the Christmas party and that's pretty much the contact you have," a senior Democrat reported. The sheer volume of contact and the extent to which this represented a change was repeatedly emphasized by congressional Democrats. "I've been to the White House more in the last six months than in the previous six years," another member said, expressing the common sentiment.

Of course, members of Congress and their staffs deal with the departments and agencies much more frequently than with the White House. Here, too, access was much greater and was facilitated by preexisting ties. "One of the big differences," a member explained, "is that now I know half of the cabinet personally, and that just does make a difference." Access furthers policy goals. A member illustrated: "There is a free flow of ideas back and forth between Congress and the administration. I talk at least weekly with Donna Shalala or Reich or Clinton's domestic policy adviser or someone of that sort, and this is very, very different from what it was like under Bush and Reagan."

It also furthers reelection goals. An aide to a junior House Democrat explained: "There is much greater access to the administration, to the bureaucracy, to talk about the problems of the district, and this is true especially since we voted for reconciliation. Now, certainly, you get a fair hearing. When the Republicans were in control, we didn't even bother."

Even powerful senior members perceived a major difference. A high-ranking staffer to a major committee chairman said: "We have a great deal more contact. Now, we can pick up the phone and tell somebody that we really need something politically. We don't have to worry that some Republican hatchet man will pick it up on the other end, realizing that you really need something, will want to make you pay enormously for that."

The more cooperative relationship with the administration changed how Democratic members pursued their goals in a number of ways. It offered new opportunities. "There are whole new areas of concern," a member pointed out. "Previously I didn't spend five minutes a week on federal appointments. Now that's an area we are very much involved in." New strategies for effectuating policy change became feasible. A senior staffer explained: "We now have open to us avenues of making changes that just were not available before; we can do things possibly through regulation, for example, rather than going the legislative route."

For some committee leaders, the change was enormous. Asked whether having a Democratic rather than a Republican president had changed his work life as a committee chairman on a day-to-day basis, one responded:

"Yes, very much so. The administration is pursuing a very aggressive agenda in our area of jurisdiction, and it reflects the agenda the committee has been pursuing for a number of years, and this is diametrically opposite to what was happening under George Bush."

But members had their complaints as well. The White House liaison people were given good marks for being savvy and attentive. But they and the White House staff more broadly were seen as being stretched too thin. "Clinton is a victim of his own campaign rhetoric about reducing the number of people in the White House and there just aren't enough people; they have a lot of trouble handling a lot of issues at the same time because there are too few people," a member said. Political appointees in the White House and the agencies, especially those who came from the campaign, were sometimes evaluated much less favorably than the White House liaison. "They brought in too many campaign people who don't understand the Hill," an experienced congressional aide said. And bureaucratic inertia and unresponsiveness annoyed some members. A Senate staffer explained:

> The administration has been very good about notifying us ahead of time when something is coming, but what we've gotten hasn't increased as much as you might think.... The bureaucracy doesn't necessarily respond, they have their own agenda, they keep doing their own things. The political people—the appointees—probably haven't been as good as they should be, as strong, and they look at the big things, and what we are asking for are little things, which they then leave to the bureaucracy and they don't come through.

Recounting member complaints but also putting them into perspective, a member of the congressional leadership said: "Members are like their constituents. They are very hard to please. There is a lot of grumbling—that it takes them too long, that they have not been very responsive on appointments, that former members of Congress haven't done that well in terms of appointments. But it's a mixed bag, and as I said, members are hard to please."

In summary, although the relationship between the administration and congressional Democrats was basically good during the 103rd Congress, there were some irritants. Furthermore, there was little the White House could do about the most basic source of friction, as a White House liaison staffer explained: "One of our problems is that we have to tell people 'no' a lot, and a lot of times legitimately. This is both on big legislative initiatives and on things for their district. During the past twelve years they were not getting anything from the administration and they saw that as political. Then after twelve years the dam burst and they found out that there was not much water there."

The incentives for cooperation are even greater for the president and the congressional leadership of his party than for the president and rank-and-file members. The congressional majority leadership, especially in the House, commands procedural, organizational, and informational resources invaluable for building coalitions. As guardians of their party's image, congressional leaders have a major stake in the president's success; and the president has resources—favors and the bully pulpit—that make him an invaluable ally.

From the beginning of Clinton's presidency, the working relationship between him and the Democratic congressional leadership was cooperative and close, if not always smooth. Both Speaker Tom Foley and Senate Majority Leader George Mitchell were convinced that congressional Democrats' fate was closely linked to the Clinton administration's success. "Nobody's going to have divided government to blame anymore," Foley said as the new Congress convened. "We will have the first opportunity we've had in a long time to prove government can work—and people will be watching."[17]

The congressional Democratic leadership met with the president at the White House frequently; "there have just been a huge number of meetings," a leadership staffer reported at the end of the first year. A number of these meetings included Republican leaders as well. The Democratic leadership and Clinton discussed the full range of their mutual concerns—scheduling, political and legislative strategy, and issues. Republicans were included in issue discussions when there was "at least a chance of bipartisanship." Clinton also often visited the Hill, at least fifteen times during 1993, according to a White House count.

Contact at below the presidential level was still more frequent. On the House side, the White House congressional liaison attended the regular Thursday morning whip meetings and the meetings of those whip task forces set up to mobilize votes on legislation of interest to the president. The Speaker provided a desk and phone in his Capitol working office to the White House liaison people. Agency liaison also worked closely with the whip operation when their legislation was under floor consideration. Similarly, on the Senate side, contact between the leadership and the top liaison people was an everyday occurrence. At the senior staff level, consultation and coordination with the executive branch became a major part of the job.

The different constituencies and different institutional perspectives of a president and the congressional leadership assure that the relationship will never be without problems. Differing electoral constituencies contributed to conflicting positions on NAFTA, as we see later. Representing the interests of the House Democratic membership, the leadership's key constituency, the House leadership disagreed with the president's position on aspects of campaign finance reform. More frequent than policy disagreements were frictions arising from different institutional perspectives. Presidents, especially those with an ambitious agenda, want to get many things done and quickly; congressional leaders know the legislative process is naturally slow and that pushing it too much can create problems, that members who, in the name of speed, are cut out of the action, will have less stake in the legislation's success, and that asking members to take too many tough votes too close together is likely to be counterproductive.

From the congressional leadership's perspective, the White House sometimes did not provide the help with public opinion that it could have. "There is not as good coordination of the message of the week between the White House and the Hill as we would like; there will be times when we could very much use a lot of real emphasis on an issue that is coming to a head, where the White House is off on something else," an aide complained. And sometimes the content of the White House message made the leadership uncomfortable. The administration sometimes came very close to Congress-bashing, the leadership believed. "There can be a problem when the administration decides to counter the Perot phenomenon as, say, with reinventing government because that inevitably poses Congress as a villain and that can cause ripples," a participant explained.

By and large, however, the relationship between the Democratic leadership and the White House was good. Clinton showed himself to be a willing and adept one-on-one persuader; he took an energetic part in vote mobilization efforts. Of course, the congressional leaders wished he had been more successful at building public support for major initiatives, but they attributed that failure primarily to larger forces. The congressional leaders, for their part, were mostly loyal and effective field commanders in the battle over the president's program.

Imperfect Honeymoon

The first months of the Clinton administration were a period of considerable policy accomplishment but frequent public relations woes. The former illustrates that united control does make a difference; the impact of the latter shows what the limits of that difference are. On 3 February the House passed family- and medical-leave legislation, a central element of Clinton's agenda and a top priority of congressional Democrats. The Senate passed the bill on 4 February and President Clinton signed it on 5 February. "Motor voter," legislation to make registering to vote easier, passed the House on 4 February, and although Republicans used Senate rules to delay and exact some concessions, it passed the Senate by mid-March. Both these bills had passed Congress before with strong Democratic support but had been killed by Bush vetoes. Congressional committees quickly began work on other legislation that had been stymied by opposition from Republican presidents —revision of the Hatch Act and reauthorization of National Institute of

Health programs, for example—and on Clinton administration initiatives. None of the president's proposals were declared "dead on arrival." Some long-sought goals of congressional Democrats were accomplished without legislation. On 22 January President Clinton signed executive orders lifting the "gag rule" prohibiting abortion counseling in federally funded family planning clinics, eliminating the ban on federal funding of medical research using fetal tissue from elective abortions, and reversing the policy barring U.S. aid to international organizations that perform or promote abortion.[18]

In the media, the early legislative successes were overshadowed by controversies that made much better news stories. The dispute over gays in the military demonstrates how limited a president's control over the media agenda is. The administration never considered the issue of top-tier importance and certainly did not want it to be portrayed as if it were the number-one priority. Yet they could not deflect the media focus and consequently had to devote enormous amounts of time to the issue when so much else needed to be done.

The controversy also highlights the extent to which Senate individualism poses a problem for presidents. Senator Sam Nunn (D-Ga.), highly respected chairman of the Armed Services Committee, opposed Clinton's proposal to lift the ban on gays in the military and, on the issue, took on the newly elected president of his party vocally and publicly; for doing so, he received an enormous amount of media attention. Although Nunn eventually played 'a key role in working out a compromise, by then a considerable amount of damage to Clinton's image had been done.

Finally and perhaps most important, the controversy over gays in the military—as well as that over the Zoë Baird nomination—illustrates that when members of Congress must choose between supporting a president of their own party and following intense constituency sentiment, constituency usually wins out. In both instances, Capitol Hill was deluged by phone calls and letters, and these messages were predominately and vociferously opposed to the president. Clinton had little choice but to compromise in a major way on gays in the military and to withdraw the Baird nomination. Even if he could have won in a showdown, as he might have on Baird, the cost would have been too high. No president can expect the members of his party in Congress to vote against strong constituency sentiment very often; and, since he had an interest in their reelection, he would not lightly ask them to do so.

"It's the Economy, Stupid!": From Campaign Rhetoric to Public Policy

As the economy was the 1992 campaign's dominant issue, the success of Clinton and the Democratic Congress in enacting an effective economic program became a key test of whether the Democratic Party could govern. The approach Clinton had outlined during the campaign was complex: it involved an immediate stimulus to jump-start a sluggish economy, major long-term investment spending in areas such as education and infrastructure, and deficit reduction through tax increases on the wealthy and spending cuts in less essential programs. Perot's showing combined with the media's inability to handle complexity resulted in the news media's painting the election as primarily a public call for deficit reduction. A sizable number of congressional Democrats, including many of the large freshmen class, believed they would be judged in terms of how much they cut spending and reduced the deficit. In contrast, Democrats from core Democratic districts tended to emphasize the stimulus and investment spending.

On 17 February Clinton outlined an economic program containing the three basic elements. In response to the political climate and strong economic growth in the fourth quarter of 1992, the direct spending part of the stimulus program was reduced to $16.3 billion. The revenue component included tax increases for corporations, the wealthy, and upper-income Social Security recipients and a broad-based energy tax.

Congressional Democrats, by and large, reacted favorably, though, given the ambitiousness of the package, they knew passing it would not be easy. Republicans immediately went on the attack, blasting the proposal for being tax heavy.[19] Opposition to any new taxes has become a core tenant of Republican ideology, and many congressional Republicans believed Bush's reneging on his "no new taxes" pledge had cost him the election. Understandably the public never wants to pay more taxes, and in a period of pervasive distrust of government, no politician will damage his reelection prospects by opposing them.

The lack of incentives for Republicans to support Clinton's program made it clear from the beginning that Democrats would have to pass it on their own. As Dick Armey, a Republican leader in the House, said of his party's hard-line opposition, "They wanted to lead, now they've got to live with the accountability. Why should we give them cover?"[20]

The legislative process is complicated, particularly so when the aim is enacting such a broad-ranging set of proposals. The stimulus package would be enacted as a supplemental appropriations bill. The enactment of the rest of the program would require several steps. First Congress would have to pass the budget resolution, which sets guidelines for total spending, revenues, and the deficit. The budget resolution may and, in this case, would have to include instructions to the substantive committees to bring law in their areas of jurisdiction into conformity with the budget resolution. For example, the tax-writing committees would be instructed to report legislation raising taxes. Once the committees had complied with their instructions, the provisions they reported would go to the chamber floor packaged into a single massive reconciliation bill. Of course, each of these steps would have to be traversed in both House and Senate and then the two chambers would have to come to agreement. Yet, as complicated as this process is, the congressional budget process makes comprehensive change easier to bring about than it was before its institution in the mid-1970s.

To serve its purpose, the stimulus package had to be enacted quickly. The Democratic leaders of the House Appropriations Committee put the proposal on a fast track. A hitch developed when continuing Republican attacks made many Democrats nervous about voting for spending increases well before they voted for spending cuts. Clinton and the congressional leadership solved the problem by agreeing on a schedule change: action on the budget resolution would be accelerated and it would be brought to the floor before the stimulus package.

On 18 March the House passed the budget resolution, and late that night it passed the stimulus package. The Appropriations Committee had reported out Clinton's stimulus package almost without change, and protected by a rule that prohibited floor amendments, it passed in that form. "Deficit hawk" Democrats had argued for cuts, but moderate and liberal Democrats held firm in support. Democratic Budget Committee leaders had added $63 billion in spending cuts to the budget resolution to get the support of deficit-hawk Democrats, but basically the resolution followed Clinton's plan closely. The budget resolution was approved on a strictly party-line vote in committee and nearly that on the floor; no Republicans voted for it, and only eleven Democrats voted in opposition. The vote on the stimulus package was also highly partisan, with only three Republicans and twenty-two Democrats defecting from their parties' positions.[21]

On 25 March the Senate approved a budget resolution very similar to the one that had passed the House; again, no Republicans supported the economic blueprint, while two Democrats also voted against it. To keep the plan intact, Democrats had to vote down a plethora of amendments, most offered by Republicans to cause Democrats maximum pain. Budget resolutions are considered under special rules, however, and while Republicans could stretch out the process and make Democrats take a series of tough votes, they could not block action.

Senate rules offered the stimulus package no such protection. Before the bill came to the floor, Democratic Senators John Breaux of Louisiana and David Boren of Oklahoma began pushing a plan to delay half the spending. Like the deficit hawks in the House, they argued that increasing spending before making significant cuts sent the wrong message to a public eager for real deficit reduction and wary of Democrats' commitment to that goal. Republicans criticized the bill as pork and found the media eager for stories about wasteful and even "ludicrous, useless" projects included in the package.[22] When the bill came to the floor on 25 March, the chair of the Appropriations Committee, Robert Byrd, attempted, through an arcane use of Senate procedure, to protect the bill from destructive amendments, but only managed to outrage Republicans and many Democrats as well. Boren took and held the floor for four-and-a-half hours, effectively preventing any progress on the bill for the week. By the following week, the White House had brought dissident Democrats back into the fold, but Republicans had decided to filibuster the bill. Majority Leader George Mitchell threatened to cancel the planned recess and keep the Senate in session until it passed the bill. Democrats had the fifty votes to kill Republican amendments but not the sixty necessary to cut off debate. After failing to impose cloture for the third time on 5 April, the Senate recessed until 19 April. Bill Clinton would have to sell the program to the American people and generate enough heat to weaken Republican opposition, or he would have to compromise. Failing at the former, the president offered to cut the bill by about 25 percent, but Republicans remained united in opposition. Democrats took one more cloture vote, this on the Clinton compromise, and when, as expected, it lost on a 56–43 vote, they gave up. (The $4 billion component for extended unemployment benefits was quickly passed as a separate bill.)

Analysts attributed the defeat to Byrd's tactics, which outraged Republicans, to Clinton's unwillingness to compromise earlier, and to an ineffective public relations campaign. All these explanations have some validity, but none was as easily remedied as the analyses implied. Senate Republicans had a common interest in showing Senate Democrats and the administration they could not be ignored. Byrd's tactics probably made unity easier for Republicans to get but did not produce it. If Clinton had negotiated early in the process with moderate Republican senators, he might have picked up enough votes to get the package through the Senate; the cost would have been great unhappiness in the House, primarily among liberal Democrats but also among those conservative Democrats who had been denied a similar deal.

The lack of a public demand for the bill allowed Republicans to kill it without great fear that they would pay an electoral price. Although the public strongly supported Clinton's economic plan initially and the president made a serious attempt to generate pressure on senators, maintaining support over the long period required from introduction to enactment is not easy, and turning support into pressure on members is even harder. Again the complexity of Clinton's program put him at a disadvantage vis-à-vis the simple Republican message of deficit reduction and opposition to pork, especially with a cynical public primed to believe that most government spending is wasteful.

This battle foreshadowed the problems ahead in enacting the economic program. Getting controversial legislation through two houses with very different memberships and very different rules can be an extremely difficult and delicate exercise. Despite his media access, the president can seldom control how he and his program are portrayed; when what he is trying to sell is both complex and contains considerable amounts of bitter medicine, favorably influencing the portrayal is that much harder, and a lack of success makes enacting the program even more difficult.

Passing the reconciliation bill would be the biggest test for President Clinton and congressional Democrats. This legislation would actually write into law the changes in economic policy outlined in the budget resolution. A massive undertaking involving hundreds of policy issues and over a dozen committees in each chamber, it would be difficult under the best of circumstances. The ambitious deficit-reduction targets that had to be met meant that inevitably many unpopular decisions would have to be made. And not only would Democrats have to pass the legislation without any Republican help, they would have to contend with a withering Republican attack on the program as consisting mostly of taxes on the middle class.

The thirteen House committees met their 14 May deadline for reporting and met the deficit-reduction targets assigned to them; although a multitude of smaller compromises were made to get the necessary majorities, the major features of Clinton's economic program were preserved. The job of passing the bill in the House became immeasurably harder when, on 20 May, Senator Boren and three colleagues announced their opposition to the BTU tax, the broad-based energy tax Clinton had proposed and the House Ways and Means Committee had approved. Since Boren was a member of the Senate Finance Committee that would have to approve the tax-law changes and since the party ratio on the committee was only 11–9, his opposition made the survival of the BTU tax and even of the broad package appear doubtful. House Democrats were leery of voting for the unpopular BTU tax only to see it die in the Senate. "We don't want to be in a position of walking the plank and then have them go over and make a compromise in the Senate," Charlie Wilson (D-Tex.) explained.[23] Boren's high-profile opposition also gave impetus to conservative Democrats' push for a cap on entitlement spending, which was in Boren's plan as well.

A deal on the entitlement cap, intimations of changes in the BTU tax in the Senate, adept procedural strategy, and an intense lobbying campaign by the House Democratic leadership and the administration produced a close win on the House floor.

Majority Leader Gephardt brokered a compromise on entitlements that satisfied conservatives without alienating liberals. The administration got some energy-state Democrats back on board by acknowledging what was becoming inevitable—that the BTU tax would be altered in the Senate. The House leadership brought the bill to the floor under a rule that allowed a vote only on a comprehensive Republican substitute; amendments to delete various unpopular elements of the package—the BTU tax and the tax on Social Security payments to high-income recipients—were not allowed. Many Democrats would have found it very difficult to explain votes against such amendments back home, especially in response to thirty-second attack ads; so allowing such amendments would have confronted Democrats with the unpalatable choice between casting a series of politically dangerous votes or contributing to the picking apart of the package on the floor.

Whip David Bonior himself headed up the whip task force set up to pass the bill. Starting work several weeks before the bill got to the floor, members of the task force and then the top leaders themselves unrelentingly pursued every House Democrat; anyone who might have influence with an undecided or recalcitrant member—state party chairmen, governors, union officials, personal friends—was enlisted whenever possible to help in the effort to persuade. The administration was very much engaged. Cabinet secretaries called and visited Democrats; Secretary of the Treasury Lloyd Bentsen, for example, came to the Texas delegation's lunch meeting. The president personally called close to sixty members—some of them repeatedly. The Speaker himself closed floor debate for his party, telling members that "this is a time to stand and deliver; this is a time to justify your election."[24]

Given the level of effort, Democrats could not fail to understand that how they voted on the bill would affect their future in the House. This vote would count heavily, everyone knew, in the leadership-maintained party loyalty scores that influence a member's chances of getting a choice committee assignment. As Representative Barney Frank (D-Mass.) said, "Nobody got a pass on this."[25] The pressure was unusually overt in this instance: freshmen circulated a petition demanding that any committee or subcommittee chair who voted against the party position be stripped of his or her position by the caucus. Within hours, more than eighty Democrats, including several influential committee chairmen, had signed.[26] Committee leaders were thus sharply reminded that they are agents of the Democratic membership and that, in their importunings, the party leadership was reflecting the wishes of the great bulk of Democrats. On 27 May the House passed the legislation by 219–213; again, not a single Republican voted in support.

The Senate Finance Committee took until 18 June to report its crucial part of the reconciliation bill. To get the eleven votes needed, Senate Democratic leaders had to agree to replace the BTU tax with a gas tax. Budget act rules protected the legislation from a filibuster, but Republicans could and did offer a series of amendments designed to put Democrats on record on the bill's least palatable provisions. Many of the votes were close, but enough Democrats held firm and no major amendment was accepted. On 25 June the Senate passed the bill on a 50–49 vote, with Vice-President Al Gore casting the deciding vote. Every Republican and six Democrats opposed passage.

Changes made to pass the bill in the Senate combined with the narrow passage margin in both chambers guaranteed that reaching a conference agreement on a version passable in both houses would be a delicate and difficult task. Liberals—especially members of the Black Caucus—were dismayed with the cuts in benefits for the poor and cities made to compensate for the revenues lost when the BTU tax was replaced by a gas tax. Many deficit-hawk Democrats in the Senate had voted for the package without enthusiasm, believing it did not do enough, and might well defect if significant changes were made. A number of western Democrats refused to support a gas tax higher than the 4.3 cents in the Senate bill.

A compromise package was nevertheless worked out and the task of selling it, already underway, intensified. Methodically and relentlessly, the House leadership pursued every Democrat. "There was whip meeting after whip meeting," a participant explained. "Members were getting really sick of being beat on, they would run when we came. But we kept after them." Clinton met personally with almost every organized group of Democrats —from the Black Caucus to the Conservative Democratic Forum—and including the women, the freshmen, and the gym users; many senators and some House members were courted individually as well.[27] While his primary arguments were policy substance and the need for Democrats to show they can govern, the president made deals when he had to. Liberals had been mollified by the conference's restoring a significant proportion of the social spending the Senate had cut. An agreement to allow a vote on further spending cuts in the fall satisfied some deficit hawks. When the mercurial Boren announced he would switch and vote against the conference report, a replacement had to be found. "After four days of feverish wooing," Dennis DeConcini (D-Ariz.) agreed to switch his vote; in return, he received several policy concessions, including a lessening of the tax bite on Social Security recipients.[28] With every vote essential in the Senate, some erstwhile supporters took advantage of their bargaining position to extract benefits for their constituents; freshman Senator Russell Feingold (D-Wisc.) cut a deal on bovine growth hormone.[29] A tête-à-tête at the White House and a promise of a commission on entitlements finally induced Senator Bob Kerrey (D-Neb.) to declare his support after he had very publicly criticized the package and indicated he might defect.

After an exhausting day of feverish, one-on-one lobbying and combative floor rhetoric, the House passed the conference package by a vote of 218–216; only Marjorie Margolies-Mezvinsky's (D-Pa.) vote switch saved the package. The next day, 6 August, the Senate passed it 51–50, with Vice-President Gore again casting the deciding vote. No Republican in either chamber voted for the legislation.

Passing the economic program represented a major legislative victory for President Clinton and congressional Democrats. Although many alterations and compromises were made during the long, complex process, the final product followed the outlines of the plan Clinton had laid out in February and, within the severe constraints imposed by the deficit, it reoriented economic policy in a direction Democrats favored. Furthermore, it showed that Democrats could govern; they could stick together enough to enact tough, comprehensive legislation addressing major problems facing the country.

Democrats accomplished this feat by working together across the institutional divide. Throughout the process, Clinton maintained an enormous amount of personal contact with congressional Democrats. From inviting every member of the House to the White House to consult with him in small groups on the components of the economic plan in early February to numerous appearances at Democratic Caucus meetings on the Hill to buck up Democrats to innumerable one-on-one conversations, the president gave congressional Democrats opportunities to influence the substance of his package and immersed himself in the process of getting it enacted. A willing participant in the whipping effort, the president learned over time how to nail down a commitment. Early on, congressional participants report, Clinton was too willing to accept excuses from members. The administration also quickly learned to deploy the cabinet and other high-ranking officials to good effect; the ties many of them had to members of Congress served them well in persuasion efforts. "White House budget director Leon E. Panetta, a former House member, and Treasury Secretary Lloyd Bentsen, a former senator, spent so much time on Capitol Hill the week of July 26 that it was easy to forget they ever left the Congress," *Congressional Quarterly* reported.[30] Throughout the process, the Democratic congressional leadership worked closely and loyally with the administration, using their resources to the maximum to effect passage.

In attempting to persuade members to vote for the package, the president and the congressional leadership consistently argued that Democrats had to pass the economic program to show they could govern. Before a key vote, Clinton told the House Democratic Caucus, "Look ... we're running this place; we have to rise to the occasion."[31] As the process went on and the stakes increased, the argument that a defeat would destroy the Clinton presidency became increasingly prevalent. "If we don't vote for this package, we cut [Clinton] off at the knees and we can't do that," said Charles Schumer (D-N.Y.).[32] To some extent, the need to resort to such arguments was inevitable. Despite voters' professed desire for deficit reduction in the abstract, a real deficit-cutting package will unavoidably contain some unpalatable provisions and is unlikely to be truly popular. But Republicans were successful at portraying the package as consisting primarily of taxes on ordinary people; polls consistently showed that the public's beliefs about what the package contained were simply wrong. Despite numerous attempts by the president and other Democrats to set the record straight, the complex real story never caught up with the simpler, more sensational portrayal. As a result, the package was broadly unpopular. When Democrats passed the reconciliation bill conference report, they did so in a context in which constituent phone calls were preponderantly negative.

"It was a crucial victory," a perceptive House Democrat said shortly after the economic program's enactment. "But this is not a model for the future." To pass legislation making major policy changes, members need public support. Despite considerable policy agreement with the president and the perception that their fate was, at least in part, tied to his, Democrats could not be expected to support his programs if their constituents oppose them. Especially on health-care reform, the battle for public opinion would be the critical one.

NAFTA: A Different Test

Although united control increases the likelihood that the president and the congressional majority will have similar legislative preferences, it does not assure it on every issue. Trade is an issue that highlights differences among congressional Democrats and between them and the president. Members from the rust belt, where jobs in heavy manufacturing have been on the decline, fear that free trade will result in more jobs being exported to low-wage countries; members from the fast-growing sunbelt and from areas with a concentration of high-technology or export-oriented industries tend to see free trade as an opportunity. Although present in both parties, the split is much more intense among Democrats; they represent a greater proportion of rust-belt districts. And organized labor, a key supporter of the party, tends towards protectionism. Nevertheless, the expert consensus in favor of free trade is so overwhelming that a Democratic presidential candidate is under great pressure to adopt that position.

In any case, Clinton during the 1992 campaign endorsed the North American Free Trade Agreement (NAFTA) that the Bush administration had negotiated. He promised if elected to negotiate side agreements on labor standards and the environment to alleviate the concerns of labor and environmental groups; but the agreements reached were not sufficient for most of these groups. When the campaign for approval began in earnest in the fall of 1993, Clinton faced an uphill battle. Organized labor was adamantly opposed and was making it a litmus-test issue; Democrats were warned that endorsements and financial assistance depended on their vote. Many environmental groups were actively working against the pact. Ross Perot, who had made opposition a major part of his presidential campaign, mounted a well-financed and highly visible opposition effort, threatening to defeat supporters at the polls in 1994.

In the House, where the decisive battle was expected to be, the Democratic Party leadership was itself split. Whip David Bonior, from a rust-belt

Michigan district, and Majority Leader Richard Gephardt of St. Louis opposed NAFTA; Speaker Tom Foley of Washington supported it. While Gephardt's opposition was relatively low key, Bonior organized and led the House effort to defeat the pact.

Under these circumstances, amassing a majority from among Democrats was never a possibility. Republicans were more likely to favor the pact, but Ross Perot made many of them nervous. The Republican leadership in the House promised to deliver half the votes needed for ratification; Democrats would have to supply the other half.

The tactics Clinton and his congressional allies used to build a winning coalition were similar to those employed in the economic policy battles: a campaign to build public support, compromises and deals to win commitments from groups of members, and an enormous amount of one-on-one lobbying. From a free-trade bazaar on the White House lawn to Clinton's appearance at a U.S. Chamber of Commerce town meeting beamed by satellite to 200 sites around the country, the public relations campaign was multifaceted and intensive.[33] To assure the support of various affected groups of members, the administration backed a worker retraining package and loans and loan guarantees to communities that lose jobs to Mexico and negotiated language changes with Mexico to protect U.S. sugar, citrus, and vegetable growers. Members of the cabinet and other top-ranking officials were again deployed to lobby House members one-on-one, and Clinton talked with members in groups and individually. A Democratic task force led by Bob Matsui (D-Calif.) and with Chief Deputy Whip Bill Richardson (D-N.Mex.) as head whip was set up in the spring and, by late October, consisted of about thirty members who were meeting daily. As they worked to line up votes, they coordinated their activities closely with the White House. As a participant explained:

> It's basically the regular sort of inside whipping: one to one, go through the names, talk to people, report to the White House and to [a Speaker's aide], see what kind of help people may need. If so and so says how they are worried about the immigration implications, maybe get Janet Reno to talk to them. Or there was a member who said Hillary was going to come to his area, one that includes five or six districts, and he has not yet come out for NAFTA and he was afraid that she might not mention his name. So I called [an official] in the congressional liaison office and made sure that Hillary mentioned the guy's name.... Or somebody says, "Gee, I'll lose the financial support of labor," and we might say, "Well, how about we arrange for Gore to come and do a fund raiser in your district."

The Republicans had their own whipping operation; the leaders of the two groupings provided necessary communication between them, but each confined itself to whipping its own party members.

In the biggest gamble of the pro-NAFTA campaign, Vice-President Al Gore debated Ross Perot on nationwide television. Perot came over badly, Gore was the consensus winner, and the polls showed an increase in public support for NAFTA. The expert consensus on NAFTA had assured it basically favorable press coverage throughout the process. Within that context, the proponents' public relations campaign generally and Gore's performance specifically were sufficiently successful to provide members with cover. They made a yes vote easier for members of both parties who were convinced NAFTA was the right policy and for Democrats who were conflicted on policy grounds but wanted to support Clinton when they could.

Because Congress had agreed during the Bush administration to consider NAFTA implementation legislation under a fast-track procedure, no amendments were allowed. When the House vote came at 10:26 P.M. on 17 November, the legislation passed 234–200; 156 Democrats voted no and 102 voted yes, a few short of the number promised. Strong Republican support made up the deficit; Republicans split 132–43 in favor. As expected, the Senate easily approved NAFTA on a 61–38 vote.

In the days after the victory, the press speculated endlessly about whether such cross-partisan coalitions would become commonplace and whether the battle would leave debilitating scars that would prevent congressional Democrats from working with Clinton in the future. An examination of context and incentives makes it clear how unlikely either outcome was. On the issue of NAFTA, Clinton and a majority of Republicans had coinciding policy views; on most issues, Republicans are far to the right of Clinton. Given that policy agreement, NAFTA gave House Republicans an opportunity to counter the criticism of being solely nay-sayers. Even so, Republicans had decidedly mixed feelings about contributing to Clinton's success, suggesting that they would seldom be willing to do so.

For Democrats, the incentives were the reverse. During the fight, the opposing members of the Democratic leadership, especially Foley and Gephardt, had shown great restraint in how they waged the battle; Gephardt, for example, never criticized the president personally; Foley, although very much engaged, kept his public role low key and did not criticize his lieutenants. Even while Bonior was leading the opposition effort, his whip office was working with the administration on other issues. After the vote, both the president and Hillary Clinton called Bonior. Although the defeat was bitter for most active Democratic opponents, the boost it gave Clinton's image was a silver lining.

Health-Care Reform: A Gamble Lost

Health-care reform was a central issue in Bill Clinton's winning presidential campaign, ranking in priority behind only the economy. Whether to undertake a major effort to overhaul health care early in Clinton's term was therefore never in question; but no one involved believed it would be easy. The United States spends about one-seventh of its gross domestic product on health care; reform would not only directly touch everyone, it would be immensely complex and would affect the economic interests of a large number of powerful groups.

Attempting a comprehensive reform of the health-care system was thus a gamble—one that the president and congressional Democrats lost. The costs of that failure were high, extending well beyond health-care legislation to a spate of other significant bills that died in the wake of the health-care debacle. Why were Clinton and the congressional Democratic majorities unable to pass a health-care reform bill? Were strategic mistakes at fault or was it contextual factors beyond their control? A brief chronology of the effort provides some answers as well as insights into the problems of attempting nonincremental change.

Promising to send Congress a health-care reform plan within one hundred days, President Clinton in January 1993 named his wife, Hillary, to head a task force to draft the proposal. Mindful of the need for congressional input, over 120 congressional staffers participated in various working groups and, in the first four months of the task force's existence, Hillary Clinton and Ira Magaziner held over 200 meetings with members of Congress. Interest groups were also consulted. By 23 April, task force staff members had met with 572 organizations.[34] The attempt to keep the task force's membership and its deliberations confidential proved to be a mistake. Interest groups that feared losing out and the press pilloried the effort, casting it as narrow and illegitimate despite the wide consultation.

Drafting a major overhaul plan in one hundred days was almost certainly an unrealistic goal. As it turned out, the defeat in April of the stimulus program made unveiling the plan in May as targeted politically unwise. The White House and the congressional leadership decided that passing the economic program required a single-minded focus on that effort. A battle to enact such comprehensive and contentious legislation is highly labor intensive and requires the undivided attention of the congressional leadership and much of the president's time. Furthermore, if several major efforts are going on at once, press coverage is even less predictable and more likely than usual to be harmful—because the press and the electronic media can choose the big story of the day and will almost always select the negative over the positive. Consequently, conducting several such campaigns simultaneously is nearly impossible.

The president did not outline his health-care program until September. When Clinton did so in a speech to a joint session of Congress, it was very well received by congressional Democrats and the public. Polls showed strong support. The legislation itself was not ready to be introduced until

November, and, in the meantime, Clinton, Congress, and the press were occupied with NAFTA.

Groups with a major financial stake in health-care reform were not distracted. Lobbying, not just in Washington but also at the grassroots, had
started early in the year. In the spring, for example, the Pharmaceutical
Manufacturers Association had orchestrated a letter-writing campaign
against price controls on drugs aimed at the tax-writing committees.[35] In the
fall the Health Insurance Association of America (HIAA), a group of smaller
insurance companies that would likely lose out under a Clinton-style plan,
launched a television advertising blitz. "Harry and Louise" saturated the airwaves with their scary stories of what the Clinton plan entailed.

In the health-care post-mortems, the administration was criticized for
writing a too-complex plan that was too hard to explain and for not responding forcefully enough to its critics, especially to the "Harry and Louise" ads. But the health-care system is complex, and many experts argue that
partial or simple solutions are only likely to make problems worse. Hillary
Clinton admits the White House underestimated the impact of the opponents' advertising campaign: "I did not appreciate how sophisticated they
would be in conveying messages that were effective politically even though
substantively wrong," she acknowledged.[36] But whether the best White
House campaign could have effectively countered an opposition with immensely greater resources is doubtful.

Congressional action on health-care reform did not begin in earnest until 1994. By then, the opposition campaign had raised a host of doubts and
reduced public support significantly. Renewed media attention to Whitewater and Paula Jones's charges took a severe toll on the president's approval ratings, which had shot up in the last months of 1993. Lobbying by
the National Federation of Independent Businesses (NFIB), which opposed
employer mandates, intensified. A trade group of small businesses, NFIB has
members in every congressional district, many of whom are influential lo-
cally. Concern that the Clinton plan went too far with employer mandates
and spending caps had already spawned alternatives in Congress, most notably a more conservative proposal sponsored by Representatives Jim
Cooper (D-Tenn.) and Fred Grandy (R-Iowa) and Senators John Breaux (D-
La.) and David Durenberger (R-Minn.). Emboldened, Senate Minority
Leader Bob Dole began to argue that no health crisis existed and so major
reform was unnecessary. Meanwhile, groups that favored the Clinton plan in
general terms spent more time and effort complaining about details they did
not like than emphasizing their support and promoting the plan.

Key decisions about how Congress would handle health-care legislation
fell to the House and Senate leaderships. Because of the complexity of the
problem and of the legislation, a number of committees had jurisdictional
claims. When a number of committees work on a bill, agreement can be-

come harder to reach, and the process takes longer. For that reason, some outside experts urged the Speaker to appoint an ad hoc committee to handle the bill. Foley declined, deciding that the problems such a committee would create were greater than any it might solve. Members not named to the committee would likely become disgruntled; "virtually every member wants to be involved," a House Democrat pointed out in late 1993.[37]

In the House, Foley entrusted primary responsibility to the committees on Ways and Means, Energy and Commerce, and Education and Labor. In the Senate, the principal committees were Finance and Labor and Human Resources. After hundreds of hearings, the committees began to try to put together legislation that would meet Clinton's criteria and could command a majority in committee and on the floor.

What members of Congress were hearing from their constituents made that task immensely difficult. Eager for change but confused and worried early in the year, constituents expressed increasing anxiety about an overhaul as they picked up more and more misinformation about the Clinton plan.[38] Groups as disparate as the Christian Coalition and the NFIB mobilized their adherents to lobby members in their home districts.

The White House and its congressional allies continued and intensified their campaign to sell health-care reform. Meetings of a health-care "message group" to coordinate the publicity efforts of the White House and of House and Senate proponents had been taking place for months. Hillary Clinton traveled extensively to promote the plan, and key cabinet members also participated in the effort. During the Easter congressional recess, for example, cabinet secretaries traveled all over the country, with Donna Shalala, secretary of health and human services, alone visiting fourteen congressional districts.[39] Interest groups that supported the Clinton plan or an even more radical change mounted an independent campaign, but most such groups are relatively poorly funded. Proponents were never able to pay for extensive television advertising or to mount the sort of grassroots campaign in every district that the NFIB was able to carry out. Even with the advantage of the White House and its bully pulpit, proponents could not compete with the massive, single-minded, and early starting effort of opponents.

Although the committees worked in an atmosphere increasingly hostile to major reform, most managed to report legislation. The House Education and Labor Committee and the Senate Labor and Human Resources Committee reported bills that broadly followed Clinton's plan, not surprising since their Democratic majorities are more liberal than Democrats as a whole. House Ways and Means, a more representative committee, reported legislation that while taking a somewhat different approach nevertheless attained universal coverage; however, the support of many committee Democrats was grudging, given in order to move the process along rather than to signal true support, and no Republican voted for the legislation. Ominously,

Energy and Commerce, the most representative of the House committees, could not report a bill. Committee Chairman John Dingell, a skillful and powerful chair with a deep personal commitment to health-care reform, could not put together a majority for any universal-coverage plan.

In early July, the Senate Finance Committee, after months of effort, finally reported a severely watered-down plan—both a real employer mandate and universal coverage were dropped; unlike the other committees, Finance had made many decisions by bipartisan votes. Because sixty votes are needed to cut off a Senate filibuster, proponents knew they needed some Republican votes, and many had argued for a truly bipartisan bill. The Finance Committee's legislation showed how high the price for Republican votes would be; a number of committee Democrats, including Majority Leader George Mitchell, voted for the bill only to move the process along; even so, only three Republicans—all moderates atypical of their party—supported the legislation; the other six committee Republicans, including Minority Leader Bob Dole, voted against even this diluted bill.

From early in the process, participants had assumed that, after the committees reported, the party leaders in each chamber would have to meld the disparate proposals into a package that could pass on their chamber's floor. In the House, Majority Leader Dick Gephardt, who had been asked by the Speaker to spearhead the effort, and Majority Whip David Bonior in May began systematically canvassing members on their health-care stance, trying to determine what kind of bill would command a majority. Democrats, especially the critical moderate members, the leaders found, were uneasy because of their constituents' anxious mood; they were under great pressure from small business on the employer mandate issue; they feared electoral retribution if Democrats did not deliver, yet were loath to commit themselves to taking a hard vote unless they were sure that the Senate would do likewise. House Democrats worried about "being BTUed" by the Senate; they feared casting a tough vote—on employer mandates especially—only to have the Senate vote for a weaker version, as had happened with the energy tax in the economic program. The watered-down bill reported by Finance only exacerbated House Democrats' worries.

The Democratic leadership plan that Gephardt put together was modeled on the Ways and Means bill and included universal coverage and employer mandates.[40] The package that Senate Majority Leader George Mitchell crafted was considerably weaker, falling short of universal coverage and containing a distant and questionable employer mandate. That Mitchell had not been able to find support for something stronger made House Democrats even more nervous; they questioned whether Mitchell would be able to pass any sort of employer mandate on the Senate floor and became even more resistant to voting before the Senate had made its decision.

Senate floor debate began on 9 August; in late August, having made no progress, the Senate suspended consideration and left town for its delayed summer recess. Republican delaying tactics had prevented votes on any of the key provisions, and Democrats lacked the sixty votes to cut off debate. In the House, health-care reform never got to the floor. Over the recess and in September, Mitchell worked with a bipartisan group of moderate senators to try to salvage something; that effort, like a number of previous attempts to form a center coalition, failed, and on 26 September Mitchell declared health-care reform dead.

Health-care reform died because no one was able to construct a bill that could command a clear majority. To be sure, the fight over the crime bill in August distracted the congressional leadership and public attention and ate up time that otherwise would have been devoted to health care. The threat of a Republican filibuster cast a pall over attempts to marshal majorities. That legislation was not brought to the Senate floor until so late in the Congress worked against its success. But the timing was the result of the difficulty of putting together majorities for significant reform, and that was the result of a lack of public support for nonincremental policy change.

Opponents' massive public relations campaigns undermined the support necessary for Congress to undertake such change. About $60 million was spent in advertising, largely to oppose reform.[41] News media coverage did little to counteract the misinformation the opposition ads purveyed. By their emphasis on conflict and on the narrowly political rather than the policy aspects of the story, the media only exacerbated the public's already deep-seated cynicism about politics and government. Americans learned little about the substantive issues that would help them make an informed decision. Between September and December 1993, a period in which health care was very much in the news, the public's ability to answer factual questions about the Clinton proposal actually dropped: thus the percentage answering correctly that the president's plan guaranteed universal coverage decreased from 64 to 54.[42] And to kill such broad-ranging nonincremental reform, opponents only had to generate serious doubts among a public with little faith in government's ability to do anything much right.

Policy and electoral goals kept Democrats working to come up with reform legislation that would pass. Most believed that some reform was necessary and many that a real overhaul was required. Most also feared that the public would punish them at the polls for failing to deliver on this central Clinton promise; that however doubtful the public was about reform, a failure to pass anything would be read as demonstrating that Democrats had not broken gridlock and that the party was incapable of governing. But without the impetus provided by strong public support, Democrats were unable to agree on a proposal that could muster majorities in both chambers. In the end, some members concluded at least by default that the danger of doing nothing was less than the danger of doing something that many powerful interests opposed and that the public was at best uncertain about.

For many Republicans, declining popular support for a major overhaul eroded the incentive to participate constructively in the process. A few Republicans—notably Senator John Chafee of Rhode Island—believed significant reform was needed and continued to work on a proposal to the very end; for many Republicans, however, a major overhaul did not represent good public policy; they believed it neither necessary nor desirable. The early consensus that something would pass gave such Republicans an incentive to get involved so as to have some substantive influence on the product and be able to claim some credit. When increasing public doubt about the Clinton plan punctured that consensus, this incentive disappeared. As time went on, Republicans became increasingly convinced they would pay no political price for simply opposing reform and even for openly obstructing it, and that by preventing action they could impose a severe electoral price on Democrats. As early as December 1993, outside Republican strategists urged congressional Republicans to deny Clinton and congressional Democrats any sort of victory on health care.[43] Dole became increasingly negative during the Congress, moving from supporting a Chafee bill that promised universal coverage to sponsoring a stripped-down proposal that represented little real change. Newt Gingrich instructed the Republican members of Ways and Means to refrain from offering amendments in committee that might make the bill easier to pass. By the end of the Congress, Senator Phil Gramm of Texas was bragging publicly about having prevented change.[44]

After health-care reform failed, some analysts argued that the administration's fatal mistake was not trying to put together a bipartisan centrist coalition from the beginning. In fact, Hillary Clinton and other White House proponents courted Chafee and other moderate Senate Republicans throughout the process. Disagreement on core elements of substance and the few degrees of freedom available because of the deficit, not an unwillingness to reach out, prevented the construction of a broad coalition. The employer-mandate issue illustrates the problem. Chafee opposed such a mandate from the beginning, and the few Republicans who had voiced some support for the notion backed off in the face of intense small business lobbying; yet the only way to fund universal health care in the absence of an employer mandate was through a huge new tax, a clear political impossibility. To have abandoned universal coverage would have required Clinton to back down on a core campaign promise, would in the view of many experts have made the reform ineffective in controlling medical costs, and would have led to the defection of a large number of congressional Democrats, probably enough to defeat such a plan. To be sure, early in the process, when Republicans still feared being labeled obstructionists, the president could probably have put together a coalition of Republicans and conservative Democrats for a bare-bones proposal, but the substantive and political cost would have been very high. The core of the Democratic Party in Congress and in the electorate would not forgive a president for such preemptive capitulation. Putting together a bipartisan majority to support meaningful reform was never a realistic possibility. "It is a big myth that somewhere there is a political center that—if the leadership would just get out of the way—could govern," a senior House Democrat observed.[45]

The lack of strong public support for such comprehensive nonincremental change was the basic problem, and if there was a fatal mistake, it was in not countering the opposition's public relations campaign quickly and effectively enough. Although certainly the proponents' campaign could have been better timed, planned, and run, the White House could not devote the single-minded attention to the issue its opponents could, its resources paled in comparison to those of its opponents, and it confronted a much more difficult job: to explain an extremely complex problem in a media environment hostile to complexity and to sell a complicated solution to a public disillusioned about government's ability to solve problems.

The End Game

The health-care debacle's costs extended well beyond the issue itself; it set the stage for a disastrous end to the 103rd Congress during which a series of major bills were killed, most often by Republicans intent on denying Clinton and congressional Democrats any victories. Because the health-care debate had so consumed the time and attention of Congress, action on much major legislation had lagged, exacerbating the usual end-of-the-session legislative traffic jam. Their success in derailing health care emboldened Republicans; it convinced them that an obstructionist strategy carried little electoral risk and potentially a big payoff in the midterm elections.[46]

Republican obstructionism in the Senate had been a problem for Clinton throughout the Congress. A Republican filibuster killed the stimulus package; Republicans used the filibuster or a threat thereof to extract concessions on a number of bills—voter registration legislation ("motor voter") and the national service program, for example. Republican attempts to kill or water-down legislation via a filibuster were not always successful, of course. For example, the Republican filibuster of the Brady bill imposing a seven-day waiting period for buying a handgun collapsed when a number of Republican senators began to fear the political price of their participation. But their early and politically costless victory on the stimulus program, Clinton's mediocre-to-poor public approval ratings, and the sheer size of Clinton's agenda, which made it difficult for Clinton to focus media attention, convinced Republicans that extensive use of the filibuster carried little risk.

Senate Republicans were not the only obstructionists during the 103rd Congress. A number of Democrats could not resist using the immense power the Senate rules give the individual, as the economic program saga showed. The enormous antipathy that House Democrats developed toward the Senate over the course of the Congress was generated by what they saw as narrowly self-serving behavior by fellow Democrats in the Senate even more than by Republican obstructionism. Nevertheless, to an extent unprecedented in American history, the filibuster became a partisan tool.

Time pressure makes obstructionism an especially effective weapon at the end of a Congress and the greater the backlog of significant legislation, the more potent any threat of delay is. With members eager to get home to campaign, depriving President Clinton and congressional Democrats of many victories required little skill, just a willingness to use the available tools blatantly and often. Republican filibusters killed campaign finance and lobbying reform bills. Although unsuccessful in the end, Republicans filibustered and tried to prevent passage of a massive crime bill, the California Desert Protection Act, and a comprehensive education bill, even though all had had considerable bipartisan support earlier in the process. Votes on implementing the GATT world trade treaty were delayed until a postelection lame-duck session by a Senate Democratic chairman's obstructionism and by the unwillingness of many House members of both parties to vote on it before the election. Republican threats of obstructionist floor tactics were major contributors to the death of important bills revamping the Superfund program, revising clean drinking water regulations, overhauling outdated telecommunications law, and applying federal labor laws to Congress. "[Republicans] are engaged in a cynical effort to discredit the Congress and then travel around the country and persuade people that Congress won't work and they should be put in charge," a frustrated George Mitchell charged.[47]

Republicans succeeded beyond their wildest dreams. The midterm elections were a catastrophe for Democrats. Not only did they lose their Senate majority, but for the first time in forty years they lost control of the House of Representatives.

United control of Congress and the presidency allowed voters to hold their government accountable. According to the news media consensus, the 103rd Congress was a dismal failure—perhaps the worst Congress in fifty years, according to an end-of-the-session editorial in the *Washington Post;* Democrats were unable to work together either within Congress or across the branches, and as a result, little was accomplished. Voters judged the performance as unacceptable and punished Democrats at the ballot box. But was the performance of the 103rd really so bad?

Did the Crime Fit the Punishment?
Assessing the Record

Despite the public's and the news media's negative assessments, the 103rd

was actually quite a productive Congress. It passed Clinton's economic program, which, in addition to achieving significant deficit reduction, increased
the earned-income tax credit for the working poor and reformed the student
loan program. A number of other important education initiatives became
law: a rewrite of the basic aid to education bill, a school-to-work transition
program, an expansion of Head Start, and the "Goals 2000" bill to set national achievement standards. Other major legislation enacted included the
abortion clinic access bill, family- and medical-leave legislation, a revision of
the Hatch Act, motor-voter legislation, national service legislation, the crime
bill, and the Brady bill. Congress approved legislation to implement
NAFTA. By passing procurement reform and a reorganization of the Agriculture Department, Congress made progress toward "reinventing government." Had Republicans not pursued a strategy of depriving Democrats of
any victories by attempts to block all important and visible legislation at the
end of the session, another half dozen or so major bills would likely have
passed, and even without the enactment of health-care reform, the 103rd
Congress would have been extraordinarily productive. Even with those defeats, of the thirty-six items that *Congressional Quarterly* identifies as the
major legislation of the 103rd, twenty-two (or 61 percent) were enacted; of
the twenty most significant, thirteen (65 percent) became law.

The Clinton administration actively supported most of this major legislation; much of the legislation was, in fact, part of Clinton's agenda. Contrast this level of agreement between president and Congress to the much
more conflictual relationship during President Bush's first two years. Bush
and the Democratic congressional majority disagreed on legislation more
frequently than they agreed. During the 101st Congress, major legislation
(as defined by *Congressional Quarterly*) tended to emerge from committee
in a form Bush disliked; the administration position clearly lost in committee
on 60 percent of the legislation in the House and 40 percent in the Senate; it
clearly prevailed on only 18 percent of major legislation in the House committees and 26 percent in Senate committees. Bush threatened to veto at
some point during the legislative process over half of the major bills. And
two-thirds of the major legislation either was subject to a veto threat or saw
the House or Senate committee and the Bush administration take directly
conflicting positions.[48]

The Clinton administration and the Democratically controlled congressional committees certainly did not agree totally on policy; often committees
altered administration proposals significantly; but, with one possible exception, the changes were not so great as to make the legislation unacceptable
to the administration (the health-care bill Senate Finance reported was unacceptable as a final product; the administration supported the committee's reporting the bill to keep the process moving). And except for his broad threat
to veto a health-care bill that did not achieve universal coverage, Clinton

never had to resort to veto threats. Shared policy preferences made this much more cooperative relationship between president and the congressional majority possible.

These shared preferences manifested themselves in high Democratic voting support for President Clinton's legislative initiatives and positions. Senate Democrats on average supported Clinton 88 percent of the time on those votes on which he took a position; House Democrats' average presidential support score was 79 percent; and, in both chambers, support was as high in 1994 as in 1993.[49]

President Clinton and congressional Democrats worked together not perfectly but reasonably well and were fairly productive legislatively. Why, then, was the public assessment so negative? Opinion polls indicate the voters were not punishing Democrats for failing to pass health-care reform, as many Democrats had feared they would; if anything, passing the economic program and advocating a comprehensive health-care reform program cost Democrats more.

The public's sour mood is not new and has its roots in the wrenching changes the U.S. economy has been undergoing for two decades as the world economy and our place in it have changed. The problems of stagnant and declining incomes and economic dislocation that stem from those macro changes are not ones government can solve easily or quickly. Yet Clinton, the first president to attempt to address the problems seriously, has certainly not benefited politically from doing so.

The first two years of the Clinton administration show again that increasingly our political system provides few incentives for elected leaders to take on the tough problems seriously.[50] The character of public discourse as shaped by the contemporary news media does not lend itself to explaining complex issues. Even the president, whose media access is incomparably better than that of any other single actor, has only a limited ability to use the media to convey messages of any complexity. With multiple media and hundreds of reporters in increasingly frenetic competition for audience, revenues, and professional advancement, the biases toward the simple and the sensational that have always characterized the mass media have become increasingly pronounced. Moreover, the healthy skepticism that is imperative if a free press is to perform its essential function in a democracy has been replaced by a poisonous cynicism that now serves as the operating premise of media coverage of government and politics. The result is a sort of Gresham's law of political discourse: the simpleminded, sensational, and cynical drive out the thoughtful and nuanced.

The character of media coverage enormously advantages the facile, negative gut argument over the more balanced, thoughtful, nuanced argument. Politicians—even the president—seldom get much time to make their own case. Soundbites have gotten shorter and shorter. Coverage of "scandals," even if of questionable provenance, tends to eclipse coverage of policy. Media coverage of policymaking emphasizes charges and countercharges, strategic maneuvering, and possible political fallout much more than policy substance and its likely real-world impacts. Public misinformation about basic facts of stories that were intensively covered and aroused considerable public interest is one important result. In 1993 the media covered the saga of Clinton's economic program exhaustively, yet poll after poll showed the public was misinformed about basic elements of Clinton's proposal, particularly about its tax provisions.

Increasingly the operating premise of most political reporting is the poisonously cynical view that all politicians are self-serving, dishonest, and incompetent. "I don't believe anything any politician says at any time, including you," a reporter said to Senate Majority Leader George Mitchell. When the policy process is portrayed as a battle among cynical manipulators seeking to win for their own sakes and never as well-meaning people trying, despite disagreements and uncertainty, to make good public policy, it is no wonder that people do not trust public officials and have no faith in the process.

Our public discourse too often places responsiveness and responsibility at odds; it provides elective leaders with little incentive for acting responsibly. Democratic theory demands that Congress act both responsively and responsibly—that it pass laws that are responsive to the will of popular majorities and laws that, on the basis of the best evidence available, will deal effectively with the pressing national problems at which they are aimed. These two criteria are distinct. Only in a perfect world would what the majority wants always accord with what policy experts deem most likely to be effective, especially in the long run. Yet for democracy to be meaningful, some reasonable balance must be attained.

Our political system provides bountiful incentives for politicians to be responsive to strong, clearly expressed popular sentiments. The incentives for responsible behavior, in contrast, are less and seem to be declining. News media that are such a poor conduit for explaining complex matters provide little incentive for politicians to try, making conflict between responsiveness and responsibility more likely. The media's—and increasingly the society's—assumption that all politicians are equally dishonest and self-serving not only further decreases positive incentives for acting responsibly but removes the penalties for irresponsible behavior. Electoral incentives for responsible behavior are largely lacking.

Legislation seriously addressing major societal problems in the comprehensive and complex way that true effectiveness requires becomes less likely to pass. Given the status quo bias inherent in a governmental system in which separate institutions share power and successive majorities are needed to enact policy, nonincremental policy change usually requires strong public support. To overcome the multiple veto points and the contrary messages from interests with a stake in the status quo, elected officials need to receive strong, clear signals from their constituents. When public discourse is dominated by the simplest argument and the most cynical interpretation, strong public support for complex nonincremental policy change is less likely to form or, if formed, to persist long enough to see such legislation through to enactment.

None of this bodes well for the 104th Congress. In their policy preferences, President Clinton and the new Republican majorities are very far apart. Combine that with the Republicans' conviction that they received a mandate for their full program and thus that compromise is neither necessary nor politically wise, and the prospects for productive cooperation between president and Congress are dim. The lessons the 103rd Congress and its denouement in the 1994 elections teach politicians are likely to have serious effects long after the 104th Congress is history. Negativism and blatant obstructionism pay off in electoral success; taking on big problems seriously and making tough choices do not.

Acknowledgments

In addition to the material cited in the notes, this chapter is based on the author's interviews with members of Congress, congressional and White House staff, and informed observers. All unattributed quotes are from these interviews.

Notes

1. See Charles O. Jones, *The Presidency in a Separated System* (Washington, D.C.: Brookings Institution, 1994).

2. Barbara Sinclair, *Legislators, Leaders and Lawmaking: The House of Representatives in the Post Reform Era* (Baltimore: Johns Hopkins University Press, 1995).

3. Barbara Sinclair, "Agenda Control and Policy Success: The Case of Ronald Reagan and the 97th House," *Legislative Studies Quarterly* 20 (August 1985): 291–314; Darrell West, *Congress and Economic Policy Making* (Pittsburgh: University of Pittsburgh Press, 1987).

4. Pamela Fessler, "If People Get Behind President, Congress Is Likely to Follow," *Congressional Quarterly Weekly Report*, 20 February 1993, 380–81.

5. David Rohde, "Variations in Partisanship in the House of Representatives: Southern Democrats, Realignment and Agenda Change," paper presented at the annual meeting of the American Political Science Association, 1989. *Congressional Quarterly Almanac*, various volumes.

6. Ibid.

7. Rohde, "Variations in Partisanship in the House."

8. Barbara Sinclair, *Congressional Realignment* (Austin: University of Texas Press, 1982), chaps. 7–8.

9. Patricia A. Hurley, "Parties and Coalitions in Congress," in *Congressional Politics,* ed. Christopher J. Deering (Chicago: Dorsey Press, 1989), 131.

10. Data are from *Congressional Quarterly Almanac,* various volumes, and from the author's calculations from data supplied by the Interuniversity Consortium for Political Research.

11. Sinclair, *Legislators, Leaders and Lawmaking.*

12. See Barbara Sinclair, *The Transformation of the U.S. Senate* (Baltimore: Johns Hopkins University Press, 1989); and Steven S. Smith, "Forces of Change in Senate Party Leadership and Organization" in *Congress Reconsidered,* ed. Lawrence C. Dodd and Bruce I. Oppenheimer, 5th ed. (Washington, D.C.: CQ Press, 1993).

13. Ibid.

14. Democratic Study Group (DSG), "A Look at the Senate Filibuster," DSG Special Report, 13 June 1994.

15. William Connelly and John Pitney, *Congress' Permanent Minority? Republicans in the U.S. House* (Lanham, Md.: Rowman and Littlefield, 1994).

16. Karen Tumulty and Michael Ross, "Clinton Expected to Dodge Carter's Problems with Congress," *Los Angeles Times,* 6 November 1992.

17. David Hess, "100 New Faces Start in Congress Today," *Riverside Press Enterprise,* 5 January 1993.

18. Beth Donovan, "Clinton Reverses Directions: Battle Begins Anew," *Congressional Quarterly Weekly Report,* 23 January 1993, 182.

19. George Hager, "President Throws Down Gauntlet," *Congressional Quarterly Weekly Report,* 20 February 1993, 355–59.

20. Fessler, "If People Get Behind President," 380.

21. John Healey and Chuck Alston, "Stimulus Bill Prevails in House, But Senate Battle Awaits," and George Hager, "House Democrats Easily Back Clinton Budget Blueprint," *Congressional Quarterly Weekly Report,* 20 March 1993, 649–58.

22. Chuck Alston, "A Fish Story," *Congressional Quarterly Weekly Report,* 27 March 1993, 737.

23. George Hager and David Cloud, "Leaders Scramble to Win Votes for Deficit-Reduction Bill," *Congressional Quarterly Weekly Report,* 22 May 1993, 1278; see also 1277–79.

24. George Hager and David S. Cloud, "Democrats Pull Off Squeaker in Approving Clinton Plan," *Congressional Quarterly Weekly Report,* 29 May 1993, 1341.

25. Ibid.

26. Ibid., 1345.

27. David Cloud and George Hager, "With New Budget Deal in Hand, Clinton Faces Longest Yard," and Janet Hook, "In Fight for Votes, White House ... Here, There and Everywhere," *Congressional Quarterly Weekly Report,* 31 July 1993, 2023–28.

28. George Hager and David Cloud, "Democrats Tie Their Fate to Clinton's Budget Bill," *Congressional Quarterly Weekly Report,* 7 August 1993, 2122–29.

29. Ibid.

30. Hook, "In Fight for Votes," 2024.

31. Eric Pianin and Ann Devroy, "Clinton Fights Revolt on Hill," *Washington Post*, 20 May 1993.

32. William Eaton and Michael Ross, "House, in Cliffhanger, Passes Clinton's Deficit-Cutting Plan," *Los Angeles Times*, 28 May 1993.

33. David Cloud, "Clinton Turns Up Volume on NAFTA Sales Pitch," *Congressional Quarterly Weekly Report*, 23 October 1993, 2863–64; and Janet Hook, "The Uphill Battle for Votes Produces a Whirl of Wooing and Wheeling," *Congressional Quarterly Weekly Report*, 6 November 1993, 3014–15.

34. Alissa Rubin, "Special Interests Stampede to be Heard on Overhaul," *Congressional Quarterly Weekly Report*, 1 May 1993, 1081–84.

35. Ibid., 1084.

36. Adam Clymer, "Hillary Clinton Says Administration Was Misunderstood on Health Care," *New York Times*, 3 October 1994.

37. Richard Cohen, "Ready, Aim, Reform," *National Journal*, 30 October 1993.

38. Alissa Rubin and Beth Donovan, "Clinton Uses His 'Veto Pen' to Draw Line in Debate," *Congressional Quarterly Weekly Report*, 29 January 1994, 174–75; Alissa Rubin, "Suspicion of Government Solutions Lingers in Small-Town America," *Congressional Quarterly Weekly Report*, 26 February 1994, 476–77; Ceci Connolly and Beth Donovan, "Messages from the Home Folks: Seek Wisdom in Moderation," *Congressional Quarterly Weekly Report*, 9 April 1994, 831–33, 839.

39. Connolly and Donovan, "Messages from the Home Folks," 832.

40. Alissa Rubin, "Leaders Using Fervent Approach to Convert Wavering Members," *Congressional Quarterly Weekly Report*, 30 July 1994, 2142–46.

41. Annenberg Public Policy Center Study, cited in Edwin Chen, "Backers of Health Care Reform Turn Spotlight on Foes," *Los Angeles Times*, 23 September 1994.

42. Thomas B. Rosensteil, "Press Found Putting Stress on Politics of Health Reform," *Los Angeles Times*, 26 March 1994.

43. Robin Toner, "Making Sausage," *New York Times*, 4 September 1994.

44. Ann Devroy, "GOP Taking Joy in Obstructionism," *Washington Post*, 7 October 1994.

45. David Cloud and Beth Donovan, "House Delays Health Care Debate as Leaders Plot Strategy," *Congressional Quarterly Weekly Report*, 13 August 1994, 2351.

46. Devroy, "GOP Taking Joy."

47. David Cloud, "End of Session Marked by Partisan Stalemate," *Congressional Quarterly Weekly Report*, 8 October 1994, 2847; see also 2848–53.

48. Data coded by the author on the basis of *Congressional Quarterly* accounts of the legislative history of each piece of major legislation as identified by CQ.

49. *Congressional Quarterly Weekly Report*, 18 December 1993, 3473; 9 December 1994.

50. For a fuller presentation of this argument, see Barbara Sinclair, "Congress, the Public and Policy Making," paper presented at the Norman Thomas Symposium at Vanderbilt University, 30 September–3 October 1994.

4

Clinton's Legal Policy and the Courts: Rising from Disarray or Turning Around and Around?

David M. O'Brien

Presidential leadership requires, at a minimum, communicating a clear and convincing political vision. It depends no less on strong and loyal staffing to carry out that vision. In his first two years, Democratic President William Jefferson "Bill" Clinton largely failed on both scores. He vacillated on important issues of public policy and moved too slowly in filling key positions within his administration. At other times, he pursued policies running contrary to campaign promises and expectations. As a result, Clinton and the Democratic Party paid a very high price in the midterm 1994 election. With the Republican takeover of both the Senate and the House of Representatives for the first time in over forty years, along with sweeping victories in races for governorships across the country, Clinton became destined to confront major uphill battles with Congress over legislation, judicial appointments, and much else.

Nowhere was Clinton's vacillating vision and failure to fill crucial positions to carry out policies more evident than in his dealing with the Department of Justice (DOJ). That was truly remarkable after twelve years of Republican rule. Presidents Ronald Reagan and George Bush had considerable success in changing the direction of law and legal policy on a range of "social–civil rights" issues, including abortion, affirmative action, and governmental accommodation of religion.[1] Expectations for change in justice policies were high among liberal interest groups and constituencies. Yet Clinton moved slowly, hesitatingly, and occasionally mistakenly, in filling positions at the DOJ. Consequently, the course of the DOJ's legal policies and the direction of the federal judiciary shifted only slightly. In addition, when Clinton moved on some legal-policy issues and appointments, he did so in directions that ran contrary to positions taken in his presidential campaign or that were unpopular. Some nominees and legal-policy goals simply appeared far too liberal for the electorate. Confusion and anger over a perceived betrayal of Clinton's campaign promises to govern as a "New Democrat" and his failure to communicate a clear vision were not the only costs and consequences. Opportunities to forge new legal policy in Clinton's first two years were forfeited and lost irretrievably.

Mistakes and mismanagement are only part of the story, though they tell much about the importance of a president's first two years in office and how they constrain later opportunities.[2] By the end of Clinton's second year in the Oval Office, the DOJ was rising above delays in staffing and personnel turnovers. The department was gradually turning course on the enforcement of antitrust laws and in other areas of civil rights and liberties. Moreover, by the end of Clinton's second year the administration had amassed a commendable record of judicial appointees. Clinton's lower court judges were on the whole noncontroversial and highly competent, and they brought diversity to the federal bench. Clinton also named to the Supreme Court two noncontroversial centrists, Justices Ruth Bader Ginsburg and Stephen Breyer. On balance, his judicial appointees fulfilled campaign pledges for greater diversity and moved the federal judiciary back slightly toward a more moderate centrist direction.

Problems of Staffing, Turnovers, and Lost Opportunities

Clinton's problems with the Justice Department arose almost immediately after his inauguration in January 1993 over the filling of the top position of attorney general. His first two nominees, Zoë Baird and Judge Kimba M. Wood, were forced to withdraw from consideration. Each became ensnarled in controversy over having hired illegal aliens. Either one would have become the first female attorney general in the nation's history, which Clinton clearly had in mind when naming them. Yet both were also rather surprising nominees because neither possessed extensive experience directly bearing on the heading of the DOJ's 95,000 employees.

Admittedly, Baird's first job had been in the DOJ during the presidency of Jimmy Carter. For two years, she worked in the department's Office of Legal Policy and later moved into the White House legal office as an associate counsel to the president. When Reagan won the 1980 presidential election, Baird went into a prestigious Washington, D.C., law firm, specializing in corporate law. In 1990, she became vice-president and general counsel for Aetna Life & Casualty Company. The forty-year-old lawyer then became the first of many embarrassments for the Clinton administration. During the Senate Judiciary Committee's confirmation hearings on her appointment, it was revealed that she had knowingly hired two undocumented immigrants as household help and had failed to pay Social Security taxes for them. By the end of the second day of the committee's hearings and under pressure from Republican and moderate Democratic senators, Baird withdrew from the nomination.

Shortly before Clinton was about to announce his second nominee for the post, federal district court Judge Kimba M. Wood, a new public uproar arose. Press reports revealed that she too had employed illegal workers in her home. Within hours of the appearance of those reports, the forty-nine-year-old judge withdrew from consideration for the post of attorney general.

Clinton's final nominee, who indeed became the first female attorney general, was not sworn into office until mid-March. Janet Reno had for fifteen years been the state attorney for Dade County, Florida, heading its office of 900 employees. Reno had a reputation for being tough on crime, but also for being a champion of "preventive" justice policies and alternatives to incarceration. She opposed the death penalty because of its lack of deterrent effect. In spite of some criticisms and questions about her administrative abilities, Reno's nomination sailed through the Senate and was unanimously approved.

The fifty-four-year-old Harvard Law School graduate quickly won over the public with her homespun, plain-spoken, common-sense approach to justice policies.[3] As attorney general, Reno won some praise for assuming responsibility for the tragedy in Waco, Texas. That fifty-one-day-long standoff between agents of the Bureau of Alcohol, Tobacco, and Firearms (ATF) and the Branch Davidian followers of religious cult leader David Koresh ended with the fiery death of dozens inside Koresh's compound.[4] Reno also spoke out about violence on television, ethics in government, community policing, the enforcement of the Americans with Disabilities Act, and much else. Demonstrating her independence, Reno undertook changes in legal policies that ran both in line and out of line with public opinion. On the one hand, for instance, the attorney general took a firm stand on allowing greater access to government documents under the Freedom of Information Act. On the other hand, Reno reversed the Bush administration's policy of limiting federal prosecutors' discretion to engage in plea bargaining, thereby permitting them and drug couriers, so-called mules, to get around severe mandatory minimum sentences.[5] She questioned publicly the congressional push for mandatory minimum sentences for criminals, and she advocated the need for crime prevention and other tough new measures. In short, Reno won high marks for her public outspokenness. Few of her predecessors have used the attorney generalship as a bully pulpit or done so quite as effectively and credibly.

To Clinton's credit, he did not name a close personal friend or campaign manager as attorney general, as have other recent presidents. With the exception of Republican President Gerald Ford, other presidents have been charged with cronyism when filling the post. Democratic President John F. Kennedy named his brother, Robert Kennedy. Republican President Richard M. Nixon chose his law partner and campaign manager, John N. Mitchell, while Reagan appointed his personal attorney, William French Smith, as his first attorney general and then another long-time friend from California, Edwin Meese III, as his second.

Nevertheless, at the end of Reno's first year at the helm of the DOJ, she was under a storm of criticism. Reno was criticized for not being a team player, for failure to delegate, and for mismanagement.[6] Reno simply was not a White House insider, and she even clashed publicly with the president over the crime bill and some nominations to the DOJ. Within the department, doubts grew steadily about her managerial competence. Reno appeared overwhelmed and disorganized as an administrator. That was most evident when her deputy attorney general, Philip B. Heymann, resigned after just seven months in office.

Heymann, a Harvard Law School professor who had served under four previous attorneys general, cited differences in "style and chemistry" between them as the reason for his departure.[7] But there were also sharp disagreements over legal policy between Heymann and the administration. Indeed, within a week of leaving office Heymann blasted the Clinton White House and Congress for imposing mandatory life sentences for three-time violent offenders and for greatly expanding the federal government's role in prosecuting street crimes. Basically, Heymann was an old-time liberal, out of sync with the New Democrats and White House aides pushing for criminal justice reform. Still, he was neither the first nor the last to leave Reno's service. A week before Heymann left, Reno's aide in charge of scheduling and correspondence had departed. Other aides subsequently moved on.

The problem of staffing the Justice Department remained one Attorney General Reno lamented repeatedly at press conferences during her first year and a half. But it was partly a problem of her own making. Reno kept a skeletal staff and initially refused to appoint a chief of staff on the ground that, as she once put it, "I don't think attorneys general should have gatekeepers." Yet that only contributed to her problems of getting control over and setting priorities for the Justice Department.

To be sure, Reno's staffing problems, not entirely of her own making, were compounded by the White House's hesitancy in filling other critical positions and misjudgments in selecting some nominees. Months passed before

JoAnn Harris was named to head the Criminal Division and Loretta Harris was picked for the Tax Division. The first year of Clinton's administration ended with many other key positions vacant, including those of assistant attorneys general for the Civil Rights and the Environmental and Natural Resources Divisions, as well as the head of the Office of Justice Programs. More than one and a half years went by before the president named the chair of the Equal Employment Opportunity Commission (EEOC), which handles complaints about job discrimination and sexual harassment. The EEOC had a record 87,000 complaints filed in 1993 alone, but no director.[8]

Clinton also confronted major controversies over some of his nominees and was forced to back away from their nominations. His first nominee to head the Justice Department's Civil Rights Division, Lani Guinier, became a lightning rod for political conflict. Guinier, a University of Pennsylvania Law School professor, was a former attorney in the Carter administration and with the National Association for the Advancement of Colored People's (NAACP) Legal Defense and Educational Fund. Guinier also had written a number of provocative articles on minority voting rights. In them, she advocated theories for advancing "authentic black representation" and for enhancing minority groups' influence in legislative bodies.[9] Although not widely influential before her nomination, the articles provided a basis for attacking Guinier's nomination.

Conservative interest groups and Senate Republicans immediately denounced Guinier as a "radical" activist who was "out of the mainstream." They called her a "quota queen" and, recalling the 1987 defeat of Senate confirmation of Reagan's nominee Robert H. Bork to the Supreme Court, vowed to "Bork" her. Consequently, Clinton faced another uphill battle. Moreover, he faced opposition to Guinier not just from conservative Republicans. The Democratic Leadership Council (DLC), a group of southern and western politicians founded in 1985 to shed the Democratic Party's liberal image, and which Clinton had chaired while serving as governor of Arkansas, strongly opposed Guinier's nomination. Clinton appeared, as he too often did, torn in two directions.

Although the president had known Guinier since their days in Yale Law School, and although Attorney General Reno stuck by her nomination, Clinton finally abandoned her. After unwisely allowing the controversy to rage on for several months, he retreated. "At the time of the nomination," he explained, "I had not read her writings. In retrospect, I wish I had. Today, as a matter of fairness to her, I read some of them again in good detail. They clearly lend themselves to interpretations that do not represent the views that I expressed on civil rights during my campaign." Concluding, Clinton said he could not "fight a battle that I know is divisive, that is an uphill battle, that is distracting to the country, if I do not believe in the ground of the battle."[10]

Clinton's retreat from campaign promises to reinvigorate civil rights policies and his reclaiming a centrist position as a New Democrat in order to avoid a polarizing public debate over Guinier and civil rights policies, however, drew sharp criticism from members of the congressional Black Caucus and activist supporters in the "civil rights community." More generally, the Guinier episode fit part of an emerging pattern that reinforced questions and doubts about Clinton's judgment and leadership abilities.

Subsequently, Clinton came very close to nominating another African American, John Payton, to head the Civil Rights Division. But Payton, corporation counsel for the District of Columbia, withdrew from consideration after losing the support of the congressional Black Caucus. Many of its members opposed Payton on the ground that he had not voted in the last sixteen years. Finally, a full year after moving into the Oval Office, Clinton named another black attorney and former NAACP litigator, thirty-six-year-old Harvard Law School graduate Deval L. Patrick. His appointment met no resistance from Republicans and had the strong support of the civil rights community. Patrick also aggressively charted a new course on civil rights. Yet the problem remained that Patrick's appointment came so late, was mired in the lingering controversy surrounding earlier nominees for the post, and represented lost opportunities.

In fairness, Clinton did move quickly when naming some top-notch appointees. After months of speculation, he finally fired the director of the Federal Bureau of Investigation (FBI), William Sessions, and named a successor within twenty-four hours. Sessions, who was appointed to the ten-year post by Reagan in 1987, had refused to step down. He did so even though the FBI's morale kept sinking amid allegations that he misused his office, had ethical lapses, and was a very poor administrator. After firing Sessions, Clinton promptly named as FBI director federal district court Judge Louis J. Freeh. Freeh had been an FBI agent before becoming a U.S. attorney and later a federal judge. Freeh commanded respect within the FBI and won unanimous consent in the Senate. Another appointee, Anne K. Bingaman, as head of the Antitrust Division was surprising because of her background, but she won high marks for her aggressive enforcement of antitrust laws. Bingaman, the wife of New Mexico's Democratic Senator Jeff Bingaman, was a Stanford Law School graduate and a Washington, D.C., litigator before assuming the position. And although former Duke University Law School professor Walter E. Dellinger III faced stiff opposition from Senate Republicans over some of his liberal views, he was confirmed by a vote of 65–34 as the head of the DOJ's Office of Legal Counsel.

Still, the prolonged and controversy-ridden process of appointing the head of the Civil Rights Division remains more emblematic of Clinton's vacillating desire for diversity and progressive tendencies, on the one hand, and his need to remain true to his New Democrat pledges, on the other hand.

The top position in the Environment and Natural Resources Division likewise remained vacant for over eighteen months. As with filling other vacancies, a series of potential candidates for that position were floated, scrutinized, and forced to withdraw for one reason or another. In addition, Clinton was much slower than former presidents Bush, Reagan, and Carter in nominating candidates for slots as general counsel to federal departments and agencies.[11] As a result, some federal agencies' legal policies drifted. By default, the Bush administration's policies continued to prevail well into Clinton's first year in the Oval Office.

During Clinton's first year or so, controversies over other personnel turnovers in key positions further dogged the Justice Department. Associate Attorney General Webster L. Hubbell, the third-highest-ranking official in the department, was forced to resign in March 1994. He followed closely the departures of Heymann and White House counsel Bernard W. Nussbaum. Nussbaum, a tough-talking former corporate lawyer from Brooklyn who had practiced on Wall Street, was a key player in the ill-fated nominations of Baird, Wood, and Guinier. But Nussbaum came under increasing fire for alleged ethical violations involving his dealings with government officials investigating the so-called Whitewater affair. The Whitewater Development Company, an Arkansas real estate venture in which the Clintons had invested, had been funded by the failed Madison Guaranty Savings and Loan, which was under investigation by the Resolution Trust Corporation for financial improprieties. Instead of distancing the president from the Whitewater controversy, Nussbaum's activities threatened to drag Clinton further into it, and Nussbaum had to resign.

Associate Attorney General Hubbell, another close friend of the president and a former law partner of Hillary Rodham Clinton, as well as a former justice of the Arkansas state supreme court, was in turn also forced to resign. He had failed to resolve what he initially described as a squabble with his former partners at the Rose law firm in Little Rock, Arkansas. The most conservative of Clinton's appointees to the Justice Department, Hubbell's close connections with the president and personal style had made him a stabilizing force with the DOJ during Reno's troubled first year. Yet, because he could not resolve the dispute over his overbilling former clients and improperly charging expenses to his law firm, Hubbell had to leave. Morale within the Justice Department fell further when in December 1994 Hubbell agreed to plead guilty to overbilling clients $390,000 and to defrauding the federal government when in private practice.

With the departures of Nussbaum and Hubbell, matters improved, first, with the temporary appointment of Lloyd Cutler, a seasoned and respected Washington, D.C., attorney, and then with his replacement by former Democratic congressman and federal appellate court Judge Abner Mikva as White House counsel. Finally, midway into Clinton's second year in office the DOJ's operation began to come together. That was due not merely to the filling of key positions within the department. No less important, two respected attorneys with close ties to the White House were transferred to the DOJ. In late February 1994, Jamie Gorelick became the Justice Department's chief operating officer and Ron Klain was detailed from the White House. Gorelick had been general counsel for the Defense Department during Clinton's first year and had been involved in the delicate negotiations over the president's proposal on homosexuals in the military. After moving into the DOJ, Gorelick brought in some outstanding personal assistants and quickly won praise for her administrative efficiency. Also well respected on Capitol Hill, Klain oversaw the passage of the controversial crime bill in 1994 and fashioned the administration's "three strikes and you're out" proposal. Klain took charge of overseeing legal policy and pushing the administration's position on pending legislation in Congress.

By the end of Clinton's second year, the Justice Department was expediting the nomination of federal judges and charting new directions in legal policy. But the lingering problem remained that the legacy of the first year and a half was largely one of controversy, confusion, and lost opportunities. Moreover, the lost opportunities and the prospect of fighting rear-guard actions over the next two years, as a result of the Republicans' takeover of the Senate, reflected more than just difficulties in staffing and personnel turnover. Indeed, the latter problems registered the president's own priorities. Clinton simply had not given the DOJ very high priority in his domestic agenda. Instead, health-care reform was given top priority. Preoccupation with that issue and the president's own vacillations on appointments and policy positions were at the root of the problems of staffing and lost opportunities in pushing legal policy in new directions.

Renewing Affirmative Action and Making the Federal Bench More Representative

Clinton inherited a record number of vacancies (109) on the federal bench when he came into office. The large number of openings resulted from two factors. First, Congress created 85 new federal judgeships in 1990 in order to handle the flood of criminal and civil cases coming into the federal courts in the late 1980s. Second, President Bush failed to nominate many judges in his last year in office. Still, Clinton was slow to fill positions during his first year, just as Bush had been. As indicated in table 4.1, there were more judicial vacancies at the end than at the start of Clinton's first year in the Oval Office.

The failure to fill more judgeships during his first year largely reflected the staffing problems in the DOJ. More than eight months of Clinton's first year in office passed before the Senate approved Eleanor Dean Acheson as

TABLE 4.1

FILLING VACANCIES ON THE FEDERAL BENCH:
THE FIRST YEAR

	Clinton	Bush	Reagan	Carter
Number of federal judges	837	757	660	509
Vacancies on coming into office	109	40	35	N.A.
First-year nominations	33	23	44	34
First-year confirmations	28	15	41	31
Vacancies remaining at end of year	113	62	33	N.A.

head of the DOJ's Office of Policy Development, which handles the screening of potential judicial nominees. Her confirmation was held up by a dispute over her belonging to a country club that had no black members and a history of discriminating against women. In the meantime, judicial appointments were handled by Nussbaum, Hubbell, White House deputy counsel Joel Klein, and Ron Klain, who had previously worked for the chair of the Senate Judiciary Committee, Delaware's Democratic Senator Joseph Biden.

The process of selecting judicial nominees also changed in some rather surprising ways. During the Reagan-Bush era, lower court judgeships were given higher priority, potential candidates were subjected to the most rigorous screening process ever, and the screening process became a larger bureaucratic operation within the Justice Department, along with greater White House supervision than in any other preceding administration.[12] In addition, both administrations followed the Carter administration in curbing the practice of "senatorial courtesy," of deferring to recommendations of homestate senators for federal district court judgeships.

By contrast, the Clinton administration initially downplayed the DOJ's role and, later, after shifting primary responsibility back to the department's Office of Legal Policy Development, downsized the judicial selection operation. Until the Senate's confirmation of Eleanor Dean Acheson as head of the Office of Legal Policy Development, the selection of lower court judges remained a White House operation. Moreover, the administration relied on District of Columbia lawyers to vet potential nominees, that is, to review their records and investigate their records and reputations. Not since the Kennedy administration has a White House relied so heavily on private attorneys, outsiders, in such a way. After Acheson, along with fourteen others in the department and two staffers in the White House, assumed responsibility for screening potential judicial nominees, the use of vetters was discontinued. Instead, department attorneys typically go over candidates' questionnaires and then, in Acheson's estimate, make forty to sixty telephone calls to judges, lawyers, and others in the jurisdiction that the candidate would sit on the federal bench.[13] In this way, the DOJ eliminated some potential judicial candidates and decided which ones it would go forward with after receiving evaluations from the American Bar Association and further interviews with DOJ attorneys.

Another major change made in the judicial selection process was the Clinton administration's decision to actively seek only *one* nominee for each federal district court vacancy from the homestate senator. That constituted a return to pre-Carter administrations' deference to the tradition of senatorial courtesy. The Carter, Reagan, and Bush administrations had curbed senatorial patronage and asserted greater presidential power and control over the selection of lower court nominees by demanding that senators provide at least three names for each vacancy. Moreover, even the preferences of homestate senators in the Republican Party were not always respected during the Reagan and Bush administrations, if their candidates were deemed too liberal on issues such as abortion or the rights of the accused.[14] The Clinton administration's return to the practice of deferring to senatorial patronage amounted to both a retreat from the past three administrations' assertion of presidential power over that of senators and a strategic maneuver designed to avoid bitter confirmation battles in the Senate over lower court judgeships.

At the end of Clinton's second year, his Justice Department had nonetheless amassed an impressive record of highly qualified judges who brought greater diversity to the federal bench. Indeed, in his second year in office Clinton appointed over 100 judges, a near-record number that had not been surpassed since 1979. In his initial two years, Clinton named a total of 129 federal judges, whereas Bush had appointed only 187 in twice that time (see table 4.2).

Moreover, 65 percent of Clinton's appointees were rated by the American Bar Association (ABA) as "well qualified," the ABA's highest ranking.[15] By comparison, 59 percent of Bush's, 55 percent of Reagan's, and 56 percent of Carter's judicial appointees were ranked "well qualified."

In addition, 58 percent of Clinton's judges were women and minorities. In other words, Clinton appointed more nontraditional federal judges than any preceding president (see table 4.3).[16] Nearly one-fourth of Clinton's judges were African Americans, 9 percent were Hispanic, and 31 percent were women. In the words of political scientist Sheldon Goldman, who has monitored judicial appointments to the lower federal courts for over thirty years, "This will undoubtedly be the benchmark against which all future administrations will be judged. This tremendous push toward ethnic and gender diversity could break all historic records."[17]

In addition to being a highly qualified and diverse group of federal judges, a larger portion of Clinton's judicial appointees than those of Bush, Reagan, or Carter had prestigious Ivy League undergraduate and law school educations. Like predecessors in both parties, Clinton favored overwhelm-

TABLE 4.2
NUMBER OF JUDICIAL APPOINTMENTS FROM EISENHOWER TO CLINTON

	Eisenhower	Kennedy	Johnson	Nixon	Ford	Carter	Reagan	Bush	Clinton
Supreme Court	5	2	2	4	1	0	4	2	2
Circuit courts	45	20	41	45	12	56	78	37	19
District courts	127	102	125	179	52	202	290	148	108
Special courts[a]	10	2	13	7	1	3	10	0	0
Totals	187	126	181	235	66	261	382	187	129

SOURCE: Department of Justice.

a. Includes the defunct Courts of Customs and Customs and Patent Appeals, and the Court of International Trade. Data for Clinton appointees are for those confirmed through 1994.

TABLE 4.3
A Profile of Presidential Appointees to the Federal Courts

	Johnson		Nixon		Ford		Carter		Reagan		Bush		Clinton	
	%	No.	%	No.	%	No.	%	No.	%	No.	%	No.	%	No.
Total number of appointees		162		224		64		258		368		185		129
Gender														
Male	98.1	159	99.8	223	98.4	63	84.4	218	92.3	340	80.5	149	68.9	89
Female	1.8	3	0.4	1	1.5	1	15.4	40	7.6	28	19.4	36	31.0	40
Ethnicity or race														
White	93.8	152	95.9	215	90.6	58	78.6	203	93.4	344	89.1	165	65.8	85
Black	4.3	7	2.6	6	4.6	3	14.3	37	1.9	7	6.4	12	24.0	31
Hispanic	1.8	3	0.8	2	1.5	1	6.2	16	4.0	15	4.3	8	8.5	11
Asian			.4	1	3.1	2	0.7	2	0.5	2			0.7	1
Native American													0.7	1

SOURCE: Sheldon Goldman, "Bush's Judicial Legacy: The Final Imprint," Judicature 282 (1993), and Department of Justice. The data for Clinton's appointees are through 1994 and were obtained from the Department of Justice.

ingly those affiliated with his own party. About nine out of ten of his judicial appointees identified with the Democratic Party. On average, Clinton's judges were 49.4 years old at the time of appointment; the average age of Bush's judges was 48.2, while Carter's judges had the oldest average age at 50.1. Goldman also found that "a majority of Clinton's judges, unlike those of the previous three administrations, came to the federal bench directly from the judiciary (as state judges, federal magistrates, or federal district judges)."[18] That aspect of Clinton's judicial recruitment reinforces Goldman's conclusion that "by ABA standards, the Clinton appointees overall are the best qualified for federal judgeships since the ABA began to rate judicial candidates in the 1950s."[19]

In short, Clinton largely fulfilled his campaign promises both to seek high-caliber appointees and to bring greater diversity to the federal bench. When he spoke to the ABA in 1992, Clinton maintained that "public confidence in our federal judiciary is furthered by the presence of more women lawyers and minority lawyers on the bench, and the judicial system and the country benefit from having judges who are excellent lawyers with diverse perspectives."[20] Clinton achieved diversity on the federal bench without sacrificing quality. Only one nominee, an African American prosecutor for Prince George's County, Maryland, Alexander Williams, was rated unqualified by the ABA. Still, Williams was unanimously recommended by the Senate Judiciary Committee and unanimously confirmed by the Senate.

Besides appointing an unprecedented number of women and minorities to the federal bench, Clinton named two highly respected disabled lawyers to the bench. Although there was no mention of his impairment at the time of his nomination, David S. Tatel became the first blind person to be named to the federal appellate bench. Appointed to the U.S. Court of Appeals for the District of Columbia, Tatel had a highly respected reputation as a civil rights attorney and advocate for poor children. He also had experience serving in the civil rights office of the Department of Health, Education, and Welfare during the Carter administration.

Another record for the federal judiciary was the appointment of the first openly homosexual federal judge. But in order not to reignite the major controversy that had erupted over Clinton's proposal to remove the ban on homosexuals in the military, the White House played down that fact, and it went largely unnoticed in the press and during the Senate confirmation process. The appointment of former Fordham Law School professor Deborah Batts nevertheless registers the Clinton administration's commitment to diversity. The appointment also reflects the difference between the Clinton and the Reagan-Bush administrations. New York's Democratic Senator Daniel Patrick Moynihan had first recommended Batts for a judgeship during Bush's administration. In spite of three interviews with Justice Department officials, she failed to get the presidential nod. Batts, an African American,

Harvard Law School graduate, and divorced mother of two, had been in private practice for six years before becoming a U.S. attorney in the Southern District of New York for five years and then joining the Fordham faculty in 1984. The forty-seven-year-old former professor was never told directly why Bush declined to nominate her. But she recalls others telling her that "Professor Batts's image of what a judge should be is not the same as what [the Bush administration's] image is."[21] Batts speculated further that the Bush administration was uncomfortable with the fact that she was a lesbian, which she is open about but does not advertise. "I'm a mother," as Judge Batts explains, "I'm an African American. I'm a lesbian. I'm a former professor. If people assume any one of these is going to predominate it would create a problem."[22]

The quest for diversity and a more representative federal judiciary basically replaced ideology in Clinton's judicial selection process. During the Reagan-Bush era, judicial philosophy and judicial candidates' stand on controversial issues such as abortion became "litmus tests" in judicial selection.[23] Some liberal interest groups expected the Clinton administration to reverse course sharply and impose its own litmus tests for judicial nominees. Instead, the Clinton administration charted a centrist course, deferring to homestate Democratic senators' recommendations for district court judges, even when they went against the president's stand on a woman's right to choose abortion, for instance.

Justice Department officials running the judicial selection process denied having a liberal litmus test. "We don't have litmus tests or judicial philosophy tests," claimed Assistant Attorney General Eleanor Acheson, adding, "but I do think we've put people on the bench who are interested in people and their problems, in being rigorously fair-minded, in making the court[s] an open and accessible place."[24] In White House deputy counsel Joel Klein's words, "We don't see courts as a vehicle for social change. It's enough to put people of demonstrated quality on the bench. We've done this across gender, race, and national origin lines. And that is a legacy that the president is proud of."[25]

Inexorably, both liberal and conservative interest groups were not pleased with the Clinton administration's strategy for judicial selection or some of its judicial nominees. To try to govern from the center inevitably invites attacks from the left and the right. "It's clear that the Reagan and Bush administrations steered the judiciary in an anti-choice direction," observed Kate Michelman, the president of the National Abortion Rights Action League (NARAL), "and I think it's important that the Clinton administration make a significant effort to correct this."[26] NARAL and other liberal groups were thus disappointed when Clinton named to the federal bench judges who had spoken out against abortion rights. Nan Aron, the executive director of the Alliance for Justice, an umbrella organization that monitors judicial appointments for a coalition of liberal "public interest" groups, agreed. In Aron's words, "We have to be true to our beliefs and principles. If the administration nominates candidates who lack a sensitivity and commitment to constitutional principles, we will work hard to make our voice heard."[27]

Liberal groups such as the Alliance for Justice and the People for the American Way were able to pressure the administration into delaying, if not ultimately abandoning, some potential judicial nominees who had been recommended by Democrats as patronage appointees. The Alliance for Justice successfully fought against the administration's nomination of Missouri appellate court Judge Gary Gaertner to a federal district court, for instance. Judge Gaertner was a long-time friend of Representative Richard Gephardt, a crucial ally for the president in achieving his legislative agenda. Yet the Alliance for Justice prepared a seven-page "background memorandum" on Judge Gaertner, accusing him of insensitivity toward the rights of criminal defendants, women, and homosexuals. The alliance lobbied hard and successfully (at least prior to the 1994 midterm elections) against his nomination.[28]

Another potential nominee for the federal bench whose appointment was delayed by liberal groups was the former mayor of Albany, New York, Thomas Whalen III. Whalen was considered for an appointment to the federal district court in the Northern District of New York. Once again, liberal groups and abortion rights advocates came out in opposition. They accused Whalen of attempting to block the placement of a Planned Parenthood clinic in Albany. By challenging his selection, they succeeded in preempting his nomination, at least during Clinton's first two years.

Liberal groups were not always successful in defeating judicial nominees they deemed too conservative. William Downes, for one, was nominated and confirmed for a seat on the federal district court in Wyoming in spite of strong opposition from liberal women's interest groups. Downes was criticized for reportedly calling abortion rights activists "bra-burners." He had as well, among other things, led a fight at the Wyoming state Democratic convention in 1988 against a plank endorsing women's abortion rights. Downes, though, was a friend and former law partner of Democratic Governor Michael J. Sullivan, an abortion opponent and the state's senior Democrat. With no Democratic senator from Wyoming, the White House deferred to Sullivan's recommendation of Downes, and his nomination was confirmed by the Senate.

Conservative interest groups and Republican senators were geared up to fight any liberal judicial nominee from the outset of Clinton's administration. Organizations such as the Free Congress Foundation, which monitors judicial appointments for conservatives, and the Washington Legal Foundation planned aggressive attacks. Not surprisingly, they were not pleased with many of Clinton's judicial appointees. In the words of the Free Congress Foundation's Thomas Jipping, who led unsuccessful fights against the confirmation of Attorney General Reno and several lower court judges: "I think there are many liberal judicial activists in [Clinton's judicial appointees], and they have been rubber-stamped by the Senate."[29] But that was hardly the case. In fact, the Free Congress Foundation and Republican senators fought against the confirmation of a few judicial nominees and delayed or derailed the nomination of others.

Republicans on the Senate Judiciary Committee put most judicial nominees through rigorous questioning. At virtually every confirmation hearing at least one Republican senator was present to ask nominees about their views on the death penalty.[30] Those who appeared too liberal were blasted during the committee's hearings by Senator Orrin Hatch of Utah or other Republicans. Martha Craig Daughtrey, the first female to sit on the Tennessee state supreme court, faced sharp opposition from Hatch. He claimed that her record on the state court was "unduly hostile to the death penalty."[31] Still, Daughtrey's judicious responses to questions reassured the Senate Judiciary Committee, and she was confirmed in 1993 for a seat on the Court of Appeals for the Sixth Circuit.

The Free Congress Foundation and ranking Republican Senators Hatch and Strom Thurmond (R-S.C.) also targeted a few judicial nominees for defeat. Two, Rosemary Barkett and H. Lee Sarokin, were specifically targeted. Senator Hatch distributed confidential reports on them to conservative columnists in order to drum up opposition, and both hearings before the Senate Judiciary Committee were marked by vintage partisan struggles.

Rosemary Barkett, a former Roman Catholic nun and the first female chief justice on the Florida state supreme court, was nominated for a seat on the U.S. Court of Appeals for the Eleventh Circuit. Barkett faced stiff opposition over Republican senators' charges that she was too soft on criminal defendants and had voted to overturn lower courts' imposition of the death penalty. At her confirmation hearing, Senator Thurmond took the offensive by reciting the gruesome details of murder cases in which Chief Justice Barkett had voted to overrule death sentences. The Judiciary Committee's chair, Senator Joseph Biden (D-Del.), countered by reviewing at length the details of other cases in which Barkett had voted to uphold death sentences. Ultimately, after Florida's Republican Senator Connie Mack threw his weight behind her appointment, Barkett won Senate approval by a vote of 61–37.

Federal district court Judge H. Lee Sarokin's proposed elevation to the federal appellate bench was also targeted by conservative groups and senators. He too faced a bitter confirmation hearing. The sixty-five-year-old judge was recommended by Clinton's long-time friend, Senator Bill Bradley (D-N.J.). Conservatives, though, deemed Judge Sarokin too liberal in his rulings on the rights of the accused and the First Amendment's protection for homeless people. They also attacked him for having received an award from an antismoking group, after having presided over a controversial cigarette manufacturer's liability case. Senator Hatch repeatedly blasted his "liberal' judicial activism," charging that "Judge Sarokin has worked to smuggle his soft-on-crime views into his criminal opinions."[32] Nonetheless, Judge Sarokin was approved by a vote of 63–35 in the full Senate.

Although conservative Republicans' two principal attacks on Clinton's judicial nominees thus failed, they were able to delay, and after the 1994 midterm election were in a position to defeat, the confirmation of others who appeared too liberal. That is what happened when the Clinton administration followed up on two judicial candidates, both Mexican Americans, recommended by California Democratic Senator Barbara Boxer. Both would have become the first Mexican Americans to serve on the federal district court in Los Angeles. But, only one, Richard A. Paez, was confirmed by the Senate. The other, Samuel Paz, became ensnarled in a controversy over his views. Both Paez and Paz described themselves as liberal. Yet they were otherwise very different and took different career paths. Paez, a Mormon and former "public interest" lawyer for the Western Center on Law and Poverty and the Legal Aid Foundation of Los Angeles, had served for thirteen years as a municipal court judge, appointed in 1981 by then Governor Edmund G. ("Jerry") Brown. In contrast, Paz was affiliated with the American Civil Liberties Union and had specialized in suits over police brutality and misconduct. Paz was also an outspoken advocate of affirmative action and had publicly defended the 1992 Los Angeles riots as a protest against political and economic inequality. Paz's legal practice and outspoken political views were an easy target for Republicans, who stalled his confirmation in the 103rd Congress and doomed chances for his confirmation afterward.

The Clinton administration's anticipation of Republican opposition to nominees who appeared (or could be portrayed as) too liberal and deference to Democratic senators' patronage recommendations for homestate district court judgeships led to the appointment of mostly moderate to conservative lower court judges. Clinton's judicial appointments, thus, on balance disappointed some liberal groups. "Reagan and Bush really changed the philosophy of the courts, and not for the better," in the view of, among others, Ninth Circuit U.S. Court of Appeals Judge Stephen Reinhardt, a Carter appointee. "Clinton had the opportunity to do the same, and he blew it. There seems to be this sense that [the administration doesn't] want to do anything to offend Hatch or [Wyoming's Republican Senator Alan K.] Simpson. You can't conceive of Bush or Reagan thinking, 'let's not do anything that could offend [Massachusetts's Democratic Edward] Kennedy.' Those of us who have waited for three decades for a Democrat to be appointing liberal judges, particularly to the Supreme Court, have been deeply disappointed," concluded Judge Reinhardt.[33]

Criticism by liberals, such as Judge Reinhardt and the Alliance for Justice, however, was largely dismissed by the administration and was certain to carry even less weight after the 1994 elections. In the words of Eleanor Dean Acheson, "Judge Reinhardt's agenda and the Alliance for Justice's agenda is not our agenda."[34] Instead of an agenda for appointing liberal judges, Acheson stressed the department's focus on the qualities of "judicial temperament," "productivity," "energy," "integrity," mental "agility," and concerns about judicial nominees' understanding of the "court as an institution," as well as the administration's goal of bringing diversity to the federal bench.

No less important, while Clinton changed the complexion of the federal judiciary with the appointment of more women and minorities, his 127 lower court judges are not likely to have a significant effect on the direction of the federal judiciary. That reflects not only his naming some conservative judges. The fact is that Clinton's appointees made only a small dent in the federal bench after twelve years of judicial appointments by Bush and Reagan. Of Clinton's 127 lower court appointees, 58 filled positions vacated by retiring judges appointed by Carter, Johnson, and Kennedy. Another 24 filled newly created judgeships. Merely 35 percent replaced (45) judges appointed by Republican presidents. Furthermore, 66 percent of the seats on the federal bench remain filled by Republican-appointed judges. Only in the District of Columbia Circuit do the number of district court judges appointed by Democratic presidents outnumber those named by Republicans, as indicated in table 4.4. Clinton and other Democratic appointees to the highly influential federal appellate bench are also outnumbered by majorities appointed by Republican presidents in every one of the thirteen U.S. courts of appeals (see table 4.5).

In sum, Clinton's appointments to the lower federal courts were largely symbolic, basically bringing cosmetic changes to the federal bench. They did not and are not likely to change the direction of the federal judiciary. The prospects for more significant change were, then, undercut by the Republicans' gaining control of a Senate majority and the turnover of the chair of the Senate Judiciary Committee to Senator Hatch. As a result, Clinton faces naming more conservative judges in order to assure their confirmation or, alternatively, courting controversy. In his last two years, Clinton is certain to confront tough battles over any judicial nominee targeted or portrayed by conservative groups and Republican senators as liberal on this or that issue. The difference between Clinton's judicial appointments during his first two years and the last two years, though, in all likelihood will be apparent at the margins. Those such as Gaertner and Whalen, opposed by liberal groups because of their conservative positions, are more likely to be nominated, while those, such as Daughtrey, Barkett, and Paz are less likely to be nominated and certain to face even more bitter confirmation hearings and, in all likeli-

TABLE 4.4
DISTRIBUTION OF JUDGESHIPS ON U.S. DISTRICT COURTS BY APPOINTING PRESIDENT, AS OF 14 October 1994

Circuits	Total seats	Vacancies	Clinton	Other Democratic	Total Democratic	Republican
District of Columbia	15	0	5	4	9	6
First	29	1	8	4	12	16
Second	62	7	18	3	21	34
Third	62	4	8	7	15	43
Fourth	52	2	7	7	14	36
Fifth	78	7	13	14	27	44
Sixth	63	2	10	15	25	36
Seventh	46	1	7	7	14	31
Eighth	43	4	8	4	12	27
Ninth	99	5	10	17	27	67
Tenth	37	2	6	7	13	22
Eleventh	63	4	8	12	20	39

SOURCE: Compiled by the author from records of the Department of Justice.

TABLE 4.5

DISTRIBUTION OF JUDGESHIPS ON U.S. COURTS OF APPEALS BY APPOINTING PRESIDENT, AS OF 14 OCTOBER 1994

Circuits	Total seats	Vacancies	Clinton	Other Democratic	Total Democratic	Republican
District of Columbia	12	1	2	2	4	7
First	6	1	0	0	0	5
Second	13	0	4	3	6	7
Third	14	0	2	1	3	11
Fourth	15	2	2	2	4	9
Fifth	17	1	3	2	5	11
Sixth	16	2	1	5	6	8
Seventh	12	2	0	1	1	9
Eighth	11	0	1	2	3	8
Ninth	28	2	1	10	11	15
Tenth	12	3	1	1	2	7
Eleventh	12	1	1	3	4	7
Federal	13	0	1	2	3	10
Totals	181	15	19	33	52	114

SOURCE: Compiled by the author from records of the Department of Justice.

hood, defeat in the Senate. Indeed, shortly after the Republicans regained control of the Senate in January 1995, Clinton abandoned the nominations of Samuel Paz and a couple of others because they were portrayed as too liberal and their confirmation certain to be defeated in the Senate.

Avoiding Controversy: Two Jewish Justices

After more than a quarter of a century in which four Republican presidents made ten consecutive appointments to the Supreme Court, Clinton had the opportunity to fill two vacancies during his first two years in office.[35] Midway through the 1992–93 term, Justice Byron White announced his decision to retire at the end of the term. Appointed by President Kennedy in 1962 at age forty-four, Justice White served for thirty-one years and remained the last appointee of a Democratic president. In his time on the bench, he established a staunchly, though by no means uniformly, conservative track record. On some of the most controversial social–civil rights issues, he voted with conservatives. Justice White dissented from the landmark ruling in *Roe v. Wade*[36] and all subsequent rulings affirming a woman's right to have an abortion. He authored the opinion for a bare majority in *Bowers v. Hardwick*,[37] rejecting an extension of the right of privacy to protect private consensual sexual relations. Except for upholding Congress's power to enact affirmative action programs, Justice White opposed such state and local programs unless adopted to remedy specific policies of past discrimination. Although supportive of First Amendment free speech claims in many cases, Justice White often dissented from the Court's decisions enforcing a rigid "separation of church and state" under the First Amendment. With respect to the rights of the accused and criminal justice matters, he also generally sided with conservatives. Justice White, for instance, dissented from the watershed ruling in *Miranda v. Arizona*.[38]

In announcing his decision to retire almost four months in advance of the end of the Court's term, Justice White gave Clinton not only a chance to fill his seat but ample time to select his successor. He may have done so for several reasons. Among others on the Court, Justice White reportedly lamented how the televised coverage of the Senate confirmation hearings for controversial nominees—in particular, the ill-fated nomination of Robert Bork in 1987 and the bitter 1991 struggle over the confirmation of Justice Clarence Thomas—denigrated the Court. Besides considerations for the Court's institutional prestige, Justice White may have wanted to ensure that Clinton had ample time to pick a suitable successor given the controversies over the withdrawal of the president's first two nominees for attorney general and the extraordinary battle that had doomed the last opportunity for a Democratic president to make an imprint on the Court. In 1968 President Lyndon Johnson's proposed elevation of Justice Abe Fortas to the seat of chief justice was defeated when Republicans and conservative Southern Democrats in the Senate forced Justice Fortas to withdraw from consideration.

For his part, Clinton immediately announced that he would search for a nominee who possessed "a fine mind, good judgment, wide experience in the law and the problems of real people," and, the president added, "who has a big heart." During his 1992 campaign when asked about filling possible vacancies on the Supreme Court, Clinton said that he would look "for someone, first of all, who was unquestionably qualified by reason of training, experience, judgment. Then I would look for someone who believed in the constitutional right of privacy ... who [is] prochoice."

Still, more than three months passed before Clinton finally settled on Judge Ruth Bader Ginsburg as his nominee to become the 107th justice of the Supreme Court. Clinton had wanted a politician, a "consensus builder,"[39] who might pull the Court in more liberal directions on some issues. But he also wanted to avoid any major controversy over Senate confirmation that might affect his plans for health-care reform. In addition, several prominent and potential nominees withdrew from consideration, including New York's Governor Mario M. Cuomo and that state's Chief Judge Judith Kaye, as well as Clinton's secretary of the Department of Education, Richard Riley. From a list of over fifty potential nominees, which included federal judges Jose Cabranes, Jon O. Newman, Amalya Kearse, and Patricia Wald, along with Tennessee's supreme court Justice Gilbert Merrit, the president and his advisers narrowed the contenders to a handful.

In the week before the announcement of his nominee, Clinton vacillated between elevating his secretary of the Department of the Interior, Bruce Babbitt—an old friend and former Arizona governor—and naming one of two other federal appellate court judges, Ruth Bader Ginsburg or Judge Stephen G. Breyer. Environmentalists wanted Babbitt to stay at Interior, and he faced strong opposition from the senior minority member on the Senate Judiciary Committee, Senator Hatch. By contrast, both Ginsburg and Breyer had the support of Hatch and Senator Edward Kennedy (D-Mass.). Moreover, each had won seats on the federal bench as last-minute appointees of Carter in 1980.

Judge Breyer had served as chief counsel to the Senate Judiciary Committee when it was chaired by Senator Kennedy in the late 1970s. Senators Kennedy and Hatch were instrumental in pushing Breyer's and Ginsburg's nominations through in 1980, when, as the presidential election approached, Republicans threatened to block all further Carter judicial appointees. Hatch knew and liked Breyer for his work as chief counsel. At that time, Hatch also agreed to meet Ginsburg, at the request of H. Ross Perot. Perot knew Hatch and had been asked to arrange the meeting by his Washington, D.C., tax attorney, who was Ginsburg's husband, Martin. Ginsburg

impressed Hatch then, and later with her thirteen years of service on the
Court of Appeals for the District of Columbia Circuit, during which time
she served with future Justices Antonin Scalia and Clarence Thomas, as well
as defeated Reagan Supreme Court nominees Judges Robert Bork and Douglas Ginsburg (who is no relation to the justice). In 1993, Hatch, though favoring Breyer, remained supportive of Ginsburg. And New York's Senator
Daniel Patrick Moynihan, Martin Ginsburg, and leaders of prominent
women's groups were among Ginsburg's strongest supporters urging Clinton
to name her.

After meeting Judge Breyer for a widely publicized luncheon amid speculation that he would get the nod, Clinton met with Judge Ginsburg the
next day. He was plainly touched by the charm and strength of the sixty-
year-old Jewish grandmother, jurist, and leader of the women's movement in
law in the 1970s. When subsequently announcing his selection, Clinton
praised Ginsburg's "pragmatism" and called her the Thurgood Marshall of
the women's movement. That comparison to the former justice who as a
young attorney had argued many of the cases brought by the National Association for the Advancement of Colored People's Legal Defense and Education Fund, however, was initially drawn by former solicitor general Erwin
Griswold. At the fiftieth anniversary of the Supreme Court Building in 1985,
he observed that "in modern times two appellate advocates altered the nation's course . . . Thurgood Marshall and Ruth Ginsburg."

Born in Brooklyn, Ginsburg went to Cornell University as an undergraduate, where she also met her future husband. Both Ginsburgs went on
to Harvard Law School, but following her husband's graduation and acceptance of a position in a New York City law firm, Ginsburg finished her third
year at Columbia Law School, where she tied for first place in the class. Following graduation, Ginsburg worked as a law clerk for two years for a federal judge. Then, in 1961, she could not find a New York law firm that
would hire her, because she was a woman. After two more years working as
a research assistant, Ginsburg was hired by Rutgers University School of
Law, where she taught until 1972, when she became the first woman law
professor at Columbia Law School.

Because no Jewish justice had sat on the high bench for almost a quarter of a century (since Justice Fortas resigned in 1969), Jewish groups welcomed Ginsburg's nomination, while also rejecting the mythology of a "Jewish seat" and emphasizing that her selection was based on merit. Women's
groups were also generally pleased, though some voiced concerns about
Ginsburg's criticisms of *Roe* v. *Wade*. In a 1993 speech at New York University Law School, Ginsburg expressed reservations about the scope, though
not the result, of that controversial ruling. In her words:

Without taking giant strides and thereby risking a backlash too forceful to contain, the Court, through constitutional adjudication, can reinforce or signal a green light for a social change. In most of the post-1970 gender classification cases, unlike *Roe*, the Court functioned in just that way. It approved the direction of change through a temperate brand of decision-making, one that was not extravagant or divisive.

Roe v. Wade, on the other hand, halted a political process that was moving in a reform direction and thereby, I believe, prolonged divisiveness and deterred stable settlement of the issue. The most recent *Planned Parenthood [of Southeastern Pennsylvania v. Casey* (1992)] decision, although a retreat from *Roe*, appears to have prompted a renewed dialogue, a revival of the political movement in progress in the early 1970s. That renewed dialogue, one may hope, will, within a relatively short span, yield an enduring resolution of this vital matter.[40]

Despite that measured criticism of *Roe* and expression of a moderate-centrist judicial philosophy, Ginsburg had been at the forefront of the women's movement in law in the 1970s. Besides teaching at Rutgers and Columbia law schools, in the 1970s Ginsburg also served as the director of the American Civil Liberties Union's Women's Rights Project, arguing six (and winning five) important gender-based discrimination cases before the Supreme Court. Ginsburg championed a legal strategy of chipping away at precedents on a piecemeal basis and building on new principles of equal protection that exposed the irrationality of gender discriminations that often resulted in men's receiving benefits that they would not have otherwise received.

Although failing to persuade the Court to recognize gender as a "suspect category" under the Fourteenth Amendment's equal protection clause, Ginsburg was victorious before the Court in *Frontiero v. Richardson*,[41] which overturned regulations that discriminated on the basis of gender in conferring benefits for dependents of military personnel; *Weinberger v. Wiesenfeld*,[42] which struck down a Social Security Act provision giving greater survivors' benefits to women with children; *Edwards v. Healy*,[43] which invalidated a Louisiana law exempting women from jury service; *Califano v. Goldfarb*,[44] which invalidated a Social Security Act provision that automatically awarded survivors' benefits to women, but not to men; and *Duren v. Missouri*,[45] which struck down a state law exempting women from jury service upon the request of attorneys.

With little opposition from Republican senators and guarded responses during her confirmation hearings, Ginsburg's nomination sailed through the Senate Judiciary Committee by an 18–0 vote. The full Senate confirmed her on a vote of 96–3, with only Republican Senators Jesse Helms (N.C.), Robert C. Smith (N.H.), and Don Nickles (Okla.), voting against. On the bench in her first term (1993–94), Justice Ginsburg proved to be an aggressive questioner during oral arguments. There was no sign of her experiencing the so-called freshman effect, and she undertook her share of the Court's opinion writing.[46] Justice Ginsburg also quickly aligned herself with the Court's centrists. She voted most often with Justice David H. Souter (77 percent of the time), and next most often with Justice John Paul Stevens (75.9 percent), followed by Justice Sandra Day O'Connor (69.8 percent). By contrast, Justice Ginsburg voted least often with those on the far right, siding with Chief Justice William Rehnquist in 66.7 percent of the cases, Justice Scalia in 62.1 percent, and Justice Thomas in only 52.9 percent of the cases. Justice Ginsburg also appeared inclined to side with liberal-leaning justices on social–civil rights issues, such as abortion, church-state relations, and equal protection, while joining conservatives in most criminal law cases, except for some involving the imposition of capital punishment.

On 6 April 1994, Justice Harry Blackmun announced he would retire at the end of the Court's term. The eighty-five-year-old justice had served on the Court for almost a quarter of a century. He was appointed as a "law and order jurist" by Republican President Richard Nixon in 1970 at the suggestion of Blackmun's high school friend, Chief Justice Warren E. Burger. Indeed, Justice Blackmun initially voted so often with Burger that the two were nicknamed "the Minnesota twins," since they both hailed from that state. But Justice Blackmun soon asserted his own independence. Over the course of his tenure on the bench, he came to vote more often on social–civil rights issues with the Court's last liberals, Justices William J. Brennan, Jr., and Thurgood Marshall. Justice Blackmun authored the controversial landmark ruling on abortion, *Roe* v. *Wade,* for which he received thousands of letters attacking him and which he repeatedly said he would carry to "his grave." Although *Roe* will overshadow his other opinions, Justice Blackmun handed down several other important rulings, including *Garcia* v. *San Antonio Metropolitan Transit Authority,*[47] on states' rights under the Tenth Amendment. He also championed the Court's extending First Amendment protection to commercial speech. On most matters of criminal procedure, however, Justice Blackmun remained a steadfast conservative, writing significant opinions for the Court that cut back on the scope of the Fourth Amendment's guarantee against "unreasonable searches and seizures."[48] The principal exception to Justice Blackmun's conservative stand on criminal justice matters was his reconsideration, shortly before announcing his retirement, of support for the death penalty.[49]

Justice Blackmun and President Clinton had become friends over the years, attending annual gatherings of the Renaissance Club in Hilton Head, South Carolina. In announcing that he would retire at the end of the term, as Justice White had done almost a year earlier, Justice Blackmun gave the president ample time to choose a successor. Clinton in turn took less time in selecting his second nominee to the Court, only thirty-seven days in contrast to the eighty-seven days that had passed before he announced his first appointee. Still, Clinton once again appeared to agonize and vacillate in making his decision. He finally settled on the noncontroversial federal Judge Stephen Breyer, whom he had passed over a year earlier, because his other top two candidates would have proven more controversial and might have set off a confirmation fight in the Senate.

Clinton had said he wanted a nominee who was an experienced "politician" with a "big heart." Once again, though, some prime candidates withdrew from consideration. Notably, Senate Majority Leader George Mitchell said he had to stay in the Senate to lead the fight over the president's ill-fated health-care reform proposal. Clinton also again decided against elevating his secretary of the interior, claiming that he "could not bear to lose him from the cabinet." In fact, Bruce Babbitt was the most liberal of Clinton's top three final candidates and would have confronted bitter opposition from Senators Hatch and Thurmond. Conservative groups were also certain to come out in opposition to Babbitt because of his liberal views and 1987 attack on Reagan's nomination of Judge Bork to the Court.

Clinton's other favored candidate and long-time friend, federal appellate court Judge Richard Arnold, presented other political problems. Judge Arnold, a Harvard Law School graduate and former law clerk to Justice Brennan, had lymphoma cancer and had recently undergone low-level radiation therapy. While Judge Arnold's cancer was not life threatening, it could have been used as a basis for Republican senators' voting against his confirmation. Clinton cited Judge Arnold's health as the reason for bypassing him, while there was much in the judge's record on the federal bench that would have invited attacks from the right and the left. In particular, liberal women's groups were likely to come out against Judge Arnold because of some of his rulings on all-male clubs and abortion rights.

In the end, Clinton went against his progressive instincts and aimed to avoid political controversy by naming a centrist jurist who enjoyed bipartisan support in the Senate. The fifty-six-year-old Jewish Judge Breyer was trained as an undergraduate at Stanford and Oxford universities. He received his law degree from Harvard Law School, where he subsequently taught administrative law for over a decade. After graduating from law school, he served as a law clerk to Justice Arthur J. Goldberg, one of the most liberal justices on the Warren Court. During that year the justice handed down his controversial and visionary opinion on the "reserved rights of the people" in the Ninth Amendment in *Griswold v. Connecticut*,[50] which held that a constitutional right of privacy bars states from denying married couples access to and use of contraceptives. Unlike the liberal justices for whom he clerked, Breyer proved to be a moderate pragmatist and legal technician during his thirteen years on the federal appellate bench. His academic writings, moreover, concerned primarily issues of administrative law and regulatory policy.[51] For that very reason the president's advisers anticipated relatively low-key confirmation hearings. Although some of Breyer's theories about risk regulation and environmental protection did come under attack from liberal senators, and Indiana's Republican Senator Richard Lugar questioned some of the millionaire's financial investments, the Judicial Committee unanimously approved him. With broad bipartisan support, the full Senate confirmed Breyer by a vote of 87–9 as the 108th justice.

In making his first two appointments to the Supreme Court, Clinton vacillated, hesitated, and sought advance assurances from Senators Biden and Hatch, among others, that his nominees would not spark controversies over Senate confirmation. Both times, Clinton appeared torn between his progressive instincts and rhetoric, on the one hand, and his other priorities as well as a deep desire to avoid confirmation battles, on the other. If a vacancy opens up in his last two years, with a Republican majority in the Senate and Senator Hatch chairing the Judiciary Committee, Clinton is certain to face even harder choices and greater obstacles in making his own imprint on the Court.

Legal Policy and Reversing Course

Shortly after being sworn into office, Clinton moved quickly to reverse course in some areas of legal policy and to fulfill campaign promises. Two days after his inauguration, he issued an executive order repealing the Reagan/Bush administrations' ban on abortion counseling by organizations receiving federal funding, which a bare majority of the Rehnquist Court had upheld in *Rust* v. *Sullivan*.[52] On the sensitive issue of abortion rights, Clinton sharply distanced his administration from that of his two immediate predecessors. He reversed the federal government's legal policies on abortion and other matters largely on his own, without assistance from Congress.

Even with Democratic majorities in both houses, the administration failed to persuade Congress to repeal restrictions on abortion funding for the poor under the Hyde Amendment, named after its sponsor, Representative Henry J. Hyde (R-Ill.). The proposed Freedom of Choice Act, which would have prohibited most state restrictions on abortion, also failed to pass. The administration did successfully help push through legislation making it a federal felony to obstruct access to abortion clinics and authorizing the Justice Department to prosecute antiabortion protestors for blocking entrance to abortion clinics.[53] Yet all other changes forged in the area of federal policies on abortion were done by the president alone. Through executive orders and directives, Clinton ordered agencies to remove bans on federal funding of medical research using fetal tissue, for example. He lifted barriers to abortions in overseas military medical facilities and eliminated a Reagan-imposed ban on aid to international organizations that perform or "actively promote" abortion. As a result, there was modest, not sweeping, change in the federal government's policies on abortion. With congressional defiance on that and other issues certain to grow in 1995–96, Clinton will either have to compromise further or rely even more on executive orders and regulatory reform, as Reagan did in his second term, to achieve legal policy changes that Congress refuses to authorize.

On other controversial issues of legal policy, Clinton appeared to turn somersaults, reversing course and then backtracking. He thereby appeared indecisive and weak in the face of heated controversy, and created confusion over where he actually stood. During the 1992 presidential campaign, for instance, Clinton denounced President Bush's policy of intercepting and returning Haitian "boat people" without first holding asylum hearings. Bush had adopted that policy after the military overthrew Haitian President Jean-Bertrand Aristide and thousands of Haitians began trying to escape to Florida. Although attacking Bush's policy during the presidential campaign as inhumane, Clinton abruptly flip-flopped after the election and embraced a continuation of the policy.[54]

Besides championing an unsuccessful health-care reform proposal, which would have had a massive impact on other legal policies and sparked years of litigation,[55] no other issue in Clinton's first year caused as great an uproar as his initial proposal to end discrimination against homosexuals in the military. Clinton had pledged in his campaign manifesto, *Putting People First,* to put an end to such discrimination. Republicans, though, had not made it an issue in the 1992 presidential election. Thus, when shortly after coming into office Clinton elevated that divisive issue to national debate, there was immediate and widespread opposition, polarizing the public. Not only did Republicans and leaders of the religious right oppose the president, but Clinton also faced a bitter fight with heads of the military and the chair of the Senate Armed Services Committee, Georgia's Democratic Senator Sam Nunn.

Moreover, Clinton mistakenly allowed the controversy over homosexuals in the military to drag on for almost a year, diverting his administration's and the public's attention from other pressing matters. During that time he searched for a compromise, floating various ideas, such as having separate barracks for homosexual and heterosexual troops. Finally, Clinton backpedaled and effectively backed down. Reaching a compromise with Pentagon officials in July, Clinton signed into law, in November 1993, orders that military personnel would no longer be asked about their sexual orientation, but still allowing the dismissal from military service of those who openly acknowledged engaging in homosexual acts. Under Clinton's "don't ask, don't tell, and don't pursue" policy, little changed legally. Homosexuals remained subject to dismissal, and no new enforceable rights against such discrimination were created.

At its best, in the words of Representative Barney Frank (D-Mass.), one of the few openly homosexual members of Congress, the new policy was "a minor advance over the current situation."[56] That "minor advance," though, came at a very high price. The White House had become embroiled in another controversy, and Clinton had been forced to retreat. Once again, Clinton appeared indecisive. The president's confusing message and about-face was further compounded when shortly before the new policy was to go into effect a federal district court held that the military's previous long-standing policy against homosexuals was unconstitutional. Judge Terry J. Hatter also barred the government from enforcing its policy, ordering a fine of "a minimum of $10,000 per day" if it continued doing so.[57] As a result, Clinton's Solicitor General Drew Days III filed in the Court of Appeals for the Ninth Circuit a request for an emergency order enjoining the enforcement of the lower court's order. Days argued not only that Judge Hatter had exceeded his authority and that his order would hinder implementation of the new policy. In contradiction to Clinton's earlier stance, Days also claimed for the administration that homosexuals in the military could cause "irreparable harm" and that the judiciary should defer to the military.

In 1994 Clinton pursued another controversial and potentially even more dangerous course when deciding to send troops into Haiti in order to restore to power that country's elected but ousted president, Jean-Bertrand Aristide. He did so without first seeking congressional approval and thereby risked an explosive controversy that could have led to impeachment charges if his decision resulted in major casualties among American soldiers. As it was, Clinton's decision to invade Haiti was sharply criticized for being unconstitutional and a violation of the War Powers Resolution.[58] In protest, a letter was sent to the president by ten leading constitutional law professors, including Stanford Law School professors John Hart Ely and Gerald Gunther, liberal constitutionalist and Harvard Law School professor Laurence Tribe, and the University of Chicago's conservative professor Philip Kurland. They argued that "the president may not order the United States Armed Forces to make war without first meaningfully consulting with Congress and receiving its affirmative authorization" and concluded, "those principles, as well as your oath of office, require you to follow President Bush's example in the Persian Gulf War: to seek and obtain Congress's express prior approval before launching a military invasion of Haiti."[59]

Senate Majority Leader George Mitchell, among other Democrats, fended off criticism and efforts to push for congressional approval. They did so because the odds were against winning support for Clinton's plan and were likely to result in another embarrassing defeat for the president. Yet Mitchell and other Democrats had to recant their own previous position when criticizing Reagan's and Bush's initial plans to send, without prior congressional approval, troops into combat in Grenada and Kuwait. In particular, before Bush's securing congressional approval for sending forces into Kuwait in order to expel the invading Iraqi army, in 1990 Mitchell claimed that "the president has no authority, acting alone, to commit the United States to war."[60] That position—that the president has only the constitutional power unilaterally to "repel sudden attacks"—is the most constitutionally defensible and the one that Democrats had held Republicans to in the past.[61] But they abandoned that position and Clinton became the first president to speed up an invasion because he could not win congressional approval. While Bush had also claimed similarly broad power, he sent troops into Kuwait and Iraq under a mandate from the United Nations. Clinton was also the first to claim the presidential power to launch an invasion even if Congress forbade it!

Before the invasion of Haiti, leading Republicans in Congress also challenged the constitutionality of Clinton's proposed action and unwillingness to seek congressional approval. In response, Walter Dellinger, who at the time was the assistant attorney general in charge of the Office of Legal Counsel, defended the invasion on three grounds in a letter sent to Republican senators. First, he contended that Congress had implicitly approved an invasion when enacting the 1994 Defense Appropriations Act, which stipulated that the president, after making certain findings and reporting them to Congress, could send troops into Haiti without further congressional authorization. Second, Dellinger claimed that the invasion did not violate the War Powers Act because the president had notified Congress of his actions. Third, Dellinger argued that the invasion would not constitute a "war" in a constitutional sense on the ground that U.S. troops were invited in by the legitimate, though exiled, government of President Aristide.[62] Nonetheless, those were slim legal reeds on which to defend Clinton in the event that massive deaths resulted and led to impeachment proceedings over charges that he had acted unconstitutionally.

Largely overshadowed by the controversies surrounding Clinton's personnel appointments, the proposed ban on discriminating against homosexuals in the military, unfolding plans for health-care reform, and the administration's successful battle to secure passage in 1994 of a tough new anticrime package were the Justice Department's accomplishments in charting new directions in legal policy. After twelve years of Republican rule, the Justice Department did turn 180 degrees from the Reagan and Bush administrations' positions on some issues of civil rights and liberties, besides abortion. Whereas the Bush administration had argued that the Civil Rights Act of 1991 should not apply retroactively to cases pending at the time of the law's enactment, Clinton's Justice Department advanced the opposite view.[63] Assistant Attorney General Patrick reversed course on the issue of affirmative action and reinvigorated the Civil Rights Division's litigation of cases involving discrimination in financial institutions' lending practices, housing, and other areas.

Notably, the about-face in the government's position on affirmative action drew national attention to a case in which the Bush administration had filed an *amicus curiae* ("friend of the court") brief in support of a white female teacher, Sharon Taxman, who was laid off because of budget cuts, while a black colleague with the same seniority retained her position. Attorneys for Taxman and the Bush administration attacked the constitutionality of her layoff and charged the school district with reverse discrimination. Patrick and Attorney General Reno took the opposite view. In Reno's words, "diversity should be a factor that employers can consider in developing voluntary affirmative-action plans."[64] Likewise, Solicitor General Days reversed course on pending cases before the Supreme Court and drew criticism from conservatives that politics was driving legal policy and the government's reversal of its positions.

Criticism that the solicitor general and the Justice Department improperly reversed direction on important issues of legal policy such as affirmative action was, of course, misdirected and wrong. As political scientist Rebecca Mae Salokar, among others, has shown, the Justice Department and the solicitor general's office are political and integral parts of the executive branch's policymaking.[65] Reversals in the direction of legal policy are to be expected with changes in administrations. Moreover, the president and his staff should fashion clear policies and vigorously pursue them. That is what Reagan's Justice Department did and what elections are about. "What do you expect?" as Bruce Fein, an assistant attorney general in the Reagan administration, put it. "If Bush lost, why should his policy prevail in the courtroom?"[66] Another former Reagan Justice Department assistant attorney general, Charles Cooper, agreed: "That's [the Clinton administration's] right, that's what we did."[67]

The underlying problem with the Justice Department's reversing direction on legal policy, as with the president's handling of the issue of homosexuals in the military and the treatment of Haitian refugees, remains that on controversial issues Clinton's administration sent confusing, mixed messages and became mired in controversy. In other words, the Justice Department reversed course, only to turn around again in face of criticism from the right and then the left. Another example of the administration's confusion, lack of coordination, and persistent pattern of sending mixed signals was the Justice Department's reversal of positions on what became a very controversial child pornography case before the Supreme Court.

The case, *Knox v. United States*,[68] involved the questions of how a 1991 statute banning "any visual depiction [of] a minor engaging in sexually explicit conduct," including "lascivious exhibition of the genitals or pubic area," should be enforced and whether it was unconstitutionally vague or overly broad under the First Amendment. Steven Knox was convicted of possessing child pornography after police discovered in his home videotapes that depicted adolescent girls in bikinis and underwear and zoomed in on their crotches. Knox appealed his conviction on the grounds that "lascivious exhibition" should apply only to the nude display of children's genitals or, alternatively, should apply only to the child's behavior, not to the mere portrayal. A panel of the Court of Appeals for the Third Circuit, however, rejected Knox's arguments and upheld his conviction, without reaching the First Amendment issues. In the appellate court's view, "nudity was not a prerequisite," and the statute applied because Knox's videotapes "clearly were designed to pander to pedophiles."[69] Subsequently, Knox appealed that ruling to the Supreme Court.

In the Supreme Court, the Bush administration filed a brief in support of the lower courts' rulings, arguing that the statute applied to exhibition of children's clothed genitals if the context was such as to draw sexual attention to the child. But Clinton's Justice Department reversed course, and reversed course more than once. Initially, the department urged the Court not to grant review and to leave the appellate court's decision standing. Yet, when the Court granted review, Solicitor General Days filed a brief basically siding with Knox. Days contended that the child pornography statute required "a visible depiction of the genitals," either clothed or unclothed, and that the children must be portrayed as "lasciviously engaging" in sexual conduct, instead of focusing on the lasciviousness of the photographer or consumer. The appellate court, according to Days, erred in upholding Knox's conviction because it "utilized an impermissibly broad standard" for defining child pornography.

When on 1 November 1993 the Supreme Court remanded the case back to the appellate court for reconsideration in the light of the standard asserted by Days for the administration,[70] the matter erupted into another controversy over the direction of the administration's legal policy. Conservative groups such as the American Family Association had already mounted a campaign over the issue, charging that the Clinton administration was weakening efforts to prosecute the commercial exploitation of children. Clinton initially tried to distance himself from the controversy, while Reno defended the department's interpretation of the statute. But within two weeks of the Court's action, the Senate unanimously passed a resolution criticizing the Justice Department's interpretation and making it clear that it intended the statute to apply to people like Knox. Within days of that resolution, Clinton ordered Reno to toughen the department's position and "to promptly prepare and submit any necessary legislation to ensure that federal legislation reaches all forms of child pornography."[71] Still, a full year passed before Reno reversed the department's position on *Knox*. Finally, two days after the November 1994 midterm elections, in a twenty-one-page brief signed by Reno, but not Days, the Justice Department supported the appellate court's original ruling and interpretation upholding Knox's conviction.[72]

Significantly, the administration not only twice reversed course but had allowed yet another controversy to simmer unnecessarily for over a year.

Conclusion

The presidency is the president, as political scientist Richard Neustadt long ago correctly observed.[73] And Clinton's administration is a reflection of Clinton. His failure to communicate a clear and convincing political vision remains at the root of the problems of staffing, turnover in personnel, giving direction to the Justice Department's legal policies, and reversal of positions on important issues. As a result, legal policy overall in his first two years appeared confusing, riddled by uncertainties, and often mired in controversy. The confusion and uncertainty in turn marked lost opportunities and distracted from the Justice Department's accomplishments. All but overshadowed and overlooked by the media were the department's successes in appointing highly qualified federal judges, including a record number of women and minorities, and moving toward stricter enforcement of antidiscrimination laws. But a president's staff, however organized and effective afterward, cannot save a president from himself.

There is no little irony that the country's oldest president, a former actor and nonlawyer, Ronald Reagan, left a major imprint on legal policy and a continuing legacy in the federal courts. By contrast, Clinton, the youngest president since John F. Kennedy, a graduate of Yale Law School, and a former teacher of constitutional law, failed to give the Justice Department very high priority in his administration. To be sure, it is impossible and unfair to compare two years with an eight-year presidency. Yet Reagan and his followers wanted to forge revolutionary change in the federal courts; in Attorney General Edwin Meese's words, "to institutionalize the Reagan revolution so it can't be set aside no matter what happens in future presidential elections."[74] By contrast, for Clinton the institutional integrity of the federal judiciary and diversity on the bench are more important than ideology. Still, even that important message of Clinton's presidency was largely lost during his first two years. And that is the point of drawing the comparison: although Reagan was largely disengaged from his presidency and delegated a great deal to others, he and those around him in the White House and the Department of Justice knew where he stood and what he stood for. That is what Clinton should have known before entering the Oval Office, and what his first two years should have taught him.

Notes

1. For further discussion of the legal policies and judicial appointments of the Reagan administration, see Charles Fried, *Order and Law: Arguing the Reagan Revolution—A Firsthand Account* (New York: Simon and Schuster, 1991); and David M. O'Brien, "The Reagan Judges: His Most Enduring Legacy?" in *The Reagan Legacy: Promise and Performance,* ed. Charles O. Jones (Chatham, N.J.: Chatham House, 1988), 60–101.

2. See, generally, Richard E. Neustadt, *Presidential Power and Modern Presidents* (New York: Free Press, 1990).

3. See, e.g., Janet Reno, "A Common-Sense Approach to Justice," 77 *Judicature* 66 (1993); and Paul Anderson, *Janet Reno: Doing the Right Thing* (New York: Wiley, 1993).

4. See NBC News–*Wall Street Journal* survey, April 1993, showing 66 percent approval for Reno's handling of the Waco incident, in *National Journal* 1256 (22 May 1993).

5. See Daniel Klaidman, "Reno Brings Back the Plea Bargain," *Legal Times* 1 (15 November 1993).

6. See, e.g., W. John Moore, "Tough Enough?" *National Journal* 1154 (15 April 1993); David Johnston and Stephen Labaton, "Doubts on Reno's Competence Rise in Justice Dept.," *New York Times,* 26 October 1993, A1; Michael Isikoff, "Reno Has Yet to Make Mark on Crime," *Washington Post,* 26 November 1993, A1; Daniel Klaidman, "Amid Plaudits, Is DoJ Drifting?" *Legal Times* 4 (27 December 1993); and David M. O'Brien, "Beyond Reno's Charisma: Mismanagement at Justice," *Los Angeles Times,* 1 May 1994, M2.

7. "Weekly Press Conference with Attorney General Janet Reno and Deputy Attorney General Philip Heymann," *Federal News Service,* 27 January 1994.

8. See W. John Moore, "A Slow Civil Rights March," *National Journal* 1160 (14 April 1994).

9. See Lani Guinier's articles "The Triumph of Tokenism: The Voting Rights Act and the Theory of Black Electoral Success," 89 *Michigan Law Review* 1077 (1991); "No Two Seats: The Elusive Quest for Political Equality," 77 *Virginia Law Review* 1413 (1991); "Keeping the Faith: Black Voters in the Post-Reagan Era," 24 *Harvard Civil Rights–Civil Liberties Law Review* 393 (1989); and "Voting Rights and Democratic Theory: Where Do We Go from Here?" in *Controversies in Minority Voting: The Voting Rights Act in Perspective,* ed. Bernard Grofman and Chandler Davidson (Washington, D.C.: Brookings Institution, 1992).

10. Quoted in "Clinton on Guinier," *New York Times,* 5 June 1993, A8.

11. See Marianne Lavelle, "Federal Legal Policies Still Unknown," *National Law Journal* 1 (14 June 1993).

12. See O'Brien, "Reagan Judges"; and David M. O'Brien, *Judicial Roulette* (New York: Twentieth Century Fund/Priority Press, 1988), chap. 3, pp. 49–65.

13. Interview with Eleanor Dean Acheson, Washington, D.C., 1 December 1994.

14. For further discussion, see O'Brien, "Reagan Judges."

15. See Sheldon Goldman, "Clinton's Nontraditional Judges: Creating a More Representative Bench," 78 *Judicature* 68 (1994).

16. For further discussion, see O'Brien, *Judicial Roulette.*

17. Quoted by Naftali Bendavid, "Adding Diversity to the Bench," *Legal Times* 7 (27 December 1993).

18. Goldman, "Clinton's Nontraditional Judges," 72.

19. Ibid.

20. Quoted by Holly Idelson, "Clinton's Unexpected Bequest: Judgeships Bush Did Not Fill," *Congressional Quarterly Weekly Report* 317 (13 February 1993).

21. Quoted by Deborah Pines, "Ex-Professor Seen Bringing Compassion to Federal Bench," *New York Law Journal*, 13 July 1994.

22. Ibid.

23. See, e.g., O'Brien, *Judicial Roulette;* and Barbara Hinckson Craig and David M. O'Brien, *Abortion and American Politics* (Chatham, N.J.: Chatham House, 1993), 157–96.

24. Quoted by Bendavid, "Adding Diversity," 7.

25. Quoted by Joan Biskupic, "Despite 129 Clinton Appointments, GOP Judges Dominate U.S. Bench," *Washington Post*, 16 October 1994, A20.

26. Quoted by Neil A. Lewis, "Clinton Is Considering Judgeships for Opponents of Abortion Rights," *New York Times*, 18 September 1993, A1.

27. Quoted by Daniel Klaidman, "Just Like Old Times? Liberals Challenge President on Some Judgeships," *Legal Times* 1 (25 October 1993).

28. Interview with Nan Aron, Washington, D.C., 27 October 1994.

29. Quoted by David G. Savage and Ronald J. Ostrow, "Clinton's Big Bench: Judges of All Stripes and Colors Appointed," *Los Angeles Times,* 16 November 1994, A5.

30. Alliance for Justice, *Judicial Selection Project Annual Report 1993* (Washington, D.C.: Alliance for Justice, 1993), 7.

31. Quoted by Lacrisha Butler, "Daughtrey Nomination Clears Judiciary Committee," Gannett News Service, 18 November 1993.

32. Quoted by Jennifer Buksbaum, "Senate Confirms Sarokin for Seat on Appeals Court Despite Fight from GOP," *The Record,* 5 October 1994, A3.

33. Quoted by Stephen Labaton, "President's Judicial Appointments: Diverse but Well in the Mainstream," *New York Times,* 14 October 1994, A15.

34. Interview with Acheson, 1 December 1994.

35. This section draws on the author's discussion in *Supreme Court Watch — 1994* (New York: Norton, 1994), 3–5.

36. *Roe v. Wade,* 410 U.S. 113 (1973).

37. *Bowers v. Hardwick,* 478 U.S. 186 (1986).

38. *Miranda v. Arizona,* 384 U.S. 436 (1966).

39. For further discussion, see David M. O'Brien, "How to Win Friends and Influence People: Life in the Supreme Court," *Los Angeles Times,* 13 June 1993, M1.

40. Ruth Bader Ginsburg, "Speaking in a Judicial Voice," 67 *New York University Law Review* 1885 (1992).

41. *Frontiero v. Richardson,* 411 U.S. 677 (1973).

42. *Weinberger v. Wiesenfeld,* 420 U.S. 636 (1975).

43. *Edwards v. Healy,* 421 U.S. 772 (1975).

44. *Califano v. Goldfarb,* 430 U.S. 199 (1977).

45. *Duren v. Missouri,* 439 U.S. 357 (1979).

46. See, e.g., Christopher E. Smith, Joyce Ann Baugh, Thomas R. Hensley, and Scott Patrick Johnson, "The First-Term Performance of Justice Ruth Bader Ginsburg," 78 *Judicature* 74 (1994).

47. *Garcia* v. *San Antonio Metropolitan Transit Authority,* 469 U.S. 528 (1985).

48. See, e.g., *California* v. *Acedevo,* 111 S.Ct. 1982 (1991).

49. For a further discussion, see David M. O'Brien, "The Death Penalty Decision: Justice Blackmun's Very Public Shift," *Los Angeles Times,* 6 March 1994, M1.

50. *Griswold* v. *Connecticut,* 391 U.S. 146 (1965).

51. See, e.g., Stephen G. Breyer, *Regulation and Its Reform* (Cambridge, Mass.: Harvard University Press, 1982); and *Breaking the Vicious Cycle: Toward Effective Risk Regulation* (Cambridge, Mass.: Harvard University Press, 1993).

52. *Rust* v. *Sullivan,* 111 S.Ct. 1759 (1991).

53. See 1994 Freedom of Access to Clinic Entrances Act, 18 U.S.C. Sec. 248(a)(1).

54. The policy was upheld by the Supreme Court in *Sale* v. *Haitian Centers Council, Inc.,* 113 S.Ct. 2549 (1993).

55. See, e.g., Rorie Sherman, "Health Plan to Have Major Legal Impact," *National Law Journal* 1 (20 September 1993); and Special Issue, "The Clinton Health Plan: A Legal Response," *National Law Journal* S1 (11 October 1993).

56. Quoted in Michael R. Gordon, "No Bar on Serving, but Engaging in Gay Sex Is Still Forbidden," *New York Times,* 23 December 1993, A1.

57. *Volker Keith Meinhold* v. *United States Department of Defense,* 808 F. Supp. 1455 (1993); and *Volker Keith Meinhold* v. *United States Department of Defense,* 808 F. Supp. 1453 (1993).

58. War Powers Resolution, 87 Stat. 555 (1973). For further discussion, see David M. O'Brien, *Constitutional Law and Politics: Struggles for Power and Accountability,* 2d ed. (New York: Norton, 1995), 278–83.

59. Quoted in Stuart Taylor, "A Betrayal of the Constitution," *Legal Times* 25 (19 September 1994).

60. Quoted in ibid.

61. See John Hart Ely, *War and Responsibility* (Princeton: Princeton University Press, 1993).

62. See Neil Lewis, "A President's Ability to Declare War," *New York Times,* 30 September 1994, A29.

63. Brief for the government in *Landgraf* v. *USI Film Products,* 114 S.Ct. 1483 (1994).

64. Quoted by Tim O'Brien, "Behind Justice's Flip-Flop in the N.J. Bias Suit," *Legal Times* 2 (19 September 1994).

65. See Rebecca Mae Salokar, *The Solicitor General: The Politics of Law* (Philadelphia: Temple University Press, 1992). For criticism that the Department of Justice and the solicitor general became too politicized during Reagan's presidency, see Lincoln Caplan, *Tenth Justice: The Solicitor and the Rule of Law* (New York: Knopf, 1987); but compare Fried, *Order and Law.*

66. Quoted by Henry Reske, "A Flap over Flip-Flops: Solicitor General Says Changing Court Stances Not Unusual or Wrong," *ABA Journal* 12 (January 1994).

67. Quoted by Pierre Thomas, "Deval Patrick and the 'Great Moral Imperative,'" *Washington Post,* 24 October 1994, A1.

68. *Knox* v. *United States,* 114 S.Ct. 375 (1993).

69. *United States of America* v. *Knox,* 977 F.2d 815 (1992).

70. *United States* v. *Knox,* 114 S.Ct. 375 (1993).

71. Quoted by Michael Isikoff and Ruth Marcus, "Clinton Enters Child Pornography Dispute," *Washington Post,* 12 November 1993, A1.

72. See Jerry Seper, "Justice Department Flip-Flops on Child-Pornography
Case," *Washington Times,* 11 November 1994, A3.

73. Neustadt, *Presidential Power.*

74. Quoted in O'Brien, "Reagan Judges," 62.

5

The Federal Executive under Clinton

JOEL D. ABERBACH

The second half of the twentieth century has been marked by a set of controversies about the nature and role of the executive branch in the United States. What should it do? How big should it be? Who should control it? How should it be staffed so that it can perform well?

Democrats built and staffed much of the contemporary administrative state during the New Deal and Great Society eras. The agencies and programs they created were identified as products of their party, providing a built-in basis, if assertive "conservative" Republicans ever came to power, for questioning not only the fundamental policies the agencies administered but the loyalty and role of their top career personnel as well. This indeed happened. The latter years of the Nixon administration and the eight years of the Reagan administration were particularly contentious, as Nixon sought to gain control of policy and administration in the face of a Democratic Congress, and Reagan, with the added advantage of a Republican Senate for six years of his presidency, sought to change the mission and shape of the executive branch.

The struggles between assertive Republican presidents and Democratic Congresses determined to thwart their influence exacerbated the normal rivalry between the branches built into our system of separate institutions, sharing powers. Congressional oversight of executive branch agencies increased noticeably in the late 1960s. It then took off in the early 1970s during a turbulent period of intense congressional conflict with the president and of internal reforms designed to increase Congress's capability to review and control the activities of the executive branch.[1]

Presidents Nixon and Reagan tried to have their way by using an "administrative presidency" strategy,[2] stressing often bizarre statutory interpretations and rule by administrative regulations written by loyal appointees. The goal was to bypass Congress when it was standing in the way of what presidents wanted to do (or, more commonly, did not want to do). Civil servants in the domestic agencies, often suspected of having Democratic sympathies, were cut off from policy influence to the maximum extent possible.[3] Political appointees to administrative positions were chosen for their total loyalty to the man (Nixon) or the cause ("Reaganism"), so that they could be manipulated at will. Congress, increasingly suspicious of the president and determined to exercise influence over agency behavior, countered with detailed laws designed to tie the hands of the administration. "Micromanagement" by Congress, the detailed specification of what agencies were expected to do, was the result.

Tensions cooled noticeably during the more moderate Bush administration. Bush refrained from "bureaucrat bashing." In fact, he praised public servants and showed interest in having a high-quality career service.[4] He was less determined than Reagan to eliminate programs. His appointees were more moderate and independent than Reagan's. And he was apparently less concerned about the beliefs of agency careerists.[5] Still, Bush's administration used such devices as the Competitiveness Council led by Vice-President Dan Quayle to control the issuance of regulations that might offend key Republican constituencies, and Congress reciprocated by continued micromanagement and other efforts to control administration.

This was the administrative setting for Bill Clinton's presidency. The debate about the scope of government, what it should do, was hardly resolved. The question of how much control the president and Congress should exercise over the administrative agencies was muted by the end of split-party control of the two branches, but, of course, the question was not answered. And issues concerning top government executives—such as criteria for selection, responsiveness, and appropriate roles of political and career executives—were still very much unresolved.

A New Democrat?

Bill Clinton sought the Democratic nomination and ran for office as a "New Democrat," a "different kind of Democrat." The label was meant to symbolize moderation, a middle-of-the-road approach to policy. Clinton promised to deal with the government's severe deficit problem, solve the nation's health-care problems in an effective and efficient manner, make long-neglected investments in human and physical capital, and reinvigorate the economy. The trademark sign in his campaign headquarters—"It's the economy, stupid!"—was taken as a symbol that his main focus as president (as well as during the campaign) would be on the nation's economic drift and stagnation, problems of major concern throughout the electorate.

Once it became clear that Clinton would be a serious candidate for his party's nomination, journalists and others spent a good deal of effort trying to discern the nature of his core political beliefs. They did not have an easy time of it, despite the New Democrat label that Clinton could claim as former head of the Democratic Leadership Council. Burt Solomon of the *National Journal*, in a preinauguration article, noted that while Clinton clearly had "policy ambitions galore," how they fit together and what his priorities might truly be was not so clear. In fact, what he found was "a persistent political ambiguity":

> To Elaine C. Kamarck, a senior fellow at the Progressive Policy Institute in Washington, a home to some key Clinton advisers, Clinton counts as a liberal, which she defines as believing in an activist government. But at the Urban Institute, senior fellow Isabell V. Sawhill regards him as "genuinely a moderate-to-conservative Democrat in terms of his values." [In brief,] a persistent political ambiguity has exacerbated the blurry picture the voters have of Clinton....
>
> If what he's trying to do proves unpopular, "he'll rethink it," said [Gloria] Cabe, who was a top aide on his gubernatorial staff and has been handling congressional relations for Clinton's campaign. "He's very pragmatic."
>
> If you ask Clinton's advisers if he'd cull priorities from his pile of domestic proposals, they'll tell you that he learned the dangers of doing too much too soon during his first, failed term as governor. Then if you ask what his priorities as president would be, they'll offer a list that doesn't quit.[6]

On issues related to race and gender, Clinton promised a more diverse administration than Bush's, but made an emphatic point of distancing himself from militants. His "deliberate, skillfully orchestrated rebuke" of a rap singer with the suggestive name Sister Souljah was, as *National Journal* noted, the "most famous moment on civil rights" of his campaign. That the statement was made at an event sponsored by Jesse Jackson underscored the point Clinton was clearly trying to communicate.[7]

At the risk of oversimplifying, it is probably fair to say that this was classic Clinton. In the same article, reporter W. John Moore noted that "Clinton has been portrayed as an ardent backer of affirmative action programs. But he ducked the issue throughout the campaign."[8] And, according to Moore, "from the New Hampshire primary to election night, Clinton delivered much the same message, praising diversity, vowing an economic transformation and promising 'full participation, full partnership' in his presidency to black and white audiences alike. But he avoided addressing such issues as affirmative action, civil rights enforcement, and race-specific remedies for discrimination."[9]

"New Democrat" Clinton won the three-way election contest with 43 percent of the vote. The problem, of course, was how he would turn the often ambiguous, centrist stands of the candidate into the policies of the president, and what the consequences of his actions would be.

Clinton and Top Civil Servants

Before turning to the question of Clinton's behavior as president, it is useful to say a few words about the fit between the agenda of the New Democrats and the policy perspectives of civil servants. How good a fit is there? Are there likely points of disagreement? What has been the consequence for career executives of a Democrat entering the White House after twelve years of Republican control of the executive branch?

Bert Rockman and I have been studying the attitudes of top civil servants and political appointees since 1970. We have data on the views of these executives (senior career civil servants in the domestic agencies of the federal government and their politically appointed superiors) in the Nixon, Reagan, and Bush administrations.

These data demonstrate that there was a substantial and continuing difference in the political views of top civil servants and political appointees during these administrations. Civil servants in the domestic agencies, much as the introduction to this chapter indicated Republicans feared would be the case, were both more likely to be Democrats and more liberal in their views on the appropriate role of government than the appointees of Republican administrations.[10] Nixon and Reagan, in particular, countered this with determined efforts to control the influence of civil servants and to change the political composition of the corps of top civil servants, with Reagan by far the more successful as a result of a variety of factors including the added tools given the president and his appointees by the Civil Service Reform Act of 1978.

The data, however, also show a shift in the party affiliations and political views of both political appointees and top civil servants across administrations. President Reagan's appointees were more Republican and well to the right of President Nixon's, but so were the top civil servants his administration had to work with. Without simplifying too much, it can be said that the two groups shifted in parallel so that the gap remained in their party affiliations and views, but the civil servants were decidedly more centrist than before, while the modal political appointee was now well to the right of center. (Bear in mind that these are not the same individuals, but samples of the incumbent political appointees and top civil servants in each administration.) The profiles changed a bit in the Bush administration, with a very slight trend to the left—at least as compared to the Reagan administration—of both groups.

The bottom line is that while Clinton did not inherit the lopsidedly Democratic and relatively liberal civil service that Nixon found when he succeeded Lyndon Johnson, he did not face a particularly Republican and conservative group either. The term "moderate" (although with significant variation about the mean) probably sums up the political views of the group of top civil servants Clinton found in place, a profile not likely to upset a New Democrat very much. With the authority granted by the 1978 Civil Service Reform Act to move members of the top corps of civil servants (those in the Senior Executive Service) around within each agency, the Clinton people had both the authority they needed to put civil servants they were comfortable with in key positions and a nucleus of civil servants with whom they should have felt comfortable available for placement.

With systematic research on the subject as yet unavailable, it is not possible to say much about how comfortable the Clinton people actually were with the top civil servants they inherited. A certain amount of tension was to be expected, of course, as political appointees and civil servants go through a testing period in any change of administration. (David Stanley's colorful image of the two "sniffing each other like dogs" at the beginning of a new administration is as true today as when he wrote the line thirty years ago.[11]) But the initial evidence is that relations were not unusually hostile or tense.

There were, not surprisingly, many indications of potential difficulties. For example, the *National Journal* ran a story in November 1992, before Clinton's inauguration, in which Lou Cordia, described as "executive director of the Reagan Alumni Association and a board member of the Bush-Quayle Presidential Appointees Association," estimated that during the Republicans' twelve-year tenure some 2,000 hard-core conservatives moved into high-level civil service jobs.[12] And the *New York Times* ran a story at the same time headlined "Clinton's Promise of Cleaning House Worries Some Civil Servants." The theme was that many "career Government employees now worry about their fate under a Clinton Administration that has pledged to dismantle the Reagan-Bush legacy the employees helped create." The story focused on some civil servants who had vigorously carried out policies in the Reagan-Bush administrations. It quoted Carol A. Bonosaro, president of the Senior Executives Association, to the effect that career employees seen as "cheerleaders" for an outgoing administration may suffer in the next. She said, "There is a real danger that [such] a career civil servant will be sent to the turkey farm—given a job with few responsibilities, few staff and no access to the boss. It is an incredible waste of talent and of taxpayers' money."[13]

But, overall, the adjustment between the higher level of the civil service and the Clinton administration appears to have gone about as smoothly as one might reasonably expect. A story profiling Ann Brown, just after she was appointed chair of the Consumer Product Safety Commission by President Clinton, contained the following response to a question repeating charges that commission inaction in the Bush-Reagan years had forced Congress and state governments to legislate remedies to problems the top career staff had tried and failed to get the commission to address:

> The commission has a terrific staff, but it has not been listened to.
>
> One of the things I've done since getting to the commission is try to invigorate the staff. I've been there 10 days, and I've had two brown-bag lunches with the [department] directors. I've opened the elevators. The staff had to use a special key card to open the elevators, and they weren't allowed to come in nights and on weekends. Imagine! Someone wants to work on a weekend and they sat on that.[14]

When I asked Carol Bonosaro about SESers' adjustment to the transition from Bush to Clinton and about the general state of relations between SES executives and the Clinton administration, she said that they varied by department but that overall they were good.[15] There had been well-publicized problems in some departments, such as Agriculture, but these were more the exception than the rule. The area where there was some tension between the association and the administration (and presumably, therefore, between many SES executives and the administration) was over the participation of senior executives in the administration's "Reinventing Government" initiative, a subject I discuss in detail later in the chapter.

Clinton's Cabinet Appointees

The Clinton administration set out to make its mark through the diversity of its appointees. While Clinton had been vague on his stand on affirmative action and many related issues during the campaign, he had often mentioned that he wanted an administration that "looked like America." It would be fair to say that just as the theme of Richard Nixon's appointments policy after the first year or two of his term was loyalty to the man, and Ronald Reagan's was adherence to the tenets of "Reaganism," the theme of Clinton's political appointments was racial/ethnic (in the contemporary usage of the terms, meaning blacks, Latinos, Asians, and like groups), gender, and even geographic diversity. This policy came to be called "EGG," and has been a source of pride and some difficult moments for the administration.

Clinton's cabinet is one of the most diverse ever appointed. As Burt Solomon of *National Journal* said in a January 1993 article entitled "Clinton's Gang": "Clinton succeeded ... in naming a cabinet that is probably more diverse in background than any in history. His choice of six women, four blacks, and two Hispanics to 23 top-tier posts eclipsed Jimmy Carter's previous standard for slighting white males."[16]

The last sentence of the Solomon quotation is a not-too-subtle version of the kind of resentment this overt policy of aggressively seeking diversity of a particular kind evidently stirred up among many in the elite as well as in the general public. Solomon went on to note: "But the diversity of Clinton's crew goes only so far. If his cabinet is to count as a mosaic of America, some pieces are missing. There are no anti-abortion activists or Asian-Americans or what retired Columbia University historian Henry F. Graff calls 'real dissenters in society.' For all of Clinton's talk about diversity, Graff said, 'you won't get Mike Royko [at] Labor.'"[17]

Solomon's piece includes a rather revealing analysis of Clinton's cabinet appointees, examining the people behind the facade of racial and gender diversity. What he found was a relative uniformity in other respects. "None is strident in ideology or anything but pragmatic," Solomon reported. "Most attended elite colleges." In general, he wrote, they were "raised in comfort." Indeed, of those "in Clinton's first wave of appointees, a higher proportion of the blacks and Hispanics were raised in comfort than of the whites."[18]

In reality, then, this was hardly an unusual or radical cabinet group, except in terms of skin pigment or chromosomes. But it was symbolically different, and in this sense represented a statement by the incoming administration. The problem was to interpret what the statement meant. David Broder, in a story headlined "Diversity Was Paramount in Building the Cabinet," noted that "several Clinton insiders said privately they were concerned that the choices suggest little about the direction of the Clinton administration." The article described Clinton's efforts to fulfill his campaign promise to have the "most diverse" top-level appointees in history: "The scramble to meet that goal produced a remarkable last-minute shuffle of people and jobs, demonstrating that for the first Democrat to win the White House in 12 years, the need to showcase the ethnic, racial and gender variety of his party overrode any ideological litmus tests, [or] any concerns about internal policy cohesion."[19]

Choosing the Subcabinet

Before the inauguration, Clinton drew in part on the model of his Republican predecessors and appointed a director of personnel

> to coordinate sub-cabinet appointments with Mr. Clinton's cabinet choices. In so doing, he seemed to be following the example of recent Republican presidents, who closely controlled appointments below the rank of cabinet secretary. By contrast, the last Democratic president, Jimmy Carter, allowed his department heads to choose most deputies, who then often pursued policies at odds with White House views—so much so that one senior Carter aide once joked about calling his memoirs: "Present at the Confusion."[20]

Not surprisingly, the way the process worked under Clinton was hardly as neat or efficient as the above statement about appointment procedures under some of his recent Republican predecessors might lead one to expect. This was in large part because the administration did not seem driven by a consistent set of policy goals, but instead seemed consumed by a desire to fulfill its diversity pledge. Thomas Friedman wrote an article in the *New York Times* in January 1993 entitled "Diversity Pledge Slows Clinton on Appointments." In it he quoted a Clinton transition official as saying in response to the charge that Reagan and Bush had filled more of the top-level subcabinet jobs at this stage in their administrations: "The process is working. There is no delay from our point of view. If we wanted to rely on the usual white boys in Washington, we would be done by now. But if you want to get beyond that, it takes a little longer."[21]

Friedman reported that Clinton and his spouse, Hillary, personally signed off on most of the top choices, causing delay because of the president-elect's tendency (carried over into other areas of his presidency) to take his time and change his mind before making a decision. Additional problems were created, Friedman said, because

> Mr. Clinton is trying to satisfy his top aides and campaign supporters, many of whom are white males, with the jobs they are seeking, while at the same time bringing in new faces and minority members to fulfill his diversity pledge. This has naturally led to people, particularly some white males, being offered jobs that they do not want or feel are inferior; they then complain, and the musical chairs start anew.[22]

Further, once the cabinet secretaries were selected, they had their own ideas about whom they wanted in subcabinet positions in their units, causing clashes between the transition team and the secretaries over the final choices.[23] The process caused all sorts of embarrassing leaks, such as the one indicating that Henry G. Cisneros, the secretary of housing and urban development, a Texan of Latino origin, "had been told that his list of proposed nominees included the names of too many New Yorkers."[24]

The White House's drive for diversity at the subcabinet level clearly yielded results. A January 1994 article in the *Washington Post* by Martha Riche, director of policy studies for the Population Reference Bureau, outlined an impressive set of statistics on Clinton's success in appointing top officials who "look like America." She summarized the data as follows: "One year into his administration, with more than three-fourths of appointments filled, it seems President Clinton has delivered—beating heavy demographic odds to do so."[25]

Riche presented the following comparisons: African Americans, 12 percent of the population, constituted 14 percent of Clinton's appointees;

Hispanics, 9.5 percent of the population, were 6 percent of appointees; Asian Americans appointees mirrored the percent of Asians in the population—3 percent; Native Americans appointees also mirrored the population—0.6 percent; and the gender split was about 50–50, with males constituting 54 percent of appointees and females 46 percent. There were some differences among the agencies, with minorities tending to be highest in agencies headed by minorities and lowest in agencies such as Defense, State, Energy, and EPA.

Evaluation of Clinton's Appointments Process and Appointees

While the overall diversity effort must be regarded as a success in its own terms, that is, Clinton's appointees did mirror the population to a remarkable extent, there were some costs associated with it.

The first was delay in putting appointees in place. The Clinton administration was noticeably slower than other recent administrations in making its appointments. As table 5.1 indicates, Clinton had fewer confirmed appointees in place at the end of his first year in office than either Reagan or

TABLE 5.1

PRESIDENTIAL APPOINTMENTS CONFIRMED BY THE SENATE,
FIRST YEAR OF EACH ADMINISTRATION,
CARTER TO CLINTON

	Clinton (1993)	Bush (1989)	Reagan (1981)	Carter (1977)
Total first-year confirmed appointments[a]	499	432	662	637

SOURCE: Executive clerk to the president.
NOTE: Data courtesy of Professor James P. Pfiffner, George Mason University.
a. Includes all full-time presidential appointments passed by and with the advice and consent of the Senate (PAS).

Carter. (He was ahead of Bush, but the Bush administration, unlike the others represented in the table, did not constitute a change in party control and therefore was able to proceed at a more leisurely pace, especially with respect to jobs below the top level.)

A study by Rogelio Garcia of the Congressional Research Service compared nominations and confirmations to policy positions in the first 100 days of the Clinton and Reagan administrations. Garcia found that Clinton had fewer nominations confirmed after 100 days, not because he had submitted fewer nominations, but because he "took longer than Reagan to submit most nominations." He concluded:

> Investigation and clearance of nominees, completions of committee questionnaires by nominees, and committee hearing procedures were similar during both administrations, so that one was not burdened more than others in the process. The Clinton administration's efforts to achieve ethnic, gender, and geographic diversity, however, may be partly responsible for its slow pace in submitting nominations to the Senate.[26]

At times, as the previously cited HUD example demonstrates, the delays caused political embarrassment. Ironically, one area where the slowness of the process was most manifest was in appointing officials to civil rights posts at the Justice Department and the Equal Employment Opportunity Commission. The EEOC was headed for more than a year by a Reagan administration holdover who, although a nominal Democrat, was widely distrusted by civil rights groups because he had headed California Democrats and Independents for Reagan in 1980.[27]

The delay in this instance was caused by the desire to name a Latino to the top job. The White House floated several names of prospective Latino nominees over the first year or more of the administration, but all were "shot down by civil rights groups who felt they lacked sufficient experience in fair-employment law."[28] Some civil rights advocates started quietly suggesting that the search be broadened to include other ethnic groups, but this caused an angry reaction by Latino advocates. A story in the *Los Angeles Times* summarized the dilemma of the situation quite well:

> In an ironic collision of symbolism and substance, the White House has left unfilled a key civil rights job for over a year while searching for a nominee that sends the right signal of racial diversity.... The civil rights community and the administration itself are now split around a pointed question: Is the symbolism of naming a Latino to the job more important than the impact of leaving leaderless the agency charged with enforcing laws prohibiting hiring discrimination on the basis of race, sex, age, or physical disability?[29]

A nominee, Gilbert F. Casellas, was finally announced in June of 1994.[30]

The delays in making appointments led the *Washington Post*, hardly an opponent of the Clinton administration's diversity policy, to write in frustration in an editorial titled "How Not to Fill a Government":

> In and out of the White House, the delays [in appointing people to top posts] are often attributed to the administration's efforts to create a government that is regionally diverse and includes a large number of women and members of

traditionally excluded minority groups. Fairness and diversity are worthy goals. But the administration has made affirmative action even more complicated than it had to. Agencies, especially early on, were expected to come up with whole "slates" for top posts. If a potential nominee who was, say, an African American or a woman or a southerner decided later not to take a job, the whole slate of which he or she was part might be rejected or juggled considerably. This was a ridiculous time consumer and left essential jobs for which there were suitable prospective nominees unfilled.[31]

Such editorials added to the trail of politically costly publicity the diversity policy caused.

A sort of conflict not unexpected when one plays the politics of numbers in appointments arises when groups declare inappropriate their share of appointees. This happened to Clinton in the case of Latinos (and, as well, in a well-publicized flap with women's groups that Clinton called "bean counters") when the National Hispanic Leadership Agenda, a "nonpartisan coalition of interest groups and Latino leaders," criticized the White House for not appointing the appropriate percentage of Latinos to high-level jobs.[32]

And the emphasis on diversity caused even the elite press to stress some non-job-related aspect of a prospective appointee, rather than the person's qualifications for the job. The *New York Times,* for example, ran a story on an intended administration nominee headlined "Lesbian to Get a Housing Post." Not until the last paragraph was there any discussion of the fact that there was some potential opposition to the appointment from public-interest housing groups concerned about the nominee's lack of experience in fair-housing law.[33]

Beyond delays in appointments attributed to the drive to select top officials who would "look like America" and whatever politically costly publicity may have accompanied this effort, there were also glitches in the process, and problems with some appointees. One of the most damaging came in the selection of attorney general. Clinton first nominated a corporate lawyer named Zoë Baird for the post, but she was forced to withdraw after it was learned that she had broken a law—one, it should be noted, almost never enforced in practice—by employing an illegal alien. This was followed by an even more embarrassing incident in which Judge Kimba Wood was dropped from consideration because she had once hired an illegal alien to care for her son, although at the time hiring such an individual did not violate the law, because the immigration statutes had not yet been revised to make the act illegal. Feminists were distressed, believing that female nominees were being held to a standard not applied to men with children and "angered that the White House had publicized what Clinton officials perceived as Judge Wood's second liability, that she had trained—for five days two decades ago—to work at a Playboy club in London while attending the London

School of Economics."[34] Clinton finally settled on Janet Reno for the attorney general's post, and she has not been a satisfactory "team player," according to most reports.

As previously mentioned, there were also problems caused by the White House's role in making subcabinet appointments. The *Washington Post* editorial on "How Not to Fill a Government," after acknowledging that a president needs loyal people in the agencies and that "cabinet secretaries sometimes propose clunkers," went on to opine that "there is a real history here of the thing working the other way around: worthy, qualified would-be nominees being sidetracked for less-qualified pals. Certain nominees seemed to require the approval of six or eight different White House staffers, some of whom hardly qualified to have an opinion—and, or course, of the president himself."[35] One of the major appointment failures of the administration revolved around the nomination of Lani Guinier to the top civil rights position in the Justice Department. Guinier had written articles holding that "majority rule is often insufficient to guarantee blacks their fair share in the political process."[36] When the articles became the focus of attention, a huge controversy ensued. Guinier's support faded away in a cloud of charges that she was a "quota queen." Clinton finally withdrew her nomination, claiming that he had not read Guinier's writings prior to the controversy and that once he did review them, he came to the conclusion that her views were at odds with his. While the claim of ignorance may not have been totally convincing, the withdrawal of the nomination was widely regarded both as a pragmatic response to the likely defeat of the nominee in the Senate and as an effort to reclaim the "middle ground" during the effort to get the Clinton economic package through Congress.

The withdrawal of the nomination led Al From, president of the centrist Democratic Leadership Council, to praise Clinton's decision in the following passage which reveals the depth of controversy in the Democratic Party and among his supporters in the presidential campaign about where the "real" Bill Clinton stood:

> Three years ago, as chairman of the Democratic Leadership Council, Gov. Bill Clinton signed a declaration of principles with this plank: We believe the promise of America is equal opportunity, not equal outcomes.
>
> In the defining speech of his candidacy, at Georgetown University in October 1991, he promised a new covenant in which "it is the responsibility of every American . . . to fight back against the politics of division and bring this country together."
>
> In her writings, Ms. Guinier has emphasized the divisions among Americans, raising questions about the legitimacy of majority rule and asserting that "racism excludes minorities from ever becoming part of the governing coalition."

When the president read her writing, he concluded that her views and his did not mesh and as a matter of conscience pulled back her nomination. Her backers assert that she is the victim of a misinformation campaign. That is wrong: the problem was her views could not pass muster with many Democrats, including the president.[37]

Scandals also consumed some of the administration's appointees. Such cases include Webster Hubbell, a former law partner of Hillary Clinton's, who was said to have dominated decisions about Justice Department appointments. Hubbell had to resign his Justice Department post in response to an investigation of his billing practices at the Rose law firm in Little Rock. (He subsequently pleaded guilty to fraud charges.) Roger Altman, a highly regarded appointee in the Treasury Department, fell victim to fallout from the Whitewater hearings. And Mike Espy, the secretary of agriculture, also resigned under a cloud.

Finally, it is necessary to consider the *Washington Post's* editorial charge that at least some of the administration's appointees were lackluster. A grading of cabinet performance about a year into the administration by the reporting team of the *National Journal,* for example, gave Secretary of State Warren Christopher an "A" for Team Play, but "C"s for Management and Salesmanship and a "D" for Innovation.[38]

That same article, however, while it rated the cabinet uneven—"stronger in its second tier but weaker in its core"—summarized the cabinet's overall talent and performance positively: "By the standards of recent history, Clinton's cabinet seems to rate as good but not great. Political scientists don't rank it with the best of modern times.... But in the main, the men and women Clinton spent untold hours hiring during the presidential transition seem personally talented and politically astute, not to mention demographically diverse."[39]

One should be cautious in accepting any rating of the cabinet, but on balance the *National Journal* assessment seems fair. People rise and fall on these ratings over time, of course, so the individual entries on the *Journal's* scorecard would look different today than they did at the end of 1993. And sometimes flaws stressed in such a rating system are not too surprising, or even necessarily meaningful if put in perspective. For example, Secretary of State Christopher is given universally low ratings for innovation in the conceptualization of what U.S. foreign policy should be in the post–Cold War world, but he is joined by most of the best minds in and out of government in struggling to define what policy should be.

An evaluation of the whole panoply of appointees, focusing on those at the subcabinet level, reached similar conclusions to the rating of the cabinet quoted above, even finding a "nagging sense of sameness about them" despite their surface diversity:

The meritocratic gleam of Clinton's decision makers may explain the nagging sense of sameness about them. They are poised, ambitious, bright, hardworking. Any oddballs among them have so far stayed out of sight. Not many of them are ideologues. At heart, they're all pragmatists. Even the ones who weren't Washingtonians seem delighted to become so and eager to take their places in the Establishment. Indeed, they bear a resemblance not only to each other but also the policy makers they supplanted.[40]

Overall, then, it seems that the Clinton administration's cabinet appointments and, from what can be gleaned from a less than systematic review, its subcabinet level appointments, should be rated at least average—some less successful than others, but not particularly bad when compared to the norm. And they have been mainly pragmatic people, hardly atypical in this respect when compared to the appointees of most previous administrations. The Clinton administration has clearly had problems with appointments to positions in the agencies, both in terms of delays in filling positions and in some of the early and well-publicized foul-ups that ended in nominees withdrawing or being withdrawn. And it has almost certainly paid a political price because of the symbolic implications of its unremitting focus on diversity. But a case can be made that the administration's underlying problem has been not with the appointees themselves, but with some of the most visible policies it has pursued or been seen as pursuing, and the public's reaction to them. (The handling of gays in the military and the health-care reform strategy are prominent examples.) From what one can tell, real responsibility for most of these policy difficulties lies primarily in the White House (and a staff "that uniquely combined hubris and incompetence," according to a *New York Times* editorial following the 1994 election),[41] not in the agencies or their appointed or career personnel.

What Kind of Democrat in Office?

One of the most interesting aspects of the stunning defeat the Democrats suffered in the 1994 midterm elections was the vigorous discussion of the "New Democrat" concept it provoked. The *New York Times* editorial of 10 November 1994 quoted earlier summarized a part of the Democrats' electoral problem as follows:

The vote plainly reflected widespread disgust with big government and impatience with government activism, two things with which the Democrats are most closely identified. The question is how Mr. Clinton, a different Democrat, came to be seen as an old-fashioned tax-and-spender. The best answer is probably the health-care reform program whose Brobdingnagian design—following as it did his successful (and justifiable) move to raise taxes in order to shrink the deficit—tagged him in the public eye as an advocate of big government.[42]

It will be a major sport of political scientists and other analysts over the next few years to analyze data gathered from this election to determine to what extent the public really is disgusted with big government, since Americans often reject the concept while accepting such existing components as Social Security, Medicare, and the like. But there is no doubt that sizable elements of the political elite interpreted the election results as the *Times* does. Moreover, few would disagree that whatever the Clinton administration did stand for was quickly lost in a sea of confusing messages.

Clinton the candidate promised to keep his eye firmly on improving the economy and dealing with the health-care problems facing the country. But Clinton the president quickly became enmeshed in a politically costly dispute about gays in the military, which at best made him appear vacillating and not focused on the key concerns expressed in his campaign. His economic stimulus package was successfully portrayed by opponents as a set of unnecessary pork-barrel projects. His health-care program took a long time to take shape and, as the *Times* editorial notes, was so complex and politically vulnerable that its well-financed opponents were successful in tarring it with the unpopular "big government" label. Amazingly, the crime bill, something that should have been politically beneficial to the president and his party—even if it might not have been expected to have that much impact on crime—became the focus of an effective attack on the social components in the legislation, changing the debate to the politically damaging tax-and-spend theme.

In short, the public saw numerous examples of an administration that seemed to stray from the New Democrat themes that dominated much of Clinton's campaign rhetoric. They seemed to ignore, downplay, or forget the areas where Clinton did, or tried to do, what he indicated he would. These included deficit control (although without the promised middle-class tax cut), trade expansion, shrinking the size of government, deregulating business, and, at least at the level of discussion, welfare reform.

Because the administration's message was so confused (the charitable would say broad and varied), and Clinton's popularity seemed mystifyingly low given the briskly recovering economy, it became a sport for pundits and politicians alike to suggest how the president should position or reposition himself. The devastating failure of the health-care reform proposal, in particular, cast a pall over the administration and brought its competence into question.

A September 1994 article in the *New York Times* quoted a person described as one of Clinton's "Midwestern strategists" as follows: "Expectations were pretty high [when Clinton assumed office]. The Democrats were going to do 100 days this, and 100 days that. But I think there's a strong image out here that he and the Democrats aren't up to this thing. I think they've got to right this ship pretty soon."[43]

The article went on to summarize Clinton's situation after almost two years of his administration as follows:

> Nobody disputes that Mr. Clinton, already adept at the quick change, needs to reinvent himself.... The president has, in fact reinvented himself before. He won office as the Democrat who stole the Republicans' best lines on food-stamp cheats, stood up to the rapper Sister Souljah and decried the "brain-dead politics" that led Washington politicians to reject progress in pursuit of partisan gain. That is the president who later pushed centrist legislation ... to set up a national service program, to move welfare recipients from dependency to steady incomes and to shrink the Federal bureaucracy. And it is the same president who said repeatedly last month that crime victims are of all political stripes, and that the importance of passing anti-crime legislation surpassed the question of which party would gain most from it.
>
> That same president, [however], was branded a social-issues liberal after unwittingly making gay servicemen's rights the first issue of his presidency, and a free-spending liberal after making a $20 billion "stimulus" of new Federal programs, financed by deficit spending, his first economic cause. Then he was branded a big-government liberal after casting his proposed health care overhaul in terms of a new Federal "right," the right to be insured against sickness, even at added taxpayer expense.[44]

With this kind of interpretation in the air, it is little wonder that after the 1994 midterm election debacle the president sent out strong signals that he was indeed going to refocus himself. In a speech at Georgetown University, Clinton returned to the phrases and themes of his presidential campaign: "With all my strength, I will work to pursue the new Democrat agenda."[45] Another article quoted Clinton as saying, "I'm not going to compromise on my convictions," but then went on to assert: "Yet Clinton has been nagged throughout his presidency by public confusion over what his convictions are. Even his friends have said that Clinton badly strayed from the centrist message that he ran on, either trading away his principles for votes or abandoning his moderate stance to embrace liberal crime and health plans."[46]

The controversy about Clinton's beliefs even had an amusing angle. Departing adviser David Gergen, a Republican who had once counseled both George Bush and Ronald Reagan, and who had been brought into the White House in mid-1993 in one of the earlier efforts to signal the pragmatic and moderate direction the administration intended to take after the gays in the military and Lani Guinier controversies, was quoted as saying that "nobody knows what he [Clinton] stands for."[47] The statement caused a mini-controversy of the type that flares up so often in Washington. The issue was whether Gergen meant, as some of his enemies in the White House supposed, that Clinton did not stand for anything, or whether he was trying to say that Clinton was a true centrist but had failed to communicate his beliefs. The only thing that seems clear at this point is that there is confusion about what Clinton does believe.

Reinventing Government

One area where Clinton has followed the New Democrat agenda clearly and consistently is in the so-called reinventing government initiative. Soon after the 1992 presidential election, the Democratic Leadership Council, through its think tank called the Progressive Policy Institute, published a volume entitled *Mandate for Change,* which was meant to provide a "blueprint for a new America." President-elect Clinton, who had helped create the Democratic Leadership Council, praised the book for charting a "bold new course," and said, in language familiar to any who knew the rhetoric of the New Democrats, that it offered "creative new ideas for tackling America's toughest problems and a new governing philosophy based on opportunity, responsibility and community."[48]

Prominent in *Mandate for Change* is a chapter by David Osborne on "Reinventing Government: Creating an Entrepreneurial Federal Establishment." This chapter, and a book with a similar title by Osborne and Ted Gaebler, provided the blueprint for the National Performance Review (NPR), commissioned by President Clinton and chaired by Vice-President Al Gore. The goal of the review was, in the vice-president's words, "to make government work *better* and cost *less*" (emphasis in original).[49] The report laid out four "key principles" for achieving these goals:

1. Cutting Red Tape—the goal is to "cast aside red tape" in order to shift "from systems in which people are accountable for following rules to systems in which they are accountable for achieving results."
2. Putting Customers First—an "effective, entrepreneurial" government must focus on meeting the needs and satisfying the customers of its services.
3. Empowering Employees to Get Results—government should decentralize authority to "empower those who work on the front lines."
4. Cutting Back to Basics: Producing Better Government for Less—reinventors should find ways to make government work better by abandoning the obsolete, ending special privileges, investing in greater productivity, and using advanced technologies.[50]

The reinvention "principles" are all attractive at first glance. It would be hard to find someone who likes red tape. All of us would like to be put first as customers of government services. It seems like a fine idea to empower those closest to the front line of service delivery, because they are most likely to understand the needs of service recipients. And who wouldn't want an up-to-date government that worked better while costing less?

But behind these seemingly simple principles lurk all sorts of problems. As James Q. Wilson points out in his critique of the key principles of the National Performance Review, what we call red tape serves a variety of real purposes in government, including ensuring that groups can get access to the administration and guaranteeing fair procedures in decision making. Groups and citizens would miss the procedures and requirements that are the core of red tape, should they lose them, and demand them back. Empowering an agency's employees by decentralizing decision making is likely to fall victim to the first significant scandal that occurs (as it inevitably will in any organization), with Congress reacting by putting restrictions in place to prevent future scandals. And the suggestion in the National Performance Review that we "eliminate what we don't need" is, as the budget debates in this age of relative scarcity have demonstrated, attractive rhetoric but very unattractive to politicians when the actual targets have to be defined.[51]

Wilson's analysis also identifies problems with the putting-customers-first notion, particularly the problem that without offering government workers a share of the revenues brought about by gains in customer satisfaction, exhortation would be the main mechanism to stimulate government workers to do what is wanted. While I think it is possible to design a form of profit sharing in some areas at least, the core assumptions behind the customer notion itself are open to serious question. As Donald Kettl points out, "defining customers is much harder than it looks," and, assuming one can successfully define them, customers of particular services may have preferences that the aggregate of citizen taxpayers do not want to support. There are also, Kettl says, problems with the service-based approach when public goods, such as defense, are what the government is providing.[52]

The underlying problem with the NPR and its recommendations is part and parcel of major unresolved problems in American government discussed in the introduction to this chapter—just who is and should be in charge of the bureaucracy? What should it do? How should it be organized (and what should the division of tasks and authority between officials be like) so that it can perform well? And what, if anything, should be done so that each incoming administration will feel reasonably confident about the capacity and cooperation of the civil service?

As Kettl notes, what the NPR implicitly does is argue

the need to transfer power from Congress to the executive branch. In the

NPR report, Congress makes few appearances except as the source of over-regulation and micromanagement, and those problems are critical to the NPR's diagnosis of government's performance problems. Reinventing government requires ending overregulation and micromanagement. That implicitly demands that Congress give up its penchant for tinkering with the bureaucracy and leave more of management to the managers.[53]

NPR also says quite explicitly that government employees need to be empowered, particularly by putting more decisions on the "shop floor." Kettl characterizes the NPR approach as "implicitly a philosophy of transferring power from Congress to the bureaucracy and, within the bureaucracy, from top-level to lower-level officials." He also notes that NPR lacks an explicit strategy for dealing with Congress, a significant problem since the support of Congress is necessary for much of what NPR calls for, and that support is by no means assured given the assumptions underlying NPR.[54]

So what the Clinton administration is doing in NPR is continuing the thrust toward executive power of its Republican predecessors, but with a twist. Rather than advocate that power be held at the center of the executive branch, particularly in the hands of the White House and a dominant (and politicized) OMB, it is endorsing a decentralization of decision making into the bureaucracy, what might be called "deregulating government." The latter is something that a Democratic administration can be comfortable with because it, unlike the Republican administration of Ronald Reagan, for example, endorses the missions of most of the agencies. But in transferring power from Congress to the bureaucracy, NPR appears to increase the opportunity for an assertive administration to recentralize power in the hands of the White House. The incentive to do so will be there in cases where there are strong disagreements about policy (e.g., Reagan), or when the president has an inordinately strong need to be in control (e.g., Nixon).

In essence, deregulating government, which is the core of the NPR's program, can work only where there is a consensus on fundamental policy among all the key actors in the system. If not, there will be a drive back to central control by an administration anxious to regulate and direct what government is doing, or intense sniping from a Congress uneasy about the course of policy and frustrated by its loss of influence, or both. What looks like an innocent and attractive reform—and many of its elements and related policies are quite attractive, especially the encouragement of innovations by federal managers and the decision by the Clinton administration to ease the heavy hand of OMB on regulations written by the departments—needs a lot of examination. Basic questions of democratic accountability are raised by NPR. If customers control the bureaucracy, what is the role of elected officials? What would happen if a ruthless president determined to follow an "administrative presidency" strategy came to office after the government had been "reinvented"? There may be good answers to these questions, but they are not satisfactorily articulated as yet.

Finally, NPR raises a host of issues about the role of the top cadre of career executives, particularly those in the SES. NPR stresses the role of those "on the floor" and downplays the role of higher career managers. This was nowhere more apparent than in the decision to form the National Partnership Council (NPC)—the body created to advise the president on all manner of personnel policy from labor-management relations to staffing and compensation—as a partnership with employee unions, excluding managers' associations from the process.[55] The tactical goal behind this maneuver was to win over the employee unions, a strong constituency of the Democratic Party and potential opponents of the cutbacks in government personnel NPR envisioned in the government that "worked better and cost less."

The tactic worked, especially because so much of the reduction in positions would be at the career management level, but the result has been, according to Kettl,

> that the short-term bargains [the reinventers] made unquestionably have hurt their ability to fashion long-term change. They have alienated many government workers, especially key managers, on whom they will need to rely to carry the flag into battle, and they have no clear strategy to get them back. Neither have they developed a strategy for building a fresh foundation for a strong and vibrant public service, upon which the future of reinvention will rest.[56]

Indeed, Carol Bonosaro, president of the Senior Executives Association, in her column in the association's newsletter reporting on the "Reinventing Summit" held in June 1993, complained that "no corporation would embark on reinventing itself without the complete involvement of its top executives. With the exception of the career executive members of the National Performance Review (NPR) staff, the partnership has not been clearly expressed, either by the White House or at the departmental and agency level."[57]

And this was not the first statement of discontent on the subject by the Senior Executives Association's president. Vice-President Gore had previously suggested that the SES had too many people in it relative to the overall size of the federal workforce. Bonosaro responded by noting that the SES was three-tenths of one percent of the 2.2 million federal workforce, and was quoted as saying: "I thought the vice president had gained a great deal of insight in the last six months. But that remark makes clear he is not fully acquainted with the SES, unfortunately."[58]

Bonosaro followed up on these expressions of the association's dissatisfaction with a letter to Vice-President Gore, and in September 1993 a meeting was held in which he "promised a formal role for SEA in the implementation of the National Performance Review (NPR) recommendations."[59] The vice-president also gave a speech at Georgetown University in March 1994 on "The New Job of the Federal Executive," urging federal executives to meet the challenge of the changes promoted by the reinvention initiative. But, as Kettl asserts in his account of the speech: "Federal managers have heard the [Vice President's] message, but the voice of large cuts in the government service has spoken even louder. Fulfilling the promise of the NPR depends on their action, but the NPR has singularly under-motivated them."[60] Aside from the larger conceptual problems of the reinvention, then, there is still a big job to do in selling it to the people who will be key actors in implementing it.

And the conceptual problems will not go away. The NPR is rich in attention to the pop organization theory precepts of Osborne and Gaebler, but it has an eerie ahistoricity about it. NPR ignores the great struggle of the past twenty-five years over administrative accountability and political control of the executive branch, as if the problems were solved and there was consensus about what the government should do. Until these conditions hold, a strategy of devolving decisions to the lower levels of the bureaucracy will not solve the problems of the executive branch. It could even make them worse.

Waiting for Godot?

As in many other areas, Clinton at midterm is still very unsettled when it comes to the federal executive.

In his selection of political appointees, he has made an indelible mark by successfully engineering the most diverse administration in the nation's history. Overall, he seems to have appointed pragmatic people who are at least as able as those selected by the average administration. Some problems have arisen, of course, but probably not an inordinate number. Indeed, it is not likely that Clinton's personnel policies are a major source of his problems, except for the possibility that his highly publicized drive for diversity was less popular with the white male public than with the core minority and female constituencies of the Democratic Party.[61]

Clinton's problem is in part environmental. He is president at a time when the economy is in flux, so that while his administration has produced high employment, real wages continue to fall, and the disorder and uncertainties of the post–Cold War continue to unsettle the population (or, at least, contribute to situations that often make a president look bad). But what seems to be at the core of the administration's problem is a failure to define itself. It can do this in part through its appointments, of course, but merely being diverse is not enough. Indeed, directionless diversity puts the emphasis on the latter, which is arguably not a net political plus.

The debate over what kind of Democrat Clinton is tells the story. Clinton does not seem to know for sure, and neither does anyone else. He has a set of appointees and a higher civil service that can fit relatively comfortably with the moderate policies of a New Democrat or even the somewhat more liberal policies of a more standard, mainstream Democrat. What they cannot do is serve to define the administration for the public at large.

After the midterm election, the chair of the Democratic Leadership Council introduced a public session of the group by saying that Clinton won the White House as "a moderate Democrat, a new Democrat. But he has governed as something else. Not as a liberal as the Republicans say, but as a transitional figure. For while Bill Clinton has the mind of a new Democrat he retains the heart of an old Democrat."[62]

Both Clinton and Gore then appeared before the council, and Gore went so far as to say: "You can and do make a powerful argument that where we have not been, we should have been."[63]

Though trying to decide what Clinton believes and to influence what he does has become part of the game for Democratic politicians, especially given their current difficulties, such statements also highlight Clinton's dilemma. In his appointments strategy, policy goals were not the key, the mosaic was the key. It was almost as if Clinton were saying: "if you build diversity, good solutions will come." But one lesson of this administration is that a government that "looks like America" is far from enough for political success. A demographically perfect group that doesn't quite know where it is headed is apt to be as lost as any other.

Acknowledgments

The author gratefully acknowledges the excellent research assistance provided by John Medearis and support from the Academic Senate and the Center for American Politics and Public Policy at UCLA.

Notes

1. Joel D. Aberbach, *Keeping a Watchful Eye: The Politics of Congressional Oversight* (Washington, D.C.: Brookings Institution, 1990).

2. Richard P. Nathan, *The Administrative Presidency* (New York: Macmillan, 1983).

3. Joel D. Aberbach and Bert A. Rockman, "What Has Happened to the U.S. Senior Civil Service?" *Brookings Review* 8, no. 4 (Fall 1990): 35–41.

4. Joel D. Aberbach, "The President and the Executive Branch," in *The Bush*

Presidency: First Appraisals, ed. Colin Campbell and Bert A. Rockman (Chatham, N.J.: Chatham House, 1991), 223–47.

5. Joel D. Aberbach and Bert A. Rockman, "The Political Views of U.S. Senior Federal Executives, 1970–92," *Journal of Politics* 57, no. 3 (August 1995): 838–52.

6. Burt Solomon, "Twixt Cup and Lip," *National Journal,* 24 October 1992, 2411–12.

7. W. John Moore, "On the March Again?" *National Journal,* 12 December 1992, 2825.

8. Ibid., 2826.

9. Ibid.

10. Aberbach and Rockman, "Senior Federal Executives."

11. David T. Stanley, *Changing Administrations* (Washington, D.C.: Brookings Institution, 1965), 87.

12. W. John Moore, "Boomtown!" *National Journal,* 14 November 1992, 2607.

13. Robert Pear, "Clinton's Promise of Cleaning House Worries Some Civil Servants," *New York Times,* 15 November 1992, N18.

14. Denise Gellene, "Child Issues High for Product Safety Chief," *Los Angeles Times,* 25 March 1994, D3.

15. Telephone interview with the author, 8 July 1994.

16. Burt Solomon, "Clinton's Gang," *National Journal,* 16 January 1993, 116.

17. Ibid.

18. Ibid., 117–18.

19. David Broder, "Diversity Was Paramount in Building the Cabinet," *Washington Post,* 25 December 1992, A1, A21.

20. Thomas L. Friedman, "Clinton Taking Big Role in Picking Cabinet Aides," *New York Times,* 18 November 1992, A12.

21. Thomas L. Friedman, "Diversity Pledge Slows Clinton on Appointments," *New York Times,* 12 January 1994, A13.

22. Ibid.

23. Ibid.

24. Douglas Jehl, "High Level Grumbling over Pace of Appointments," *New York Times,* 25 February 1993, A8.

25. Martha Farnsworth Riche, "The Bean Count Is In!" *Washington Post,* 23 January 1994, C2.

26. Rogelio Garcia, "Nominations and Confirmations to Policy Positions in the First 100 Days of the Clinton and Reagan Administrations," Congressional Research Service Document 93–540 *GOV,* 24 May 1993.

27. Stephen Labaton, "Administration Leaves Top Civil Rights Jobs Vacant: Anti-Bias Groups Are Frustrated with the White House's Pace," *New York Times,* 31 October 1993, N1.

28. Robert Brownstein, "Key Civil Rights Post Left Empty as Search Falters," *Los Angeles Times,* 22 May 1994, A1.

29. Ibid.

30. "Choice for Rights Post," *New York Times,* 16 June 1994, A18.

31. "How Not to Fill a Government," Editorial, *Washington Post,* 14 March 1994, A18.

32. Sam Fulwood III, "Latinos Denounce Clinton Appointment Record," *Los Angeles Times,* 18 May 1993, A12.

33. *New York Times,* 25 January 1993, A11.

34. Catherine S. Manegold, "Women Are Frustrated by Failed Nominations," *New York Times,* 7 February 1993, L22.

35. "How Not to Fill a Government," A18.

36. Neil A. Lewis, "Aides Say Clinton Will Drop Nominee for Post on Rights," *New York Times,* 3 June 1993, A11.

37. Al From, "Guinier Had to Go. Now," *New York Times,* 5 June 1993, N15.

38. Special Report, "Cabinet Scorecard," *National Journal,* 6 November 1993, 2634–44.

39. Ibid., 2634.

40. Burt Solomon, "Clinton's Meritocracy," *National Journal,* 19 June 1993, 1453.

41. "Dr. Fell's Election," Editorial, *New York Times,* 10 November 1994, A14.

42. Ibid.

43. Michael Wines, "Cramming: So Many Minds to Be Changed, So Little Time," *New York Times,* 11 September 1994, E1.

44. Ibid., E1, E3.

45. Paul Richter, "Clinton Hints at Pursuing a Less Liberal Agenda," *Los Angeles Times,* 11 November 1994, A1, A20.

46. John M. Broder, "Demoralized White House Begins Urgent Reassessment," *Los Angeles Times,* 12 November 1994, A1, A21.

47. Al Kamen, "Ganging Up on Gergen," *Washington Post,* 2 December 1994, A29.

48. Will Marshall and Martin Schram, eds., *Mandate for Change* (New York: Berkeley Books, 1993).

49. Al Gore, *Creating a Government That Works Better and Costs Less* (New York: Plume, 1993), xxxviii.

50. Ibid., xxxviii–xl.

51. James Q. Wilson, "Reinventing Public Administration," John Gaus lecture delivered to the American Political Science Association, New York City, 2 September 1994. Published in *PS: Political Science & Politics* 27, no. 4 (December 1994): 667–73.

52. Donald F. Kettl, *Reinventing Government? Appraising the National Performance Review* (Washington, D.C.: Brookings Institution, 1994), esp. 39–40.

53. Ibid., 22.

54. Ibid., vi.

55. Ibid., 14.

56. Ibid., 21.

57. Carol A. Bonosaro, "What I Learned at the Philadelphia Summit," *ACTION* 13, no. 8 (September 1993): 8.

58. Stephan Barr, "Gore Sees Larger Cuts in Staffing," *Washington Post,* 28 July 1993: A17.

59. Carol A. Bonosaro, "Administration Opens Dialogue with SEA," *ACTION* 13, no. 9 (October 1993): 1.

60. Kettl, *Reinventing Government?* 17.

61. In the 1994 House elections, 62 percent of white men voted for the Republicans, compared to an average of 52.5 percent in the previous seven elections. The comparable numbers for white females are 55 percent and 48.5 percent respectively. See "Portrait of the Electorate: Who Voted for Whom in the House," *New York Times,* 13 November 1994: Y15.

62. Robert Shogan, "Centrist Ally Calls Clinton 'Old Democrat,'" *Los Angeles Times,* 7 December 1994, A30.

63. Douglas Jehl, "Group's Head Says Clinton Broke Faith," *New York Times,* 7 December 1994, A12.

6

The Parties, the President, and the 1994 Midterm Elections

HAROLD W. STANLEY

Midterm elections are almost always hard on the president's party. The 1994 elections were particularly harsh for President Bill Clinton and the Democrats. High Democratic hopes after the 1992 presidential election made the midterm losses all the more painful. Republicans gained, but the election also stimulated questions about the health of the two-party system and the electorate's attachment to it. This analysis of Clinton and the political parties during the first two years of his presidency discusses the extent to which the midterm elections were a referendum on the Clinton presidency, whether the elections signaled a partisan realignment, and how the results might affect the parties and the presidency in the last two years of Clinton's term.

The 1992 Election

The 1992 and 1994 elections bracketed the first two years of the Clinton presidency. The 1992 elections put Clinton in the Oval Office with Democratic majorities in both houses of Congress. The 1994 elections provided, in part, a judgment by voters on how well Clinton and his fellow partisans had met the expectations raised by the 1992 elections. Thus, understanding the 1994 elections requires consideration of the 1992 elections.

The 1992 election results offered at least a temporary end to divided government—Republican presidents and Democratic control of at least one house of Congress—that had characterized the national government for twenty of the previous twenty-four years. This divided government, as 1992 campaign rhetoric had it, produced legislative gridlock from which Clinton and Democratic legislative dominance promised relief.

Clinton, from a place called Hope, centered his Democratic nomination acceptance speech around the theme of hope. While desire for change from "politics as usual" struck a responsive chord among many voters, Clinton's victory also gave hope to Democrats that the Democratic Party might reestablish winning ways in presidential elections—a presidential victory had eluded Democrats in five of the six previous elections. Beginning with the Reagan years, Republican candidates had found greater favor, and partisan trends eroded the Democratic lead among partisan identifiers. Perhaps under Clinton's presidential leadership the Democratic Party could end the ebbing of its support and refashion a new majority coalition.

George Bush's 1992 presidential loss had underscored the variability of public support. In early 1991, in the aftermath of the Persian Gulf War, President Bush enjoyed record-breaking levels of public approval for his performance as president. Less than two years later, Bush could not marshal enough support for reelection in a three-way contest.

The record-breaking public approval for Bush in early 1991 had discouraged prominent Democratic presidential challengers from seeking the presidency, leaving the field to six lesser-known Democrats: former California Governor Jerry Brown, U.S. Senator Tom Harkin of Iowa, U.S. Senator Bob Kerrey of Nebraska, former U.S. Senator Paul Tsongas of Massachusetts, Virginia Governor Doug Wilder, and Arkansas Governor Bill Clinton. Clinton prevailed over these contenders, but his road to the White House was a rocky one.

The volatility of support for Clinton—his ability to bounce back in the polls—reflected his political resiliency. Throughout his quest for the presidency, questions about his personal character dogged Clinton. Allegations about Clinton's draft dodging and extramarital affairs received extensive publicity immediately before the first-in-the-nation New Hampshire primary and threatened to knock him out of the running. But Clinton's strong second-place showing in New Hampshire allowed him to label himself the "Comeback Kid," seize the media's attention, and thus secure a viable position for the subsequent primaries and caucuses in other states.[1]

Political support for Clinton hit rock bottom before recovering. In May 1992, as Clinton was sewing up the Democratic nomination, polls revealed that the presumptive Democratic nominee placed no better than third, trailing both Bush and Perot in national polls. Two months later, in the midst of the Democratic National Convention, Perot dropped out of the presidential race, citing as one reason a revitalized Democratic Party. When the convention closed, the Clinton–Gore ticket led Bush–Quayle by 24 percentage points.[2] A skillful general election campaign, along with some luck, allowed Clinton to triumph in November.[3]

Bush's high approval ratings in 1991 masked problems he could not avoid in the months leading up to the 1992 elections. The Republican right's displeasure with Bush's presidential performance and a broader-based discomfort over the performance of the economy under Bush combined to bedevil his reelection bid.

Conservatives—never embracing Bush as one of their own—were chafing over Bush's stewardship of the presidency.[4] In the fall of 1990 Bush broke his 1988 campaign pledge of "Read my lips. No new taxes." Conservative Republicans were particularly angered and provided stronger than expected support for political commentator and former Nixon speechwriter Pat Buchanan's right-wing challenge to Bush's renomination. The need to quell the disquiet among the more conservative Republican elements diverted Bush's attention during his renomination struggle and made the Republican National Convention more of a shoring up of Republican core supporters than a reaching out to the moderate middle.

The 1992 general election hinged on economic concerns. Prior to the early 1980s, this was an area of Democratic advantage due in part to the legacy of the New Deal and the Great Depression. But since the end of Reagan's first term, economic issues were increasingly favorable grounds for Republicans. Between late 1983 and early 1991, in public assessments about which party would do a better job of keeping the country prosperous, Republicans held a solid advantage, something they seldom had enjoyed between 1952 and 1980.[5] The Bush presidency squandered that recently acquired partisan advantage. Indeed, one commentator, F. Christopher Arterton, claimed that "from the perspective of strategy, . . . the story of the 1992 campaign is fundamentally shaped by the failure of Bush's campaign to address voter concerns about the economy."[6] By contrast, Clinton campaign strategists keyed on the economic issues, best symbolized by the sign George Stephanopoulos posted in Clinton campaign headquarters proclaiming, "It's the economy, stupid!"

Personal economic anxieties abounded, but the inference that the public was moved by a concern for personal economic welfare should be tempered by the realization that collective judgments about national economic conditions were politically devastating to Bush's reelection: "Instead of self-interest, the key element of the economic issue was a concern for the national welfare."[7] A majority of voters thought that their personal economic conditions were the same or better than four years previously; only a third saw themselves in personal economic difficulty. But 80 percent thought national economic conditions were "poor" or "not so good" and voted heavily against Bush's reelection.

Bush's strong suit, foreign policy, failed to move voters toward supporting him. Ironically, foreign policy successes during the Reagan and Bush presidencies—such as the end of the Cold War and the Persian Gulf War —reduced international tensions and left voters freer to focus on domestic issues, such as the state of the economy. Some voters viewed Bush's foreign policy performance as part of the problem: the president seemed more inter-ested in events abroad than at home.[8] The Persian Gulf War stopped short of removing Saddam Hussein from power. Events in Iraq kept Hussein in the news in the United States and led to one of the more barbed bumper stickers of the campaign: "Saddam Hussein has a job. Do you?"[9]

Democrats triumphed in 1992 and had grounds for ecstasy. The results also gave Democrats grounds for concern. Clinton's popular vote percentage in a three-way contest did not mark expansion of the Democratic base of support. Indeed, it only matched the level averaged by losing Democratic presidential candidates since 1968.[10] For reelection, Clinton must build on the support secured in 1992 or count on a serious independent candidate cutting into the Republican support base in 1996 more than draining sup-port from the incumbent president.[11]

The volatility of popular support worked in 1992 to put the Democrats back in power. That volatility worked against the Democrats in 1994 and may not work to their advantage in 1996.

In 1992 "change" was the watchword, and even Bush as the incumbent president promised to deliver change to a public disenchanted with legisla-tive gridlock and "politics as usual." Redistricting following the 1990 census changed many congressional district lines, encouraging some incumbents to retire rather than tackle the difficult task of learning and courting a new dis-trict. Congress suffered in public esteem as a result of the House Bank scan-dal, which revealed that members of Congress enjoyed—and some abused —overdraft privileges unavailable to the public.[12] The contentious Senate hearings over Clarence Thomas's nomination to the Supreme Court mobi-lized many, particularly women, who were angered by the all-male Judiciary Committee's handling of Anita Hill's charges of sexual harassment.[13] Perot personified and harnessed much of the public disenchantment to amass 19 percent of the vote in the general election—an impressive, nearly unprece-dented total for an independent candidate. Clinton pitched his campaign to-ward the middle of the political spectrum rather than core elements of the Democratic coalition such as labor and minorities, banking on their eventual support, while claiming to be a "New Democrat" and promising change from the politics of the recent past.[14]

1994 Midterm Elections

The 1994 midterm elections delivered an enormous political setback to the Democratic Party. Clinton had won the presidency with a plurality of 43 percent of the vote; the midterm results revealed that he had failed to ex-pand that support base. The midterm voters may have meant to reject the Democrats more than they endorsed the Republicans,[15] but when the dust settled, the Republican gains had transformed the political landscape.

For the first time in forty-two years the Republican Party, picking up 53 seats, had won a majority in the House of Representatives, 231–203. House Republicans won a majority of seats and a majority of the nationwide vote, a feat they had not accomplished since 1946. In a general election in which the "ins" were being tossed out, 35 Democratic incumbents lost, but not a single Republican incumbent lost.[16]

In the Senate, Republicans regained the majority control they had lost in 1986. The election results provided 52 seats. The day-after-the-election partisan switch by Senator Richard C. Shelby of Alabama boosted that total to 53. (The subsequent switch by Senator Ben Nighthorse Campbell of Colorado made it 54 in March 1995.) Again, no Republican incumbent lost a bid for reelection, but two Democratic incumbents did. Republican Senate majorities, while more recent than a House majority, have not been common. In the sixty-two years before 1995, the Republicans had a majority in only ten years.[17]

Republicans made sizable inroads at the state level as well. The number of Republican governors rose from nineteen to thirty, giving Republicans their first majority of governorships since 1970. Five Democratic incumbents lost; no Republican incumbent did.[18]

Republicans made substantial headway in state legislatures, too, picking up more than 100 state senate seats and about 370 state house seats. These seat gains gave Republicans control of 17 more legislative chambers. Before the election Republicans had majority control in only 31 of the 98 partisan state legislative chambers (Democrats had 64, and three were tied). After the election Republicans controlled 48, Democrats 47, and three were tied. Moreover, Republicans controlled both chambers in more states (19) than Democrats (18), with split partisan control in 12 others.[19]

Republicans were quick to interpret the election as a negative referendum on Clinton's presidency. Haley Barbour, chairman of the Republican National Committee, claimed that "what the American people did tonight is they rejected President Clinton's policies."[20] Political science literature questions such a strong emphasis on issues voting, but even Democrats acknowledged voter disappointment with Clinton and the Democrats. Clinton's pollster characterized voters as "still very open to the Clinton presidency, even as they are enormously critical of his results in the first two years."[21] Barbour's Democratic counterpart, David Wilhelm, noted that the Democratic recapture of the White House along with Democratic majorities in the House and Senate had given voters reason to expect an end to partisan gridlock and a serious start on the nation's most important problems. But since 1992, Wilhelm conceded, "Democrats failed 'to govern with discipline or unity' and paid the price for that failure in the election.... 'The American people hoped for and expected an end to gridlock.... As the governing party, Democrats did not meet that test often enough.'"[22]

Was the 1994 midterm election a referendum on Clinton's presidency? Exit polls offer helpful insight.[23] As in the cases of Bush and Reagan in previous elections, most midterm voters claimed that President Clinton was not a factor in their voting decisions. A 52 percent majority said Clinton was not a factor in 1994. Of those for whom the president did matter, as many had voted to support the incumbent president as to oppose him in 1982 or 1990. But in 1994, more opposed (27 percent) than supported (18 percent) the president. Moreover, as Kathleen Frankovic, director of surveys for CBS News noted, "for the 16 percent of voters who said Clinton's performance was one of the two most important reasons for their vote, the impact was even more negative: 72 percent of those voters voted Republican, and only 28 percent voted Democratic."[24] (This group alone yielded an overall advantage of 7 percentage points to the total Republican national vote.)

Why, for the minority of voters citing the president as a factor in the vote, did Clinton provide more drag than lift for the Democrats? Clinton and the Democrats had delivered too little of what they had promised. Partisan gridlock and economic anxieties continued. Moderate, centrist moves were few and eclipsed by more salient, ultimately unsuccessful proposals on health care and gay rights. Elected with only a plurality of the popular vote, Clinton's activism required political capital he had yet to acquire. Initial proposals encountered difficulties—both in being delayed and in being opposed—and nominations were withdrawn, giving an impression of political bungling. Throughout his presidency, allegations about extramarital affairs and financial improprieties ("Whitewater") swirled around Clinton, fueling lingering doubts about his character and denting his presidential stature.

The same themes that Clinton had captured in the 1992 presidential election—change and economic recovery—cut against the Democrats in 1994. Candidate Clinton had promised change, but the partisan bickering of gridlock continued, and not enough change occurred to content voters. A Republican Senate filibuster derailed Clinton's economic stimulus package.[25] Clinton had campaigned on the economy in 1992 and claimed in 1994, as Bush had before him, that the economy was recovering. Yet improving economic indicators did little to allay voter anxieties about jobs in an economy marked by corporate downsizing and layoffs.

Exit polls showed that attitudes toward the economy played a vital role in 1994, as they had in 1992. The politics played out differently: in 1992, voter despair over the economy advantaged the Democrats; in 1994, the Republicans. Despite signs of economic recovery by 1994, voter anxieties about the economy, particularly wages and salaries, were prominent.[26] Seventy-five percent of the voters in 1994 said they were not better off today than they were two years ago; 43 percent said that they were "working harder and earning less." In 1992, 79 percent of the voters thought the economy was in bad shape, and 62 percent of these voters supported Democratic House candidates. In 1994 a smaller majority of voters thought the economy was in bad shape (57 percent), but the same share (62 percent) supported Republican House candidates.[27]

Democratic campaign emphasis on the improving economy had been drowned out, in part by prolonged consideration of Clinton's health-care initiative, which ended in failure in late September 1994. As Clinton's pollster noted in retrospect, despite the importance of fulfilling a 1992 campaign promise, "health care had a very debilitating effect.... People watched a year-long political battle. They saw it as just partisan bickering, people's interests being crowded out, special interests reigning free. At the same time, [there was] ... what they saw as big government being talked about for a year."[28] More than a failed proposal, Clinton's health-care reform suggested to some voters that he was a big-government Democrat, seeking another large government program, paid for by the middle and working classes, in this case to guarantee universal heath-care coverage.

Such impressions undermined Clinton's status as a New Democrat from the 1992 campaign. As a former chair of the Democratic Leadership Council, a group within the Democratic Party designed to bring the Democrats back toward the mainstream, Clinton had seemed likely to reveal more moderate tendencies once in office.[29] Clinton had run as a New Democrat in 1992, but once in the Oval Office governed more as a traditional Democrat. The middle-class tax cut, promised in the campaign, abandoned once in office, hampered growth of Clinton support among a group the Democrats needed to court.[30] The midterm campaign themes moved away from 1992's New Democrat themes and targeted the traditional party bases by raising the specters of Republican threats to Social Security and civil rights.

Early in his administration Clinton pushed for the right of gays to serve in the military. By prompt action on this campaign pledge, the Clinton administration reinforced the image of Democrats as backing social-activist minorities against the cultural and economic interests of the mainstream.[31] Clinton's early advocacy of gay rights signaled priorities at odds with the thrust of the presidential campaign, a political miscalculation from which he was unable to recover. Opponents of his gays in the military policy ultimately diluted the president's proposal, meaning that Clinton pleased no one in the process and raised doubts about his political productiveness. The president's position did help mobilize opposition by the religious right, a group alienated as well by simmering allegations concerning Clinton's extramarital affairs and Whitewater. Additionally, pronouncements of Surgeon General Joycelyn Elders, a Clinton appointee, on sex education and drug legalization also angered social conservatives and the religious right.[32] Such anger had political consequences—among midterm voters, conservatives made up 37 percent of the voters, up from 30 percent in 1992.[33]

Not every move Clinton made was that of a liberal, traditional Democrat. To the degree that moderation had been exhibited in Clinton's presidency through deficit reduction, this proved a difficult campaign theme for congressmen to drive home in the midterm elections.[34] Ratification of the North American Free Trade Agreement (NAFTA) succeeded with Clinton's forceful lobbying, despite having to go against a bulwark of the Democratic Party, the labor unions. What had seemed hopeless at the start passed comfortably, but this was a rare example of a major proposal on which Clinton began the process in the middle by seeking a bipartisan coalition, instead of staking out a position on the left and edging toward the center to pick up needed votes.[35]

Despite the NAFTA success, Clinton's inability to deliver on health care raised doubts about his ability to deliver generally. Even ultimately successful passage of a crime bill in August 1994 had required special legislative efforts that called into question the president's ability to work with a Democratic Congress.[36]

Clinton and the Democratic congressional majorities did not succeed in restoring an image of competence in governing. The electorate's support for government activism, as well as its trust in government, continued to erode. When asked if government should be doing more or if government was doing too many things better left to businesses and individuals, only 41 percent of the midterm voters thought government should do more; 56 percent said it was doing too much. In 1992 the figures were 49 and 41. Fewer trusted government in Washington to do the right thing most of the time: in 1994, 25 percent did; in 1990, 33 percent had.[37]

These negative attitudes toward government accompanied low approval ratings for Clinton. The low ratings were not unusual: Clinton's ratings resembled those that Carter and Reagan (first term) had achieved at their midterm elections. Among all voters, Clinton had 45 percent approval of the way he was handling his job as president, the same figure Carter held in 1978 and about the level of Reagan's approval in 1982 (49 percent), but below Bush's 58 percent in 1990.[38] Ironically for a president who had stressed domestic issues, foreign policy successes such as the averted invasion of Haiti proved to be bright spots.[39] But as Bush and Carter had learned, foreign policy successes rarely compensate for domestic discontent.

Figure 6.1 tracks Clinton's 1993 and 1994 approval ratings according to the Gallup poll. After a brief honeymoon period, public approval slid sharply from the mid to high 50s to the high 30s in June 1993, then rose to hover around majority approval from fall 1993 to early summer 1994 before falling to 39 percent approval in August and September. Anemic presidential approval often occurs, but for a president elected with a plurality vote, growing support from favorable public reaction to on-the-job performance is politically essential. Clinton's term did not trigger that public response.

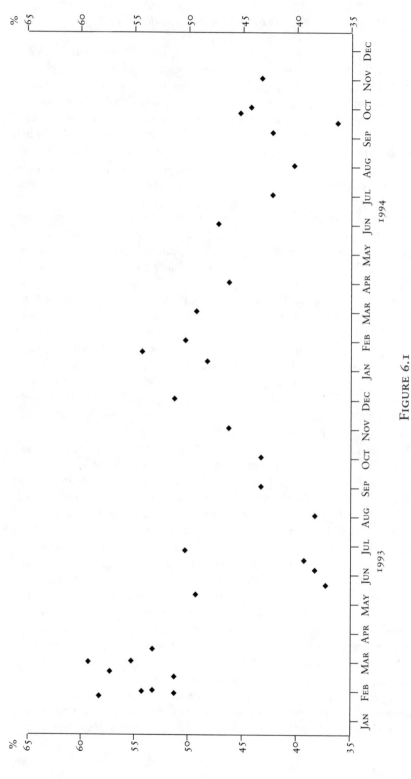

FIGURE 6.1

CLINTON'S PRESIDENTIAL APPROVAL RATINGS, 1993–94

SOURCE: Gallup poll data provided by the Gallup Library.
NOTE: Interviewees answering "approve" to the question, "Do you approve or disapprove of the way Clinton is handling his job as president?"

Realignment or Dealignment?

Did the midterm elections signal partisan realignment, dealignment, or the breakup of the two-party system?[40] Solid answers to such questions require the passage of time: future elections will provide readings of the durability of electoral patterns and the benefits of hindsight, but some insights can be offered with only the midterm results in hand.

Realignment, a much-used and abused term, speaks to a fundamental shift in the support coalitions for the parties. Dealignment concerns a decline in the centrality of parties to political behavior and attitudes. Elements of both appeared in the midterm results: the continued slide of the white South toward the Republicans suggested realignment; however, the volatility apparent when contrasting 1994 with 1992 suggests parties are slipping as electoral moorings loosen. If the new Republican congressional majorities fail to perform satisfactorily and negative verdicts like those of 1992 and 1994 are rendered against Republicans in 1996, the electoral beneficiaries may be not Democrats but independent or third-party candidates. Perot's 19 percent of the vote in 1992 was the highest for any independent or third-party candidate in seventy years. Taken together, this evidence indicates the current two-party system will be sorely tested in the years ahead.

Did the Republican "Contract with America" and smashing Republican victories in the 1994 midterms signal an emerging Republican majority coalition? No, but Republicans, like Democrats after 1992, can hope that happens. Several partisan trends favor the Republicans: political developments in the South, redistricting, and the likely change in campaign contributions. Neither party has a dominant position. The rough Democratic–Republican parity in the number and loyalty of partisan identifiers suggests electoral outcomes can be in the hands of voters who consider themselves independent of the parties, signaling continuing prospects for volatility in those outcomes.

In 1994 Republicans, unlike Clinton, courted these independents, Perot supporters prominent among them. The Contract with America, announced on 27 September 1994 and signed by more than 300 Republican House members and candidates, listed "the ten bills Americans would see in the first 100 days of the first Republican controlled House in 40 years." Addressing the sense of futility voters felt in holding representatives accountable, Republicans boldly stated, "The contract will allow people to hold us accountable, measure our performance and, if we break the contract, throw us out." The contract promised votes on a balanced-budget amendment, a line-item veto, congressional term limits, and a middle-class tax cut, as well as votes on proposed reforms in policy areas affecting crime, welfare, children, national security, senior citizens, capital gains, legal reforms, and product liability.[41]

The Contract with America "was designed to touch the Perot constituency's hot buttons."[42] Perot voters, who would have split evenly between Clinton and Bush in 1992 if Perot had not run, supported Republican House candidates by a 67–33 margin in 1994.[43]

The Contract with America helped nationalize the campaign and countered Tip O'Neill's axiom that "all politics is local," but its impact should not be overstated. Surveys revealed limited public awareness of the Republican Contract with America. Items within the contract—such as the balanced-budget amendment, limitations on welfare, and term limits—have enjoyed widespread popular support, but even after the election two-thirds to three-quarters of survey respondents were unaware of the contract.[44] The existence of the contract, coupled with substantial Republican victories, cannot be read as evidence of a mandate or the emergence of a new Republican majority coalition among voters.[45] Richard Bond, a former chairman of the Republican National Committee, said it best. Bond did not read the 1994 results as revealing "some long-lasting preference for the Republican Party. What it is is a reaffirmation of the message of change.... Bill Clinton and the Democratic Congress failed to deliver fundamental change in political reform, in economic reform, in institutional reform, and in cultural reform, and they were fired. The Republicans have been given two years to now produce it and, if they don't, they're out too."[46]

A durable Republican majority did not emerge in 1994, but several trends favor the Republicans. Most auspicious are the southern partisan developments. The emergence of southern Republicans has been a decades-long story, with Dixiecrats and "Democrats for Eisenhower" being among the first signs of break-up in the Solid South. Continuing disaffection with the national Democrats since the 1960s and the appeal of Reagan in the 1980s also worked to Republican advantage.

In the South in 1994 the Republicans gained a majority of both House seats (64, to 61 for the Democrats) and Senate seats (12, to 10 for the Democrats). Thirty years earlier, after the 1964 election, Republicans had held only 2 of the 22 southern Senate seats and 16 of the 106 southern House seats. Although the reliance of Democratic majorities on southern seats has been reduced in recent years, the tilt of the South toward the Republicans has ominous overtones for reestablishing Democratic congressional majorities. Even after the 1992 elections, Democrats held a 77–48 edge in southern House seats. This 29-seat net regional edge made up more than half of the Democratic margin of control in the House.

Democratic recovery in the South is not assured. Of the 61 Democrats who won, 14 received less than 55 percent of the vote, 31 less than 60 percent.[47] To be sure, Republicans also had close wins, but further Democratic slippage seems likely, since southern Democratic congressional candidates have lost a principal argument to their mostly conservative constituents. The notion that despite a more liberal national party, southerners should send

Democrats to Congress because Democrats controlled Congress has lost its force. Southern Democratic incumbents who could deliver for constituents because of seniority now find themselves in a diminished minority, stripped of the presumption of majority status. One result of this predicament may be a rightward movement with greater emphasis on issues by southern Democratic congressmen. But since the conservative Democratic voter in the South is truly an endangered (if not extinct) species, another result may be further Republican gains.[48]

Partisan ideological polarization in Congress seems likely to sharpen as a result of the rise of southern Republicans and the decline of southern Democrats. As Walter Dean Burnham notes, southern Republicans have been firmly on the right of their party. "On the Democratic side, the disappearance or defection of the party's right wing will inevitably mean that the party's congressional caucus will find its center of gravity shifted to what passes for the left in this country."[49]

Recent redistricting has aided Republicans.[50] Following the 1990 census, the creation of majority–minority districts spurred on by the Voting Rights Act altered the partisan configuration of congressional and state legislative districts. The suspicion is strong that in partisan terms Republicans benefited more than Democrats. Pooling black voters, typically very loyal Democratic supporters, into one congressional district inevitably left two or three surrounding districts less Democratic. The resulting brighter Republican prospects in the surrounding districts helped bring forth higher-quality, better-financed Republican candidates.

Majority–minority districts served to insulate minority officeholders from pro-Republican trends. In the South, for instance, Republicans gained sixteen seats held by white Democrats; none of the region's seventeen black members of Congress lost. Yet the Democratic Party, even in the South, has not become a party resting basically on support from racial minorities. Despite the relatively greater presence of black Democrats among southern Democratic House members, almost three-quarters of southern Democratic congressmen are nonblack. Exit polls suggest that blacks made up about 15 percent of the southern voters in 1994 and, supporting Democrats at a 91 percent loyalty level, provided 30 percent of all Democratic House votes in the South. Thus, nonblacks, who made up about 85 percent of southern voters, furnished about 70 percent of all Democratic House votes in the South. Even within the South, the Democratic Party remains biracial in composition, both in terms of its elected officials and its supporters.[51]

Along with redistricting and the move of the South toward the Republicans, another contributor toward continued Republican political success will be the likely shift of corporate campaign donations toward Republicans. Corporate political action committees (PACs), like PACs in general, have shown a marked preference for contributing to incumbents.[52] When Democrats controlled Congress, most incumbents were Democrats, and Democratic campaign coffers fared well. With fewer Democrats, and stripped of the presumption of majority control, Democrats are likely to find corporate PACs funneling funds more in line with their policy preferences and in recognition of the Republican majority in Congress.[53]

In the quest for PAC and other dollars, Republicans gained an organizational edge over Democrats with the revitalization or the National Republican Congressional Committee (NRCC) under Representative Bill Paxon of New York. Taking over the NRCC after the 1992 elections, Paxon inherited a debt of $4.5 million and a withered potential donor list. Paxon trimmed the NRCC staff by a third and revived the financial capacity of the NRCC, wiping out the long-term debt and raising $18 million.[54] The Democratic organizations also improved on past performance, but continued to lag far behind the Republicans. In terms of "hard dollars" reported by the federal accounts of the six national party committees, Democrats doubled their fund raising in 1994 compared with the 1990 midterm; yet Republicans raised twice again as much as did the Democrats.[55]

The gains Republicans registered in the 1994 midterms were prefigured by earlier election results. After losing the White House in November 1992, Republicans won all six major elections: Georgia's U.S. Senate runoff, the Los Angeles and New York City mayoralty elections, the U.S. Senate special election in Texas, and the New Jersey and Virginia governorships.[56] In 1994 special elections for U.S. House seats in Kentucky and Oklahoma were captured by Republicans despite both districts being two-to-one Democratic in voter registration.[57]

These pro-Republican election results did not spring from substantial shifts in Republican Party identification. Trends in partisanship during Clinton's presidency gave Democrats some signs of hope, fleeting though these proved to be. Figure 6.2 charts party identification from the CBS News/ New York Times polls since 1981, the start of Reagan's presidency. The Democratic advantage of the early 1980s has narrowed, with Republicans occasionally achieving parity with the Democrats.[58] After Clinton's initial year, survey data on partisanship indicated that "for the first time since 1976, the Republican Party is no longer gaining at the expense of the Democrats."[59] Clinton was taking some of the steam from Republican rhetoric on certain issues. In early 1994 one Republican analyst assessed the Democrats' gains under Clinton as follows: Democrats are "getting credit for going back to the center.... If you broke out issues [on] which the Democrats made the most gains—you'd get crime and welfare reform. That gives them a booster shot."[60] These Democratic partisan leads (as much as 17 percentage points in some polls) proved unstable; during 1994, Republicans bobbed back to parity. In November 1994 the Democrats enjoyed a slim 3-percentage-point lead.

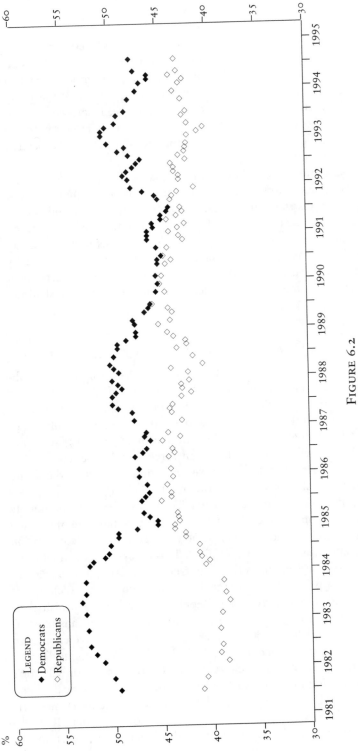

FIGURE 6.2

DEMOCRATIC AND REPUBLICAN PARTY IDENTIFICATION, 1981–94

SOURCE: CBS News/*New York Times* polls press releases.

NOTE: Graphs show the percentages of Democratic and Republican identifiers as a moving five-poll average from 104 surveys between January 1981 and November 1994. Partisans include those who answered "independent" or "don't know" to the initial question but thought of themselves as closer to a party in response to the follow-up question. Initial question: "Generally speaking, do you usually consider yourself a Republican, a Democrat, an independent, or what?" Follow-up if independent or don't know: "Do you think of yourself as closer to the Republican Party or to the Democratic Party?"

Consideration of partisanship may be irrelevant if fickleness rather than durable partisan support for party nominees characterizes voters. Partisanship still matters: in 1994 Republicans voted Republican, Democrats backed Democrats. Indeed, voters identifying with a party were somewhat less likely to defect from their party's nominee in 1994. On average, 16 percent of each party's identifiers who voted failed to support their party's House nominee from 1980 to 1992, but only 7 percent of Republican voters and 10 percent of the Democrats defected in 1994.[61]

Partisans were more loyal, but, being similarly sized, Democrats and Republicans offset one another. This rough parity of partisan identifiers, which varies across districts and states, makes the proportion and preferences of independent voters critical.[62] The 1994 electoral results swung on the turn of the independent voters toward the Republicans in 1994, unlike 1992. Independents, having gone Democratic in 1988, 1990, and 1992 by 54–46 percent, switched to Republicans by 56–44 in 1994.[63] Independent voters as the swing group heralds an electoral volatility that overshadows durable partisanship.

Political Prospects

The public appetite for "politics as usual" has been seriously curbed: substantial congressional turnover has marked recent years. The freshman class in the House after the 1992 election numbered 110, after 1994, 87. For the Senate, the corresponding figures are 14 and 11. In 1995, 183 members (42 percent) of the House will have been first elected in 1992 or 1994.[64] One-fourth of the Senate will have had less than three years' experience.[65] The newcomers may not last, but such turnover is both a product of the desire for change and a contributor toward further political change.

While Republicans triumphed in 1994, Democrats have no monopoly on the political perils ahead. President Clinton faces the challenge of steering a sensible course over the next Congress between conflict and cooperation with the new Republican majorities. While White House insiders might like to see the congressional Republicans self-destruct by catering too strongly to extremely conservative elements in the Republican coalition, such hopes may prove misguided as congressional Republicans seek to refurbish their credentials as the governing party. Both Democrats and Republicans must be combative enough to define contrasting agendas but cooperative enough to avoid the appearance of prolonging the political ineffectiveness of gridlock.

Will bipartisan cooperation characterize the remainder of Clinton's term? Clinton is being urged by some to move toward the political center. The same logic applies to congressional Republicans. Just as Democratic boll weevils held sway in Reagan's first two years, more moderate Republican House members could frequently hold the balance of power in the

104th Congress. The strains of holding together a majority coalition could give moderate Republicans more clout.[66] Nevertheless, various considerations, discussed later, suggest partisan polarization and conflict are more likely to prevail than bipartisan cooperation.

Whether Democrats or Republicans will gain or both will lose ground before 1996 is an open question. With Republican control of Congress and a Democrat in the White House, divided government can make determining political responsibility—who's to blame, who's to praise—a shell game. If partisan gridlock continues, third-party or independent candidates may benefit, further straining the two-party system.

How might Democrats recover the ground lost during the first two years of the Clinton administration? Any Clinton argument in 1996 about the need for change to a Democratic majority in Congress will ring hollow. He had that majority for 1993–94 and could not deliver the change he had promised during the 1992 campaign. Will the country need a New Democrat in 1996? They elected one in 1992 and he resembled an Old Democrat in 1993–94. If voters still want change in 1996, should they change the president? Presidential elections are about choice. You cannot beat someone with no one, and the 1996 contrast between Clinton and the leading alternative(s) will be critical. The ability of an incumbent to run a negative campaign is limited—a positive message seems essential. Clinton, like Bush in 1992, may find "my opponents could be worse" to be an uninspiring, unavailing campaign theme (even though Truman fared well with such a theme in 1948).

Clinton and the Democrats will not lack for advice, most of it unsolicited. Advice about the course Clinton and the Democrats should take falls into three broad categories: go left, go right, and go away.

Those urging Clinton or the Democrats to "go away" are not of one mind. One group thinks the Democratic ticket will be better off in 1996 without Clinton at its head,[67] another thinks the Democrats and the two-party system should be rejected so that more meaningful party alignments can emerge.[68]

Those urging Clinton to go left are not primarily concerned with Clinton's political prospects for 1996. These commentators read the midterm results as punishment for straying from core, liberal Democratic principles.[69] A return to basic Democratic values, these commentators suggest, will re-energize the party's base, connect with the disconnected, and restore the party's fortunes. Moving toward the Republicans will be self-defeating because, if forced to choose between a Republican and a Republican imitator, voters will choose the real thing over the copy.

Those urging Clinton to go right, toward the political center, read the midterm results as punishment for governing as a traditional Democrat after having run as a New Democrat. The New Democrat course, these commentators contend, has not been tried, much less rejected. Returning to the campaign themes of 1992 will be the best way to restore the Democratic Party and Clinton's political support.[70] Advocates of a centrist course see the 1994 midterm election setback as "liberating" for Clinton, since the traditional Democratic factions have reduced political clout. During the presidential campaign, Clinton had taken on some elements of the party coalition, the Sister Souljah incident being one of the more prominent. As president, he parted with the labor unions over NAFTA. Clinton's tendency to shift positions may not make the moderate course the clear choice of the administration.

Presidential politics for 1996 seem apt to contribute to ideological polarization and combativeness. For partisan reasons, Clinton may find the moderate course a politically difficult one. Given the nature of Democratic primary electorates and the earlier scheduling of California and New York in 1996, Clinton, like Carter in 1980, seems more vulnerable to challenge from the Democratic left than from the center. Jesse Jackson, for one, has hinted that he might mount that challenge, perhaps from outside the party as an independent candidate.[71]

Presidential campaign dynamics also affect the Republicans. Senate Majority Leader Robert Dole, marked by more moderate tendencies than House Speaker Newt Gingrich, must court the right of the Republican Party, a faction that figures prominently among Republican presidential primary voters. If presidential politics pulls Clinton to the left and Dole to the right, more interparty combat, less bipartisan cooperation seems apt to characterize Congress after the 1994 elections.

The political pitfalls and problems are not all Democratic ones. Will two years of a Republican congressional majority make Democrats more attractive? The Republican tactics that worked in opposition need not ensure retaining a majority: championing discontent to win the reins of government does not suffice for a winning position once in government. The Republican "contract" provides some attractive political positions, but legislating them into policy may prove divisive or counterproductive for Republican growth. The political consequences that flow from the contrasts between position taking and policy making can be enormous.

The 1994 midterm was a Republican triumph, but the numbers give some grounds for concern. Turnout was relatively high in 1994 for a midterm election. In 1992 turnout had also picked up relative to recent presidential levels. More than the mathematics matters, but 51 percent of the 38.7 percent 1994 midterm turnout does not denote broader-based support than Clinton's 43 percent plurality of the 56.8 percent 1992 turnout.[72] The congressional Republicans must reach out expansively to prevail in the larger turnout of 1996.

The Republican coalition has its internal contradictions, most notably between its social and economic conservatives.[73] Republican gains in the South in 1994 were the culmination of long-term trends that were more ideologically or socially driven than based on economic anxiety. In the Midwest, however, the voters who switched to support the GOP in 1994 were typified by younger, white, working-class men motivated by economic issues. These voters do not share the socially conservative positions that have been winning Republican converts in the South. Reagan wrestled with these divisions by talking a socially conservative line while legislating an economically conservative one. Gingrich and Dole must also finesse these divisive divisions, lest Democrats exploit the Republican differences.

Congressional Republicans, with majority control of both chambers for the first time in more than forty years, face daunting challenges. Clinton's approval ratings may be deemed low, but those ratings are stratospheric when compared with public approval of Congress. Republicans are likely to find that such disapproval was not linked to Democratic control, but adheres to the institution.[74] Republicans delivered a stunning political setback to the Democrats in 1994, but 91.6 percent of the House incumbents who sought reelection won.[75] As Richard Fenno showed, pursuit of individual self-interest produces serious collective action problems. Congressional incumbents run for Congress by running against Congress: constituency relations are bolstered by establishing political goodwill and empathy between individual incumbents and constituents, but running down the institution as a whole.[76] There is little reason to think that Republican incumbents will place the party above their own reelection bids. Political careers are at stake, and individual enhancement in what has been a candidate-centered era may not resolve the collective action problems faced by the congressional parties.

Republicans in power can energize Democratic bases. Just as Clinton's support of gays in the military mobilized the religious right in opposition, some Republicans can be painted as villains to stir up the Democrats.[77] In the immediate aftermath of the election, House Speaker Gingrich and Senator Jesse Helms of North Carolina gave Clinton and the Democrats easy openings for appearing presidential and statesmanlike.[78]

While Republicans have the potential to embarrass themselves, control of Congress also gives them the power to embarrass Clinton. Investigations into Whitewater may gain ground now that Republicans call the shots on Capitol Hill. The steady glare of publicity about such allegations may serve to sap Clinton's reputation and distract attention from other topics.

During the remainder of Clinton's term, further political change seems likely. Democratic revitalization could make the Republican gains in 1994 short-lived, akin to Truman's bouncing back from the 1946 setback to victory in 1948. Clinton may turn his fortunes around, giving life once again to the "Comeback Kid" label, but in the aftermath of the 1994 midterm, it seems more likely that Clinton will be the sixth one-term president of the last eight. Resurgent Republicanism could produce further Democratic decline. Or, Republican and Democratic floundering could yield even greater discontent with the two-party system. The resilience of the current two-party system will be sorely tested in the years ahead.

Notes

1. Tsongas, from the neighboring state of Massachusetts, had been expected to win New Hampshire and did, with 33.2 percent of the Democratic vote to Clinton's 24.7 percent. Charles D. Hadley and Harold W. Stanley, "Surviving the 1992 Presidential Nomination Process," in *America's Choice: The Election of 1992*, ed. William Crotty (Guilford, Conn.: Dushkin, 1993), 31–44; Harold W. Stanley and Richard G. Niemi, eds., *Vital Statistics on American Politics*, 4th ed. (Washington, D.C.: CQ Press, 1994), 91.

2. On 1 October 1992 Perot reentered the race as an independent presidential candidate. Barry C. Burden, "Chronology of the 1992 Presidential Campaign," in *Democracy's Feast: Elections in America*, ed. Herbert F. Weisberg (Chatham, N.J.: Chatham House, 1995), 323.

3. Clinton's luck involved continuing indications of poor economic performance and the timely release in late October 1992 of a report by the Iran-*contra* special prosecutor, which contradicted Bush's statements that he been "out of the loop" of decision making on Iran-*contra*. F. Christopher Arterton, "Campaign '92: Strategies and Tactics of the Candidates," in *The Election of 1992: Reports and Interpretations*, ed. Gerald M. Pomper (Chatham, N.J.: Chatham House, 1993), 86–87.

4. Ross K. Baker, "Sorting Out and Suiting Up: The Presidential Nominations," in Pomper, *The Election of 1992*, 40–42; and Walter Dean Burnham, "The Legacy of George Bush: Travails of an Understudy," in Pomper, *The Election of 1992*, 28–30.

5. Stanley and Niemi, *Vital Statistics*, 168.

6. Arterton, "Campaign '92," 77.

7. Gerald M. Pomper, "The Presidential Election," in Pomper, *The Election of 1992*, 145–46.

8. Similarly, some skeptical voters saw Republicans' questioning of Clinton's character as an effort to distract attention from the real issue, the economy. For a discussion of voter attitudes during the campaign, see Kathleen A. Frankovic, "Public Opinion in the 1992 Campaign," in Pomper, *The Election of 1992*, 110–31.

9. The ability to reduce complicated choices to a memorable, punchy line is a hallmark of campaign professionals. One of the better Republican bumper stickers in 1992 urged voters: "Annoy the media. Reelect Bush–Quayle."

10. Michael Nelson, "Conclusion: Some Things Old, Some Things New," in *The Elections of 1992*, ed. Michael Nelson (Washington, D.C.: CQ Press, 1993), 184.

11. Exit polls in 1992 suggested that Perot's presence did not cost Bush the election. If Perot had not been on the ballot, some Perot supporters would have stayed home, others would have split their votes between Bush and Clinton. In only three states did the exit polls suggest Bush would have won. The margin of

error given the sample sizes of the exit polls in those states qualify this conclusion, but the swing of electoral votes from these three states would not have changed the outcome. Pomper, "The Presidential Election," 142, 155 n.11.

12. Marjorie Randon Hershey, "The Congressional Elections," in Pomper, *The Election of 1992*, 162–65, 175–77.

13. Burnham, "The Legacy of Bush," 25–26; Hershey, "The Congressional Elections," 177–80.

14. Baker, "Sorting Out," 66; Arterton, "Campaign '92," 102–3.

15. Samuel Kernell's concept of "negative voting" may best explain the Democratic midterm loss. See "Presidential Popularity and Negative Voting: An Alternative Explanation of the Midterm Congressional Decline of the President's Party," *American Political Science Review* 71 (1977): 44–66.

16. *Congressional Quarterly Weekly Report,* 12 November 1994, 3232; 3 December 1994, 3460.

17. *Congressional Quarterly Weekly Report,* 12 November 1994, 3240.

18. David S. Broder, "Vote May Signal GOP Return as Dominant Party; Victors Push Beyond Solid Southern Base," *Washington Post,* 10 November 1994, A1; *Congressional Quarterly Weekly Report,* 12 November 1994, 3247.

19. Nebraska, not included in these totals, has a nonpartisan, unicameral legislature. National Conference of State Legislatures, "Preliminary Partisan Composition of the State Legislatures," 15 November 1994.

20. As quoted in Richard L. Berke, "G.O.P. Candidates Show Early Gains in Senate Races," *New York Times,* 9 November 1994, B4.

21. Stan Greenberg, speaking at the Democratic Leadership Council press conference, National Press Club, 17 November 1994, Federal News Service transcript.

22. As quoted in Edward Walsh, "After the Vote, the Party Planning; Democrats Wonder Whether Sea Change Is Plea for Centrism," *Washington Post,* 10 November 1994, A27. More succinctly, Wilhelm admitted, "We got our butts kicked." As quoted in Dan Goodgame, "Right Makes Might," *Time,* 21 November 1994, 52.

23. The discussion of exit polls benefits from communications to the H-Pol electronic discussion group by Kathleen Frankovic, director of surveys for CBS News, "Election Post-Mortem," 13 November 1994; and Gary Langer, senior polling analyst for ABC News, "'94 Vote: Republicans Seize the Reins of Discontent," 11 November 1994.

24. Frankovic, "Election Post-Mortem." In another exit poll a majority of voters (59 percent) said their vote was about Clinton but almost as many supported as opposed him: 28 percent of the voters said their House vote was in support of Clinton, 31 percent said against, and 38 percent said it had nothing to do with Clinton. Mitofsky International exit poll of 5,260 voters as reported in the *New York Times,* 10 November 1994, B4.

25. Chuck Alston, "The Minority Strikes Back," *Congressional Quarterly Weekly Report,* 10 April 1993, 908; Jon Healey, "Democrats Look to Salvage Part of Stimulus Plan," *Congressional Quarterly Weekly Report,* 24 April 1993, 1001–4.

26. Peter Passell, "Economic Scene: Why Isn't a Better Economy Helping Clinton's Popularity?" *New York Times,* 3 November 1994, D2.

27. Langer, "'94 Vote."

28. Stan Greenberg on CNN, "Inside Politics," 17 November 1994.

29. Richard L. Berke, "Centrists Are Wary of Clinton Tilting," *New York Times*, 3 December 1993, 24.

30. Chuck Alston, "The President's Position on Taxes: Reversal or 'Healthy Evolution'?" *Congressional Quarterly Weekly Report*, 20 February 1993, 384–86.

31. Walter Dean Burnham, "Realignment Lives," chapter 12 of this volume.

32. Scott Shepard, "Outspoken Surgeon General a Lightning Rod for GOP Storm of Scorn," *Atlanta Journal and Constitution*, 23 September 1994, 15. A month after the midterm election, Clinton forced the resignation of Surgeon General Elders over her suggestion that schools consider teaching masturbation as one way of limiting the spread of the AIDS virus. Douglas Jehl, "Surgeon General Forced to Resign by White House," *New York Times*, 10 December 1994, 1.

33. Frankovic, "Election Post-Mortem."

34. Adam Clymer, "GOP Appears Set to Make Big Gains in Race for House," *New York Times*, 7 November 1994, A1, B10.

35. David S. Cloud, "Decisive Vote Brings Down Trade Walls with Mexico," *Congressional Quarterly Weekly Report*, 20 November 1993, 3174–79; and Robert W. Merry, "Voters' Demand for Change Puts Clinton on Defensive," *Congressional Quarterly Weekly Report*, 12 November 1994, 3207–8.

36. Ironically, in Clinton's first year, congressional support of his positions rivaled the postwar highs for Eisenhower in 1953 and Lyndon Johnson in 1964. Phil Duncan and Steve Langdon, "When Congress Had to Choose, It Voted to Back Clinton," *Congressional Quarterly Weekly Report*, 18 December 1993, 3427–31.

37. Frankovic, "Election Post-Mortem."

38. Figures are from ibid. Before the election, surveys reported an increase in Clinton's approval ratings. For example, see Stephen Labaton, "Bolstered Clinton Campaigns for Allies: Rising in the Polls, President Becomes an Attractive Stump-Mate," *New York Times*, 1 November 1994, A20.

39. R.W. Apple, Jr., "Clinton's Gain: The Big Stick Speaks," *New York Times*, 12 October 1994, A11; and Douglas Jehl, "Clinton Adjusts Itinerary, and His Campaign Focus: Mideast Trip Highlights Foreign Policy," *New York Times*, 19 October 1994, A12.

40. For a review of the realignment and dealignment literature in the light of political developments through the Reagan years, see Paul Allen Beck, "Incomplete Realignment: The Reagan Legacy for Parties and Elections," in *The Reagan Legacy: Promise and Performance*, ed. Charles O. Jones (Chatham, N.J.: Chatham House, 1988), 145–71.

41. *Congressional Quarterly Weekly Report*, 12 November 1994, 3216–18.

42. Merry, "Voters' Demand."

43. Langer, "'94 Vote." Langer notes that "Perot's own clout shouldn't be overestimated. His voters made up just 13 percent of the electorate, down from 19 percent in 1992. And all voters were asked if they 'agree with Ross Perot on most issues.' Just 15 percent said they did."

44. Kathleen Frankovic, "The Republicans' Honeymoon," CBS News poll press release, 29 November 1994.

45. Clyde Wilcox, *The Latest American Revolution? The 1994 Elections and Their Implications for Governance* (New York: St. Martin's Press, 1995), 21; E.J. Dionne, Jr., "A Shift, Not a Mandate," *Washington Post*, 22 November 1994, A21; and Richard L. Berke, "Victories Were Captured by G.O.P. Candidates, Not

the Party's Platform," *New York Times,* 10 November 1994, B1, B4. For a detailing of changes in the party coalitions through 1992, see Harold W. Stanley and Richard G. Niemi, "Partisanship and Group Support, 1952–92," in Weisberg, *Democracy's Feast,* 220–40.

46. Richard Bond on "Morning Edition" (National Public Radio), 18 November 1994.

47. The South is defined here as the eleven states of the former Confederacy, which entails revision of Congressional Quarterly figures based on a thirteen-state South in Rhodes Cook, "Dixie Voters Look Away: South Shifts to the GOP," *Congressional Quarterly Weekly Report,* 12 November 1994, 3231; and Dave Kaplan, "Southern Democrats: A Dying Breed," *Congressional Quarterly Weekly Report,* 19 November 1994, 3356. Jack Bass and Walter DeVries, *The Transformation of Southern Politics: Social Change and Political Consequence Since 1945* (New York: Basic Books, 1977), 36–37.

48. Hastings Wyman, Jr., *Southern Political Report,* 22 November 1994, 1. On the decline of southern Democratic conservative voters, see Edward G. Carmines and Harold W. Stanley, "Ideological Realignment in the Contemporary South: Where Have All the Conservatives Gone?" in *The Disappearing South? Studies in Regional Change and Continuity,* ed. Robert P. Steed, Laurence W. Moreland, and Tod A. Baker (University, Ala.: University of Alabama Press, 1990), 21–33.

49. Burnham, chapter 12 of this volume.

50. Abigail Thernstrom, "Redistricting, in Black and White: By Any Name, It's a Quota," and Allan J. Lichtman, "Quotas Aren't the Issue," in *New York Times,* 7 December 1994, A23. For a general discussion of this phenomenon finding that "plans which advantage blacks also can be expected to advantage Republicans," see Kimball Brace, Bernard Grofman, and Lisa Handley, "Does Redistricting Aimed to Help Blacks Necessarily Help Republicans?" *Journal of Politics* 49 (1987): 169–85.

51. Calculations with exit poll data from *New York Times,* 13 November 1994, 15. Some states differ from the regional patterns. As Hastings Wyman, Jr., points out, "In the 3 contiguous states of North Carolina, South Carolina, and Georgia, for example, there are 29 U.S. Representatives—19 white Republicans, 6 black Democrats, and 4 white Democrats. The same trend is occurring in other states, in state legislative as well as congressional races. When the GOP has a good year, the Voting Rights Act operates so that white, not black, Democrats lose." *Southern Political Report,* 22 November 1994, 2.

52. Corporate PACs have, in the aggregate, favored Senate Republican candidates over Senate Democrats but have contributed more to House Democratic candidates than to House Republicans since 1987–88. Federal Election Commission figures as reported in Stanley and Niemi, *Vital Statistics,* 182–83.

53. Jennifer Babson and Kelly St. John, "Momentum Helps GOP Collect Record Amounts from PACs," *Congressional Quarterly Weekly Report,* 3 December 1994, 3456–59; Peter H. Stone, "The GOP's New Gold Mine," *National Journal,* 3 December 1994, 2869.

54. Robert Pear, "Creating a Republican Wave, Then Riding It In," *New York Times,* 15 November 1994, B10; John Machacek, "Paxon Is Already Eyeing '96," *Rochester Democrat and Chronicle,* 20 November 1994, 10A.

55. In terms of monies raised outside the restrictions of the Federal Election

Campaign Act ("soft money"), Democrats and Republicans reported about $43 million each. Federal Election Commission, "Democrats Increase Pre-election Activity," 2 November 1994; and Weston Kosova, "The Party's Over," *New Republic*, 20 June 1994.

56. Dave Kaplan and Elizabeth A. Palmer, "As Voters Clean House Again, Democrats Are Left in Dust," *Congressional Quarterly Weekly Report*, 6 November 1993, 3065. Commenting on the 1993 November elections, Kaplan and Palmer write: "Out with the in; in with the out. That simple message continued to reverberate across the political landscape.... Much as in 1992, voters signaled their dissatisfaction with incumbents in general and with governmental business as usual. This year, however, the main victims of the house-cleaning were the Democrats...."

57. *Congressional Quarterly Weekly Report*, 14 May 1994, 1242; 28 May 1994, 1410.

58. To smooth fluctuations from poll to poll, figure 6.2 presents a five-poll moving average of Democratic and Republican partisanship. In individual CBS News/*New York Times* polls the percentage of Republican partisans has equaled or surpassed the percentage of Democrats in November 1984; August 1986; September 1989; June and August 1990; January, April, May, and September 1991; and January and April 1994.

59. Richard L. Berke, "Tides That Brought Democrats to G.O.P. Have Turned," *New York Times*, 20 February 1994.

60. Kevin Phillips, quoted in Berke, ibid.

61. Calculated from network exit polls as reported in *New York Times*, 13 November 1994, 15.

62. Republicans and Democrats each made up 37 percent of the voters in 1994 in the Voter News Service exit poll (*National Journal*, 12 November 1994, 2631); Democrats 41 percent and Republicans 35 percent in the Mitofsky International exit poll reported in the *New York Times*, 13 November 1994, 15.

63. Langer, "'94 Vote."

64. *Congressional Quarterly Weekly Report*, 12 November 1994, 3214.

65. Donna Cassata, "Freshman Class Boasts Résumés to Back Up 'Outsider' Image," *Congressional Quarterly Weekly Report*, 12 November 1994, special report, 9.

66. Norman J. Ornstein, "The Rising Republican Centrists: Congress's New Power Brokers," *Washington Post*, 20 November 1994, C3.

67. Robert Shogan, "Post-Election Turmoil Grips Democratic Party from Top to Bottom," *Los Angeles Times*, 21 November 1994, A17; R.W. Apple, Jr., "Clinton's Grip on '96 Ticket Not So Sure," *New York Times*, 21 November 1994, A1, B8; Jack W. Germond and Jules Witcover, "Replace Clinton? Don't Count on It!" *National Journal*, 3 December 1994, 2863.

68. For example, see Theodore J. Lowi, "Still Angry, Voters? Why Not a Third Party?" *USA Today*, 9 November 1994.

69. For example, Michael Lind, "What Bill Wrought: Liberalism's Second Chance," *New Republic*, 5 December 1994, 19–22; and Daniel Cantor and Juliet Schor, "A Populist Manifesto," *New York Times*, 5 December 1994, A19.

70. For example, see the statements of Al From, president of the Democratic Leadership Council, and Will Marshall of the Progressive Policy Institute at the Democratic Leadership Council Press Conference, National Press Club, 17 No-

vember, 1994, Federal News Service transcript. To reclaim "what Arthur Schlesinger, Jr., called the 'vital center' of American politics," advocates of this position urge a new Democratic agenda that breaks out of the "old debates between left and right." See Will Marshall, "Democrats, Arise! (Which Way Is Up?)," *New York Times*, 5 December 1994, A19.

71. Walsh, "After the Vote," A27; and Carl P. Leubsdorf, "Will Clinton Change His Approach?" *Dallas Morning News*, 10 November 1994, A31.

72. The Committee for the Study of the American Electorate estimated 1994 turnout at 38.7 percent of voting-age population (personal communication, 7 December 1994). The 1992 turnout figure is from Walter Dean Burnham (personal communication, 1 March 1993).

73. David Lauter, *Los Angeles Times*, 10 November 1994.

74. Frankovic, "Election Post-Mortem": "Only 16 percent of voters [in 1992] approved of the way Congress was handling its job, but only 20 percent approved in the 1990 exit poll." See also Hershey, "Congressional Election," 164.

75. Republican incumbents registered a 100 percent reelection rate (157 of 157); Democratic incumbents had an 84.4 percent success rate (190 of 225). *Congressional Quarterly Weekly Report*, 12 November 1994, 3232.

76. Richard F. Fenno, Jr., *Home Style: House Members in Their Districts* (Boston: Little, Brown, 1978).

77. Neil A. Lewis, "Liberal Groups Banking on Republicans for Renewal," *New York Times*, 28 November 1994, A15.

78. Gingrich opined that a quarter of the White House staff had used drugs in the past. Helms suggested that the military had no respect for Clinton as commander-in-chief and that if Clinton visited military bases in North Carolina, he had better have a bodyguard.

7

The Clinton Administration
and Interest Groups

GRAHAM K. WILSON

Presidents and Interest Groups: Conceptualizing
Administration–Interest-Group Relations:
Context, Party, Style, and Policy

William Jefferson Clinton came to a Washington often criticized by his fellow citizens for being dominated by "special interests." Running, like so many of his predecessors, against Washington, Candidate Clinton had promised to change this situation. But what have President Clinton's relations with interest groups been like in practice?

Any description of the relationship between presidents and interest groups swiftly encounters two problems that are characteristic of the interest group system: variety and change.

There is enormous variety in the interest-group system. We use the term "interest group" to refer to organizations as diverse as churches, business corporations, universities, the American Automobile Association (AAA), the Sierra Club, and labor unions. These organizations differ in the resources available to them, their internal structures, and their strategies for dealing with the rest of the political system. An administration's relationship with one interest group often will not be the same as its relationship with another; a president who is on cordial terms with environmental groups for that very reason may be on less cordial terms with business groups, or vice versa. Some interest groups will pursue strategies based on discrete and technical discussions with an administration's representatives; other interest groups will pursue a protest strategy, mobilizing against an administration instead of engaging in dialogue with it.

The second problem in describing the president's relationship with the interest-group system is that it changes. During the past thirty years new interest groups such as those representing environmentalists and feminists have become established as major actors in Washington and are particularly important for Democrats. Business has invested heavily in improving its representation in Washington. Other interest groups have declined in importance. We once used to think of the interest-group system as static. We now recognize that the system, like the society it represents, is always changing. Presidents themselves alter—Skowronek would say disrupt[1]—the patterns of politics in Washington, including interest-group politics. A new administration may be more or less favorably disposed toward a particular interest. The new president's goals, policies, and style may also require more or less cooperation from interest groups. A president such as Nixon operating a policy that requires the cooperation of interest groups (such as his attempt to run an incomes policy in 1971) is obliged to adopt an approach to relevant interests (especially unions) that is very different from that of a president such as Reagan, whose policies consisted mostly of the word no. President Johnson's style, perhaps driven by complex psychological factors as well as by political calculation, drove him to seek the company and approval of interest-group leaders; the president of the American Federation of Labor–Congress of Industrial Organization (AFL-CIO) was one of many interest-group leaders regularly courted by Johnson.[2]

The combination of the enormous variety of the interest-group system and the considerable changes occurring within it results in a very complicated, indeed confusing, situation. We may reduce some of the confusion that results from the richness, variety, and impermanence of interest-group relations with presidents by focusing on four factors: context, party, style, and policy. Together these factors explain much in an administration's dealings with interest groups.

Context

President Clinton came to a Washington in which the scale and visibility of interest-group activity in policymaking was greater than ever. The importance of interest-group activity has been a recurring theme in commentary on American politics for at least 150 years. Yet the degree to which interest groups are well organized and respected participants in policymaking varies. Empirical studies suggest that in the 1950s, when academics were more likely than today to interpret American politics in terms of interest-group politics, even business interest groups were poorly financed and organized.[3] Numerous interest groups that we take for granted today, such as Common Cause, Friends of the Earth, and Greenpeace, simply did not exist. President

Clinton's hero, John F. Kennedy, faced fewer and weaker organized interests than Clinton does.

There is no doubt that the number of interests represented effectively in Washington has grown dramatically in the past thirty years.[4] Interests that long seemed unable to organize into groups overcame the difficulties confronting them. Most political scientists, following the work of Mancur Olson,[5] had supposed that collective goods that are in the interests of all —such as a healthy environment, satisfactory consumer goods, and honest government—could not stimulate the organization of groups because if the groups were successful, members and nonmembers alike would receive the public good produced. Despite this skepticism, a huge growth in environmental, consumer, and good-government groups proved that the difficulty could be overcome. Partly in reaction to the perceived threat to their interests that this development posed, business interests also mobilized, modernizing long-established organizations such as the Chamber of Commerce and the National Association of Manufacturers (NAM) while forming new but quickly visible groups such as the Business Roundtable and the National Federation of Independent Business (NFIB). Individual corporations decided that politics was too important to leave to business organizations, however, and the number of corporations that maintained their own offices in Washington increased dramatically.[6] The Merck corporation, which manufactures pharmaceutical drugs, now has twice as many lobbyists itself as the Pharmaceutical Manufacturing Association (PMA), which represents the whole industry.[7]

Numerous explanations have been advanced for this explosion in the number of interests represented in Washington. The activities of interest-group entrepreneurs,[8] the support of patrons such as foundations,[9] and technological developments such as computerized mailing lists and cheaper long-distance phone calls have all been advanced as explanations for the growth of public interest groups. The growth of business interest groups has been explained in terms both of a desire to ward off the attacks of public interest groups[10] and a quest for federal contracts.[11] All are agreed, however, that the interest-group sector of American politics has grown dramatically.

Some impression of the scale and range of interest groups setting up in Washington can be gained from specialized journals such as the *National Journal,* which reports on interest-group politics. A single week's issue in 1993 reported the opening of Washington offices for interests as diverse as the Women's Mining Coalition, the Society of Manufacturing Engineers, and the National Telecommuting and Telework Association. The next week the *National Journal* reported that dentists had diagnosed a need for more lobbyists, adding two lobbyists to their existing strength. Students enrolled at Rutgers, Harvard, Princeton, Vanderbilt, MIT, or the campuses of the University of California system might be surprised to learn that their universities maintain Washington lobbying offices. A lobbying firm, Cassidy and Associates, specializes in helping universities have Congress "earmark" federal research funds for them so that they do not have to try to obtain those funds through a process of competitive and expert evaluation ("peer review") run by bodies such as the National Science Foundation.[12] While some declining industries and corporations have reduced their Washington representation —the Tobacco Institute was forced recently to cut employment at its Washington office—the general trend has been for more and more interests to hire more and more lobbyists to represent them.

The growth in the number of interest groups has been accompanied by an increase in the visibility of interest-group activity. Interest-group contributions through political action committees (PACs) are a crucial and visible part of most politicians' campaign funds. Journalistic accounts of policymaking on controversial issues in Washington such as tax reform,[13] gun control,[14] and health insurance stress the number and centrality of lobbyists involved. The interest groups themselves have tended, like presidents, to "go public," seeking to expand their attentive constituencies around the country not only by mobilizing members through mass mailings or satellite hookups to local branches but by appealing to the general public through television commercials. The famed "Harry and Louise" commercials attacking the Clinton health-care proposals were the most successful (though rarely shown outside the Washington, D.C., area) in an interest-group advertising campaign that cost over $60 million. This was more than the candidates spent on the 1992 presidential election campaign and yet only part of an estimated $300 million spent by interest groups in trying to influence the politics of health insurance.

Recent presidents, starting with Carter, have responded to the increased activity of interest groups and their own needs to mobilize a constituency for their programs by devoting greater staff resources to interest-group liaison.[15] All presidents have contacts with interest-group representatives. But since Carter, a unit in the White House staff has been given primary responsibility for this task. The standing of this unit within the White House has varied, but recent presidents have decided that they are unwilling to rely on the old methods of personal contact or on assigning a White House staffer informally to liaise with an interest group. Within the Clinton White House, the Office of Public Liaison (as the unit is called) has been one of the more stable parts of the White House staff, with the same person, Alexis M. Herman, in charge from the beginning of the administration. Herman has sixteen people working for her, specializing in contacts with different interests. Herman's own "beat" is black interest groups and business. Unlike some of her predecessors in other administrations, Herman seems to have managed to maintain easy access to the president by having a reputation for being "the first aide to jump into the limousine with the president when he was on his way to an event."[16]

Even though interest groups are more numerous and active, and their links to the presidency are more institutionalized, they are not necessarily more powerful than in the past. The number and variety of interest groups ironically contains important checks on their power. The popular perception that Washington is increasingly dominated by "special interests" (a phrase used to describe interest groups with which one disagrees or to which one does not belong) has created the opportunity for politicians to run against interest groups. Millionaire Senator Herb Kohl (D-Wisc.) could claim to be "no one's Senator but your own" because he could afford to finance his election campaigns from his own large bank accounts; Ross Perot applied this strategy to presidential politics. Once elected, politicians are able to capitalize on public distrust by claiming the credit for "standing up to the special interests." Giving in to interest groups is not the only way to succeed politically.

In practice, politicians are rarely in danger of having to oppose *every* interest group. The increased number and variety of interest groups in Washington makes it even more likely than in the past that a politician can find a sympathetic interest group to support his or her position on a policy issue. While some interest groups are much more powerful than others, the likelihood has increased of equal and opposite interest-group forces opposing each other on a particular issue; the National Rifle Association (NRA) now confronts an effectively organized if less well financed coalition of groups opposed to gun violence. In their study of interest-group politics in the 1950s, Bauer, Pool, and Dexter noted that in interest-group politics, equal and opposite forces cancel each other out.[17] In the 1990s, the American interest-group system is closer than it once was to the antidote for interest-group power that James Madison suggested in *Federalist* No. 51 at the founding of the Republic: interest must be set against interest so that they hold each other in check.

The plethora of interest groups also provides opportunities for the White House. We often imagine that interest groups respond quickly and predictably to policy proposals. The process is rarely so automatic. Even the best equipped interest groups have trouble tracking the vast numbers of bills and regulations under consideration in Washington. Even the best staffed groups have difficulty assessing the impact of new policy proposals on their interests. An important element in supporting or opposing new policies in Washington is mobilizing interest groups. Groups may need their attention drawn to policy proposals, or more probably, to details of policy proposals that they may have missed. The skilled politician will try to persuade groups to interpret a policy proposal's impact on their interests in a way that suits the politician's purposes. To borrow from the terminology of international relations, groups' definitions of their self-interests are often constructed in a political process.

In addition, most interest groups today campaign as part of an alliance. Interest groups usually need to combine to contest important legislation, but as interest groups become more numerous and varied, combining becomes more difficult. In many campaigns, such as those on tax reform in the 1980s, political consultants provide the necessary integration, creating new, deliberately short-lived interest-group confederations intended to last only as long as the legislative battle.

The White House Office of Public Liaison (OPL) is ideally situated to influence the mobilization of interest groups, the process of constructing their understanding of their self-interest, and the creation of interest-group alliances. With the help of lobbyists in other parts of the executive branch, OPL has the resources to mobilize interest groups in support of administration policies. Supported by the expertise of the executive branch, OPL can work to convince groups that their interests would be advanced by administration policies. OPL can constitute the core of a coalition around which interest groups can coalesce. As is the case in the president's dealings with other parts of the political system, these advantages may be used more or less effectively.

Two other factors in the context in which the Clinton administration took office influenced the prospects for interest groups. First, there was widespread agreement that the very large budget deficits created under President Reagan must be reduced and should be reduced at least in part by reducing government expenditures. The climate was not, in short, conducive to any large increase in government expenditures, a simple fact of considerable importance for interest groups in domestic politics. In contrast, the ending of the Cold War provided new opportunities for foreign policy interest groups. As the United States no longer had a single, generally overriding foreign policy objective, the containment of the Soviet Union, groups were less constrained in pressing their concerns. President Clinton's willingness to accede to demands from American supporters of the Irish Republican Army (IRA) that the leader of its political arm, Gerry Adams, be admitted to the United States before the IRA's suspension of terrorism reflected in part that Britain's loyal support for the United States during the Cold War was no longer needed. The calculus that had caused American presidents to avoid unnecessary offense to Britain no longer applied.

Party

Political parties are generally linked to interest groups, and American political parties are no exception. President Clinton, like many politicians, asserted his willingness to stand up to "special interests," but he came into office with the support of interest groups allied to the Democratic Party.

The Democrats' interest-group coalition is both diverse and changing.

Ever since the New Deal, Democratic presidents have been supported by labor unions, particularly industrial unions such as the United Auto Workers (UAW). In the 1992 election, as in every presidential election since the 1930s bar one (1972) and in numerous congressional contests, unions had been important sources of money and campaign assistance for the Democrats. Union support for the Democrats was particularly strong in 1992 because of the desperate times on which unions had fallen. Union membership had dropped to around 16 percent of the workforce, and only 12 percent in the private sector. Apart from their support for policies advocated by Clinton during the campaign that would affect the population as a whole, such as national health insurance, unions had good reason to believe that their very institutional survival depended on an end to Republican control of the White House. Reagan and Bush nominees to bodies such as the National Labor Relations Board (NLRB) and the federal courts had reinterpreted federal labor laws in a manner highly disadvantageous to unions. While other factors, such as changing employment patterns and their own failings, contributed to the weakness of unions, changes in federal labor law and in the regulatory environment were probably essential preconditions for a revival of the labor movement in the United States. Neither could be achieved without Democratic control of the White House.

Yet the weakness of the unions also made them less desirable partners. Even when unions were much stronger, as in the 1950s and 1960s, they had failed to secure changes in *labor* legislation they favored. Labor's victories in that period, such as the 1964 Civil Rights Act and the 1965 Voting Rights Act, had come as part of coalition partnerships. On labor issues, even many Democrats treated unions as just another interest group. Now, with unions much weaker, this tendency could be expected to be stronger.

Moreover, for many Democrats of Clinton's generation, unions were not a group that attracted instinctive emotional support. Unions, to Democrats under age fifty, had links to the Mafia or were led by crusty, intolerant old men who had supported American involvement in Vietnam. Newer interest groups such as feminists, environmentalists, and civil rights groups were more likely to attract support. The defining political issues for Clinton's generation had been ones such as Vietnam. Clinton's own unwillingness to fight in the war, so typical of college-educated people of his generation, had been a major topic in the campaign. Although some unions, such as the UAW, had also been against American involvement in Vietnam, most had supported it. For many years after the war, the political resources commanded by unions had made it politic to forget these differences, but the newer interest groups commanded vast resources. EMILY's List, the feminist organization that provides female candidates with cash, is now one of the nation's largest PACs. In response to the antienvironmental attitudes of President Reagan and some of his appointees, such as Interior Secretary James

Watt, environmental interest groups had grown throughout the 1980s, while unions declined. It was no longer clear that the balance of political power in the Democratic interest-group coalition lay with the unions. On some issues, such as family-leave legislation, which President Bush had vetoed and Clinton supported, the newer interest groups in the Democratic coalition and the unions agreed. On other issues, such as protecting endangered species or departing from seniority in laying off or promoting workers, unions and the newer members of the Democratic interest-group coalition were likely to differ.

President Clinton therefore faced a series of dilemmas in relation to his interest-group constituency.

First, how close did Clinton wish to be to *any* interest group, given the popularity of attacks on "special interests" in 1992? Although the attacks were general, the Democrats felt particularly vulnerable, perhaps because of the interests with which they were identified, and perhaps because of the success congressional Democrats had in attracting PAC contributions from such a wide variety of interests, including business. The PAC dependency of Democrats made them look as though they were up for sale. Clinton sought to challenge this image as a candidate. In Arkansas, Clinton had secured not only one of his policy triumphs, educational reform, but also political success by confronting one of the interest groups to which he had previously been close, the teachers' union. Similar opportunities would occur in Washington.

Second, would President Clinton give priority to the traditional members of the Democratic coalition, the unions and their concerns, or would he devote scarce political resources to addressing the concerns of the newer members of the Democrats' interest-group coalition? Clinton's victory reflected his success in winning back the Reagan Democrats, blue-collar workers repelled by the social values of many of the newer interest groups, such as Hillary Clinton's favorite cause, the Children's Defense Fund, which emphasized supporting single-parent families. The emphasis on economic issues—embodied in the apparently misquoted slogan from Clinton campaign headquarters, "It's the economy, stupid!"[18]—was much more attractive to union members than the liberal foreign policy or social values with which nearly all Democratic presidential candidates had been identified since 1972. Yet, apart from the closeness of the Clintons to the Children's Defense Fund, their awareness of how political resources had shifted to the newer members of the Democratic interest-group coalition was illustrated by the determination with which Clinton sought contributions for his campaign from homosexual groups, particularly in Hollywood. Clinton faced the danger of disappointing either his traditional Democratic supporters or newer social-reform groups.

Presidential Style

Neither by conviction nor personality was President Clinton attached firmly to particular policies or positions. Clinton had promoted himself as a "New Democrat," one who sought new ideas with which to tackle old problems. Historians might have noted that ideological rigidity had never been a hallmark of the Democrats during the New Deal and that almost every Democratic presidential candidate since Truman had claimed to be a "New Democrat." Nonetheless, Clinton's promotion of himself as someone who was open to fresh thinking and was not committed to past policies made him open to arguments from interest groups, among others. Clinton has been described by both friends and critics as a "policy wonk," a president who somewhat unusually enjoys debating the details of domestic policy proposals. From the perspective of interest-group lobbyists, here was a president whose mind could be changed.

Critics of President Clinton, such as the journalist Michael Kelly, have suggested that this openness to argument is accompanied by less admirable personal characteristics such as irresoluteness and an almost desperate desire to please.[19] President Clinton vacillates, in this view, partly because he cannot make up his own mind and partly because he wants to please the last group to have spoken to him. The eminent political scientist Richard Fenno has suggested that Clinton is an "easy touch" for those who bargain with him: "Even before you say trick or treat you get the candy."[20] The New Republic noted that this flexibility can have startling consequences for American foreign policy. The United States, having committed itself to the independence of the small Macedonian republic of the former Yugoslav Federation, deployed 600 American troops to act as a "trip wire" in the event of an attack on the infant state. An arcane dispute between Macedonia and Greece about the republic's name resulted in the mobilization of the Greek American lobby against Macedonia. Clinton's senior aide, Greek American George Stephanopoulos, brought a delegation of Greek American lobbyists to see the president at a meeting from which the State Department was excluded. Clinton, who had approved a decision to open a legation and deploy troops in Macedonia, now agreed to the delegation's requests not to recognize Macedonia. The United States was left in the somewhat unusual position of having sent troops to protect a country it did not recognize. As the New Republic journalist Hanna Rosin commented, "such flip flops are nothing new, but this one was particularly instructive. It shows what happens when a well organized Democratic interest group meets a president, who, at least when it comes to foreign policy, just can't say no to anyone."[21]

Macedonia was part of a pattern of vulnerability to foreign policy interest groups, as Rosin had argued. The decision to grant Gerry Adams a visa before the IRA's suspension of terrorism was similarly the result of last-minute pressure from American sympathizers with the IRA. The State Department had advised that the established American policy of refusing visas to supporters of terrorism be maintained; at the last moment, the White House overruled it. Even the decision to invade Haiti was in part the result of pressure from African American lobbyists and the congressional Black Caucus, which understandably argued that if President Clinton was prepared, as he claimed, to intervene in the Balkans to save Europeans from atrocities, he should be prepared to do the same in the Caribbean to save people of African descent from equally dreadful treatment.[22] In one of the most bizarre twists in his presidency, Clinton agreed to receive at the White House Salman Rushdie, the British author threatened with death by Iran for blasphemy in his novel *The Satanic Verses.* No sooner was the meeting over than Clinton tried to reduce criticism of his gesture from Islamic groups by describing it as an encounter in a hallway, not a real meeting at all.[23]

Thus, as a result of either open-minded flexibility in his thinking or a chronic desire to please in his personality, President Clinton presented an attractive target for lobbyists. If the president disagreed with an interest group at the outset, it was entirely possible he would agree with them by the end.

Policy

The final element in our analysis is the policies that the president has advocated. As noted earlier, some forms of public policy are based on close cooperation and partnership between business, labor, and government; such forms are known as corporatism. The Clinton administration did have a corporatist streak in its thinking, represented most clearly by Secretary of Labor Robert Reich. The Clinton administration developed close links to Detroit, pleasing the "Big Three" auto manufacturers not only by reducing the CAFE (corporate average fuel economy) standards expected from the cars they produce but by entering into a somewhat corporatist partnership with them in providing resources for research on fuel efficiency. In another example of a collaborative relationship with business, the Department of Transportation dropped a lawsuit aimed at forcing General Motors to recall trucks whose fuel tanks were thought likely to explode in accidents in return for a contribution of $50 million by General Motors to the department's research on safety. Yet the opportunities for corporatist partnerships between economic interests and government are few in the United States,[24] and the corporatist tendency in the administration's thinking was reflected more in the labor secretary's rhetoric than in public policy.

In contrast, a large number of administration policies could be counted on to mobilize interest groups. President Clinton's leading domestic commitment, the creation of a national health insurance scheme, was a case in point. Every major proposal to reform the American health-care system—

from President Truman's unsuccessful proposal for a national health scheme to President Johnson's successful promotion of government health-care assistance for the elderly to President Carter's vain attempt to contain health-care costs—has been accompanied by a major battle between interest groups. As a leading scholar of American health politics, Theodore Marmor, has written, "National health insurance generates an ideological intensity matched by few other issues in American politics. The antagonists in the debate are well defined and well known, and they have remained remarkably stable over time."[25] The medical industry has some of the best-known and best-organized lobbies in Washington, including the insurance industry, the American Medical Association (AMA), and the hospitals, not to mention the unions, which have been the bedrock of the campaign for national health insurance. All these groups have very large PACs, together contributing to the vast majority of representatives and senators.

Other equally obvious battles would result from the administration's attempts to reduce environmentally damaging subsidies (in the form of low rents) for ranchers raising cattle on federal lands in western states and for corporations extracting valuable minerals from under these lands. The administration was to lose both these proposals as a result of opposition from the interests affected. Other issues that became very prominent for the administration, such as gays in the military and the North American Free Trade Agreement (NAFTA), were likely to attract extensive lobbying.

Relations with interest groups were, or at least should have been, of considerable importance for the administration. As we noted earlier, the legislative process in Washington is accompanied by the creation of temporary, ad hoc coalitions organized around either political entrepreneurs ("contract lobbyists") or a coalition formed by the administration. While few would pretend that interest-group politics alone determines the fate of legislation, the administration's success or failure in forging interest-group alliances would have a considerable impact on its prospects for success.

Stumbling, Succeeding, and Losing

One of the oddities of the first eight months of the Clinton administration was its apparent sharp tilt toward the newer members of the Democratic interest-group coalition. This tilt carried with it severe potential consequences: the loss of the Reagan Democrats won back by the campaign emphasis on "the economy, stupid!" Conversely, it gained little inasmuch as the newer groups being favored had no prospects of supporting Republicans or being supported by them. It is hard to imagine it was anything other than an unintended consequence of the administration's policies, a result of what Elizabeth Drew described as the unintended consequence of changes in the administration's agenda order. "What most of the Clinton people—including

Clinton—didn't realize until later was that ... the president, who had run for office as a centrist, was placing himself on the left side of the spectrum, appearing to be responding to interest groups on that side."[26]

The speedy discovery that the campaign promise to produce a health-care plan within a hundred days could not be kept, and the decision to give second place to welfare reform, scarcely an attractive issue for the Democrats, left a gaping hole in the political agenda. Journalists needed issues about to which to write, and the administration gave them a series that appeared to emphasize its links to the new interest-group members of the Democratic coalition.

The first of these issues was that of gays in the military. President Clinton had promised gay groups, which he courted during the election campaign, that he would end the ban on gays serving in their nation's armed services. Perhaps because Clinton failed to act forthrightly, by ordering the armed services to admit gays in the same manner that President Truman had ordered them to end racial segregation, the issue became more prominent. Both congressional Republicans and conservative Democrats, especially the powerful chair of the Senate Armed Services Committee, Sam Nunn (D-Ga.), took advantage of Clinton's hesitation to assert their own strength. Although the president retreated to a policy in which gays could serve as long as they concealed their sexual orientation (a practice termed "don't ask, don't tell"), his identification with gay rights was reinforced even while he disappointed gay interest groups.

A second set of controversies that reinforced this apparent tilt arose from President Clinton's choices for executive branch posts. During the campaign, Clinton had promised to appoint an administration "that looked like America." In practice, this easily lampooned pledge—for the criteria for "looking like America" could be many and, in the hands of late-night comedians, bizarre—meant that he would appoint more racial minorities, Hispanics, and women than President Bush did. Moreover, the administration interpreted this policy to mean that the people appointed should not only be from relevant demographic groups (women, African Americans, etc.) but should be acceptable to the Washington offices of interest groups that claimed to speak for those sections of the population. Being a woman would often not be enough; having the endorsement of the National Organization for Women (NOW) was also required. The administration soon found itself defending choices that made perfect sense to the Washington representatives of the newer interest-group members of the Democratic coalition (such as NOW) but that were harder to sell to the country as a whole. Many of the posts involved were minor, but the political costs were significant. The choice of Sheldon Hackney to chair the National Endowment for the Humanities—a man who as president of the University of Pennsylvania had overseen the adoption of a highly "politically correct" set of policies including a very restrictive speech code—produced one of the few Senate debates ever on a nomination to that post. Above all, the nomination of Lani Guinier to serve as assistant attorney general for civil rights appeared to demonstrate—however she attempted to define her views—a commitment to precisely those policies of placing affirmative action ahead of core American values that had lost the Democrats so much support in the previous twenty years. For good measure, the abrupt decision to abandon Guinier before she had an opportunity to defend her views publicly made the president seem weak at best, and at worst, disloyal to a friend.

The impression that the president had tilted toward the new liberal interest groups in the Democratic coalition was also reinforced by the accident of Clinton's inheriting NAFTA from his Republican predecessor. In an inversion of the historical pattern, freer trade became identified as a more conservative and Republican, rather than a liberal and Democratic, issue. Above all, labor, especially the AFL-CIO, had drifted from a general support for freer trade in the 1960s (when the AFL-CIO supported reciprocal tariff reduction) to a strong protectionist position in the 1990s. Unions made opposition to NAFTA their major legislative goal in 1993. Whose side was the president on? Not unusually, it was hard to tell. Clinton had criticized NAFTA during the 1992 campaign, and throughout 1993 his attitude remained ambivalent. The president's ambivalence allowed opponents of NAFTA to make progress, as Democratic leaders in the House such as Representative Richard Gephardt of Missouri were free to organize the opposition to the treaty without seeming to oppose a president of their own party. In the end, Clinton turned, perhaps reflecting that even an American president as little interested in foreign policy as he could not ignore the damage to the prestige and authority of the United States that rejection of NAFTA would cause. A determined presidential campaign around the nation as well as in Washington produced a last-minute victory that was an impressive achievement for the president, even though its difficulty had been increased by his own prevarication.

Yet victory came at the cost of a major breach with the unions. After NAFTA was approved, the AFL-CIO made dire, if unrealistic, threats of the revenge it would exact on Democrats who had betrayed it. A breach with labor was not a disaster for a Democratic president. As Hillary Clinton reminded people, a fight with the teachers' union had done wonders for their standing when Bill was governor of Arkansas: "You show people you are willing to fight when you fight your friends."[27] Coupled with areas where the president had been willing initially to take political hits to please his constituents, such as gays in the military or appointing people "who look like America," the president's willingness to upset labor seemed to demonstrate his tilt toward the newer liberal interest groups in the Democratic alliance. He seemed willing to placate gays while upsetting labor. Yet the administration needed the support of unions as part of its coalition for health-care reform. A rare—and highly successful—example of the use of Hillary Clinton as a conciliator was to have her sit next to the aged president of the AFL-CIO, Lane Kirkland, during the president's State of the Union speech to Congress.

In contrast, the fight for NAFTA brought the administration closer to a number of business groups. Administration lobbyists worked in partnership with business lobbyists; a group of thirty leading business lobbyists met representatives of the administration every Monday at the Washington offices of Allied Signal to coordinate strategy.[28] The U.S. Chamber of Commerce also campaigned hard for NAFTA, using the "high tech" equipment of which it is proudest, its satellite link to branches across the country, to rally support for the treaty.[29] In its first year, the administration's interest in recruiting corporations to fight for health-care reform (discussed later), NAFTA, and the tendency to stress deficit reduction more than new programs, as described by Bob Woodward,[30] created an impression of a Democratic administration that might be at odds with labor but that was trying to be close to business.

Health Care

As noted earlier, health-care reform was both the major and the most predictable battle of the first half of Clinton's first term. The president had staked his reputation on achieving health-care reform based on universal, irrevocable coverage for all Americans. It was obvious that achieving health-care reform of this nature would require a skillful strategy for dealing with well-organized interests.

The president had several strategies to consider for dealing with interest groups on health reform. One would have been a strategy of confrontation, "going public" to use Kernell's term,[31] enjoying the support of obvious allies such as labor unions and attempting to overpower opposition. This was a high-risk strategy, and two considerations precluded it. First, the administration was unable to coordinate the political campaign for the measure with the policymaking process. Like a World War I general who ended the artillery barrage hours before the infantry advanced, Clinton delivered a masterful speech on health-care reform long before the administration's plan was ready. Moreover, the plan, when unveiled, proved to be so complicated that it was politically unsalable to a mass public. Second, as we have seen, relations with health-care reform's most obvious allies—unions—had been complicated by the decision to make the ratification of NAFTA such a high priority.

A second and very different plan would have been to rely on an "inside the Beltway" strategy that would have incorporated a wide variety of interest groups into a health-care reform coalition. It was easier to imagine a diverse coalition being assembled in the 1990s than ever before, notwithstanding the constancy of past divisions on health care that Marmor noted. Labor unions had been in favor of national health insurance since the idea was first proposed in the United States. But two of the idea's long-time opponents were now potential allies. Doctors, irritated by constraints on their cherished "freedom to practice" imposed by private insurance companies, viewed the threat of government-mandated health insurance with less alarm than had their predecessors, when the AMA fought the "socialized medicine" of Medicare with such ferocity in the 1960s. Smaller insurance companies faced the threat of extinction as market forces resulted in the rapid expansion of HMOs (health maintenance organizations) owned by the largest insurance companies.

Most tempting of all was the possibility of an alliance with big business. Corporations such as the auto manufacturers, long used to paying for ever more expensive health-care insurance for their workers, had come to realize that they were in effect also paying for the uninsured. If only because of federal requirements, American hospitals were in practice not free to refuse to treat people who came to their emergency rooms, whether or not they had health insurance. Moreover, tight cost constraints in some sectors of the health industry (e.g., Medicare, many HMO agreements) resulted in costs being transferred to other sectors, especially those paid for through the health plans of large corporations, where cost controls were less stringent. As a result, according to Cathie Martin's brilliant description,[32] there existed among the more sophisticated officials of large corporations a large constituency for health reform. Even the U.S. Chamber of Commerce—which has opposed almost every extension of the welfare state—was for a time on record in favor of government's mandating health insurance coverage by employers.

There is no doubt that managing an "inside the Beltway" coalition in favor of health reform would have been difficult. Business groups offer their members many veto rights over changes in policy, so that offending a single large corporation or industry was likely to result in business organizations representing large corporations sitting out the fight. The well-organized National Federation of Independent Business (NFIB) was always likely to oppose national health insurance; NFIB was renowned for both its pugnacious style and its ability to stir up opponents of legislation in most congressional districts. Courting the AMA would also have presented challenges. The more conservative members of its House of Delegates allied with the head of its Washington office, Lee Stillwell (a former employee of the NFIB), against its vice-president in Chicago, John Crosby, who was to accept quite radical changes in the health-care system.[33]

Yet the administration's failure resulted primarily from swinging uneasily between a conciliatory strategy and confrontation. While the administration could see the advantages of a "Coalition for Health" led by a chief executive officer of a large corporation, it could not in the end bring itself to follow a coalition approach. The vast task force led by the administration's most thorough "policy wonk," Ira Magaziner, failed to involve a number of crucial interest groups such as the AMA in its deliberations. This may have been the result of an entirely reasonable calculation that no administration could win the support of all the groups with a stake in the vast health-care industry. Yet some of the groups that were excluded, such as the AMA, which had become progressively more disenchanted with the bureaucracy of private health insurers, were not necessarily opposed to change. Other excluded groups, such as the Health Insurance Association, which represented the smaller insurance companies, moved quickly onto the offensive.

The opponents of health-care reform who felt their incomes threatened could indeed mobilize vast resources. Even before the president's health-care plan as a whole had died, important elements of the reform package had been abandoned in the face of vigorous attacks by interest groups. An important part of the administration's case for health-care reform had been that the existing system cost everyone—patients, government, and employers—too much; the proportion of gross national product (GNP) devoted to health care in the United States (about 14 percent) was far higher than in any other country. Yet by the summer of 1994, cost containment had disappeared. Cost containment succumbed to what has been termed Newman's law of health-care reform: every dollar of what some people call waste is someone else's income. Groups that felt threatened by cost containment created a special coalition, the Health Care Leadership Council. The activities of the council provide a classic example of how a modern interest campaign operates both within and outside the Beltway. Related PACs contributed $26 million to representatives and senators. One firm, the Ridley Group, run by a former aide to Senator Frank Lautenberg (D-N.J.), was hired to produce commercials attacking cost containment. Another firm, Bonner and Associates, which specializes in grassroots campaigning, was hired for $2 million to stir up protest across the country. Bonner and Associates employed ten veteran Democratic organizers to work in seventy "swing" congressional districts, often working with local chambers of commerce. Radio advertisements urged outraged voters to telephone a number that was in fact Bonner's; the staff of Bonner and Associates then "patched" each phone call to the office of the relevant representative. Focusing more on local opinion leaders, Senator Paul Tsongas was hired to spend a few days a month to make the pitch to the editorial boards of newspapers. While it is never possible to prove that an interest-group campaign destroyed a policy proposal, all this activity must have given legislators pause.

In contrast, the forces favoring health-care reform were much less visible. The AFL-CIO favored reform, yet was nowhere near as visible in campaigning for it as it had been in campaigning for Medicare in the early 1960s. Individual unions, such as the UAW, found that some of the specific proposals developed by Hillary Clinton's and Ira Magaziner's task force could even be to the disadvantage of their members, who already had high levels of health insurance. No groups appeared to campaign as vociferously in favor of health-care reform as its opponents campaigned against it. Whether more enthusiastic support could have been obtained from unions had the administration done less to offend them is an intriguing if unanswerable question. In practice, the mobilized interest groups were skewed heavily against health reform.

Meanwhile, the administration stumbled in its attempts to run an "inside the Beltway" campaign. A key element in this strategy had been recruiting big business to the cause of health-care reform, a strategy that seemed promising. In part, this reflected a general failing of the administration's lobbyists. The Office of Public Liaison has been criticized for its failure to develop the links to business groups that had seemed to be strengthening in 1993. Martin quotes a corporate lobbyist: "Outreach to them [the Office of Public Liaison] means access to those who have been with them from the beginning and shutting out everyone else."[34] Above all, while the prospect of a deal with business remained, Hillary Clinton switched to a strategy of popular mobilization, singling out insurance companies and pharmaceutical manufacturers as the villains of health care. While this strategy made sense in terms of a confrontational strategy—as interest groups well know, mobilization generally requires a villain to oppose—it resulted inevitably and predictably in the collapse of efforts to create a coalition for health-care reform that included business. Organizations such as the Business Roundtable refused to fight in alliance with an administration that was attacking some of their members. The issue was recast, to the disadvantage of the administration, as one of big government versus industry. Business groups that had earlier supported health-care reform speedily retreated from their commitments, and by the end of the summer, the administration's health-care plan was dead.

The failure to secure health-care reform resulted from many factors. One of them was the incoherence of the administration's strategy for dealing with the numerous and well-equipped interest groups that everyone with Washington experience knew would be active on this issue. Hillary Clinton argued after the fight was lost that "this battle was lost on paid media and paid direct mail."[35] Yet both could have been expected, and a strategy for getting health-care reform should have included a plan for dealing with such predictable interest-group activities. The Clintons claimed to be willing to make deals with interest groups on the issue, yet they struck most groups and observers as inflexible from the moment their plan was developed by a task force that shut out of its deliberations some of the most vitally concerned groups. The Clintons, particularly Hillary Clinton, zigzagged between a conciliatory approach and attempts at a strategy based on popular mobilization,[36] a strategy that, when tried, was pursued with striking incompetence. In the end, the administration seemed unwilling to deal yet unable to fight.

The best possible interest-group strategy that could have been devised might not have resulted in the adoption of national health insurance. But the interest-group strategy followed by the Clintons was not the best possible strategy. It is clear that the White House failed to take advantage of the possibilities open to the presidency in the contemporary interest-group system. These are in general the opportunities to mobilize groups, to define the issues to groups, and to form alliances centered on the White House Office of Public Liaison. All these opportunities existed in the health-care debate. In the early 1990s, the configuration of interest groups on the health-care issue was unusually fluid. Contrary to Marmor's picture of stability in the predispositions and alliances of interest groups involved in health-care politics, every major interest was both unsure of where its own advantage lay and how it should react to the Clintons' plan. Unions worried about the implications for their members' existing benefits, big business teetered between a reflexive opposition to "big government" and its self-interest in escaping paying a disproportionate share of the costs of the nation's health-care system, and the medical profession itself doubted that the present system should continue. Not surprisingly, major interest groups such as the AMA were deeply divided internally.[37] Even the insurance industry, sections of which mobilized against the plan, was deeply divided between smaller companies who paid for the "Harry and Louise" commercials through the Health Insurance Association of America (HIAA) and large companies for whom the Clinton plan promised to be, in the words of a public interest group's letter to the *New York Times*, "the deal of a lifetime."[38]

In the face of such divisions and uncertainties among interest groups, the administration should have been able to define the issues involved for interest groups in a manner that suited its own advantage. The opportunities had never been greater for construction of new interest-group alliances, disrupting the old grouping against national health insurance. An incomplete mobilization of even the natural supporters of national health insurance such as labor unions left a minority of interest groups, notably the NFIB and the HIAA, dominating the political stage. Ironically, even the HIAA was dissatisfied with the outcome, believing that some reforms in the current system were necessary. The administration had, however, not devoted much thought to the politics of health; its plan had been constructed, in the words of a *New York Times* reporter, "with a zealous attention to detail and a deaf ear to politics."[39] The administration's Republican opponents did not make the same mistake. Republican leaders such as the then minority whip in the House of Representatives, Newt Gingrich, worked assiduously to get wavering interest groups such as the AMA back in line. Gingrich, for example, contacted all 450 members of the AMA House of Delegates to persuade them to reverse their association's support for employer mandates.[40] The presidency had far more resources than the minority whip for such political persuasion and mobilization; the Clinton administration failed to use them.

Conclusion

It may seem harsh to emphasize the fate of the administration's health plan in assessing its competence in dealing with interest groups. Yet this was the largest domestic issue facing the administration, and the necessity for a strategy to deal with interest groups in this area was evident. Nor should we assume that this period reflected the limits of the administration's accomplishments in either health care or relations with interest groups more generally. As a consequence of the change in the political landscape produced by the Republican victories in the 1994 elections, health care in the form proposed by the Clintons would not be revived in 1995. The administration may well have the capacity for developing better strategies with interest groups, particularly if it is able to win a second term. (In 1995, the administration mended fences with traditionally Democratic interests such as unions by taking a tough stand on trade with Japan.) President Clinton may make errors, but as his critics acknowledge, he is eager to learn. The extensive changes in the White House staff in the fall of 1994 demonstrated an awareness of the need to integrate the work of the White House staff and the administration's strategies. On taking over as chief of staff, Leon Panetta told the *New York Times* that his task was to transform the White House staff from a campaigning to a governing organization.[41] The administration's relations with interest groups demonstrated the scope available for improvement.

Government is not only influenced by interest groups, but it in turn influences them. While the Clinton administration has scarcely had time to change the interest-group system profoundly, it has exerted a modest influence. The Clinton administration presented new opportunities to lobbyists with better access to the new administration than their rivals. The law firm of Akin, Gump, Strauss, Hauer and Feld could capitalize on the contacts of partners such as former Democratic National Committee chairman Robert Strauss and Vernon Jordan better than when the Republicans held the White House. Clients as diverse as American Airlines and the governments of Chile, South Korea, and Colombia retained the law firm to capitalize on its continuing political links; Jordan, for example, chaired a dinner for the Democratic National Committee in July 1994 that raised $3.5 million.[42] Almost amusingly, the Rose law firm in which Hillary Clinton had worked in Arkansas opened an office in Washington in an attempt to capitalize on its contacts, only to be overtaken by the Whitewater affair.[43]

Shifts in influence between lobbyists follow any change of administration. But what of the administration's impact on the interest-group system as a whole? There has been an impact, but not of the type the president wished for when, in his speech to Congress presenting his first budget, he warned that "special interests" would be fighting him all the way. The Clinton administration's attempts, in very difficult circumstances, to bring about long-awaited reform in areas such as health care have contributed to a further growth in the interest-group system. Jack Bonner, who made his living from organizing "grassroots" campaigns for interest groups against the Clintons' health-care plan, realized as early as February 1993 that the president was good for at least one industry: lobbying.[44]

Sympathizers with the Clinton administration may argue that this is exactly the point. As Stephen Skowronek has written, different presidents take different tests.[45] This chapter gives support to one of Skowronek's arguments about the modern presidency: presidents today are surrounded by a thicker structure of constraining institutions (in this case, interest groups) than their predecessors were. We might also argue that an activist president necessarily faces more difficulties in dealing with interest groups than a president who is not trying to change policy much. Clinton, so goes the argument, faced a tougher exam than, for example, President Reagan. Yet this alluring argument overlooks the radicalism of contemporary conservativism. Deregulation, budget cutting, and tax changes—all policies of the Reagan administration—can result, and in the 1980s did result, in a firestorm of interest-group activity; Reagan's first interior secretary, James Watt, was seen as the ideal recruiting sergeant for liberal environmental groups. Most recent presidents, Republican and Democratic, have come to Washington set on changing policies in ways that are bound to matter to interest groups. Skillful presidents will arrive in Washington knowing that they need a strategy that will overcome these difficulties.

Notes

1. Stephen Skowronek, *The Politics That Presidents Make* (Cambridge, Mass.: Harvard University Press, 1993).

2. Joseph Goulden, *Meany* (New York: Atheneum, 1973).

3. Raymond Bauer, Ithiel de Sola Pool, and Lewis Anthony Dexter, *American Business and Public Policy* (New York: Atherton Press, 1963).

4. Jeffrey Berry, *The Interest Group Society* (Boston: Little, Brown, 1984); Kay Lehman Schlozman and John Tierney, *Organized Interests and American Democracy* (New York: Harper & Row, 1986); Graham K. Wilson, *Interest Groups in the United States* (Oxford: Oxford University Press, 1981).

5. Mancur Olson, *The Logic of Collective Action: Public Goods and the Theory of Groups* (Cambridge, Mass.: Harvard University Press, 1968).

6. Wilson, *Interest Groups in the United States;* and David Vogel, *Fluctuating Fortunes: The Political Power of Business in America* (New York: Basic Books, 1989).

7. *National Journal*, 23 October 1993, 2526.

8. Robert H. Salisbury, "An Exchange Theory of Interest Groups," *Midwest Journal of Political Science* 13 (1969): 1–13.

9. Jack Walker, "The Origins and Maintenance of Interest Groups in America," *APSR* 77 (1983): 390–406.

10. Wilson, *Interest Groups in the United States;* Vogel, *Fluctuating Fortunes.*

11. Graham K. Wilson, "Corporate Political Strategies," *British Journal of Political Science*, 20 (1990): 281–88.

12. *National Journal*, 11 December 1993, 2949.

13. Jeffrey H. Birnbaum and Alan S. Murray, *Showdown at Gucci Gulch* (New York: Vintage Books, 1987).

14. Osha Davidson, *Under Fire: The NRA and the Struggle for Gun Control* (New York: Holt, 1994).

15. Martha Joynt Kumar and Michael Baruch Grossman, "Interest Groups and the Presidency," in *The Presidency and the Political System*, ed. Michael Nelson (Washington D.C.: CQ Press, 1984), 282–312.

16. *New York Times*, 30 August 1994, A8.

17. Bauer, de Sola Pool, and Dexter, *American Business and Public Policy.*

18. See Bob Woodward's account of the source of this catchphrase as one element of the Clinton campaign's "three-pronged message." *The Agenda: Inside the Clinton White House* (New York: Simon and Schuster, 1994), 54.

19. Michael Kelly, *New York Times Magazine*, 31 July 1994. For another example of this interpretation of Clinton, see Elizabeth Drew, *On the Edge: The Clinton Presidency* (New York: Simon and Schuster, 1994).

20. Quoted in the *National Journal*, 5 November, 1993, 2676.

21. Hanna Rosin, "Why We Flip-Flopped on Macedonia: Greek Pique," *New Republic*, 13 June 1994.

22. *National Journal*, 28 May 1994, 1269.

23. Drew, *On the Edge*, 354–55.

24. Robert H. Salisbury, "Why No Corporatism in America?" in *Trends Toward a Corporatist Intermediation*, ed. Philippe Schmitter and Gerhardt Lehmbruch (Beverly Hills, Calif.: Sage, 1979); Graham K. Wilson, "Why Is There No Corporatism in the United States?" in *Patterns of Corporatist Policymaking*, ed. Gerhardt Lehmbruch and Philippe Schmitter (Beverly Hills, Calif.: Sage, 1982).

25. Theodore Marmor, Judith Feder, and John Holahan, *National Health Insurance: Conflicting Goals and Policy Choices* (Washington D.C.: Urban Institute, 1980), 7.

26. Drew, *On the Edge*, 42.

27. Woodward, *The Agenda*, 110.

28. *National Journal*, 30 October 1993.

29. *National Journal*, 16 October 1993.

30. Woodward, *The Agenda.*

31. Samuel Kernell, *Going Public: New Strategies of Presidential Leadership* (Washington, D.C.: CQ Press, 1986).

32. Cathie Martin, "Mandating Social Change: The Struggle within Corporate America over National Health Reform," paper presented to the annual meeting of the American Political Science Association, New York City, 1-4 September 1994.

33. "The Health Care Debate: The Doctors," *New York Times*, 5 August 1994, 18.

34. Martin, "Mandating Social Change," 27.

35. *New York Times*, 3 October 1994, A9.

36. Hillary Clinton, for example, described her plan as "very threatening to those who currently control the insurance market." *New York Times*, 7 November 1993, sect. 4, 14.

37. Julie Kosterlitz, "Stress Fractures," *National Journal*, 19 February 1994, 412.

38. Letter from Sidney Wolfe and Sara Nichols of Public Citizen to the *New York Times*, 7 November 1993.

39. "What Went Wrong? How the Health Care Campaign Collapsed," *New York Times*, 29 August 1994, 1.

40. "The Health Care Debate," 18.

41. *New York Times*, 30 August 1994.

42. *National Journal*, 2 July 1994.

43. *National Journal*, 27 November 1993, 2844.

44. *National Journal*, 15 February 1993, 328-33.

45. Skowronek, *Politics That Presidents Make.*

8

Frustration and Folly:
Bill Clinton and the
Public Presidency

George C. Edwards III

The Clinton administration is the ultimate example of the public presidency, one based on a perpetual campaign to obtain the support of the American people and fed by public opinion polls, focus groups, and public relations memos. Within the White House the political consultants who ran Clinton's presidential campaign have had a presence and influence that has not been seen before. George Bush spent $216,000 for public opinion polls in 1989 and 1990, while Clinton spent $1,986,410 in 1993 alone. This included three or four polls and three or four focus groups per month.[1]

On the Saturday after Clinton took office, Paul Begala, Stan Greenberg, and James Carville began almost daily meetings in the White House with Clinton or his aides to review strategy. On the following Tuesday they re-created the Little Rock "war room" central command in the Old Executive Office Building next to the White House. "This is going to be a presidency that integrates its policy goals and its communications abilities," declared Greenberg.[2]

Two forces destined the Clinton presidency to be a public presidency. First was the president's operating style. Having governed in Arkansas with frequent elections and public relations campaigns on behalf of his reform proposals, it was only natural that he continue the campaign mode inside the Beltway.

Second, the conditions of his election undermined any claims to his having received a mandate for his policies. With only 43 percent of the national vote and only one state, Arkansas, giving him more than 50 percent of the vote, running behind all but five members of Congress, and with Democrats losing ten seats in the House and, ultimately, one in the Senate, there was little perception in Congress that he possessed either a mandate or long coattails. Democrats were not impressed, and Republicans were not intimidated in the least. Moreover, much of the president's vote was anti-Bush rather than pro-Clinton, and exit polls found that 54 percent of the electorate preferred lower taxes and fewer services to higher taxes and more services,[3] hardly the policy thrust of an activist Democratic president.

Clinton had his work cut out for him in trying to lead a badly divided public. At the time of the election, 46 percent of the public favored government involvement "in trying to help business create jobs and compete productively," but 45 percent were opposed. Opinion was about equally split on spending the "peace dividend": 38 percent wanted to reduce the deficit, 23 percent wanted to finance domestic programs, and 23 percent wanted to reduce taxes.[4]

Thus the new president's strategic position was not one in which he was in a position to structure the choices of Congress as being for or against a president who had the clear support of the people. Obtaining public support, then, was inevitably going to be a constant preoccupation of the Clinton administration. As Clinton pollster Stan Greenberg put it, "We need popular support to keep the pressure on Congress to vote for change."[5]

Yet this administration, headed by one of the most capable and politically skilled presidents, has found it difficult to achieve public support for its leader and his policies. As a consequence, it has struggled (and often stumbled) in its efforts to govern.

Public Approval

At the foundation of the public presidency is public approval of the president. Public approval operates mostly in the background and sets the limits of what Congress will do for or to the president. Widespread support gives the president leeway and weakens resistance to presidential policies. It provides a cover for members of Congress to cast votes to which their constituents might otherwise object. They can defend their votes as support for the president rather than support for a certain policy alone.

In addition, public support makes the president's other leadership resources more efficacious. If he is high in the public's esteem, the president's party is more likely to be responsive, the public is more easily moved, and legislative skills become more effective. Thus, public approval is the political resource that has the most potential to turn a situation of stalemate between the president and Congress into one supportive of the president's legislative proposals.

Lack of public support strengthens the resolve of those inclined to op-pose the president and narrows the range in which presidential policies re-ceive the benefit of the doubt. In addition, low ratings in the polls may cre-ate incentives to attack the president, further eroding an already weakened position. It did not take long for Bill Clinton to experience these problems.

Clinton began his tenure as president with 58 percent approval, seven points higher than either Ronald Reagan or George Bush received in their first polls. He fell to 51 percent within days, however, as controversial issues such as abortion, gays in the military, and the Zoë Baird nomination domi-nated the headlines in his first week in office. Recovering to the highest rat-ing of his tenure, 59 percent, in late February 1993, he fell steadily until June, hitting a low point of 37 percent. Then the president benefited from a rally after the bombing of Iraq at the end of June and ultimately rose to 56 percent in September following his address on health care. He ended the year at 54 percent approval (see figure 8.1).

In 1994 he rose to a high point of 58 percent in late January, but saw his support slowly erode so that by mid-August he had reached 39 percent, rising to the 40s by the end of the year. This is not an impressive perform-ance for a president finishing his second year in office, but it is not unprece-dented. Ronald Reagan bottomed out at 35 percent approval in January 1983. Gerald Ford, Jimmy Carter, and Richard Nixon were around the 50 percent mark. Eisenhower, Kennedy, Johnson, and Bush were all in the 60–70 percent range after two years in office.

THE FRIENDS OF BILL

President Clinton may bill himself as a new kind of Democrat, but the presi-dent's core support is the same as that for Kennedy, Johnson, and Carter: Democratic Party identifiers, liberals, nonwhites, and those with lower in-comes. Gender first appeared as an important influence on presidential ap-proval in the Reagan years and persisted under George Bush. In those cases, men were more supportive of the president, but women give Clinton some-what more support than men do (see table 8.1).

Easterners are more supportive, and those in the South and West are less so, largely because of differences of ideology. Clinton, unlike Jimmy Carter but like LBJ, has not been able to retain the backing of his own re-gion. Neither age nor education distinguishes public attitudes toward the president.

Because his approval levels have not been high, there is less potential to discriminate between supporters and nonsupporters. Nevertheless, the presi-dent has polarized the public along partisan lines. The 50 percentage point difference in the approval levels of Republican and Democrat identifiers is similar to the 53 percentage point difference for Ronald Reagan—the most polarizing of modern presidents. (The average difference between the parties

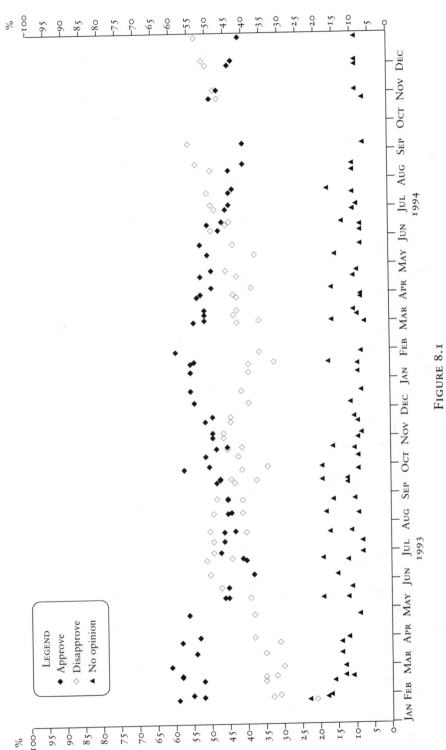

Figure 8.1
Clinton Presidential Approval

TABLE 8.1
AVERAGE CLINTON APPROVAL, 1993–94

	Approve	Disapprove	No opinion
Overall	48%	41%	11%
Party			
Republican	22	70	8
Democrat	73	18	9
Independent	45	43	13
Ideology			
Conservative	32	61	8
Moderate	54	37	9
Liberal	68	25	8
1992 Vote			
Bush	16	77	7
Clinton	80	13	7
Perot	35	56	10
Race			
White	45	45	10
Nonwhite	68	21	12
Sex			
Male	46	45	9
Female	50	38	12
Age			
Under 30	49	40	10
30–49	48	42	10
50 and over	47	41	12
Income			
Less than $15,000	52	35	13
$15,000–$29,000	49	39	11
$30,000–$49,000	47	44	9
$50,000–$74,000	46	46	8
$75,000 and over	44	49	7
Education			
High school, incomplete	48	38	14
High school graduate	47	41	11
Technical or trade school	46	44	10
College, incomplete	46	44	10
College graduate	49	44	7
Region			
East	52	37	10
Midwest	48	41	11
South	44	45	11
West	47	43	10

SOURCE: Gallup poll.

in support for Presidents Eisenhower through Carter was only 35 percentage points; the difference was 37 percentage points for President Bush.)

This disparity is not surprising, as fiscally and culturally conservative Republicans who are skeptical of government are unlikely to appreciate the president's efforts to raise taxes, allow gays to serve in the military, and overhaul health care.

When a president receives only 43 percent of the vote, he must enlarge his coalition of supporters to govern effectively. On Clinton's first full day in office, Stan Greenberg told the Democratic National Committee, "This election is not in any way a realigning election." "We need to understand that the Republican coalition collapsed in 1992, but we have not yet formed a new Democratic coalition." "We need to take those Perot voters very seriously."[6]

Yet Bill Clinton's support in the fall of 1994 looked a lot like his support in November 1992. Only 13 percent of those who voted for George Bush and 27 percent of those who supported Ross Perot approved of Clinton's performance as president. Nevertheless, 75 percent of those who voted for him still supported him.[7]

Thus the president's problem is not so much that he has lost ground (although he has lost more than he would like) as that he has not gained any. By way of contrast, in 1968 Richard Nixon also won office with 43 percent of the vote, but he was able to add to his support substantially throughout his first term.

CREDIT WHERE CREDIT IS DUE?

The president's lack of public support is particularly puzzling to many because he has battled hard for major policy change, and the country has experienced both peace and prosperity during his tenure. From the perspective of the conventional wisdom, Clinton should be rather high in the polls. As Republican pollster Frederick Steeper put it, "He's breaking all precedents. He should be at 60 percent approval."[8] What has gone wrong?

One of the most interesting aspects of the public's evaluations of Bill Clinton is the extent and strength of opposition to him. Within ten days of taking office, he had 32 percent disapproval. So much for a honeymoon. In mid-1994, Gallup found that 19 percent of the public "strongly" approved of his performance as president and 23 percent approved "not strongly." But 34 percent of the public "strongly" disapproved of him, and another 15 percent disapproved "not strongly." Thus, fully a third of the public intensely opposed the president, not an auspicious environment for future gains in the polls.[9]

Much of the public is unaware of the president's success—or refuses to believe it. For example, at the end of October 1994, 59 percent of the public thought the economy was still in recession! Only 34 percent knew the deficit had decreased since Clinton became president, and 65 percent thought taxes on the middle class had increased during that period.[10] Adding insult to injury, a poll in September found that only 24 percent felt his economic plan and budget had helped the economy.[11] At the same time, 70 percent of the public thought former President Jimmy Carter should get most of the credit for the agreement between U.S. and military leaders in Haiti that avoided a U.S. invasion of the island. Only 15 percent credited Clinton for the accord.[12]

Part of the problem may be frustration over what people perceive as the president's inability to get things done. The failure of a string of major bills to pass at the end of the 103rd Congress in 1994 fed this perception, but sometimes even the president's legislative successes have contributed to it. His most notable legislative victories have been harrowing, ugly not clean. The instability of the president's coalitions has meant that they are prone to falling apart, making crises and abject pleading inevitable.

For example, on the 1994 crime bill, Clinton turned what should have been an easy triumph—a crime bill in an election year—into a near political fiasco. He allowed the bill to balloon in size and shape to attract Democratic votes and then had to compromise with Republicans after being humiliated by losing on a rule to bring the bill to the House floor. Thus, instead of getting credit for being tough on crime and taking on the National Rifle Association and winning, the news was about what he had to give up to eke out a victory. Similarly, the White House was slow to mobilize support for the GATT free trade agreement and had to cut a last-minute deal with Republican Senator Robert Dole to avoid embarrassment. Dole received credit as a statesman, while Clinton was left in the supplicant's role.

People are also apparently unwilling to grant credit to a president they do not respect. It has been rare for Clinton to receive even 50 percent approval for his handling of the economy, ostensibly his greatest success.[13] In September 1994 he had only 43 percent approval. In the same poll only 36 percent approved of his performance on health care, his highest priority, while 60 percent disapproved. Foreign policy, neither a Clinton priority nor an area of substantial achievement, at least until late in his second year, has been especially dismal for the president. Although he was given high marks early in his term, by August 1994 he received only 34 percent approval for his handling of foreign affairs. This rose to 43 percent in October following success in dealing with difficult situations in Haiti, Kuwait, and North Korea.[14]

There seems to be an almost visceral level of mistrust and dislike for Clinton, a rejection of him not as a leader or politician but as a person. Much of the aversion to Bill Clinton appears to be based on cultural issues such as gays in the military, abortion, and doubts about the president's character. These controversies broke early and set the tone of the administration for many, and the issue of character is never far from the headlines.

THE QUESTION OF CHARACTER

The covenant between the president and the people is a fragile one, worn thin by the lies of Watergate and Vietnam and suspicions about politicians that linger and are reinforced by the awesome speed and impact of the modern media. The atmosphere on inauguration day was supportive for the new president, but the image of "Slick Willie" was not buried. Nor was the public's discontent with politics as usual. When asked to choose between a president who set a good moral example for the country and one with whose political views it generally agreed, the public chose the former by 59 percent to 32 percent.[15]

To increase his public support beyond his electoral coalition, Clinton had to avoid questions of character. These included appearing evasive, cynical, too anxious to please (two-faced, hypocritical), too inclined to back off his principles (too "political"), and too inclined toward scandalous behavior. In other words, this president had to show the public that he could be trusted.

More frankness is expected as the press has become more adversarial, but Clinton's credibility has been tested by perceptions of evasiveness. Before his inauguration, he spoke of a new relationship with Saddam Hussein and then the next day back-tracked on his own words. Decisions regarding Haitian refugees, the middle-class tax cut, Bosnia, China's most-favored-nation status, Travelgate, and the nomination of Lani Guinier, for example, have made him vulnerable to criticism and given the press a theme that has set a negative tone for coverage of the Clinton administration.

Charges of cynicism and hypocrisy have also hurt the president. In *The Agenda*, Bob Woodward reported that during the campaign Clinton knowingly exaggerated revenues from raising taxes on foreign corporations, essentially made up numbers for health-care savings, knew that his proposed middle-class tax cut was intellectually dishonest, and (according to future OMB director Alice Rivlin) made "dishonest" and "untrue" statements about the direction of the deficit. Once in office, he described his own economic plan as a "turkey."[16]

It has also been difficult for many to reconcile the populist, anti-Washington candidate with the president sending his daughter to private school, having his hair cut by a very expensive Hollywood stylist, holding the largest and most grandiose inauguration in history, and setting new records for raising "soft money" for the Democratic National Committee. Moreover, the image of the culturally conservative New Democrat seems at odds with gays in the military, a politically correct cabinet, Surgeon General Joycelyn Elders's incendiary remarks regarding sex, drugs, and abortion, and big government policies, especially the defining issue of health-care reform.

The Clinton White House has a tendency toward self-righteousness, which some see as arrogant and hypocritical. Hillary Clinton appeared on the cover of the *New York Times Magazine* with an accompanying article headlined "Saint Hillary." The administration portrayed the health-care system as failing because of greedy insurers, drug makers, and doctors, and justified the 1993 tax increase on the wealthy as appropriate for those who had prospered in the 1980s. To many, however, there is a contradiction between the politics of virtue and the behavior of the Clintons. Hillary Clinton's seeking authorization for an unusual stock offering for Madison Guaranty Savings and Loan, owned by Whitewater partner James McDougal, from regulators appointed by her husband; her lucrative sweetheart dealings in the commodities market; and the financing of the Clintons' investment in Whitewater indicated that before they arrived in the White House, they were cashing in themselves.

There is nothing worse than pictures of administration officials with their right hands in the air, and by the time of the summer 1994 Whitewater hearings, people were ready to believe the worst. In the end the Whitewater investigation was less important for identifying possible criminal violations than for shedding light on the ethical norms in the White House. The hearings left an ugly impression of political expedience over integrity: a *Time* magazine poll found that 51 percent of the people thought the Clintons were hiding something about their role in Whitewater. Only 35 percent believed them. Similarly, 46 percent felt there were improper contacts between the Treasury Department and the White House, while only 31 percent thought the contacts were proper.[17]

A mid-1994 Gallup poll found that 39 percent thought Clinton was honest and trustworthy (56 percent did not); 30 percent said he keeps his promises (67 percent said he does not); only 50 percent felt he was a man of strong convictions.[18] A Wirthlin poll taken at about the same time found that only 31 percent of the public responded that Clinton's moral values mirrored their own.[19] It is very difficult for a president to win public support when the public views him as untrustworthy, vacillating, evasive, and unprincipled. It is equally difficult to overcome these persistent judgments about character.

FOREIGN POLICY

In 1992 Bill Clinton attacked George Bush for "a basic pattern of reactive, rudderless and erratic U.S. diplomacy." He claimed that Bush displayed "activism without vision, prudence without purpose and tactics without strategy."[20] His remarks did not make much of an impression at the time, but the irony is that he now faces these same criticisms—and people are listening.

This may come as a surprise to those who note that the public has not put foreign policy high on its list of concerns. Yet the national press pays much more attention to foreign than to domestic policy. The *Tyndall Report* measures the network television weekday coverage for the top ten stories each week. In 1994 (through September), among these stories, health care received 448 minutes of coverage, about the same as the 432 minutes for natural disasters and only slightly more than Whitewater received. The economic recovery received only 77 minutes and the crime bill only 119 minutes of coverage, while Bosnia, Cuba, Haiti, North Korea, and Rwanda received a total of 1,621 minutes of coverage. (O.J. Simpson's trial received 614 minutes of coverage, more than any other single matter.)

The press has a strong influence on the criteria people employ when they evaluate the president, and the coverage of issues that Clinton is not seen as handling well (in mid-July 1994 only 39 percent saw him as an effective world leader, while 59 percent felt he was not)[21] naturally feeds the perception that he is not up to one of the primary roles of the presidency. It also reinforces the perception of his "waffling" on domestic issues.

The president just cannot win in the foreign policy arena. In July 1994, 39 percent of the public felt he was spending too much time on foreign policy and not enough on domestic policy![22]

THE CLINTON RALLY

On 26 June 1993, President Clinton ordered the U.S. Navy to launch twenty-three Tomahawk cruise missiles at Iraq's intelligence headquarters in downtown Baghdad. The U.S. attack was in response to Iraq's role in a conspiracy to assassinate former President George Bush during a visit to Kuwait. General approval of the way he was handling his job as president surged in the CBS News/*New York Times* poll from 36 percent before the attack to 50 percent immediately following it.

More than patriotic fervor was involved in this rally, however. Conservatives were not more likely to rally behind the president's use of force, despite their frequent advocacy of a "tough" foreign policy. Those who rallied were those with the lowest thresholds to overcome to move to support of the president: Democrats, those who gave him economic and foreign policy support, and those who approved of his qualities of leadership and empathy.

Thus Bill Clinton was not able to add new groups to his coalition of supporters through the use of military force. Even more important, the rally dissipated rapidly. By early August he was back to 38 percent approval in the CBS News/*New York Times* poll.

On 23 September 1994, U.S. troops intervened in Haiti. The Gallup poll taken on 6–7 September showed Clinton with a 39 percent approval level, while the poll of 23–25 September found Clinton with a 44 percent approval rating, only five percentage points higher than before U.S. troops went ashore. An overnight poll taken on 23 September showed an approval level of 48 percent, so the strongest positive impact of the Haiti intervention policy dissipated very rapidly.

Dependent on public support to pass its large legislative agenda, the Clinton administration has had to govern without the support of public opinion, and sometimes in spite of widespread public opposition. The president's lack of approval has diminished his ability to govern; it also has limited his ability to obtain public support for his policies, which is central to governing in the public presidency.

Leading the Public

Public support provides the ultimate leverage for presidential leadership. It is difficult for others who hold power to deny the legitimate demands of a president with popular support. Yet the Clinton White House has typically been unable to move the public to support the president's policies.

Recognizing that political leadership is a process of education and persuasion, Bill Clinton began wooing the public even before his inauguration. He hosted a carefully staged two-day economic conference in Little Rock on 14–15 December 1992. The economists who spoke supported Clinton's basic economic policy stands. There were no advocates of supply-side economics or of the basic Republican precept of low taxes and small government. Similarly, the business executives in attendance were almost all from prosperous, growing companies. Those such as General Motors and IBM that were laying off thousands of workers were not represented. Although a variety of perspectives were offered, especially on international trade, Clinton and the speakers seemed determined not to challenge one another or raise sore points.

The goal of the conference was to create a political mood, a national consensus that the economy was in structural decline and that there was no quick fix. Clinton also wanted to portray himself as engaged in finding a solution. The overarching goal, however, was for public opinion to provide a context in which Congress would pass whatever he proposed. Although the president-elect obtained agreement that the economy had problems requiring governmental attention and showed himself to be a master of the details of economic policy and fully involved in finding solutions to economic problems, there was little preparation for a specific recovery plan.

When the president's first major economic proposal, the fiscal stimulus plan, was introduced, it ran into strong Republican opposition. During the 7–19 April 1993 congressional recess, Clinton stepped up his rhetoric on his fiscal stimulus bill, counting on a groundswell of public opinion to pressure moderate Republicans into ending the filibuster on the bill. (Republicans, meanwhile, kept up a steady flow of sound bites linking the president's package with wasteful spending and Clinton's proposed tax increase.) The groundswell never materialized, and the Republicans found little support for any new spending in their homestates. Instead, they found their constituents railing against new taxes and spending. Thus, by the time Clinton proposed a 25 percent cut in the bill's spending package on 16 April, it was too late to matter.[23]

The president's next major legislative battle was over the budget. On 3 August 1993, he spoke on national television on behalf of his budget proposal, and Senate Republican leader Robert Dole spoke against the plan. A CNN overnight poll following the president's speech found that support for his budget plan *dropped*.[24] Several million calls were made to Congress in response to Clinton and Dole, and the callers overwhelmingly opposed the president's plan.[25] A late-July talk-show-style news conference on expansion of the earned-income tax credit was largely ignored by television network news.

The White House had more success on NAFTA. The debate between Vice-President Al Gore and Ross Perot on *Larry King Live* was a shrewd gamble. The show had the highest rating for any regularly scheduled program in the history of cable television. In addition, it was carried on broadcast stations, so perhaps 20 million people watched the show. Among the 357 adults Gallup found who had watched the debate, support for NAFTA increased from 34 percent to 56 percent and opposition decreased from 38 percent to 36 percent. The vice-president succeeded in convincing many undecided voters, and Perot's negatives rose from 39 percent to 51 percent after the debate.[26] Thus, Gore had provided political cover for members of Congress who feared a Perot-led backlash against their support for NAFTA and had weakened the threat of Perot at the polls. Even here, however, the White House's ability to move public opinion was limited. Gallup polls taken on 2–4 November and on 15–16 November (just before the House vote on 17 November) both showed only 38 percent of the entire public in favor of the trade agreement. (Opposition diminished from 46 to 41 percent, however.)

When the rule on the 1994 crime bill was voted down in the House, the president immediately went public. Speaking to police officers with flags in the background, he blamed special interests (the NRA) and Republicans for a "procedural trick," but his appeal did not catch fire. Meanwhile, Republicans were talking about pork, tapping public resentment. Clinton's public push yielded only the votes of three members of the Black Caucus. So he had to go to moderate Republicans and cut private deals.

As we discuss later, the president was unable to sustain the support of the public for health-care reform, despite substantial efforts. Nevertheless, the White House held out against compromise with the Republicans and conservative Democrats, hoping for a groundswell of public support for reform. But it never came.[27] Indeed, by mid-August 1994, only 39 percent of the public favored the Democratic health-care reform proposals, while 48 percent opposed them.[28]

FOCUSING ATTENTION

An important element of a president's legislative strategy is to set the agenda of Congress. In the public presidency, this means setting the agenda of the public first. An important component of agenda setting is establishing priorities among legislative proposals. If the president is not able to focus attention on his priority programs, they may become lost in the complex and overloaded political environment. Setting priorities is also important because the White House can lobby effectively for only a few bills at a time. Moreover, the president's political capital is inevitably limited, and it is sensible to focus it on the issues he cares about most.

Setting the agenda requires first limiting it and then keeping a focus on priority items. From its first week in office, the Clinton administration did a poor job at both. The president promised to have legislation ready for improving the economy at the very beginning of his term and to propose a comprehensive health-care package within his first hundred days in office. Neither program was ready on time, creating a vacuum filled with controversies over issues of lower priority, such as gays in the military, the bungled nominations of Zoë Baird and Kimba Wood, and public funding for abortion. These issues left an impression of ineptitude and alienated many in the public whose support the president would need for his priority legislation—hardly an auspicious beginning for an administration that had come to office with only 43 percent of the vote.

The president's public standing recovered when he presented his economic program to the public in February 1993 and, once again, after he delivered his health-care message in September 1993. Yet after each speech he lost control of the agenda, and public support for himself and his programs dropped notably.

Health-Care Reform.—The defining issue of the Clinton presidency is (or was to have been) health-care reform, and the White House's handling of this issue further illustrates the difficulties the administration has had in focusing attention on its priority legislation.

It is difficult to maintain focus on a proposal until a bill is written. The Clinton administration set and then badly overshot its deadline for delivery of a health-care reform plan, first arousing and then dissipating public interest. It was not until 22 September 1993, more than eight months after taking office, that the president made a national address on health-care reform, his highest-priority legislation.

The speech was well received, and polls showed that the public was overwhelmingly supportive of his efforts.[29] Six days later, Hillary Clinton began her testimony on health-care reform before five congressional committees, captivating and dominating her audience. But still there was no bill. The pace of rhetoric was out of sync with the pace of lawmaking. The president's September speech had the effect of peaking attention in a legislative battle before the introduction of the bill.

It was not until 27 October 1993, more than nine months after the president appointed his wife to head a panel to prepare health-care legislation, that Clinton submitted his plan—1,342 pages of it—to Congress. At that point public support was divided evenly, with 45 percent both for and against his bill.[30] Even at this late point, many technical revisions and corrections were required on the 1,342-page bill, further blurring the focus on the plan. In addition, the congressional leadership had to sort out committee jurisdiction problems before it could figure out when formally to present the bill. Finally, on 20 November, two months after the president's national address, his health-care reform proposal was introduced in both houses of Congress.

In the meantime, there were important distractions from the president's bill. Clinton's appearance on a ninety-minute program from a Sacramento television station ended up focusing on a wide range of issues and concerns, leaving the president little room to lobby for his health-care plan. Then, on 3 October, eighteen American soldiers were killed on a peacekeeping mission in Somalia, and others were wounded or missing in an exchange with a local faction. Americans were horrified to see pictures of a dead soldier being dragged through the streets of Mogadishu. So the president returned from his health-care trip to California and focused on events abroad. Americans seemed to lose interest in health care at this point. Bill McInturff was doing daily tracking polls from the time of the president's 22 September speech. From that date, "awareness of the plan was going up. Support for the plan was going up." But on 3 October it stopped.[31]

Other distractions occurred in October as well. Democratic Representative Jim Cooper (D-Tenn.) introduced his own, considerably more modest, health-care proposal in the House, and Democratic Senator John Breaux (D-La.) introduced a similar bill in the Senate. In addition, the president had to devote his full attention and all the White House's resources to obtaining passage of NAFTA, which dominated the news for weeks. Moreover, on 11 October the *USS Harlan County*, carrying U.S. troops as part of a UN plan to restore democracy in Haiti, was forced to turn around and leave in the face of pro-military gunmen.

Thus, the administration did not use the September–November period as fully as it had hoped to educate the public and develop support for health-care reform. It was another example of the imperfect transition from the campaigning mode to governing in the Clinton administration.

Obstacles to Focusing the Agenda.—The Clinton White House does not receive high marks for focusing attention on its high-priority issues. Yet the fault lies not only in the White House's execution of a communications strategy. It is also in the administration's conception of the possibilities of such a strategy. It is one thing to *try* to focus attention on only a few priority items. But success in this endeavor will be determined to a large extent by the degree to which issues, including international crises, impose themselves on the president's schedule and divert attention, energy, and resources from *his* agenda.[32]

In the summer of 1994, as the White House entered the final negotiations over its high-priority bills on crime and health-care reform, it had to deal first with the Whitewater hearings and then with a huge influx of Cuban refugees. When the White House tried to put off focusing on welfare so as not to undermine its massive health-care reform proposal, Senator Daniel Patrick Moynihan (D-N.Y.) criticized the president for not being serious about welfare reform. Moynihan, chair of the Senate Finance Committee, which had to handle much of health-care reform, threatened to hold health care hostage, so the White House had to devote at least some attention to welfare reform.[33]

When the president tried to press themes he had articulated in his 1994 State of the Union message by hitting the road, he was caught up in other issues, such as the trade war with Japan, possible military action in Bosnia, criticism by former Justice Department officials over the crime bill, and cleaning up a last bit of mess from the "Tailhook" scandal.

There is often not much the White House can do in such situations. As George Stephanopoulos put it, "on the campaign trail, you can just change the subject. But you can't just change the subject as president. You can't wish Bosnia away. You can't wish David Koresh away. You can't just ignore them and change the subject."[34]

Yet part of the problem is the president himself. Clinton and his advisers understand the virtue of a clear, simple agenda,[35] and the president knows that his defining issues have been overwhelmed as he has engaged in issue proliferation.[36] As he admitted in 1993, "what went wrong was I was not able to keep the public focus on issues that we're working on after I gave the State of the Union address."[37] "It's hard to get more than one message a day across on the evening news to the American people."[38]

He cannot contain himself, however. For example, he rarely focused on his fiscal stimulus package for more than a few days at a time. On 13 November 1993, the last weekend before the NAFTA vote in the House, Clinton made headlines with an emotional appeal in a black church in Memphis on stopping crime. Naturally, this speech, not NAFTA, received the headlines in the Sunday papers and news programs. Shortly after the midterm elections, the president traveled to Indonesia to sign an agreement regarding free trade among Pacific Rim nations. Yet he overshadowed his own success with an off-the-cuff comment on school prayer. Compounding the problem, he made news again the following day as he backed away from his own words.

The president has an undisciplined personal style, tremendous energy, a desire to please many sides, a mind stuffed with policy ideas, and a party of interest groups clamoring for policy. Clinton came into office with a large agenda (just read his prime-time address of 17 February 1993), and Democrats had a laundry list of initiatives that had been blocked by George Bush, ranging from family and medical leave to motor voter registration and health-care reform. He and his fellow partisans believe in activist government and are predisposed toward doing "good" and against husbanding leadership resources.

But no good deed goes unpunished. The more the White House tries to do, the more difficult it is to focus the country's attention on a few priority issues. And it is equally difficult to receive credit for his achievements when there are so many issues that lie ahead. "I'm the most impatient person on earth," the president declared. "I've tried to do so many things that sometimes when I do things, no one notices. Most Americans don't know we did family leave or motor voter or national service or changed the environmental policy, because I was always in some other controversy that was getting more ink."[39]

STRUCTURING CHOICE

Every president not only wants the country and Congress to focus on his priority issues; he also wants the debate to be on his terms. Framing issues in ways that favor the president's programs may set the terms of the debate on his proposals and thus the premises on which the public evaluates them and on which members of Congress vote on them. As one leading adviser to Reagan put it, "I've always believed that 80 percent of any legislative or political matter is how you frame the debate."[40] Often this involves portraying policies in terms of criteria on which there is a consensus and playing down divisive issues.

One of the most serious limitations of the Clinton administration has been its lack of rhetorical definition. The administration's failure to structure choice effectively for the public and for Congress is a consequence of its ill-defined projections of itself. It is not the result of an administration that has been unaware either of the importance of projecting a strong, clear vision of its policies or of its failure to do so. Nevertheless, it has not clearly defined what it is about. The failure to do that has left the Clinton administration vulnerable to the vicissitudes of events and to definition by its opponents.

From the start of the administration, the major players in the White House understood the need for communicating the central values of the Clinton presidency in a coherent fashion. In the early months, they were especially concerned with crafting an organizing idea for their economic program. They also knew that they were not succeeding in doing this. Side

issues such as gays in the military were getting in the way, resulting in cari-
catures of Clinton and the administration.[41]

As the months went by, the White House continued to suffer from a
lack of coordination between its policy and its political messages. Clinton
could not seem to create a simple, central message, relating each policy to an
overall theme.[42] As is his nature, the president continued to seek help in
communicating, at one point complaining to Paul Begala that "you gave me
a week's worth of strategy [to sell his economic plan] and I needed three
months."[43]

On his first major legislative proposal, his fiscal stimulus package, the
White House allowed the Republicans to define his economic program in
terms of pork barrel. On his budget, the president's political consultants
complained that the Republicans had succeeded in focusing public debate on
tax increases rather than economic growth or deficit reduction.[44] Clinton
tried to present the issue of taxes as one of fairness, but there is little evidence that this perception was widely shared. When he said his own proposal lacked enough spending cuts and challenged anyone to find more, the
discussion focused on whether there were enough cuts rather than economic
stimulus or deficit reduction. "The Clinton administration has lost control
of its agenda," complained Stan Greenberg.[45]

In June 1993 Greenberg wrote to Clinton regarding the administration's
contradictory messages. Should it emphasize deficit reduction or economic
growth? Should it have a Wall Street message that would not spook business
or a populist message that would appeal to middle-class allergies to taxa-
tion? Should it pursue a legislative focus according to Congress's agenda or
focus on a broader message for influencing Congress through public opinion? Should Clinton define himself as a social liberal (gay rights, abortion,
quotas) or a new kind of Democrat focusing on middle-class values such as
rewarding work and responsibility?[46]

We do not know if Clinton ever replied to the memo, but we do know
that the president was well aware of his inability to set the terms of the debate over his proposals. When asked why he was having such a difficult time
obtaining the support of the "new" Southern Democrats, Clinton responded, "One reason is that in their own districts and states, they've let the
Republicans dominate the perception of what we're trying to do ... the Republicans won the rhetorical debate."[47] (It is worth noting that the president
blamed his potential supporters instead of himself.)

Clinton could not reach the American people—and it frustrated him.
Six months after taking office the president reflected on the unexpected dimensions of his job on *Larry King Live:* "The thing that has surprised me
most is how difficult it is ... to really keep communicating what you're
about to the American people." "That to me has been the most frustrating
thing." A few months later he confided to a friend, "I did not realize the im-

portance of communications and the overriding importance of what is on the evening television news. If I am not on, or there with a message, someone else is, with their message."[48]

Health-Care Reform.—Health-care reform again illustrates the difficulties the Clinton administration has had in governing through the public presidency. Sometimes it seemed the president was in an impossible position. On 22 September 1993, he made a very effective speech outlining his health-care proposal. He articulated six principles as the foundation for his plan: "security, simplicity, savings, choice, quality, and responsibility," and he emphasized security. This was an attempt to set the terms of debate over health care and to depict the plan in comforting, affordable terms.

Before the speech, he briefed bipartisan groups of members of Congress for two days, brought 250 talk-show hosts to the White House, and hosted a lunch for select journalists. The day following the speech, the president and his cabinet went on the road to sell the plan to the country, reinforcing a sense that this was the start of a historic process that would culminate in fundamental change. In late September the Gallup poll found the public split 59–33 percent in favor of Clinton's health-care program.[49] It appeared that Clinton had changed the premises of decision from whether to overhaul health care to how to do it.

Opponents did not play dead, however. An aggressive advertising campaign characterized the president's plan as expensive, experimental, providing lower quality and rationed care, and a job killer. So it was important that Clinton keep the country focused on his terms.

But he did not. Instead, the White House failed to follow up effectively on the momentum and national focus of the initial launch of health care, and public support eroded. He gave the critics a chance to organize while the country waited for the details of the plan in October. Calculating that by not offering details in September, he was depriving critics of a target, the president ended up giving them an easy target—the suspicion that he could not figure out how to pay for it.

When the health-care reform bill was introduced, the White House decided to keep its sales pitch focused on themes rather than specifics. This seemed like a reasonable approach because the legislation was so complicated. The public was not willing to make a leap of faith, however; its attention generally focused less on the goals of the president's plan and more on the means he proposed to achieve them. Details such as health alliances had to be defended, even to likely allies. But the White House resisted inquiries about how health alliances would work and talked about its six principles. By November, commentator William Schneider was pointing out the pitfalls of such an approach,[50] but the administration persisted.

The White House was unable to keep the public's attention focused on the inadequacies of the health-care system and the broad goals of reform. The dominant public response to the plan was confusion. The bill's complexity made it difficult to explain. Competing plans in Congress heightened the confusion, as did a myriad of health-care industry voices with a deluge of direct mail, radio spots, and advertising, picking out pieces of the plan to oppose. Instead of revolving around a central theme, then, public debate focused on the reform's pitfalls.

The White House's most prominent rhetoric focused on obtaining universal coverage for the 15 percent of the public without access to health care (largely those earning $15,000 to $30,000 a year). The greatest concerns of the middle class (who had some form of health-care insurance)—rising insurance costs, fear of a government takeover of health care, rationed health care, and fear of losing coverage—were rarely emphasized.[51]

Because the White House health-care reform plan was bureaucratic and complicated, it was easy for opponents to label it a government takeover of the health-care system. This threatened the middle class. Gallup polls in August 1994 found that the public saw Clinton's health-care reform proposal as a typical Democratic social welfare program, one that helps the poor, hurts the middle class, and creates bigger government. In the end, people were more worried about what would happen if health-care reform passed than about losing their health insurance: too much government was a bigger concern than too little health insurance.[52]

So despite unveiling his health-care plan with an impressive flourish, the president made little progress in convincing Americans that he had the correct approach. As he lamented in March 1994, "one thing we have not done in an organized and coherent way for the last couple of months is to be very positive in getting out the same message over and over again, and in asking people to compare the alternatives."[53]

The White House recast its six principles to five catch phrases—guaranteed private insurance, choice of doctor, real insurance reform, preservation of Medicare, and guaranteed health benefits at work—but things did not get any better. By August 1994, most Americans wanted to give up and start over again the next year.[54] Which is exactly what happened.

Even worse, the president's health-care bill projected an image of Clinton as a proponent of big government and inflicted substantial damage to his image, especially among Independents.[55] The White House saw the results in the midterm elections.

Obstacles to Structuring Choice.—Some administrations lend themselves to structuring choice better than others. It is especially difficult to convey a consistent theme when the president has a large, diverse agenda—as Bill Clinton has. He thinks of his legacy primarily in terms of passing legislation, and he wants to do it on all fronts, as we have seen.

In addition, the president's views are a complex blend of populism and traditional values. His critics emphasize his liberal stances such as that on health care and "investments." He was branded a social-issues liberal after gays in the military and abortion became the first issues of his administration. Then he was labeled a free-spending liberal after he proposed a $20 billion fiscal stimulus bill as his first economic policy proposal. Yet Clinton also took many conservative, "New Democrat" stances in budget deficit reduction, the crime bill, welfare reform (or its early thrusts), and the like—reflecting traditional values of family, responsibility, work, and reciprocal obligation.

This combination has made it difficult to establish a central organizing theme for the Clinton administration. It is a challenge for the White House to lead Democrats in the public or Congress with deficit reduction at the core of its policy. As Clinton himself declared sarcastically to aides, "We're Eisenhower Republicans here, and we are fighting with Reagan Republicans. We stand for lower deficits and free trade and the bond market. Isn't that great?"[56] A year later he might have added the crime bill. Thus it is not surprising that the administration's agenda has failed to resonate with the public.

It is challenging to structure choice on more specific policies as well. The White House had to make a strategic decision regarding which to push first, the president's budget or his fiscal stimulus bill. Some Democrats wanted Congress to pass the president's budget with its spending cuts before they were asked to vote for spending increases in the stimulus bill. Although it made sense to provide these Democrats with political cover from the deficit hawks, the move also injected tax increases into the debate over the fiscal stimulus bill. Senate Republicans pointed to tax increases repeatedly in their successful effort to defeat it.[57] Structuring choice is rarely easy.

Success in Structuring Choice.—The Clinton administration has not been without success in structuring choice. When it appeared that Congress might not vote for NAFTA, the White House repackaged the issue and secured an important legislative victory. It shifted from emphasizing the trade agreement's impact on jobs and began to stress arguments that failure to pass it would undermine U.S. foreign policy. President Clinton told a news conference that if Congress voted down NAFTA, "it would limit my ability to argue that the Asians should open their markets more." "More importantly, my ability to argue that the Asians and the Europeans should join with me and push hard to get a world trade agreement through ... by the end of the year will be more limited."[58] Al Gore went even further: "the consequences of a defeat for NAFTA in the foreign policy arena would be really catastrophic."[59] This strategy increased the stakes of the vote, and thus the risks of losing, but it worked.

The White House also emphasized that support for NAFTA represented a willingness and ability to tackle the future with confidence. As one of Clinton's strategists put it,

> We learned something from Ronald Reagan, finally. You need to be right on more than the merits of the case; you need to be right on the presentation. We started to do better when we got off statistics and cast it more broadly ... as a choice between the future and the past, optimism and pessimism, hope and fear, embracing the modern world and trying to hide from it.[60]

The Limits of the Public Presidency

The belief in the importance of communication is not surprising for a president who has at times demonstrated great skills as a communicator and for White House political advisers who employed communication techniques adeptly during the 1992 presidential campaign. Yet there are important differences between campaigning and governing, and the president must adjust if he is to succeed.

The transition is rarely smooth. As Charles O. Jones put it, "after heading a temporary, highly convergent, and concentrated organization" in a presidential campaign, the winner moves into the White House and becomes the "central figure in a permanent, divergent, and dispersed structure."[61] As we have seen, communication becomes more difficult as the president loses control of his agenda and has to convince people not that he is superior to his opponent(s)—a relatively simple comparative judgment—but that his calls for specific change deserve support. At the same time, his opponents need only to cast doubt on the president's proposals in order to kill them.

In such an environment, it is important for the White House to have a clear understanding of the potential of governing through the public presidency. To start, there are very real limits to what public support can do for the president. The impact of public approval or disapproval on the support the president receives in Congress occurs at the margins of the effort to build coalitions behind proposed policies. No matter how low presidential standing dips, the president will still receive support from a substantial number of senators and representatives. Similarly, no matter how high approval levels climb, a significant portion of Congress will still oppose certain presidential policies. Members of Congress are unlikely to vote against the clear interests of their constituencies or the firm tenets of their ideology out of deference to a widely supported chief executive. Public approval gives the president leverage, not control.[62]

There are equally important limitations on using the bully pulpit to lead public opinion. Take the case of "the Great Communicator," Ronald Reagan. Numerous national surveys of public opinion have found that support for regulatory programs and spending on health care, welfare, urban problems, education, environmental protection, and aid to minorities increased rather than decreased during Reagan's tenure.[63] On the other hand, support for increased defense expenditures was decidedly lower at the end of his administration than when he took office.[64] (This may have been the result of the military buildup that did occur, but the point remains that Reagan wanted to continue to increase defense spending, but the public was unresponsive to his wishes.)

In the realm of foreign policy, Reagan was frustrated in his goal of obtaining public support for aid to the *contras* in Nicaragua.[65] But the problem for Reagan was broader than this. Whether the issue was military spending, arms control, military aid and arms sales, or cooperation with the Soviet Union, public opinion by the early 1980s had turned to the left—*ahead* of Reagan.[66]

Finally, Americans did not move their general ideological preferences to the right.[67] Indeed, instead of conservative support swelling once Reagan was in the White House, there was a movement *away* from conservative views almost as soon as he took office.[68] According to William Mayer, "whatever Ronald Reagan's skills as a communicator, one ability he clearly did not possess was the capacity to induce lasting changes in American policy preferences."[69] As press secretary Marlin Fitzwater put it, "Reagan would go out on the stump, draw huge throngs and convert no one at all."[70]

Yet despite the history of failures and frustrations of the public presidency, the Clinton White House continued to assign strategic primacy to communications. In a discussion of his problems in his first year in office, the president declared that he needed to do a better job of *communicating.* "There have been times when I've been surprised by my inability to shape the agenda on a daily basis or to shape the message that's going out to the folks.... It's always frustrating to feel that you're misunderstood ... and you can't quite get through."[71] A year later the president sounded the same theme as the solution to his political problems: "what I've got to do is to spend more time communicating with the American people about what we've done and where we're going."[72]

Ever ready to discuss his performance in public, the president told a national newspaper audience the weekend before the midterm elections that "if I had to say what I needed to do to improve as a leader, it would be to find ways to be able to share with the American people what I know to be the facts here, what we're doing, and to give them some sense that I'm listening to them and they have some input, but that I'm moving the country in the right direction."[73]

So when the president felt it was time to reorganize the White House in the summer of 1993, he turned to communication specialist David Gergen. A year later, when Clinton needed to improve yet again, he turned to Leon

Panetta, whose two main concerns became *focus* and *message*. When he was having problems with foreign policy, he nominated journalist Strobe Talbott as undersecretary of state and moved Gergen to the State Department. He also quadrupled the size of foreign policy press offices and devoted more public appearances to foreign policy. At midterm, he reflected that one of his major changes in handling foreign policy was in *explaining* it to the public.[74]

Yet there are more to Clinton's problems with the public presidency than communication techniques. As Zbigniew Brzezinski, President Carter's national security assistant, told CNN, "the problem is not only the message—the problem is also substance." No communication strategy can overcome the image of the *USS Harlan County* and its cargo of would-be UN peacekeepers retreating from the coast of Haiti, backed down by a handful of armed thugs on the docks of Port-au-Prince. An obsession with public relations and blunting short-term domestic criticism is no substitute for a steady, coherent foreign policy based on a conceptual framework for post–Cold War international order.

After the failure of health-care reform, Hillary Clinton reflected that the most frustrating failure was not getting the country to understand that the plan was an opening offer—a problem of communications. "It was described as an ultimatum by our opponents and therefore used to undermine the process of reaching agreement," she complained. "This battle was lost on paid media and the paid direct mail."[75] Similarly, the president claimed that health-care reform did not pass because "people who are making a huge amount of money out [of] the system . . . have spent a lot of money to terrify the people who do have health care today into thinking that if our bill passed it would make it worse and it would lead to more government intervention in the health-care system."[76]

Yet research has found that the negative advertising opposing the president's health-care plan, advertising that was indeed often misleading, had little impact on the general public.[77] And there was never any visible effort to compromise until it was too late. Democratic congressional leaders were unwilling to break with Clinton's goal of universal coverage and thus made no meaningful compromise offer. Moreover, adherence to that goal drove the administration to stick with employer mandates and cost controls, which were necessary to make universal coverage affordable but which also doomed the bill.

Ultimately it was the nature of the president's proposal itself that precluded his succeeding. As Martha Derthick put it:

> In many years of studying American social policy, I have never read an official document that seemed so suffused with coercion and political naïveté . . . with its drastic prescriptions for controlling the conduct of state governments, employers, drug manufacturers, doctors, hospitals, and you and me.[78]

Clinton and the Public in Perspective

It is ironic that the Clinton administration, whose orientation toward governing has revolved around the public presidency, has had to govern without the support of public opinion, and sometimes in spite of public opposition. We have seen that the White House has found it difficult to maintain public support or move the public to support its policies. Sometimes, it is seems that the president and his aides could have performed more effectively. At other times, the frustrations the White House encountered were probably inevitable. In either event, we must be cognizant of the unfavorable context in which Bill Clinton is trying to govern.

The climate for effective communication with the public is not favorable. Clinton put it well in a midterm assessment of his presidency: "Leadership ... is getting things done and moving the country forward. Now, the one thing I do believe is that a leader also is able to communicate with people in any environment. And I find it is an incredible challenge to ... communicate with the American people while in the midst of these constant battles with Congress and in this sort of attack-journalism format that dominates so much of American life."[79]

Even the most persuasive of presidents must reckon with an environment for policymaking that is not conducive to major reform. It would be very difficult for any activist administration to be successful in the 1990s. The lack of resources drives the president's policy choices, as it has since at least 1981. Bill Clinton cannot make the "investments" in education, training, and physical infrastructure that he desires; he had to choose the fiercely opposed employer mandates and cost controls on private-sector spending to finance health care; and he has had little to trade for votes. In the presidency of Lyndon Johnson, the president may have been able to form coalitions by providing benefits for a wide range of interests, but in the 1990s the president wins by *subtracting* from bills, not adding to them.

Any president elected with only 43 percent of vote should not expect to pass far-reaching social legislation without involving the other party, especially when the public is dubious and well-organized interest groups are fervently opposed. Moreover, the greater the breadth and complexity of the policy change the president proposes, the more opposition it is likely to engender. In an era when a few opponents can effectively tie up bills, the odds are clearly against the White House.

None of these challenges are likely to be lessened in the third and fourth years of Bill Clinton's term. Moreover, the blurring between campaigning and governing that has marked the Clinton legislative style will be of less use in an environment in which Republicans are in the majority in both houses of Congress and are invigorated by their electoral success. Campaigning is by definition partisan, and the president is now dependent on Republican votes.

Clinton's tendency to carry the campaign mode to governance by demonizing opponents such as medicine and the drug and insurance industries has only activated Republican counterattacks and negative advertisements. The "us against them" approach to policymaking that encouraged the president to develop his health-care plan in Democrats-only secrecy and pursue a left-in coalition-building strategy instead of a center-out one will have to be altered if the president is to have any chance of success.

The need for reaching across the aisle need not be reason for despair for those seeking substantial policy change. Most major domestic legislation, including the Social Security Act of 1935, the Civil Rights Act of 1964, the Voting Rights Act of 1965, Medicare (1965), the Clean Air Act of 1970, and the Tax Reform Act of 1986, were passed with broad bipartisan support. It is not likely that Bill Clinton will enjoy similar success, given the orientation of Newt Gingrich and his Republican colleagues toward confrontation and their expectations of retaking the White House in 1996. For the president to have any chance of success, however, he must adapt the politics of his presidency to the potential of his resources and the challenges he faces.

Notes

1. James M. Perry, "Clinton Relies Heavily on White House Pollster to Take Words Right Out of the Public's Mouth," *Wall Street Journal*, 23 March 1994, A16.

2. James A. Barnes, "The Endless Campaign," *National Journal*, 20 February 1993, 460.

3. Voter Research and Surveys exit polls.

4. October 1992 poll for the *Los Angeles Times*, reported in "Opinion Outlook," *National Journal*, 5 December 1992, 2806.

5. James A. Barnes, "Polls Apart," *National Journal*, 7 July 1993, 1750.

6. Gwen Ifill, "Democrats Get a New Chairman, and a Warning," *New York Times*, 22 January 1993, A9.

7. Gallup poll of 7–9 October 1994.

8. Quoted in Burt Solomon, "Clinton, Down but Not Out, Stares at the Specter of a Single Term," *National Journal*, 8 October 1994, 2360.

9. Gallup poll of 15–17 July 1994.

10. *Newsweek* poll, 28–30 October 1994, cited in "The Problem with the President," *Newsweek*, 7 November 1994, 42. We do not know whether the public was thinking of income taxes, which were *not* raised on middle-class incomes, or energy taxes, which were increased.

11. CBS News/*New York Times* poll of 8–11 September 1994.

12. Gallup poll for CNN/*USA Today*, 19 September 1994.

13. It is worth noting, however, that the Census Bureau reported that median family income *fell* in 1993 and the poverty rate increased slightly.

14. Gallup poll of 6–7 September 1994.

15. Gallup poll of 3–6 June 1994.

16. Bob Woodward, *The Agenda: Inside the Clinton White House* (New York: Simon and Schuster, 1994), 31, 46, 47, 114, 214.

17. Poll of 4 August 1994, reported in *Time,* 15 August 1994, 18.

18. CNN/*USA Today* Gallup poll of 15–17 July 1994.

19. Cited in the *Wirthlin Quorum* 5 (June 1994): 2.

20. Quoted in William Schneider, "Clinton's Wobbly Foreign Policy Way," *National Journal,* 28 May 1994, 1274.

21. CNN/*USA Today* Gallup poll of 15–17 July 1994.

22. Peter Hart and Robert Teeter for NBC/*Wall Street Journal,* reported in "Opinion Outlook," *National Journal,* 6 August 1994, 1882.

23. "Democrats Look to Salvage Part of Stimulus Plan," *Congressional Quarterly Weekly Report,* 24 April 1993, 1002–3.

24. Woodward, *The Agenda,* 285. A CBS News/*New York Times* poll with before-and-after samples on 2 and 3 August found that support for the president's budget remained unchanged even in the immediate aftermath of the speech, but that opposition weakened.

25. "Switchboards Swamped with Calls over Tax Plan," *New York Times,* 5 August 1993, A18.

26. Gallup poll, 9 November 1993.

27. "Health Care Reform: The Lost Chance," *Newsweek,* 19 September 1994, 32.

28. Gallup poll, 15–16 August 1994.

29. Gallup poll, 24–26 September 1993.

30. Gallup poll, 28–30 October 1993.

31. Quoted in "For Health Care, Time Was a Killer," *New York Times,* 29 August 1994, A8.

32. The president seemed to recognize this in an interview in the summer of 1993. See Jack Nelson and Robert J. Donovan, "The Education of a President," *Los Angeles Times Magazine,* 1 August 1993, 39.

33. Jason DeParle, "Moynihan Says Clinton Isn't Serious about Welfare Reform," *New York Times,* 8 January 1993, 8.

34. Quoted in Thomas L. Friedman and Maureen Dowd, "Amid Setbacks, Clinton Team Seeks to Shake Off the Blues," *New York Times,* 25 April 1993, sec. 1, p. 12.

35. Woodward, *The Agenda,* 241.

36. Thomas L. Friedman, "Scholars' Advice and New Campaign Help the President Hit His Old Stride," *New York Times,* 17 November 1993, A10; Nelson and Donovan, "Education of a President," 14.

37. "Excerpts from Clinton's Question and Answer Session in the Rose Garden," *New York Times,* 28 May 1993, A10. See also David S. Broder and Dan Balz, "Clinton Finds Change Harder Than Expected," *Washington Post,* 14 May 1993, A11.

38. Nelson and Donovan, "Education of a President," 14.

39. Quoted in Jann S. Wenner and William Greider, "President Clinton," *Rolling Stone,* 9 December 1993, 80.

40. Quoted in Gerald M. Boyd, "'General Contractor' of the White House Staff," *New York Times,* 4 March 1986, A22.

41. Woodward, *The Agenda,* 110–11, 171–72, 245.

42. Ibid., 235, 245, 314–15, 325.

43. Ibid., 214. See also Broder and Balz, "Clinton Finds Change Harder Than Expected," A1.

44. Woodward, *The Agenda*, 243, 247–48.

45. "Pollster: Mistakes Made," *Bryan–College Station Eagle*, 23 May 1993, A8.

46. Woodward, *The Agenda*, 226–27; see also 241, 247–48, 250.

47. Wenner and Greider, "President Clinton," 43.

48. Woodward, *The Agenda*, 313.

49. Gallup poll of 24–26 September 1993.

50. "A Fatal Flaw in Clinton's Health Plan?" *National Journal*, 6 November 1993, 2696.

51. Darrell M. West and Diane J. Heith, "Harry and Louise Go to Washington: Political Advertising and Health Care Reform," paper presented at the annual meeting of the American Political Science Association, New York, 1–4 September 1994, 10.

52. Polls of 8–9 August 1994 and 15–16 August 1994.

53. Quoted in Adam Clymer, "Poll Finds Public Is Still Doubtful over Costs of Clinton Health Plan," *New York Times*, 15 March 1994, A1.

54. "Health Care Reform: The Lost Chance," 28–32. The *Newsweek* poll of 8–9 September 1994 found that 28 percent of the public wanted health-care reform passed in 1994, while 66 percent preferred to start over again the next year. See also "Will Reform Bankrupt Us?" *Newsweek*, 15 August 1994, 51.

55. This was a finding in a poll taken by White House pollster Stanley Greenberg for the Democratic Leadership Council. Discussed in Richard L. Berke, "Centrist Democrats' Poll Warns Clinton of Unrest," *New York Times*, 18 November 1994, A10.

56. Woodward, *The Agenda*, 165.

57. "Democrats Look to Salvage Part of Stimulus Plan," 1002.

58. "As NAFTA Countdown Begins, Wheeling, Dealing Intensifies," *Congressional Quarterly Weekly Report*, 13 November 1993, 3104.

59. David E. Rosenbaum, "Both Sides Emphasize Stakes of the Trade Vote," *New York Times*, 15 November 1993, C16.

60. Quoted in R.W. Apple, Jr., "A High Stakes Gamble That Paid Off," *New York Times*, 18 November 1993, A14.

61. Charles O. Jones, *The Presidency in a Separated System* (Washington, D.C.: Brookings Institution, 1994), 294.

62. George C. Edwards III, *At the Margins: Presidential Influence in Congress* (New Haven: Yale University Press, 1989), chaps. 6–7.

63. Seymour Martin Lipset, "Beyond 1984: The Anomalies of American Politics," *PS* 19 (1986): 228–29; William G. Mayer, *The Changing American Mind* (Ann Arbor: University of Michigan Press, 1992), chaps. 5–6; Benjamin I. Page and Robert Y. Shapiro, *The Rational Public* (Chicago: University of Chicago Press, 1992), 133, 136, 159; William Schneider, "The Voters' Mood 1986: The Six-Year Itch," *National Journal*, 7 December 1985, 2758. See also "Supporting a Greater Federal Role," *National Journal*, 18 April 1987, 924; "Opinion Outlook," *National Journal*, 18 April 1987, 964; "Federal Budget Deficit," *Gallup Report*, August 1987, 25, 27; "Changeable Weather in a Cooling Climate," 261–306. See also CBS News/*New York Times* poll (news release, 27 October 1987), tables 16, 20.

64. Lipset, "Beyond 1984," 229; Mayer, *Changing American Mind,* 51, 62, 133. See also "Defense," *Gallup Report,* May 1987, 2–3; "Opinion Outlook," *National Journal,* 13 June 1987, 1550; CBS News/*New York Times* poll (news release, 27 October 1987), table 15.

65. Ronald Reagan, *An American Life* (New York: Simon and Schuster, 1990), 471, 479; Page and Shapiro, *Rational Public,* 276. See also CBS News/*New York Times* poll (news release, 1 December 1986), table 5; CBS News/*New York Times* poll (news release, 27 October 1987), table 17; "Americans on Contra Aid: Broad Opposition," *New York Times,* 31 January 1988, sec. 4, p. 1.

66. Page and Shapiro, *Rational Public,* 271–81; John E. Reilly, ed., *American Public Opinion and U.S. Foreign Policy 1987* (Chicago: Chicago Council on Foreign Relations, 1987), chaps. 5–6; Mayer, *Changing American Mind,* chaps. 4 and 6.

67. See, for example, John A. Fleishman, "Trends in Self-Identified Ideology from 1972 to 1982: No Support for the Salience Hypothesis," *American Journal of Political Science* 30 (1986): 517–41; Martin P. Wattenberg, "From a Partisan to a Candidate-Centered Electorate," in *The New American Political System,* ed. Anthony King (Washington, D.C.: American Enterprise Institute, 1990), 169–71; Martin P. Wattenberg, *The Rise of Candidate-Centered Politics* (Cambridge, Mass.: Harvard University Press, 1991), 95–101.

68. James A. Stimson, *Public Opinion in America: Moods, Cycles, and Swings* (Boulder, Colo.: Westview, 1991), 64, 127.

69. Mayer, *Changing American Mind,* 127.

70. R.W. Apple, "Bush Sure-Footed on Trail of Money," *New York Times,* 29 September 1990, 8.

71. Quoted in Nelson and Donovan, "Education of a President," 14. See also "The President at Midterm," *USA Weekend,* 4–6 November 1994, 4.

72. White House transcript of interview of President Clinton by WWWE Radio, Cleveland, 24 October 1994.

73. "The President at Midterm," *USA Weekend,* 4–6 November 1994, 4.

74. Interview entitled "Blending Force with Diplomacy," *Time,* 31 October 1994, 35.

75. Adam Clymer, "Hillary Clinton Says Administration Was Misunderstood on Health Care," *New York Times,* 3 October 1994, A9.

76. WWWE Radio transcript.

77. West and Heith, "Harry and Louise Go to Washington." But the ads may have played an important role in reinforcing opponents' efforts to frame the debate on health-care reform.

78. Quoted in George Will, "Forrest Gump on the Potomac," *Newsweek,* 19 September 1994, 76.

79. "The President at Midterm," *USA Weekend,* 4–6 November 1994, 4.

9

Domestic Policy: The Trials of a Centrist Democrat

PAUL J. QUIRK AND JOSEPH HINCHLIFFE

The central claim of Bill Clinton's 1992 presidential campaign was that, in contrast with Republican President George Bush's preoccupation with foreign affairs, he would concentrate on solving the nation's domestic problems. He would create jobs, cut the budget deficit, promote investment and economic growth, reform the health-care system, change welfare, and stand tough against crime, among other things. As important as these particular commitments were, Clinton also stressed a general orientation toward the role of government. Rather than defend the orthodox big-government liberalism of his party, he would approach domestic issues as a more conservative "New Democrat." Promising a "New Covenant" between the people and their government, he emphasized traditional values such as individual responsibility. In fact, he borrowed Republican rhetoric to distinguish himself from the "tax-and-spend" liberals.

This centrist posture was crucial to Clinton's success in winning back many middle- and working-class white voters who had abandoned the Democrats in the three preceding presidential elections. Along with a loss of public confidence in President Bush, this posture was the key to Clinton's victory in the election. But the success of the New Democratic platform in the election by no means guaranteed that President Clinton would be able to stick with a centrist agenda and implement it—or, in other words, that it would prove a viable program for governing. Even more important, the New Democratic posture did not guarantee that Clinton would be a skilled or effective president.

A number of obstacles stood in the way. To begin with, Clinton faced all the usual difficulties of presidential leadership in contemporary American politics—the independence of Congress, the weakness of party organization, and the adversary press.[1] In addition, Clinton came into office with limited public support, his image tarnished by a number of scandals and controversies during the campaign, and having won only a modest plurality of the popular vote.

Clinton also faced obstacles that pertained specifically to his centrist, New Democrat agenda. First, any centrist program requires overcoming the normal tendencies toward partisan and ideological conflict in national policymaking. To move his centrist program through Congress, Clinton would have to assemble coalitions of moderate Democrats and moderate Republicans. But such coalitions are vulnerable to combined opposition from both ends of the ideological spectrum. Moreover, the difficulties of building centrist coalitions in Congress have grown in recent years.[2] The realignment of the electorate has virtually eliminated conservative Democrats in the South and liberal Republicans in the North and so has increased the ideological polarization of the congressional parties and diminished the number of congressional moderates.[3] In formulating his own positions, the president naturally encountered heavy pressure from liberal Democrats and their constituency groups to sign on with the ideological mainstream of the party. Significant for the liberals' claims on Clinton's loyalties, Hillary Clinton was a prominent spokesperson for liberal causes.

Second, some of the important elements of Clinton's agenda, although connected with popular goals, required overcoming strong resistance among the voters. Reducing the budget deficit required cutting spending or raising taxes; promoting job growth, in the opinion of most economists, required free trade; reforming health care required controlling costs and thus, realistically, limiting services; reforming welfare required spending money on the underclass to restore deteriorating benefit levels or at least to administer workfare provisions and create jobs; reducing crime required a focus on workable measures as opposed to symbolic gestures. In all these areas, the requirements of a responsible moderate program ran up against predictable public skepticism or opposition. As some commentators have pointed out, American policymaking institutions in recent decades have become increasingly "plebiscitary"—that is, exposed to close public observation and dependent on immediate mass approval.[4] In conducting policy debate, policymakers and especially presidents have relied increasingly on popular rhetoric. And they have become more responsive to immediate public sentiment, even though such sentiment is often misguided or uninformed.[5]

These trends toward polarization and popularization came together in shaping the strategy of the congressional Republicans. Rather than try to work with Clinton to find common ground and achieve mutually beneficial policy change, Republicans were disposed to block his initiatives and attack them with popular rhetoric. Although at times Clinton's own partisanship contributed to this tendency, the Republican strategy may signal the emergence of a more combative, less constructive role for the opposition party in Congress.

In his first two years in office, President Clinton's response to the resulting challenges of domestic policy leadership was notable, above all, for its inconsistency. At different times, Clinton provided either forceful leadership or shameless pandering; his efforts ranged from strategic virtuosity to comical bungling. He seemingly forgot, at times, that he was supposed to be a New Democrat. He also had some bad luck. And his results were mixed. With respect to policy change, Clinton won some battles, lost others, and ended up with a substantial record of achievement. Politically, however, he lost the war. The Republicans' attack strategy combined with Clinton's self-inflicted political wounds to hand the Democrats a disastrous defeat in the 1994 congressional elections.

Ironically, the Republican control of both the House and the Senate creates some opportunities for Clinton's centrist approach in the second half of his term. At least, it gives the Republicans a harder choice between policy accomplishment and mere obstruction.

A Problematic Mandate

In several ways the results of the 1992 elections created special challenges for Clinton's leadership in domestic policy. In his campaign, he emphasized strongly his claim to be a New Democrat. Although he built the campaign largely on the economy ("It's the economy, stupid!" said a famous sign in campaign headquarters), he embraced moderate-to-conservative positions on a variety of social issues. He supported the death penalty, advocated a tough version of welfare reform, and stressed his credentials as the popular governor of an impeccably conservative southern state. Even while seeking to unify the party after a difficult battle for the nomination, he made a point of demonstrating independence from traditional liberal Democratic constituencies. He chastised Jesse Jackson's Rainbow Coalition for giving a platform to black rap singer Sister Souljah, whose remarks Clinton portrayed (somewhat unfairly) as calling for the killing of whites. He supported the North American Free Trade Agreement (NAFTA) despite the opposition of labor unions. He vigorously fought off attempts to portray him as a "tax-and-spend liberal."

Speaking after the election on what it meant to be a New Democrat, Clinton said: "Above all, we must honor those basic values of opportunity, responsibility and community, of work and family and faith. This is what it means, in my view, to be a New Democrat. I was proud to campaign as one. I'm proud to govern as one."[6]

Inevitably, this stance created tension between Clinton and the party mainstream, which he was fashioning as "old." The split between New and Old Democrats, in Clinton's sense, dates at least to the 1984 Democratic Party convention, when traditional Democrats supported Walter Mondale and centrist or "neoliberal" insurgents favored Gary Hart. Broadly speaking, Old Democrats believe that the party should represent the poor, the working class, and minority groups; they want to protect or expand entitlement programs. New Democrats, in contrast, believe that the party should mainly represent the middle class; they want to extricate the party from its association with liberal values and "big government."

New Democrats arguably have been ascendant in Democratic presidential politics since Mondale lost to Ronald Reagan in 1984.[7] They captured the nomination in 1988, with Michael Dukakis, and in 1992, with Clinton. More important, many commentators and party activists have written off liberal Democrats as incapable of winning general elections.

But centrist Democrats are a minor factor in congressional election politics. Most Senate and especially House races lead to the election of either liberal Democrats or conservative Republicans. As a result, there is a disjunction between the positions required for a Democratic candidate to win the presidency and the commitments of most Democrats in Congress—and a New Democrat president will have trouble governing with a Democratically controlled Congress. As Senator John B. Breaux (D-La.) pointed out:

> After you become president, the normal pressures from the left become very active and very visible. People who really didn't support Bill Clinton in the primaries at all now feel that since he is a Democratic president, he has to follow the same rules that old-style Democrats used to.[8]

Beyond the tension with mainstream Democrats, the 1992 election created additional difficulties for Clinton and his New Democrat platform. First, even though Clinton enjoyed a solid margin of about 6 percent over Bush, he won only 43 percent of the popular vote, with almost 20 percent going to Ross Perot. The last president to win election with such a small proportion of the popular vote was Woodrow Wilson in 1912. Opponents could argue with some justice that Clinton's candidacy had been rejected by a sizable majority of the electorate and that his claim to lead was correspondingly vitiated.

Second, even as the Democrats won the presidency for the first time since 1976, they lost power in Congress. The Democrats lost ten seats in the House of Representatives and broke even in the Senate, giving Clinton an unusually slight partisan margin for a modern Democratic president. Clinton began his term with only 58 Democratic senators, 4 fewer than Jimmy Carter had enjoyed, and 258 Democratic representatives, 34 fewer than in

Carter's first Congress.[9] Party control of the government was unified, there-fore, but it was just barely so. Particularly in the Senate, where the rules gen-erally give minorities considerable leverage, the Democrats were not neces-sarily able to dictate outcomes.

Finally, the election shifted the ideological balance within this dimin-ished congressional Democratic Party away from the conservative or centrist Democrats—Clinton's natural supporters—and toward the liberals. In par-ticular, it replaced a number of conservative white males with women, Afri-can American, or Hispanic members. In the Senate, the number of women members tripled. In the House, the number of women rose from twenty-eight to forty-seven, the number of African Americans from twenty-five to thirty-eight, and the number of Latinos from eleven to seventeen.[10] Because women and minorities are prone to liberalism, these changes moved the con-gressional Democratic party to the left. Thus the same election that pro-duced a New Democrat president enhanced the position of underrepresented demographic groups and strengthened the Old Democrats (in ideological terms) on Capitol Hill.

Although more liberal than in the past, the Democrats of the 103rd Congress were also splintered, with several organized groups representing different ideological tendencies. The congressional Black Caucus—with forty members, nearly all of them House Democrats, and chaired by Kweisi Mfume (D-Md.)—was the most cohesive force on the left wing of the Dem-ocratic caucus. The Democratic Study Group, though larger and less cohe-sive, also advanced a liberal agenda.[11] The House Mainstream Forum, headed by Dave McCurdy (D-Okla.), was a branch of the Democratic Lead-ership Council (DLC), the national group of centrist Democrats in which Clinton had come to prominence as a New Democrat.[12] (The group's claim was, of course, to be in the "mainstream" of national, not Democratic Party, opinion.) Even farther to the right, the Conservative Democratic Forum (CDF), headed by Charles W. Stenholm (D-Tex.) and sometimes known as "the red neck caucus," represented mainly the dwindling group of southern Democrats.[13] The Democratic Budget Group, led by Representative Timothy J. Penny (D-Minn.; reportedly called "Scrooge" by his children), sought to advance hawkish positions on reduction of the budget deficit.[14] Despite the strongly liberal central tendency, therefore, the range of organized opinion within the small Democratic congressional majority was very broad.

Fortunately for Clinton, the Democratic congressional leadership and even the rank and file recognized the party's collective stake in proving that it could resolve its internal differences and govern effectively. Senate Major-ity Leader George Mitchell noted that it was in the "self-interest" of con-gressional Democrats to support the president. Speaker of the House Thom-as S. Foley warned that if the Democrats did not succeed in working together, they would be subject to "harsh criticism."[15]

But the Democrats' spirit of intraparty cooperation was offset by a spirit of interparty confrontation on the other side of the aisle. The Republicans came away from the election prepared to challenge Clinton's leadership immediately. Out of power in both branches, they could take the view that building a coalition to govern the nation was the Democrats' problem. And they stressed the limitations of Clinton's mandate, from their standpoint the redeeming feature of the election. On election night, Senate Minority Leader Bob Dole boldly claimed to represent the majority of Americans who had not voted for Bill Clinton. Although he wished the new president well, Dole promised, "it's not going to be all a bed of roses for Governor Clinton."[16] House Minority Whip Newt Gingrich accentuated the negative in describing the Republicans' posture toward the governing Democrats: "Our goal should be cooperation without compromise. Our role in the minority is to offer new ideas, to offer intelligent criticism of their dumb ideas, and to cooperate when we have common ground."[17]

In fact, the Republicans found very little common ground with Clinton and the Democrats. On most issues, they adopted the simple strategy of opposing the Democrats and building the case for electing Republicans in 1994 and beyond. With this strategy, partisanship climbed to an all-time high.[18]

In short, ready support for President Clinton and his centrist domestic agenda was in short supply. Much of the available support depended on the willingness of congressional Democrats to back the president largely for partisan reasons; and their disposition to help him out was balanced by Republicans' inclination to give him grief for the same reasons.

Targets of Opportunity, Real and Imagined

On taking office, Clinton tried to hit the ground running by taking action on several measures that mostly represented a standard liberal Democratic agenda but that either had demonstrably strong public and congressional support or could be adopted by executive order, without legislation. This effort produced several easy victories but also one wrenching, ignominious defeat.

The easy victories came on several popular liberal bills passed by the previous Democratic Congress but vetoed by President Bush. With a new president eager to sign them, Congress quickly passed the bills again, and Clinton had significant policy achievements in the first months of his term. The Family and Medical Leave Act required employers to grant their employees unpaid family or medical leave of up to twelve weeks. The Motor Voter Registration Law simplified voter registration, a convenience for voters and a presumptive electoral boost for Democratic candidates. The National Service program provided scholarships for students who perform qualified community service. The Handgun Waiting Period Law, or "Brady bill" (named for the White House aide disabled during an assassination attempt on President Reagan), required a five-day waiting period for the purchase of a handgun.[19]

The defeat came on Clinton's effort, in fulfillment of a campaign promise to gay and lesbian supporters, to remove the ban against homosexuals serving in the military. Often overlooked by critics of Clinton's decision making on this subject, his position on this issue was not a focus of controversy or even of much Republican criticism during the campaign. Nevertheless, when Clinton announced his intention to remove the ban by an executive order in one of his first acts as president, the negative reaction was strong and swift. High military officers, including the chairman of the Joint Chiefs of Staff, General Colin Powell, and military experts in Congress, especially the chairman of the Senate Armed Services Committee, Sam Nunn (D-Ga.), attacked Clinton's plan, pleading that the open presence of homosexuals in the services would hurt morale and weaken performance. Once media and public attention had been drawn to the subject by the controversy, it rapidly became apparent that most of the public strongly supported the military's view. To avoid the danger that Congress would override an executive order and enact the ban on homosexuals into law, Clinton backed away from his initial, firm stance and entered into a negotiation with the military to develop a compromise plan.

After extensive talks conducted amid acrimonious public debate, Clinton accepted a slightly liberalizing and quite confusing revised policy on homosexuals, helpfully summarized as "don't ask, don't tell." Under the policy, homosexual activity remains a cause for expulsion from the military. But the services are to refrain from investigating a service member's possible homosexuality (hence, "don't ask") as long as he or she avoids proclaiming or demonstrating it ("don't tell").[20]

The debate on homosexuals in the military was a political disaster for Clinton. In a single episode, he identified himself with an unpopular liberal stance on a controversial social issue, he ended up grievously disappointing his gay and lesbian supporters, and by caving in to resistance from Congress and his nominal subordinates in the military, he raised doubts about the strength of his leadership.

The Economic Program

The centerpiece of Clinton's domestic program was economic policy. His campaign had relegated every other issue, with the partial exception of health care, to the periphery to permit an unrelenting attack on the Bush administration's economic performance. Even though the economic picture was improving in the last half of 1992, the public in January 1993 still saw the economy as the nation's most important problem.[21] Its two main concerns were creating jobs and reducing the budget deficit. In fact, when Clinton moved into the White House, the country had an only moderately high unemployment rate of about 7 percent. But the federal government was running a massive annual deficit of $290 billion, and the national debt had just exceeded the $3 trillion mark for the first time.[22]

The substantial, even though incomplete, adoption of Clinton's 1993 economic program was the major domestic policy achievement of his first two years. He managed to address the public's concerns about jobs and the deficit. For the most part, he remained faithful to the centrist strategy and made good on his renunciation of "tax-and-spend" economics. The undertaking, however, was politically costly in the long run. The Republicans exploited their minority status to avoid responsibility for tough decisions and to launch punishing attacks on Clinton and the Democrats.

THE 1993 BUDGET RESOLUTION AND THE STIMULUS PACKAGE

President Clinton set forth his economic program, including the outlines of his first budget, in a speech to Congress on 17 February 1993. The program had three parts. First, he proposed a $30 billion economic stimulus package that was intended to create 500,000 new jobs. The bulk of the stimulus was to come from new spending for highway construction, extended unemployment benefits, and community block grants. Second, he proposed an investment package designed to correct an infrastructure deficit that allegedly had arisen under the preceding Republican administrations. The investment package contained $230 billion in spending and tax breaks to improve highways, bridges, and other structures needed for economic growth. Finally, Clinton called for $704 billion in deficit reduction over five years—to be accomplished through $375 billion in spending cuts and $328 billion in new taxes.[23] Out of concern for the deficit, Clinton quietly dropped his campaign promise of a middle-class tax cut. But he asserted that the new taxes would fall mainly on the wealthy and that "98.8 percent of American families" would face no increase in income tax rates.[24]

Initially, "Clintonomics" had widespread public support. In particular, 79 percent of the people who had heard Clinton's characteristically skillful speech supported his economic plan.[25] Republicans nevertheless attacked it vigorously from the beginning. They derided the new spending as mere "pork barrel"; they claimed that the proposed spending cuts were inadequate; and they warned that the new taxes would harm the economy. Some Democrats echoed these charges. Congressional leaders had originally planned to move the stimulus package quickly. But a group of Democratic "deficit hawks" objected strongly and successfully demanded a commitment from the leaders to complete action on a deficit-reducing budget resolution before taking up the stimulus measure.

The Clinton administration's vulnerability to partisan criticism in pushing painful measures to reduce the deficit was apparent from the outset of congressional action on the concurrent budget resolution, the stage in budgeting in which Congress sets general guidelines for taxing and spending. Testifying at a budget hearing, Office of Management and Budget (OMB) Director Leon Panetta pointed out that there was no easy way to accomplish deficit reduction: "There's no magic here, folks. You've got to do defense, non-defense, entitlements, and revenues."[26] Despite the unpleasant consequences, the president kept up the pressure to achieve a substantial reduction, warning that "we all understand the price we're going to pay if we continue with this deficit."[27]

Much of the debate over the budget consisted of partisan posturing for public consumption. Republicans, along with some conservative Democrats, criticized the administration for not making deep enough spending cuts but did not recommend any particular further cuts. In a testy session before the House Budget Committee, Panetta challenged such critics to "put up or shut up."[28] But they refused to take the bait. When Panetta was testifying before the Senate Budget Committee, Trent Lott (R-Miss.) made the remarkable claim that he had a list of $216 billion in "basically painless budget cuts" that could be made in the first year of the Clinton administration. Panetta demanded to see the list. Lott replied, "I'm going to keep it right here," patting his breast pocket, "until I see yours."[29] Representative Barney Frank (D-Mass.) lampooned the critics. "Yes, we have no specifics," he intoned (adapting the lyric of the old standard, "Yes, We Have No Bananas"). "We have no specifics today."[30] But the Republicans stood firm in exercising the prerogative of a minority party. When asked for a Republican budget plan, Senator Dole declined to offer one and justified the refusal by pointing out, "Well, we're not the government."[31]

At the same time, the Clinton plan was also under attack from liberal Democrats, who felt that the deficit was mostly the result of the extravagant tax cuts of the Reagan era. Opposing demands for more spending cuts, they blamed the deficits on the Republicans and conservative Democrats who had helped pass the Reagan program. "What is tough for me to swallow," said House Appropriations Committee chairman David Obey (D-Wisc.), "is that some of the same people in our party who brought us the debacle [of the 1981 tax cut] are lecturing us now."[32]

With the Republicans playing it safe and refusing to be drawn into a discussion of specific plans, Clinton and the Democrats were forced to assume the entire burden of passing a budget. To do so required difficult negotiations to overcome the large differences between liberal and conservative Democrats and reach the virtually unanimous agreement that would be needed to pass a budget with few or no Republican votes. In the House, the Democrats incorporated additional spending cuts to placate party conservatives and eventually agreed on a budget resolution within the party caucus. Sticking to the agreement in the floor debate, the Democrats defeated both a hastily assembled Republican budget and an alternative proposal offered by the Black Caucus. After weeks of "no specifics today," the Republican budget was slapped together so quickly that the document contained marginal notes and phone numbers (creating some risk, one supposes, that a staff member would have his or her phone number enacted into law).[33] With the ability of the Democrats to govern the country clearly at stake, Democratic critics on both the left and the right swallowed their objections and passed the budget resolution without the benefit of Republican votes.

Senate Democrats went through a similar process to pass the budget resolution, bridging their differences and fighting off Republican amendments designed mostly to multiply the tough votes for the Democrats. The Democrats' collective stake in appearing effective was again a large factor in gathering support. As one Senate Democrat remarked, "This kind of loyalty is not always going to be there.... These are high profile votes for a new president at the beginning of his administration and he deserves support."[34] Republicans recognized the fears of many Democrats in voting on the budget resolution. Looking ahead to the decisions on actual tax increases and spending cuts yet to come in the reconciliation process, Dole warned, "We start shooting with real bullets from here on."[35]

In the debate on the stimulus package, it was especially Clinton and the Democrats who tailored their strategy for the requirements of the next election campaign. But in this case, the Republicans were able to defeat their plans. After the adoption of the budget resolution, the Democratic leadership moved quickly to bring up the previously postponed stimulus measure. Because income and employment had been growing steadily without fiscal intervention for almost a year, the economic case for further stimulation was, at best, dubious. But the Democrats went ahead with it anyway— largely, no doubt, to help the president make good on his campaign promise of such a measure and to remind voters of the difference, on this issue, between Clinton and Bush. Republicans, however, seized on the improved economic conditions to refute the argument for stimulation. They argued, plausibly, that the real purpose of the bill was to shower benefits on favored constituencies.[36]

Taking advantage of the majoritarian procedures of the lower chamber, House Democrats ignored the Republican complaints and passed the measure. Under the rules and norms of the Senate, however, the minority can far more easily prevent action, and Republicans chose to block action on the stimulus package by filibustering. After four failed attempts by Senate Democrats to invoke cloture and end debate on the bill, the leadership conceded defeat and withdrew the bill. In the end, Congress passed a stripped-down bill, which omitted all of Clinton's spending proposals except the extension of unemployment benefits. Politically, Congress's rejection of the stimulus package was a significant defeat for President Clinton. Economically, the Republicans arguably did Clinton a favor. Their obstruction of the stimulus package helped him to escape from an inconvenient campaign promise, keep from adding to the budget deficit, and avoid overheating an already vigorous economy.

THE RECONCILIATION BILL

The debate on the reconciliation bill—the measure that brings actual taxing and spending into line with the budget resolution—largely repeated the political pattern of the budget debate. Clinton and the Democratic leadership pushed hard to carry out the planned deficit reduction. Republicans attacked the Democrats' tax increases while avoiding responsibility for a specific plan. And the Democrats negotiated among themselves and made extraordinary demands on party loyalty to pass Clinton's plan.

The Republicans had a rhetorical field day with the tough issues facing the Democrats. Said Senator Dole of the Clinton proposals, "This plan is not just the largest tax increase in American history. It's the largest tax increase in world history."[37] (He failed to mention that the tax increase was being imposed on the largest economy in world history.) Former Republican OMB Director David Stockman, a long-time advocate of deficit reduction, criticized the Republican rhetoric in a magazine article:

> The full-throated anti-tax war cries emanating from the GOP since February 17 amount to no more than deceptive gibberish. Indeed, if Congressman Newt Gingrich and his playmates had the parental supervision they deserve, they would be sent to the nearest corner ... until this adult task of raising taxes is finished.[38]

But Stockman's wounded scruples did not diminish the popular appeal of those antitax war cries.

For many Democrats, cuts in domestic spending were just as threatening as tax increases. In the House, which customarily acts first on spending bills, Democrats feared that if they voted against popular constituency benefits, the Senate would undercut them and restore the spending. Clinton collected their votes by promising, "You go out on that limb and I'll go out with you."[39]

Rather than try to orchestrate the negotiations on the massively complex bill from the White House, Clinton sensibly relied on the Democratic leadership to put together a feasible bill. "I'm promoting the principles," Clinton said. "These guys are going to work it out."[40] With a great deal of effort they succeeded in doing so, though by a close call in each chamber.

In the House, the Democratic caucus cut deals and issued threats within hours of the vote on the reconciliation bill to secure its passage. The leadership gave conservative Democrats additional cuts in entitlements and agreed to drop or change the energy tax. Turning up the pressure for party loyalty, a group of junior Democrats circulated a petition to strip committee chairs of their posts if they voted against the bill. In a roll call whose result was uncertain until the last votes were cast, the House passed the bill, 219–213.[41] Similar eleventh-hour negotiations in the Senate led to a number of significant policy changes: scaling back business tax breaks, reducing the earned income tax credit, making capital gains subject to a surtax, and dropping empowerment zones.[42] The reconciliation bill passed the Senate, 50–49, with Vice-President Al Gore casting the deciding vote.

With Republicans keeping up the political heat, even passage of the final House–Senate conference committee bill was in doubt. Representative Dick Armey (R-Tex.) called the compromise reconciliation bill "a recipe for disaster," and Minority Whip Newt Gingrich predicted that the tax increases would produce "a job killing recession."[43] Every Republican in both the House and the Senate lined up against the reconciliation bill. So did some Democrats. And many more Democrats wavered in their decision. In the end, Democrat Bob Kerrey of Nebraska, who was the last senator to announce his position, appeared to have the deciding vote. Speaking before a national television audience, he told President Clinton, "I could not and should not cast the vote that brings down your presidency."[44] In the final roll calls, Clinton's program passed the House, 218–216, and the Senate, 51–50, with the vice-president's vote again required.

Speaking of the party pressure on Democrats to support the president, one senator complained, "Both my arms feel twisted."[45] Many anticipated paying a political price for their party loyalty. Representative Marjorie Margolies-Mezvinsky, an already vulnerable freshman Democrat from a Republican district in Pennsylvania, cast one of the last "yea" votes needed to pass the bill. As she did so, Republicans jeered, "Good-bye, Marjorie."[46]

As finally enacted, Clinton's economic program fell short of his aspiration to reduce the deficit by more than $700 billion over five years. But it imposed tax increases of $241 billion and, consistent with the New Democrat platform, even greater spending cuts of $255 billion—for a total deficit reduction of almost $500 billion. For the most part, the program extracted the new taxes from corporations and the wealthy, Republican constituencies that had fared well under Reagan–Bush tax policies. It also taxed some Social Security benefits and raised the gasoline tax. The major spending cuts came from reductions in Medicare and Medicaid, reforms of the student loan program, a delay in pension increases for federal retirees, and a freeze on all federal discretionary spending.[47]

The next year, the White House budget built on the pattern established in 1993. "The real purpose of this budget is to stay on track with what was done last year," OMB Director Panetta said.[48] Treasury Secretary Lloyd Bentsen, more prophetically than he could have realized, added, "This is a tough budget. There's a lot of pain in it. A lot of blood on the floor."[49]

Health-Care Reform

After the economy, the problem that most Americans wanted government to address, as Clinton became president, was health care.[50] In fact, there were two distinct yet related problems about health care. One was coverage: fifteen percent of all Americans lacked health-care insurance, and many more were vulnerable to losing their coverage if they lost or changed their jobs or sometimes even if they got sick.[51] The other problem was costs: after many years in which increases in health-care costs greatly exceeded the rate of inflation, these costs accounted for 12 percent of GNP in 1990.[52] From 1971 to 1991, federal health-care spending—largely on Medicare and Medicaid—grew from 9 percent to 21 percent of total federal revenues.[53]

The two problems were linked because to expand coverage without taking serious steps to control costs would push the nation's health-care bill through the roof. Unfortunately, the only effective way to control costs was, directly or indirectly, to reduce services—for example, by encouraging managed care plans that weighed the benefits and costs of tests, treatments, and visits to specialists before providing them. The politics of the issue were exceptionally difficult. Physicians, hospitals, health maintenance organizations (HMOs), insurance companies, labor unions, and state governments, among other well-organized groups, vigorously defended their particular interests. Moreover, any health-care reform bill perceived as raising taxes or insurance premiums or as reducing the quality of health care was likely to encounter resistance from the public.

For President Clinton to develop an affordable health-care reform plan that solved these problems and to create sufficient consensus to get the plan adopted within two years would have been a signal accomplishment and a noteworthy feat of political leadership. But he did not come close. Clinton established an unworkable advisory process to develop a proposal. He then recommended a highly bureaucratic and extraordinarily expensive plan with no convincing means of controlling the costs or, indeed, of paying for them. In contrast with his leadership on his economic program, he strayed well to the left of his New Democrat rhetoric, and he avoided facing the pertinent hard truths and explaining them to the American public.

To begin the campaign for health-care reform, the president as one of his first official actions put his wife, Hillary Rodham Clinton, together with his friend, Ira Magaziner, at the head of a White House Task Force on National Health Care Reform, with instructions to produce a plan in a hundred days. Magaziner, an author of books on industrial policy, came to the job with a history of recommending sweeping reforms. One such recommendation was a 1,000-page, $250 million-dollar industrial development policy for Rhode Island that the state's voters rejected by four to one.[54] In the same way, Magaziner insisted on designing a sweeping reform of the health-care system.

Neither Magaziner nor Hillary Clinton had prior experience with presidential advisory processes, and in their attempt to manage one, they adopted an unorthodox, if not bizarre, approach. They assembled an unprecedentedly large and unwieldy task force of some 500 experts, from within and outside government, divided into numerous distinct working groups. They then tried to keep the deliberations and even the membership of the task force secret. (Because of the nongovernmental participants, the plan for secrecy was later overturned as a violation of a federal law that requires open meetings for advisory committees.) Evidently assuming that a workable plan could best be developed by experts insulated from political pressures, the task force avoided consulting with congressional leaders or representatives of many affected interests. According to an internal memorandum by a disaffected participant from the Treasury Department, it also ignored serious objections from within the task force about program costs.

Five months after the supposed deadline, the task force proposed a monumentally complex 1,350-page Health Care Security Act that redesigned much of the existing health-care system. Submitted to Congress in October 1993, the Clinton plan required employers to provide health insurance ("employer mandates"); guaranteed a very generous package of benefits (comparable to those received by employees of major corporations) to all Americans; and established new bureaucratic structures, called "alliances," to coordinate purchases of coverage and services. The plan sought to slow the growth of health-care costs mainly through price controls on insurance policies—an unconvincing strategy in a plan that promised gold-plated health care for all Americans.[55]

In his January 1994 State of the Union address, Clinton raised the stakes that were riding on the adoption of his approach to health-care reform. He reminded the audience of the health-care crisis and made health-care reform the top priority for his second year in office. Holding his pen aloft, he vowed to veto any health-care bill that did not provide universal coverage. The gesture was effective from the standpoint of public relations; his plan enjoyed a spurt in public support after the speech. But the unconditional demand for universal coverage deprived Clinton of the flexibility to negotiate a feasible bill.

With its complexity, high cost, and obtrusive bureaucracy, the Clinton health-care proposal was an easy target for Republicans. Rather than seek a negotiated solution with the White House—an approach that Clinton's posture may have made impossible anyway—Republicans returned to the attack mode. An influential party strategist, William Kristol, recommended that Republicans "consistently and aggressively debunk the Administration's 'crisis' rhetoric."[56] Following this advice, Senator Dole said, "Our country has health-care problems, but no health-care crisis."[57] Republicans attacked the plan as a costly, bureaucratic nightmare that would reduce the quality of care, raise insurance premiums, hamper employment, and greatly increase the federal budget deficit. The Republican criticism was reinforced by an onslaught of critical television advertising sponsored by the insurance industry and other interest groups opposed to the Clinton plan.

For the same reasons, the Clinton health-care plan elicited criticism from moderate and conservative Democrats. Senator Daniel Patrick Moynihan (D-N.Y.), chairman of the Senate Finance Committee, challenged the president's choice of priorities. "We don't have a health-care crisis in this country," he said, echoing the Republicans. "We do have a welfare crisis."[58] He added that the Clinton plan's financing scheme was a "fantasy." Representative Pete Stark (D-Calif.), chairman of the Ways and Means Health Subcommittee, disputed the need for elaborate new organizations. "Things like mandatory alliances, and all that whoop-de-do, are duplicative and unnecessary," he said. "I'm more inclined to use existing institutions."[59]

In fact, both more liberal and more conservative rival plans had significant support among congressional Democrats. Many liberal Democrats preferred a more radical yet arguably simpler and cheaper "single-payer" plan, in which the federal government would take over all funding of health care and provide coverage for all Americans. More conservative plans called for slower movement toward universal coverage, less demanding mandates for employers, or voluntary participation in purchasing alliances.[60] Commenting on the infighting among advocates of competing plans, a Democratic Party leader remarked, "We're headed for a train wreck unless we stop talking about how bad the other plans are and start talking about where the common ground is."[61] At this point, Magaziner was little help, suggesting that the task of sorting out the politics of health-care reform was the lawmakers' job and not his.[62]

With few members lined up behind any one approach, the legislative process descended into chaos. The health-care bills were referred to ten different congressional committees. The liberal-leaning Senate Labor and Human Resources Committee, chaired by Senator Edward Kennedy (D-Mass.), and the House Education and Labor Committee both reported health-care proposals that generally followed the president's plan. But other committees were less helpful to the administration. The bellwether House Energy and Commerce Committee, chaired by John Dingell (D-Mich.), was so divided that it was unable to report a bill.[63] The two revenue committees, with their special responsibility for financing, produced conservative bills. The Senate Finance Committee bill rejected employer mandates and did not purport to achieve universal coverage. The House Ways and Means Committee, even though stacked with Democrats, could barely pass a compromise bill by a vote of 20–18. As committee chairman Sam Gibbons(D-Fla.) noted, some Democrats were saying that the bill was too liberal; others that it was too conservative.[64]

Because no coherent plan had emerged from the committees, the Democratic House and Senate leaders tried to find a formula that could pass the Congress. House Majority Leader Richard Gephardt and Senate Majority Leader George Mitchell each put together their own plans and pressured party moderates to sign on with them.

As with the economic program, the leadership appealed to Democratic Party loyalty. Said House Rules Committee chairman Joe Moakley (D-Mass.), "We're talking about rallying around the flag; we need to stick together."[65] But as Representative Jim McDermott (D-Wash.) pointed out, "This is not an issue where the leadership can say to people, 'Trust me.' ... This bill affects every person in every member's district."[66] Moreover, public opinion had turned against the Democratic proposals. By July 1994, a majority of the public, 55 percent, disapproved of Clinton's plan. By August, even though 57 percent still wanted health-care reform, only 39 percent favored the plans offered by Democratic leaders in Congress.[67]

With the Democrats in disarray and their proposals lacking popular support, the Republicans adopted the strategy of sending them home to face the voters "empty-handed" on health-care reform.[68] It did not require much effort. The Democratic leadership made little progress in building a party coalition for a health-care bill before adjournment. In late September, Senator Mitchell, who was retiring from the Senate and who earlier had refused nomination to the Supreme Court because of his aspiration to pass health-care reform in his final session, announced that the bill was dead for the 103rd Congress.

We cannot assume that Clinton's missteps had prevented him from delivering on his campaign promise to reform health care. Under any presidential strategy, the barriers to consensus would have been formidable. But Clinton's failure to develop a responsible, centrist approach to health-care reform—one with less governmental intrusion and more genuine concern for cost—doomed the effort. Instead of winning a victory or at least claiming the high ground on a popular issue, Clinton gave the Republicans more ammunition for the 1994 campaign.

Crime

Another item with high priority on Clinton's domestic agenda was new legislation to fight crime. In the 1992 campaign, Clinton had promised to put 100,000 new police officers on the streets of American cities. He also advocated a popular, though substantively dubious, "three-strikes-and-you're-out" sentencing policy—under which a third felony conviction would automatically result in a sentence of life imprisonment.[69] In his 1994 State of the Union address he called for a crime bill that was "tough and smart." Because the Democrats had the unfortunate image among many voters of being "soft on crime," such a bill was potentially a central ingredient in a successful New Democratic domestic strategy.

In contrast with his drift to the left on health-care reform, Clinton staked out a centrist position on crime. As a result, he was able to build a New Democrat-style coalition of Democrats and moderate Republicans to pass major legislation on the subject.[70] Even so, the fragility of such coalitions, in a congressional setting that tends toward polarized ideological conflict, was apparent.

In the six years preceding the Clinton presidency, Congress had repeatedly debated major crime bills without reaching a resolution. The bills raised a host of issues—several of which (like the death penalty and gun control) were symbolically charged or ideologically salient and thus were hard to compromise. Fundamentally, liberals and conservatives had different views on how to deal with crime. Conservatives wanted more police, more prisons, longer sentences, and the death penalty. Liberals doubted the worth of these strategies and favored drug treatment, gun control, and social programs to prevent crime. Neither Republican presidents nor congressional Democratic leaders had made concerted efforts to bridge these differences.

In August 1993, Clinton outlined the elements of a quite conservative crime bill: money to hire 100,000 new police officers, the "three-strikes-and-you're-out" sentencing policy, authorization of the death penalty for an expanded list of federal crimes, and a procedural reform of death-row appeals. He also endorsed liberal proposals for gun control, including a ban on assault weapons. With a president who was pushing to bridge liberal-conservative differences on the crime issue, legislative action was facilitated. Congressional Democrats added the sweetener of a $28 billion anticrime spending package, and both chambers passed versions of an omnibus crime bill by the following spring.

Trouble came in the later stages of the legislative process. Although the Senate and House bills both contained combinations of liberal and conservative features, they differed in important respects. In particular, the Senate bill contained an assault weapons ban; the House bill contained a provision allowing the use of statistical evidence to challenge death sentences as racially discriminatory. In reconciling the two bills, the House–Senate conference committee split the difference, ideologically: it dropped the antidiscrimination provisions, pleasing conservatives, but kept the assault weapons ban, pleasing liberals.[71] But both decisions left important, strongly committed groups of legislators severely dissatisfied.

The result was nearly a successful coalition of the left and the right to block action by the center. In the House, Republicans, Democratic opponents of gun control, and members of the Black Caucus unexpectedly joined forces and defeated the procedural measure (called the "rule") to bring the conference committee bill to the floor for a final vote. The last-minute roadblock threatened to kill the president's crime bill.[72]

The Democratic leadership worked feverishly to find a compromise and save the bill. As with the economic plan, many Republicans attacked the crime bill for its spending provisions, such as funding for inner-city midnight basketball programs, which they discounted as mere pork-barrel. "We swallowed a little pork last fall," said Senator Dole. "We can't swallow the whole hog."[73] But President Clinton, who had been stumping for the crime bill and needed a domestic success to make up for the impending failure on health care, redoubled his rhetorical efforts to demand action.

Ultimately, the political appeal of taking action on crime in an election year—and indeed, taking several actions that had enthusiastic constituencies—carried the day, and a compromise bill passed both houses and was signed by the president. The final bill cut $3.3 billion from the original conference report, with about $2 billion of the cuts coming from crime prevention programs and the rest from prison construction and law enforcement. The bill contained an assault weapons ban, authorization of the death penalty for new and existing federal crimes, "three-strikes-and-you're-out" sentencing, and authorization for criminal prosecution of juveniles as adults in the federal court system. In a defeat for the Black Caucus, the antidiscrimination provisions were omitted.[74]

Welfare Reform

One of Clinton's boldest campaign promises was to "end welfare as we know it." His rhetoric suggested a centrist or conservative approach to welfare reform. "Work is the best social program this country has ever devised," he proclaimed.[75] In his speech accepting the Democratic presidential nomination, Clinton said, "welfare should be a second chance, not a way of life."[76]

Clinton's general approach to welfare reform seemed to have widespread potential support. In an April 1994 Gallup poll, 68 percent of the public said that most people receiving welfare payments are taking advantage of the system. Much of the public endorsed radical changes in welfare policy: 54 percent said that welfare spending should be reduced or ended altogether; a large minority, 36 percent, felt that the welfare system should be replaced entirely. Important for a centrist approach to welfare reform, 68 percent of the public favored creating a new welfare system to get poor people off welfare, even if it cost more money than the current system.[77]

In office, Clinton stuck with and elaborated his centrist view of welfare reform. But Clinton's welfare strategy was heavily invested in simplistic measures to reduce welfare dependency, so to speak, at the stroke of a pen. In any event, largely because of competing domestic priorities, Clinton was not willing to allocate sufficient funds or sufficient time and attention on the part of his administration and especially Congress to make possible a serious effort at welfare reform.

From the beginning of his administration, Clinton sought to appeal to both liberal and conservative Democrats on welfare reform. For the liberals, Clinton called for welfare recipients to receive expanded health care, child care, and education or job-training opportunities. For the conservatives, he advocated a crackdown on fathers who do not pay child support, and he called for a two-year limit on welfare payments.[78] Much like the "three-strikes-and-you're-out" sentencing policy in the crime bill, the two-year limit on welfare benefits was more clearly suited to pleasing a mass constituency than to providing a workable solution to welfare dependency.[79] More bluntly, Senator Daniel Patrick Moynihan accused Clinton of using welfare reform as "boob bait for Bubbas."[80]

In any event, Clinton kept most of his eggs in other baskets and largely sacrificed welfare reform to his other domestic priorities, especially deficit reduction and health-care reform. Because the House Ways and Means Committee and the Senate Finance Committee had central responsibilities for both health-care reform (owing to their jurisdiction over Medicare and Medicaid) and welfare reform, and because both subjects were enormously complex and controversial, for Clinton to push a welfare bill could easily have undermined his chances for action on health care. Probably for that reason, the Clinton administration went slow on welfare reform, taking until mid-1994 to unveil a specific legislative proposal—and prompting Senator Moynihan's remark, quoted earlier, suggesting that Clinton had invented a health-care crisis and overlooked a real crisis in welfare policy.

Because a workable approach to welfare reform was likely to require additional spending for education and job training, job placement, day care, enforcement of child-support obligations, and administration of workfare, among other things—with some estimates of $6 billion per year in additional costs—it was also in conflict with deficit reduction. In its policy planning, the Clinton administration maintained its commitment to deficit reduction, at some cost to the prospects for welfare reform. In draft proposals leaked in early 1994, the administration's welfare task force called for "deficit-neutral" financing of welfare reform—with additional spending on welfare to be matched by reduced spending in other areas.[81]

As the Clinton administration lumbered toward offering a centrist approach to welfare reform, it again experienced intense pressures from both ends of the ideological spectrum. Representative Dave McCurdy (D-Okla.)

and others associated with the Democratic Leadership Council urged Clinton to keep the notion of time limits on welfare benefits and to squeeze the money for welfare reform from other programs. Republicans suggested cutting food programs and benefits to immigrants. Liberal Democrats complained that time limits would "increase poverty and hurt needy families."[82] And they objected strongly when the administration floated proposals of paying for welfare reform by taxing food stamps, welfare benefits, and housing assistance. "You're taking money away from poor people to hire social workers," said Representative Robert Matsui of California.[83]

The sharp ideological differences between the parties and within the Democratic Party made it unclear whether sufficient consensus could be reached to pass a major, centrist welfare reform bill. In contrast with the crime issue, no angry public was clamoring for action and forcing rival factions to resolve their differences or be blamed for obstruction. According to Joe Califano, a former Democratic cabinet secretary with sad experience in the matter, "welfare reform is the Middle East of domestic politics."[84]

In any case, Clinton finally announced his welfare reform proposal in June 1994—far too late for serious consideration in the 103rd Congress. The Clinton plan required that a minor parent live with a responsible adult, required welfare recipients to increase their employability, and set a two-year limit for cash assistance. It also required states to establish paternity for children born out of wedlock and collect child support from absent fathers. Secretary of Health and Human Services Donna Shalala explained, "Under our plan, it will be clear to all teenagers, young men and young women, that having a child is an immense responsibility—not an easy route to independence."[85] The question of how to finance reform was largely sidestepped through the expedient of a gradual, indeed very slow, phase-in. The plan would cover only 8 percent of welfare recipients by 1999.

Republicans were quick to denounce the Clinton welfare reform plan as mere tinkering. Coming when it did, and with the hard choices about financing set aside for the future, the plan appeared to be more a campaign document than a policy proposal.

The Electoral Verdict and Its Aftermath

The first stage of the trial of Clinton's New Democrat presidency ended with the delivery of a clear, dramatic, and negative verdict by the voters in the 1994 midterm elections. For the first time since the presidency of Harry S Truman, a Democratic president would face a Republican Congress.

With Clinton's popularity starting low and mostly descending even lower through 1993 and 1994, the Republicans decided early to make the 1994 midterm elections, as much as possible, a referendum on his presidency. During the election campaigns, Republican candidates made much of

Bill Clinton's unpopularity and took delight in portraying their Democratic rivals as "Bill Clinton's man from Montana,"[86] "just another vote for Bill Clinton's policies,"[87] or "President Clinton's lapdog."[88] Exit polls demonstrated the success of this strategy. Twenty-seven percent of the voters explained their vote in the House elections as a vote against Clinton, compared with only 18 percent who explained it as a vote to support him.[89] Many of the Republicans' campaign assets in this strategy concerned weak points in Clinton's image or performance unrelated to domestic policy: from a long string of scandals and gaffes to resentment of Hillary Clinton's prominence in government to a widely criticized disarray in foreign policy.

But, to a great extent, the Republican campaign focused precisely on Clinton's domestic policies. Republican candidates had a field day with Clinton's sponsorship of gay rights, his tax increases and broken promise of a middle-class tax cut, his alleged pork-barrel spending, and his big-government approach to health-care reform, among other things. Moreover, led by Representative Gingrich, Republicans campaigned for control of the House on the basis of a multipoint "Contract with America" that drew a sharp distinction between the Republicans' domestic policy vision and that of Clinton and the Democrats. They promised a balanced budget amendment to the Constitution and a line-item veto; a capital gains tax cut along with several other cuts, credits, and incentives (some of them directly reversing Clinton's tax increases); even tougher sentencing guidelines and more death-penalty provisions than those in the Clinton crime bill; an outright prohibition of welfare benefits to minor parents; cutbacks in federal regulation of business; and other measures.[90]

The extraordinary Republican takeover of both houses of Congress represented in some degree the voters' actually embracing the Republican domestic strategy and, so to speak, signing the contract. But even more clearly, the sweeping victory was interpreted as such a mandate after the fact.

In the aftermath of the election debacle, Clinton had to pick up the pieces of his presidency and decide how to deal with a conservative-dominated Republican Congress that felt entitled to set the national agenda. His first inclination was to accommodate the Republican agenda. He called for "bipartisan cooperation."[91] And he began to renew some conservative positions that he had soft-pedaled or bargained away in the first half of his term—even flirting briefly with supporting the Republican demand for a constitutional amendment on school prayer. Meanwhile, he also searched for ways to reclaim the initiative in policymaking—proposing, within days of the election, a major restructuring of the division of responsibilities between the states and the federal government; and a generous middle-class tax cut that ended, arguably, Clinton's politically ill-fated commitment to deficit reduction and fiscal responsibility. But the White House also attacked some of the more draconian Republican ideas for welfare reform.

Whether a president who had difficulty defining himself consistently in the first half of his term would find a workable posture and stick with it under radically new and uncertain circumstances in the second half was much in doubt.

Conclusion: The Requirements of Leadership

In an old joke, a doctor reports that "the operation was a success, but the patient died." In the first two years of his presidency, Clinton's New Democrat strategy for domestic policy was a partial success. But President Clinton, at midterm, was a clear-cut political failure. The contrast between the two judgments points to some lessons about the requirements of presidential leadership.

The New Democratic agenda enabled Clinton to achieve a considerable amount of significant policy change. For one thing, the centrist general stance did not interfere with his successful promotion of several liberal measures that had widespread public support: the family- and medical-leave bill, the motor voter bill, the National Service program, and the Brady bill. More directly reflecting New Democrat themes, Clinton was also able to push through an economic program with a significant deficit-reduction package, which balanced spending cuts with tax increases on upper-income groups. He secured a major crime bill and related measures that incorporated both liberal and conservative methods of fighting crime. And although Clinton fell far short of obtaining a health-care reform bill and did not get much beyond conversation about welfare reform, he arguably made some progress toward identifying feasible options in both areas. One suspects that if, at the beginning of his term, Clinton had been offered a guarantee of this much midterm accomplishment, he would have been tempted to take it.

Nevertheless, the New Democratic agenda was shown to have a shaky foundation in congressional politics. The economic program was passed with no Republican support, by the narrowest margins, and only through extraordinary appeals to party loyalty among congressional Democrats. Even at the time, it appeared that some Democrats were making the ultimate political sacrifice to pass the program. The crime bill was almost killed by a coalition of the left and the right against the center, even though it contained a variety of popular anticrime measures. The health-care bill was, in fact, killed; and welfare reform was never really born. There was no evidence of a sustainable coalition of moderate Democrats and Republicans that would reliably implement a centrist, fiscally responsible domestic program. Instead, the Republican attack on Clinton's policies demonstrated the serious obstacles posed for such a program by an increasingly polarized and plebiscitary political environment.

Moreover, the fact that the same party controlled both the presidency and Congress—the circumstance that many hoped would end "gridlock" and restore effectiveness to American government—did not clearly help with implementing a responsible centrist agenda, and may have hurt. The Republicans took advantage of their minority status to excuse themselves of responsibility for governing. Yet, when the Democrats tried to assume that responsibility, the Republicans were sometimes able to block action, especially in the Senate, or to impose unacceptable political costs on the Democrats through effective partisan attacks. The lesson of the 1993 budget process, arguably, was that a majority party in control of both branches can substantially reduce the budget deficit—but only if it is willing to risk becoming a minority party.

Conceivably, Clinton will have a more productive relationship with congressional Republicans in the second half of his term. On the one hand, the Republicans won an extraordinary political victory by taking a confrontational approach in the first half of his term; they certainly may try to increase their winnings by using the same approach in the second half. On the other hand, with control of both houses and a share in the accountability for results, they will also face greater opportunities for policy accomplishment and greater dangers in being held responsible for deadlock.

More generally, Clinton's experience points to a strategic dilemma for future presidents: barring major changes in partisan or ideological alignments among the voters, Democratic presidential candidates will rarely be competitive in general elections unless they campaign as centrists. Although strong conservatives may have somewhat better chances than strong liberals, Republican presidential candidates will also face pressures to seek the center. But it is unclear whether, in the current state of congressional politics, a centrist presidential agenda can be a viable basis for governing. In view of the mixed results under Clinton, the jury is still out on that question.

Despite the inherent difficulties of a fiscally responsible centrist strategy, however, the reason that Clinton was an apparent political failure after two years—with well under 50 percent public approval and a stunning defeat for his party in the midterm elections—was mainly his own deficiency as a political leader. Beginning in the 1992 campaign and continuing into his presidency, Clinton was plagued by numerous scandals—concerning claims or admissions about his avoidance of the draft, his smoking of marijuana (and dubious statements on that subject), extramarital affairs, financial improprieties in the Whitewater matter, administrative improprieties in connection with the Whitewater investigation, and the removal of files after the suicide of a White House aide. His first two years in office were dominated by a series of mistakes and manifestations of mismanagement: repeated difficulties winning confirmation of cabinet nominees, a clumsy partisan takeover of the White House travel office, amateurish press relations, a reported $200 haircut that held up traffic on an airport runway, indifference and drift on critical issues of foreign policy, frequent criticism of an inexperienced White House staff, and several staff reshufflings, among others. At bottom, Clinton's troubles seemed to derive from a few key personal shortcomings: in particular, an apparent tendency to cut corners on matters of personal and professional ethics and a lack of awareness or concern about the requirements of effective decision making and management in the White House. Such weaknesses have effects on a presidency that overwhelm those of strategy and positioning.

Some of Clinton's miscues had a direct bearing on his domestic program and its political reception. The premature commitment on homosexuals in the military dissipated public and congressional support. An aspect of the staffing problem—namely, a dearth of centrist Democrats on the White House staff—contributed to the leftward drift that produced an untenably costly and bureaucratic health-care proposal. As one consequence of this drift, the centrist Democratic Leadership Council was a frequent and severe critic of Clinton. More important, the political mistakes on gay rights and health care—along with the conscious political risk taking of the tax increase—provided important ammunition for the Republicans' campaign attack on Clinton and the Democrats. Quite possibly, Clinton's domestic record, overall, was a liability in the election.

In the end, however, the main effect of Clinton's scandals, mistakes, and mismanagement was not on the progress or reception of his domestic program but on the voters' trust in his competence and integrity. This trust died a "death by a thousand cuts." In our view, a president who, along with presiding over a healthy economy, was trusted personally by the voters would have weathered the political storms of Clinton's domestic policy. That is, the voters reacted far more negatively than they otherwise would have to Clinton's positions on gay rights, taxes, and health care, among other issues, and they gave him far less credit for the healthy economy—precisely because they did not trust him. Simply stated, Clinton's standing with the public undermined his domestic program, not the reverse.

Acknowledgment

The authors are grateful to Stella Herriges Quirk for helpful comments and editing.

Notes

1. For an insightful recent discussion, see Charles O. Jones, *The Presidency in a Separated System* (Washington, D.C.: Brookings Institution, 1994).

2. The polarization of political conflict is described in E.J. Dionne, Jr., *Why Americans Hate Politics* (New York: Simon and Schuster, 1991).

3. David W. Rohde, *Parties and Leaders in the Postreform House* (Chicago: University of Chicago Press, 1991); Roger A. Davidson, *The Postreform Congress* (New York: St. Martin's Press, 1992).

4. Theodore J. Lowi, *The Personal President: Power Invested, Promise Unfulfilled* (Ithaca: Cornell University Press, 1985); Paul Brace and Barbara Hinckley, *Follow the Leader: Opinion Polls and the Modern Presidents* (New York: Basic Books, 1992).

5. Jeffrey Tulis, *The Rhetorical Presidency* (Princeton: Princeton University Press, 1987); Joseph Bessette, *The Mild Voice of Reason: Deliberative Democracy and American National Government* (Chicago: University of Chicago Press, 1994).

6. William Schneider, "Class Differences Dividing Democrats," *National Journal,* 11 December 1993, 2976.

7. Ibid.

8. *Los Angeles Times,* 29 May 1993.

9. Moreover, the Democrats lost two House seats and two Senate seats in special elections prior to the 1994 midterm elections.

10. Gary C. Jacobson, "Congress: Unusual Year, Unusual Election," in *The Elections of 1992,* ed. Michael Nelson (Washington, D.C.: CQ Press, 1993), 153–82.

11. "103rd Congress: Diversity and Power," in 1993 *Congressional Quarterly Almanac* (Washington, D.C.: CQ Press, 1994), 16–18.

12. Viveca Novak, "After the Boll Weevils," *National Journal,* 26 June 1993, 1630–34.

13. Ibid.

14. Eliza Newlin Carney, "Pesky Critters," *National Journal,* 29 October 1994, 2507–11; Novack, "After the Boll Weevils"; James A. Barnes, "His House in Order, but ...," *National Journal,* 1 January 1994, 45.

15. Richard E. Cohen, "Leadership Test," *National Journal,* 13 November 1993, 606–10.

16. *Washington Post,* 5 November 1992.

17. William Sternberg, "Housebreaker," *Atlantic Monthly,* 271 (June 1993): 26–42.

18. "With Democrat in White House, Partisanship Hits New High," in 1993 *Congressional Quarterly Almanac* (Washington, D.C.: CQ Press, 1994), 14C–21C; Richard E. Cohen and William Schneider, "Choosing Sides," *National Journal,* 22 January 1994, 179–89.

19. "Assessing the 103rd Congress ... What Passed and What Didn't," *Congressional Quarterly Weekly Report,* 5 November 1994, 3146–47.

20. "New President Faces Gay-Soldiers Conflict," in 1993 *Congressional Quarterly Almanac* (Washington, D.C.: CQ Press, 1994), 454–62.

21. "A Nation Turns Expectant Eyes to Clinton," *U.S. News & World Report,* 25 January 1993, 32.

22. *Economic Report of the President,* January 1993, 244, 266, 383.

23. "Clinton Throws Down Gauntlet," in 1993 *Congressional Quarterly Almanac* (Washington, D.C.: CQ Press, 1994), 85–89.

24. "Clinton Outlines His Plan to Spur Economy," in 1993 *Congressional Quarterly Almanac* (Washington, D.C.: CQ Press, 1994), 7D–12D.

25. Lydia Saad, "Immediate Public Reaction Boosts 'Clintonomics' Stock,"

Gallup Poll Monthly 341 (February 1993): 26–28.

26. "Clinton Throws Down Gauntlet," 87–88.

27. William Schneider, "The Deficit Has Its Uses, Clinton Finds," *National Journal*, 2 January 1993, 54.

28. Graeme Browning, "The Old Shell Game?" *National Journal*, 27 March 1993, 746–48.

29. Ibid.

30. Ibid.

31. "Budget Resolution Embraces Clinton Plan," in 1993 *Congressional Quarterly Almanac* (Washington, D.C.: CQ Press, 1994), 102–7, at 103.

32. Richard E. Cohen, "Doing Business," *National Journal*, 12 June 1993, 1394–98.

33. Viveca Novak, "Apportioning Pain," *National Journal*, 8 May 1993, 1103–6.

34. "Budget Resolution Embraces Clinton Plan," 33.

35. Ibid., 106.

36. "Fiscal 1993 Stimulus Bill Killed," in 1993 *Congressional Quarterly Almanac* (Washington, D.C.: CQ Press, 1994), 706–9.

37. *New York Times*, 4 August 1993.

38. David A. Stockman, "America Is Not Overspending," *New Perspectives Quarterly* 10 (1993): 12–14.

39. "Deficit Reduction Bill Narrowly Passes," in 1993 *Congressional Quarterly Almanac* (Washington, D.C.: CQ Press, 1994), 107–39.

40. Ibid., 114.

41. Ibid., 111–14.

42. Ibid., 118–19.

43. Ibid., 122–23.

44. Ibid., 123.

45. Ibid., 124.

46. *New York Times*, 7 August 1993.

47. "Deficit Reduction Bill," 120–21; Richard E. Cohen, *Changing Course in Washington: Clinton and the New Congress* (New York: Macmillan, 1994).

48. George Hager, "Clinton's Bid to Shift Priorities Constrained by Fiscal Limits," *Congressional Quarterly Weekly Report*, 12 February 1994, 287–93.

49. David S. Cloud, "Clinton's Cuts May Be Too Much for Lawmakers to Digest," *Congressional Quarterly Weekly Report*, 12 February 1994, 294–96.

50. Robert J. Blendon, Mollyann Brodie, Tracey Stelzer Hyams, and John M. Benson, "The American Public and the Critical Choices for Health Care Reform," *Journal of the American Medical Association* 271 (1994): 1539–44.

51. *Economic Report of the President*, 1994, 150.

52. *Economic Report of the President*, 1993, 132.

53. *Economic Report of the President*, 1994, 150.

54. Jonathan Rauch, "The Idea Merchant," *National Journal*, 12 December 1992, 2833–37.

55. William Schneider, "A Fatal Flaw in Clinton's Health Plan," *National Journal*, 6 November 1993, 2696; Alissa J. Rubin et al., "Clinton's Health Care Bill," *National Journal*, 26 February 1994, 492–504.

56. James A. Barnes, "What Health Care Crisis?" *National Journal*, 29 January 1994, 265; Jon Meacham, "The GOP's Master Strategist," *Washington*

Monthly 26 (September 1994): 32–39.

57. William Schneider, "No Score So Far on Health Care Game," *National Journal*, 12 February 1994, 398.

58. Jeffrey L. Katz, "Clinton Urged to Slow Down," *Congressional Quarterly Weekly Report*, 22 January 1994, 119.

59. Julie Kosterlitz, "Ready for Relaunch," *National Journal*, 27 November 1993, 2857.

60. Alissa J. Rubin et al., "Two Ideological Polls Frame Debate over Reform," *Congressional Quarterly Weekly Report*, 8 January 1994, 23–28; Beth Donovan, "Betting Big on Public Backing, Clinton Stands Firm on Veto," *Congressional Quarterly Weekly Report*, 25 June 1994, 1703–6; Alissa J. Rubin, "Uncertainty, Deep Divisions Cloud Opening of Debate," *Congressional Quarterly Weekly Report*, 13 August 1994, 2344–53.

61. Richard E. Cohen, "Into the Swamp," *National Journal*, 19 March 1994, 642–46.

62. Julie Kosterlitz, "The Big Sell," *National Journal*, 14 May 1994, 1118–23.

63. Beth Donovan, "Leaders to Forge New Bill from Committee Efforts," *Congressional Quarterly Weekly Report*, 2 July 1994, 1792–1801.

64. David S. Cloud, "Gibbons' Patched-Together Health Bill Now Faces Test on the Floor," *Congressional Quarterly Weekly Report*, 2 July 1994, 1793–98.

65. Alissa J. Rubin, "Leaders Using Fervent Approach to Convert Waivering Members," *Congressional Quarterly Weekly Report*, 30 July 1994, 2142–46.

66. Ibid.

67. Lydia Saad, "Public Has Cold Feet on Health Care Reform," *Gallup Poll Monthly*, 346 (August 1994): 2–9.

68. "GOP Master Strategist," 36; Alissa J. Rubin, "Chances for Limited Measure Slight as Congress Returns," *Congressional Quarterly Weekly Report*, 10 September 1994, 2523–24; David S. Cloud, "Support Erodes as Key Backers Voice Little Hope for Passage," *Congressional Quarterly Weekly Report*, 17 September 1994, 2571–72.

69. Critics of "three-strikes-and-you're-out" note that most three-time felony convicts are approaching the age when they are likely to retire from criminal activity. Putting them in prison for life, at that point, is very expensive and prevents only a modest amount of crime.

70. David Masci, "$30 Billion Anti-Crime Bill Heads to Clinton's Desk," *Congressional Quarterly Weekly Report*, 27 August 1994, 2488–89; Phil Kunz, "Hard Fought Crime Bill Battle Spoils Field for Health Care," *Congressional Quarterly Weekly Report*, 27 August 1994, 2485.

71. Holly Idelson, "More Cops, Jails: House Takes a $28 Billion Aim at Crime," *Congressional Quarterly Weekly Report*, 23 April 1994, 3142–45; Holly Idelson, "$33 Billion Crime Measure Heads to Last Hurdles," *Congressional Quarterly Weekly Report*, 30 July 1994, 2137–40.

72. Holly Idelson, "Clinton, Democrats Scramble to Save Anti-Crime Bill," *Congressional Quarterly Weekly Report*, 13 August 1994, 2340–43.

73. Holly Idelson and Richard Samman, "Marathon Talks Produce New Anti-Crime Bill," *Congressional Quarterly Weekly Report*, 20 August 1994, 2449–53; Masci, "$30 Billion Anti-Crime Bill," 2484–2493.

74. Masci, "$30 Billion Anti-Crime Bill," 2488–92.

75. Jeff Schear, "Pulling in Harness," *National Journal,* 4 June 1994, 1286–90.

76. Ibid., 1286.

77. Leslie McAneny and David W. Moore, "Public Supports New Programs to Get People Off Welfare," *Gallup Poll Monthly* 344 (May 1994): 2–5.

78. *New York Times,* 3 February 1994.

79. The main problem with the two-year limit is that few poor, single female heads of families can increase their income sufficiently to become independent within two years (or much longer). Cutting off benefits to these families punishes the women, which many people may support, but also punishes the children, which hardly anyone supports.

80. *New York Times,* 8 January 1993.

81. *New York Times,* 3 February 1994.

82. *New York Times,* 5 December 1993.

83. *New York Times,* 10 November 1994.

84. *New York Times,* 3 February 1993.

85. Rochelle L. Stanfield, "Growth Curve," *National Journal,* 23 July 1994, 1728–32.

86. Margaret Kriz, "Shoot-Out in the West," *National Journal,* 15 October 1994, 2388–92.

87. Dick Kirschten, "McClinton v. McGingrich," *National Journal,* 5 November 1994, 2592–93.

88. Graeme Browning, "Double the Trouble," *National Journal,* 5 November 1994, 2593–95.

89. William Schneider, "Clinton: The Reason Why," *National Journal,* 12 November 1994, 2630–32.

90. "Republicans' Initial Promise: 100-Day Debate on Contract," *Congressional Quarterly Weekly Report,* 12 November 1994, 3216–19.

91. *New York Times,* 10 November 1994.

10

Clinton's Foreign Policy
at Midterm

LARRY BERMAN AND EMILY O. GOLDMAN

In a preceding volume entitled *The Bush Presidency: First Appraisals,* the authors of a midterm assessment of that incumbent's foreign policy began by observing, "when scholars look back at the Bush presidency, they will probably note the extraordinary events that characterized President Bush's first twenty-four months in office."[1] The dramatic political and military transformation of Europe ended the Cold War and ushered in what President Bush described as a "new world order where diverse nations are drawn together in common cause." In his 1991 State of the Union address, President Bush declared the goals of a new world order: "to achieve the universal aspirations of mankind: peace and security, freedom and the rule of law."

Time magazine designated President George Bush its 1991 Man of the Year for leading a worldwide coalition victory in the Persian Gulf and for providing "a commanding vision of a new world order." Yet, a little more than a year later, Bill Clinton defeated the commander-in-chief who had drawn a line in the sand to stop Iraqi aggression. By election day 1992, the glow of victory in the Persian Gulf and the accompanying unprecedented public approval ratings for President Bush had been replaced by "It's the economy, stupid!" The presidency of George Bush had lost its domestic core. As the authors of the aforementioned article forewarned, "the fate of the foreign policy George Bush may be much more closely intertwined with the domestic policy George Bush than he, who would much rather lead the world than the nation, would prefer."[2]

Throughout the 1992 presidential campaign, candidate Clinton made it clear that, if elected, he would provide long-needed leadership on the neglected domestic and economic fronts. Clinton promised to "focus like a laser beam" on the economy. Lacking experience and interest in foreign policy, the presidential candidate believed that if a battle was to be fought, resources of intervention deployed, it would be in a war against domestic problems, not foreign enemies. On this domestic ground, and not on faraway soil, Bill Clinton hoped to stake his presidency. In November 1992, with Democratic majorities in the House and Senate, the new administration had good cause for optimism.

Two years later, virtually all optimism was gone. In the wake of the 1994 midterm elections that swept Republicans into majority control of both houses, with health-care reform stalled in Congress, and questions abounding about the president's character and leadership, foreign policy appears to have become more important to Clinton than it had been. Indeed, from the president's perspective, his prospects for influence over policy now appear greater in the Middle East than in the Congress of the United States. Dealing with Prime Minister Rabin of Israel or President Assad of Syria might prove less difficult than working with Newt Gingrich and Bob Dole on the Republican Contract with America. The presidential role of chief diplomat seems to offer more room for success and possible reelection than that of chief legislator of a Republican contract.

Yet whatever private illusions President Clinton may hold, his political prospects in foreign policy actually depend not as much on his well-documented learning curve as on the Serbs, the North Koreans, the Haitians, and other international actors who may have already taken their measures of the differences between Bill Clinton's rhetoric and his commitment. As Secretary of State Warren Christopher once observed, "foreign policy is always a work in progress," but the progress report for the first twenty-four months has been characterized by vacillation, indecision, and the lack of a guiding principle or compass that might provide bearing for leaders and a direction for followers on a set of policies or a Clinton doctrine.

To date, the Clinton presidency has confronted a series of difficult policy options in Bosnia, Somalia, Haiti, Europe, and Russia. The results have been decidedly mixed. "William the Waffler" was a well-earned caricature for his administration's inconsistency in linking rhetoric with policy on human rights violations in China to most-favored-nation renewal; on the flood of refugees from Haiti and Cuba; and in Bosnia, where the policy one day was to bomb the Serbs, the next day's commitment was to lift the arms embargo against Bosnian Muslims, then the hope was that the United Nations or NATO would find a solution. Brent Scowcroft, national security adviser under President Bush, derisively characterized Clinton policy in Bosnia as "peripatetic foreign policy at prey to the whims of the latest balance of forces."[3]

Nevertheless, by late 1994, the "Comeback Kid," as some analysts have described President Clinton,[4] was sitting atop a run of good fortune in foreign policy (and an accompanying deluge of good press), which included ratification of the General Agreement on Tariffs and Trade (GATT), a comprehensive Middle East peace process, and a Haiti policy in which the threat of force and its actual deployment led to the departure of the military junta of Raoul Cedras. In the Persian Gulf, Operation Vigilant Warrior constituted a clear and firm response to Saddam Hussein's deployment of 20,000 troops to the Kuwaiti border; Saddam blinked, not Bill Clinton.[5] By late 1994, Jordan and the Palestine Liberation Organization (PLO), two former allies of Iraq in the Gulf War, were now part of the Middle East's comprehensive plan for peace and sided with President Clinton. "Clinton 2, Bullies 0" proclaimed a *New York Daily News* headline in reference to Cedras and Hussein. A successful meeting of the Asian Pacific Economic Cooperation (APEC) led the *New Republic* to identify a new Clinton *in the making* —Leader of the Free World.[6]

This chapter delineates the character and substance of Clinton's foreign policy at midterm. In doing so, the tenuous nature of drawing conclusions from secondary source observations of midterm presidents, especially in foreign policy, needs to be acknowledged. In 1982, for example, midterm assessments of Ronald Reagan revealed that the president's Cold War rhetoric directed at the Soviet Union had created in the general populace a fear of nuclear confrontation. By 1988, Ronald Reagan and Mikhail Gorbachev were strolling together in Red Square amid the bliss of *glasnost* and *perestroika*. President Reagan's strongest approval ratings were now in the arena of reducing the chance of nuclear war. The Reagan two-term legacy was quite different from the observations of President Reagan midway through his first term. No doubt, the presidential legacy of Bill Clinton is similarly in the making.[7]

The Post–Cold War Environment

Assessments of Bill Clinton's handling of foreign policy must first be placed in their appropriate international context, that of the dramatically altered world environment that emerged in the wake of the Cold War. The most distinctive characteristic of the post–Cold War era and the one that separates it from the recent past is the absence of a threat as a central organizing principle. While controversy existed during the Cold War over the nature of the Soviet threat, the mere presence of an overarching strategic imperative or compass provided an anchor for U.S. foreign policy and imposed a set of priorities that (for better or worse) defined the parameters within which U.S. leaders acted in the world and resorted to force in the defense of national interests. The pre-1989 period seems far clearer in retrospect, but indisputably the Cold War provided a known and relatively predictable adversary, a familiar structure of conflict, and a set of important external constraints on U.S. action.

Today, instead of a well-defined threat to anchor U.S. foreign policy, pervasive uncertainty faces the world's sole remaining superpower as it attempts to anticipate the future foreign policy environment, establish a new psychological basis for engaging the nation in the world, and develop principles to guide the use of diplomatic, economic, and military tools abroad. For the United States, the post–Cold War world is characterized first and foremost by threat uncertainty—the disappearance of a known and familiar adversary. Certainty about the enemy has been supplanted by questions about the identity of future adversaries, their goals and capabilities, and the time frame within which future challenges are likely to arise. Post–Cold War U.S. leaders face a set of novel, diffuse, and unfamiliar foreign policy problems such as small peripheral states armed with weapons of mass destruction threatening regional and global security, and unconventional challenges posed by narco-terrorists, religious fundamentalist movements, and ethnic and nationalist violence. Of these, however, none ranks in significance, even in the foreseeable future, to replace the strategic bellwether that disappeared along with the Soviet Union.

U.S. leaders also confront problems of alliance uncertainty. Who will be our future alliance and coalition partners? Is it more desirable to build on firm alliances or to rely on flexible partnerships, collective security arrangements, or ad hoc coalitions? The absence of a hegemonic challenger has weakened the U.S. commitment to firm alliance arrangements such as NATO. Unconventional challenges, such as those posed by ethnic and nationalist violence, do not engender sufficient public concern or political resolve. The civil war in Bosnia bears witness to this, its most recent casualties being the United Nations and NATO, both of which failed to meet the challenge of the Bosnian Serbs over Bihac. Finally, complex regional dynamics, like those in the Middle East, can exacerbate alliance uncertainty given the absence of either a broader structure of conflict, such as the Cold War rivalry with the Soviet Union, or clear regional villains like Saddam Hussein. The ability of Clinton's administration, with the assistance of Congress, to surmount this obstacle and capitalize on the Arab states' loss of their Soviet patron to promote the peace process in the Middle East represents one of Clinton's greatest foreign policy successes.

A third dimension of uncertainty is resource related, namely, how to manage the economy to preserve the ability of the nation to operate in the international system and respond to future threats and challenges. The United States confronted resource uncertainty during the Cold War, though the magnitude of it has significantly grown in the Cold War's aftermath, particularly with the dramatic contraction of defense resources. At the most general level, national leaders must weigh the tradeoff between current de-

fense and defense-related spending to retain the capability to meet unantici-
pated threats in the short run and long-term economic growth to meet unan-
ticipated challenges in the more distant future. If the greatest risk to the
nation is seen to be economic rather than military in nature, which is the
view of this administration, it makes sense to shift resources away from
defense and toward long-term economic growth.

Finally, the post–Cold War environment raises questions about what
type of conflict the United States should prepare for. The question becomes
one of managing tradeoffs between preparing for high-intensity conflict,
such as another Gulf War, for low-intensity peace enforcement and nation-
building missions like those in Haiti and Somalia, or for peacetime noncom-
bat missions of humanitarian assistance and disaster relief. In the real world,
these neat distinctions blur. Bosnia, Somalia, and northern Iraq reveal the
difficulty of separating humanitarian assistance, relief missions, and peacekeeping operations from the combat dimensions of peace enforcement.[8] The
issue is one of relative emphasis, and for the Clinton team it means deciding
whether a regional engagement like the Gulf War, the first major conflict of
the post–Cold War era, represents an anomaly and exception or a prototype
of future conflicts, as the administration's Bottom-up Review assumes. It is
also necessary to decide whether planning should be geared toward the long-
term objective of shaping the international environment (be it regional or
global), toward the midterm goal of deterring threats, or toward the imme-
diate-term task of contingency response.[9]

In sum, we have entered a period in which allies and enemies can no
longer be defined by their status in the Cold War, and military objectives can
no longer be reduced to the containment of communism while avoiding nuclear conflict. Defining a strategic vision for the post–Cold War world
eluded George Bush, who was accused of lacking the "vision thing," and it
has so far eluded Bill Clinton, who has been accused of lacking the "conviction thing." This may be understandable given the indeterminacy of the
post–Cold War international environment, but the practical implication is
that U.S. policy abroad has been cast adrift, buffeted by political calculations with only minimal evidence of coherence and consistency.[10]

Clinton and the Presidency: Who Is the Rest of Me?

In *On the Edge: The Clinton Presidency,* Elizabeth Drew reconstructs the effort made in summer 1994 by White House Chief of Staff Leon Panetta to restore the president's sagging approval ratings by emphasizing the importance
and stature of the presidential office. In accepting Panetta's advice, Clinton concluded, "I've got to be more like John Wayne."[11] The president's analogy to the
tough and rugged movie hero is revealing by itself, but assumes greater signifi-

cance for understanding Clinton when contrasted with a similar invocation made by the country's most recent two-term president, Ronald Reagan. Following the 1980 San Francisco debate with then-President Jimmy Carter, candidate Reagan was asked, "Governor, weren't you intimidated by being up there on stage with the President of the United States?" "No," replied Reagan. "I've been on the same stage with John Wayne."[12]

These two references to John Wayne provide clues to both men and their respective presidencies. Ronald Reagan and Bill Clinton actually shared several political circumstances. Both were governors who positioned themselves as "outsiders" when they sought the presidency against an incumbent president. Neither Reagan in 1980 nor especially Clinton in 1992 could claim a strong popular-vote mandate. Both lacked extensive, if any, preparation or experience in foreign affairs, and both sought to restore the American public's faith in the economy while reshaping domestic priorities.

In retrospect, we know that Ronald Reagan understood that a president with a carefully defined policy agenda can achieve success by using the persuasive and command powers of the presidency. Reagan was indeed a great communicator, but he became "the Great Communicator" because he believed in something, and if he could not exactly explain its details or even be interested in those details, he was clearly able to convince the American public to follow his lead. Reagan, like Franklin D. Roosevelt, understood that much of the president's leadership challenge is tied to educating the public not on the details of policy but on the president's commitment to a course. The presidency did not engulf the man who had been on the same stage with John Wayne; but it frequently appeared to engulf the one who wanted to be more "like" John Wayne. This is so because in the realm of foreign policy, one of the primary and most important jobs of a president, Clinton has provided little consistent leadership and no convincing purpose for the nation in the post–Cold War world.

Clinton and the Presidency: Leadership and Purpose

A hallmark of the present foreign policy environment is the lack of a systemic, or external, imperative (such as the Cold War) confronting the United States. The nation faces a situation of choice instead of compulsion.[13] We have witnessed a transition from a well-ordered world we thought we understood to one that has very different properties and fosters little consensus. In evaluating Clinton's foreign policy, we must appreciate this context of "peacetime strategic uncertainty," which is the primary external driver of foreign policy vacillation and drift. But "internal" factors have exacerbated, rather than mitigated, the disarray and confusion that at present characterize U.S. policy.

One internal driver of foreign policy drift lies in the absence of a clearly articulated and compelling national purpose for the United States in the post–Cold War world. "It is not acceptable," writes Gaddis Smith, "to say that the world has become such a confusing place that each issue can be dealt with only in isolation and when circumstances force a response."[14] What do we mean by stating that what is lacking is something that, if present, would matter significantly? A national purpose expresses a people's orientation toward the world and understanding of their society's role in it. A clear sense of national purpose is crucial for building public consensus at home and generating credibility among friends and potential enemies abroad. A national purpose provides the basis for setting strategic priorities when external compulsion is at a minimum, when, in the words of Colin Gray, "the dynamic state of the world does not have self-evident meaning for the identity and intensity of U.S. national interests."[15] To date, President Clinton has not succeeded in articulating a national purpose sufficiently compelling to convince a skeptical and uninformed public about what the nation should be doing abroad.

One reason why a sense of purpose has eluded this president, and a persistent critique leveled at his foreign policy in general, has been Clinton's continuing failure to conceptualize and then explain the dangers in the world. Leadership has become more difficult because in the absence of a dedicated enemy that can stage a strategic attack on the United States or its allies, conceptualization must precede leading and following. President Clinton, like his predecessors, recognizes that the United States cannot be isolationist, that it must be selective in its involvement and engagement of U.S. forces. Yet he has yet to formulate his thinking on what is and is not a vital interest to the United States in an era where the gravest challenges are within rather than between nations. Nor has he conceptualized a rationale for restoring order as a component of a vital U.S. interest.

This lack of innovative thinking is further compounded by President Clinton's propensity to act indecisively and to engage himself intermittently in foreign affairs. From Bosnia to Haiti to Somalia, the lack of an overarching rationale for intervention has produced indecision and led to policy shortcomings, if not failures. In lieu of policy, the administration has offered a series of disconnected themes. In Somalia, it was the delivery of *only* humanitarian aid as a pretext for intervention with U.S. troops. The Balkan crisis, while no immediate physical threat to the United States, is clearly important, yet the president cannot decide how important the crisis *will* be. While he waffles, splits in NATO grow wider, Jimmy Carter proposes his version of a cease-fire, and the world community anticipates a renewed offensive because the Serbs fear neither Bill Clinton, NATO, nor the United Nations.[16]

Foreign policy drift, particularly on questions relating to the use of force, also stems from the fact that national-purpose orientations vary in the extent to which they discriminate across threats and challenges. Different national purpose orientations imply differing priorities to guide decisions about the extent and nature of involvement abroad. In public statements and documents, Clinton has defined the U.S. national purpose as one of domestic renewal. Historically, domestic orientations have gained salience when risks from threats abroad are perceived to be slight, making possible a reduction in the costs associated with the nation's foreign policy in order to invest greater resources at home. A domestic purpose has traditionally been associated with isolationism, detachment, neutrality, and other inward-looking approaches to strategy, but it need not imply noninvolvement. A domestic purpose is consistent with close bilateral ties to key economic actors essential to the world economy.[17] It is also consistent with multilateralism, but tends to favor followership and dependence on international institutions when responding to crises abroad rather than unilateralism or leadership. It should also be noted that a domestic purpose does not preclude selective unilateralism, as exemplified by the bombing of Iraq's intelligence headquarters in mid-1993 in retaliation for a terrorist plot to assassinate former President Bush during his visit to Kuwait.

Clinton's domestic national-purpose orientation locates the chief threats to U.S. interests in the domestic economic and social condition of the nation. While laudable for the home front and a necessary corrective to the Bush administration's myopia, a domestic-purpose orientation provides a very limited type of guidance for U.S. engagement abroad. In an important sense, a domestic purpose explains what coherence there is in Clinton's foreign policy. Clinton has consistently responded to societal cues about foreign economic policy by making the improvement of economic performance and international competitiveness his top priority. By stressing a competitive United States integrated into the world economy, Clinton has grasped an important dimension of world politics today; he may be praised for it in the future. Still, a domestic purpose cannot discriminate effectively across noneconomic threats, challenges, and opportunities that emerge from outside the state. For this reason, it fosters a vacuum in foreign policy priorities in key areas such as whether and under what conditions risking the use of force is appropriate. Foreign policy needs external (what we want to achieve abroad) as well as internal (what we want to achieve at home) anchors. Absent the former, the Clinton administration has achieved continuity only from the latter. Leslie Gelb of the Council on Foreign Relations notes that Clinton has shown conviction, but only in the area of international trade. And "a foreign economic policy is not a foreign policy and it is not a national security strategy."[18] Hence, many of Clinton's foreign policy decisions have not flowed from a strategic outlook but have been ad hoc responses to developments at home and abroad and attempts to satisfy domestic constituencies. As Arthur Schlesinger, Jr., put it, "since policy makers have not yet found a new guiding concept, foreign policy lobbies based on domestic constituencies rush to fill the vacuum."[19] Under pressure from the congressional Black Caucus, for example, the Clinton administration gave Haiti far higher priority than it might have had otherwise, backing the president into a military action he desperately hoped to avoid.

In sum, a domestic orientation such as President Clinton's can establish clear foreign policy priorities but only in selective areas, for several reasons. First, an internal focus implies that less attention need be devoted to thinking systematically about, and devising strategies to respond to, challenges that originate outside the nation, let alone to devising strategies that shape the external environment. Second, domestic consensus for foreign policy is always an issue in a democratic polity. But a domestic orientation subordinates foreign policy to domestic priorities more than other national-purpose orientations, illustrated by a lack of presidential attentiveness to the outside world and by a tendency to hold foreign policy hostage to domestic constituencies. Society's estimation of the costs of engagement abroad cannot be ignored, nor can allies' and adversaries' estimations of U.S predictability and resolve. The problems associated with a domestic-purpose orientation are further exacerbated in Clinton's case by his leadership qualities in foreign policy: indecisiveness and sporadic engagement. In this sense, the problem is less that of the importance of domestic politics and more that Clinton has chosen to follow rather than lead. In other words, Clinton has room to maneuver, but his foreign policy leadership style has precluded him from maximizing his leverage.

President Clinton's personal presidential style in foreign policy has been characterized by a high degree of energy and rhetoric, an appetite for information, and a preoccupation with detail. These qualities, however, have been overshadowed by the more dominant characteristics of *indecisiveness* and *sporadic engagement*. The president persistently has been unable to make hard decisions on policy because he has wanted to have it both ways. "Clinton is an omnidirectional placater," writes Garry Wills. "He wants to satisfy everyone, which is a surefire way to satisfy no one."[20] Nor has the president been engaged in or interested in the foreign policy shaping process. Mary McGrory described a typical Clinton operation as "riven with controversy, confusion, questions, loose ends, unanswered questions, eleventh hour histrionics, mad overstatements...."[21]

There seems to be agreement that Clinton's style is at once ad hoc and overly cautious. He relies very heavily on the advice of his foreign policy team, but also responds readily to domestic public opinion. Thus, the impression exists of a president who is unsure and inconsistent on foreign policy matters, and who is even conducting foreign policy with only domestic goals in mind. Clearly, Clinton aims to please. Whereas Bush was often commended for his flexibility and belief that "goodwill begets goodwill," Clinton is criticized for not holding firm to the administration's stated foreign policy aims. The difference seems to lie in the perception that although Bush would negotiate, it was he who set the terms of the debate. In Clinton's case, the perception is that he lets his adversaries (at home as well as abroad) set the terms, to which he will then respond. Where Bush was "proactively flexible," Clinton is "reactively flexible." This perception of stylistic differences between Clinton and Bush (although they are, in many ways, substantively similar) is the difference between appearing strong and appearing weak in foreign policy.

During his first year, the president's principal foreign policy advisers included Secretary of State Warren Christopher, Defense Secretary Les Aspin (later replaced by William Perry), and National Security Adviser Anthony Lake. The group of like-minded men met for lunch most every Wednesday in Lake's West Wing office. "Clinton wanted to avoid the open warfare of the Carter administration between Secretary of State Cyrus Vance and National Security Adviser Zbigniew Brzezinski," writes Elizabeth Drew. "In Tony Lake, Warren Christopher, and Les Aspin, he thought he had put together a smoothly working team. But it didn't turn out that way."[22] Drew explains that tensions soon developed based on "conflicting ambitions, divergences of outlook, and differences in style." The Bosnia policy, discussed later, would further divide the team, but it was the president's sporadic engagement that would be the chief contributing factor to drift and public perception of indecisiveness. "Clinton's failure to pay sufficient attention to foreign policy," writes Elizabeth Drew, "was a form of self-indulgence and costly ... as on domestic issues, the successes were far overshadowed by negative developments and mishandling of certain foreign challenges. By the spring of 1994 the danger Clinton had been courting materialized: the lack of public confidence in his handling of foreign policy spilled over into a lack of confidence in his presidency as a whole."[23] Guidance for engagement abroad can come from either strategy or leadership. To date, this administration has displayed very little of either.

The Clinton Presidency's Record of Intent

What, then, does President Clinton believe with respect to foreign policy? First, Clinton's view of foreign policy is tied inextricably to domestic renewal. The GATT and NAFTA, two policies inherited from the previous administration and requiring bipartisan support for passage, reveal a Clinton worldview that domestic growth depends on a foreign economic policy that promotes U.S. exports and world trade.

Reinforcing Clinton's domestic renewal theme, National Security Adviser Lake, in his 21 September 1993 Johns Hopkins University speech—one of several speeches delivered by top-level administration officials sketching a foreign policy vision of enlargement[24]—emphasized that "above all, [the U.S. is] threatened by sluggish economic growth." The strategy of enlarging the world's community of market democracies recognizes an active international role for the United States, but domestic revival is its fundamental prerequisite. Peter Tarnoff, undersecretary of state for political affairs, more forcefully iterated this theme in his comments of 25 May 1993, stating that for the United States, "economic interests are paramount. We simply don't have the leverage, we don't have the influence, we don't have the inclination to use military force, we certainly don't have the money ... to bring to bear the kind of pressure that will produce positive results." While Tarnoff was speaking specifically of Bosnia, and while the rest of the administration denied that Tarnoff's views represented official policy, the Clinton administration has displayed equally little inclination to lead on other post–Cold War crises or shape the external environment, though international events have prevented it from focusing inward as much as it would have liked.

Like Woodrow Wilson, Clinton believes that democracy can be implanted in hostile soil, and this also underlies the strategy of enlargement. Like Theodore Roosevelt and Woodrow Wilson, Clinton believes in using the rhetorical bully pulpit of the presidency to press his case. But this president has actually "turned TR on his head by speaking loudly and carrying a small stick."[25] In the areas of democratization and human rights in particular, Clinton has postured but reversed himself on all too many occasions. Where Bush was criticized by candidate Clinton for doing "business as usual with those who murdered freedom in Tiananmen Square,"[26] President Clinton talked all too loudly but then extended most-favored-nation trading status indefinitely. It may have been the correct political decision, but the president looked bad making it. The lesson was lost on Clinton who, Elizabeth Drew reports, asked David Gergen how it was that Ronald Reagan had been unscathed after the tragedy in Beirut in October 1983, when 219 Americans were killed in a suicide bombing of the Marine barracks. Gergen replied, "Because two days later we were in Grenada, and everyone knew that Ronald Reagan would bomb the hell out of somewhere."[27]

President Clinton also believes in the virtues of multilateralism. He came into office calling for strengthening the United Nations and regional security groups and was initially willing to subordinate U.S. decision making to multinational organizations.[28] On 3 May 1994, Clinton tried to articulate such a policy by stating that while the United States "cannot turn our backs on the rest of the world," it "cannot solve every problem and must not become the world's policeman." Nevertheless, the United States has "an obligation to join with others to do what we can to relieve the suffering and restore the peace" to those areas that need assistance. When confronting ethnic conflicts and peacekeeping activities, Clinton initially played down the need for NATO intervention, instead of using the opportunity to shore up NATO with a redefined mission more attuned to the post–Cold War era.[29] Reflecting a cooperative security approach, Clinton has preferred to make international response the norm, leaning toward U.S. followership, even if it has meant at times ceding leadership on Bosnia to the Russians.[30] National Security Adviser Lake took great pains in his Johns Hopkins speech to point out that the United States "should act multilaterally where doing so advances our interests—and we should act unilaterally when *that* will serve our purpose." In other words, multilateralism is a means, not an end. But the Clinton administration narrowly circumscribed the conditions under which the United States would act unilaterally.

The series of speeches delivered by administration officials in September 1993 all claimed the United States would remain engaged in the world, and even lead. Enlarging the space for democracies and markets would not only feed the U.S. economy but also operate as an important hedge against war. Yet equally significant were the host of caveats accompanying the strategy of enlargement, which included domestic renewal and UN reform, particularly with respect to peacekeeping. As Madeleine Albright, U.S. representative to the United Nations, summarized, the goal "is to ensure that we refrain from asking the UN to undertake missions it is not equipped to do and to help the UN to succeed in missions we like it to do." The United States should not get involved in every UN mission and in fact refused to authorize the immediate deployment of over 5,000 troops to Rwanda on 17 May 1994. While the sentiment for multilateralism is greater in this administration than perhaps in any other since Woodrow Wilson's, it is tempered by the realization, learned on the harsh battleground of Somalia, that the United States must limit involvement with the United Nations when that body is moving too quickly into a situation with insufficient planning and organization.

The blueprint of the administration's defense policy and more clues to its foreign policy orientation appear in the "Bottom-up" intensive strategic review of military programs launched by Defense Secretary Les Aspin in February 1993 and endorsed by his successor, William Perry.[31] The Bottom-up Review (BUR) assessed the post–Cold War environment and laid out a defense strategy and force structure to support it. Conceived as a guide for defense planning into the next century, the BUR evolved out of a series of position papers produced by Aspin's staff while he was chair of the House Armed Services Committee. The BUR employs a building-block approach to force sizing, with each building block designed to respond to a particular, and noticeably historical, hypothetical contingency such as another Desert Storm or another Operation Restore Hope. The core of the Clinton military strategy is contingency response, the assumption being "that such performance is sufficient for deterrence and for assuring regional stability."[32] Less concerned with shaping events and with molding the overall structure of international relations so that hypothetical threats are minimized, the BUR approach focuses on reacting after diplomacy and deterrence have failed.[33] It is a strategy with a short time horizon, of five to ten years, a strategy of insurance consistent with Clinton's greater interest in focusing on domestic priorities.

According to the BUR, the four fundamental dangers to U.S. interests are the proliferation of weapons of mass destruction, regional conflict, internal threats to democracy in the former Soviet Union and developing world, and "economic dangers to our national security, which could result if we fail to build a strong, competitive and growing economy." For the first time, U.S. economic strength has formally become a part of the security lexicon, echoing the priorities of a domestic national purpose.

The Clinton administration's chief foreign policy themes—domestic renewal, enlargement, and multilateralism—are woven together in the so-called En-En document, the *National Security Strategy of Engagement and Enlargement,* which articulates most extensively President Clinton's foreign policy strategy for the post–Cold War world. The document bears many hallmarks of a domestic orientation, chiefly in its concern with domestic renewal and its reliance on collective and multilateral institutions to meet international challenges and crises. The primary objectives of the Clinton policy, according to the document, are to enhance U.S. security, bolster the nation's economy, and promote democracy. Enlarging the community of market democracies earned a place in the document's title, but fell behind promoting economic prosperity in the hierarchy of strategic goals. The document stresses the importance of U.S. leadership, but a selective leadership that implies selective engagement, "focusing on the challenges that are most relevant to our own interests and focusing our resources where we can make the most difference."[34] U.S. security, the document maintains, will be promoted by a strong defense capability and through cooperative security measures. "No matter how powerful we are as a nation, we cannot secure these basic goals unilaterally.... The threats and challenges we face demand cooperative, multinational solutions. Therefore, the only responsible U.S. strategy is one that seeks to ensure U.S. influence over and participation in collective decisionmaking in a wide and growing range of circumstances."[35] The document incorporates a watered-down version of the controversial Presidential Review Directive (PRD) 13, drafted in August 1993, which identified the United Nations as the primary peacekeeping vehicle and laid out a framework for committing U.S. forces to a permanent UN army under foreign command. In PRD 13, multilateral operations were viewed as a way to save money and spread political and military risks.[36] That same sentiment for multilateral approaches, though tempered and surrounded by calls for U.S. leadership, reappears in the En-En document.

At the heart of the Clinton strategy is the belief that "the line between our domestic and foreign policies has increasingly disappeared—that we must revitalize our economy if we are to sustain our military forces, foreign initiatives and global influence, and that we must engage actively abroad if we are to open foreign markets and create jobs for our people."[37] The conclusion of the report reveals clearly the logic of the Clinton orientation. "While the Cold War threats have diminished, our nation can never again isolate itself from global developments. Domestic renewal will not succeed if we fail to engage abroad in open foreign markets, to promote democracy in key countries, and to counter and contain emerging threats."[38] In other words, engagement abroad to promote global prosperity, enlarge democracy, and contain threats is designed to serve the ultimate goal and linchpin of U.S. strategy: domestic renewal.

The Clinton Presidency's Record of Action

President Clinton's foreign policy emerged piecemeal as his administration wrestled with some of the most fundamental questions of engagement abroad: For what purpose and in what manner should the nation resort to the use of military force? How far up the agenda should human rights sit? How can the United States meet one of the gravest challenges of the post–Cold War era—the proliferation of weapons of mass destruction? How should the United States reconfigure its relations with its former adversaries and its traditional allies? These are precisely the kinds of questions the administration is still struggling to come to terms with.

THE USE OF FORCE

With the end of the Cold War, questions about when, how, and for what purpose the United States should commit military forces have taken on new dimensions of complexity. The Clinton administration's answers to these questions begin to emerge when one examines the collage created by U.S. policy toward Bosnia, Haiti, Somalia, and Iraq.

First, considerable waffling and inconsistencies regarding when force should be used suggest the lack of a "strategic" anchor. Clinton came into office urging tough action against the Serbs, arguing that Bush administration officials had outlined a false choice by asserting Washington faced the unpalatable decision of either sending hundreds of thousands of ground troops or standing on the sidelines. Candidate Clinton embraced forceful intervention in the Bosnian civil war, proposing a plan for a U.S.-led military effort to punish Serbian aggressors. Through the UN Security Council, the international community would charge Serbian leaders with crimes against humanity, the U.S. Navy would tighten the UN embargo on Serbia and Montenegro, and the United States would participate in air strikes against those attacking the relief effort in Sarajevo. President-elect Clinton continued this "interventionist" theme by calling on the United Nations to "turn up the heat a little" on Yugoslavia.[39] But despite tough talk, President Clinton back-pedaled in February 1993. The administration's long-awaited Balkan policy called for U.S. direct involvement only in humanitarian actions, and participation in an international peace process, the Vance-Owen negotiations, that acknowledged Serb territorial gains.[40] Retreating from the stance of using air power immediately against Serb militias, Secretary of State Christopher announced that the United States was prepared to employ ground forces as peacekeepers only to enforce a peace settlement.

In April 1993 the administration returned to a position advocating air strikes and in May proposed "lift and strike," only to abandon that policy ten days later in the face of both European opposition and Clinton's misgivings.[41] By late May the administration settled into a policy of containment: sending 300 U.S. troops to Macedonia as part of UNPROFOR and signing onto a UN policy to protect six Moslem "safe areas" within Bosnia. When the Serb siege of Sarajevo intensified in July, the Clinton administration again threatened air strikes to save Sarajevo and other safe areas from strangulation. NATO members finally agreed to a gradualist plan for bombing, but lack of will on the part of the United States and its allies, and clever Serb tactics—allowing just enough supplies through and participating in peace talks—combined to ensure that air strikes never occurred.[42] In December 1993, Christopher announced the doubling of U.S. humanitarian aid to Bosnia.

In a policy of general confusion, the administration, in its first year, moved close to military intervention on a number of occasions, only to back off each time for fear of alienating the Europeans or offending the Russians. As Drew summarizes: "The President of the United States looked feckless. He had talked and talked about the moral imperative of doing something about Bosnia, and done nothing. He had said publicly that he would be coming up with a strong policy, one that could well involve military action, and had failed to do so. He had reacted to what he saw on television, and his mind seemed easily changed. He had also claimed, disingenuously, to be closer to an agreement with the Europeans than he was. Whatever the policy should have been, Clinton's way of making it didn't engender confidence."[43]

Somalia revealed similar confusion regarding the use of force. In December 1992 President Bush sent 25,000 troops to Somalia for a humanitarian mission. As 1993 progressed, Operation Restore Hope, the shipping of food and medicine to starving Somalis, became a UN mission more intent on peacemaking and nation building than on humanitarian assistance. Throughout the summer and into the early fall, the Clinton administration's plan for Somalia seemed confused. Was it a humanitarian effort to feed starving people or was it a military effort to capture warlord Mohammed

Farah Aideed? In October 1993, under congressional pressure, Clinton announced the eventual withdrawal of American troops by 31 March 1994. The deaths of eighteen American servicemen and intense political pressure from both Democrats and Republicans forced Clinton to articulate specific goals for U.S. troops stationed in Somalia: self defense; keeping communications routes for UN officials and relief operations open; "keeping the pressure" on local forces that had attacked U.S. personnel; and "through that pressure and the presence of our forces, help making it reasonably possible for the Somali people, working with others, to reach agreements among themselves so that they can solve their own problems." While the original policy was one of humanitarian aid, Clinton had allowed UN Secretary-General Boutrous Boutrous-Ghali to transform the humanitarian effort into a complex scheme of nation building, culminating in the firefight in Mogadishu and Congress's attempts to limit U.S. involvement. Congressional and political outrage over the administration's loss of touch with the original mission forced Clinton to find his way back to that goal. By 31 March 1994, most American troops had left Somalia.

In Haiti, as well, the administration was waffling and indecisive on the question of using force. One of the most serious errors occurred in October 1993. The *USS Harlan County* steamed into Port-au-Prince with 200 lightly armed U.S. and Canadian military engineers, the vanguard of a UN mission overseeing the restoration of Haitian President Jean-Bertrand Aristide to power under the Governor's Island agreement. Met by a hundred rioters—apparently under the control of the Haitian military—shouting, waving machetes, and yelling, "We are going to make this another Somalia!"[44] the *Harlan County,* with its contingent too meagerly armed to protect itself, was ordered to retreat. The United States sought to reimpose trade sanctions, and Clinton continued to threaten Haiti's generals. But U.S. [in]action only convinced Cedras and company that they could defy Clinton and get away with it. In the end, the extent of President Clinton's discomfort with the military option was vividly revealed in his willingness to subcontract out foreign policy at the last minute to Jimmy Carter, who held out the hope of a peaceful resolution in Haiti. The Carter negotiations, in turn, led to another reversal of U.S. policy, allowing Haiti's military leaders to remain in the country after they had stepped down and even to seek political office.

Despite the diplomatic breakthrough, which no doubt is a short-term success, decision making remains reactive, a day-to-day approach that can be tweaked again at the last minute by the use of independent contractors to resolve foreign policy crises, particularly emissaries who are not team players.[45] Furthermore, the flip-flops on Haiti and the decision to use force there raise concerns about what former Secretary of State Henry Kissinger calls a "crisis-oriented management style" that "did not allow time to think through the long-term implications of U.S. moves to restore Haiti's elected government," such as providing a precedent for the Russians to intervene in former Soviet republics.[46]

A second insight into Clinton's approach to the use of force, stemming in part from the lack of a strategic anchor and reinforcing the tendency toward waffling, is that decisions about if, when, and how force should be used are frequently "crisis driven" in response to events both at home and those televised from abroad. Pressured by members of the congressional Black Caucus and constituents in Florida, Clinton authorized the use of military force in Haiti. Notably, even before the dramatic threat of military confrontation in Haiti, the administration had changed its policy on returning refugees in response to domestic political pressures. On Bosnia, the twists and turns of Clinton's policy were more the product of emotional reactions to the televised crisis of the day than of steady leadership on the issue. In mid-April 1993 it was televised pictures from the siege of Srebrenica and the opening of the Holocaust museum in Washington—both of which brought ethnic cleansing home—that drove the president to a new policy: lift and strike.[47] In July 1993, once again it was pictures of siege, this time of Sarajevo, that pushed Clinton to reconsider the use of U.S. ground troops.[48] Finally, it took a mortar bomb killing sixty-eight people in Sarajevo's central market in February 1994, and considerable French prodding, for Clinton and the Western allies to set up an exclusion zone around Sarajevo, issue an ultimatum to the Serbs, and authorize air strikes. According to Drew, some administration officials "spun that the new policy had been decided upon before the marketplace bombing—but that wasn't quite the case."[49] One Democratic congressional aide called it "foreign policy by CNN."[50] On Somalia, as well, U.S. policy displayed similar reversals tied to events rather than strategy. The deaths of U.S. Army Rangers produced the most dramatic example, transforming as well the administration's orientation toward the use of force in general. Now, the United States presumably will concede to low-risk, low-cost peacekeeping operations while eschewing the more arduous task of peacemaking.

Because a domestic national purpose provides weak guideposts for setting all but economic strategic priorities abroad, it increases the likelihood that much of U.S. foreign policy will be reactive to pressures at home and crises abroad. The risk is that strategy will be imputed from precedents that themselves were not grounded in strategy. So a quasi strategy emerges from a set of ad hoc policies that suggest a United States in retreat: withdrawing when things get too tough, as in Somalia, and placing so many conditions on intervention, as in Bosnia, that effective action is rendered impossible. All this is likely to encourage others to test U.S. resolve.

A third insight into President Clinton's orientation toward the use of force stems from his initial romance with multilateralism, with a posture of followership abroad, and with the United Nations as the global peacekeeper of the future. Multilateralism fit well with the president's domestic orientation. If the United Nations dealt with crises abroad, Clinton could focus on crises at home. In April 1992 candidate Clinton endorsed UN Secretary-General Boutrous Boutrous-Ghali's proposal for creating an international army whose troops would be ready to risk their lives for peace.[51] U.S. Ambassador to the United Nations Madeleine Albright reinforced the administration's commitment to "assertive multilateralism" and to multinational military cooperation with the United Nations as illustrated by Somalia. The deaths of eighteen Army Rangers in an intense firefight in Mogadishu on 3 October 1993 disenchanted Clinton with UN operations, and with the confusing command and control structure established in Somalia.[52] The romance with the United Nations has soured, and in the meantime a new Republican Congress has promised to impose a new set of constraints on U.S. foreign policy. The National Security Revitalization Act, part of the Republican Party's Contract with America, seeks to impose drastic restrictions on U.S. participation in, and funding for, UN peacekeeping activities. Yet while Clinton has backed away from assertive multilateralism, he has yet to find another rationale for how to use force in the post–Cold War period that makes sense to him.

President Clinton, however, should be credited for demonstrating learning when it comes to using force. His quick and decisive response to Hussein's movement of troops south to the Kuwaiti border was an exemplary demonstration of coercive diplomacy. And his administration did eventually come to realize the serious costs of ceding command of military operations to the United Nations.

HUMAN RIGHTS

Candidate Clinton said that human rights as an instrument of foreign policy would be fundamental to his presidency. In two key areas, Clinton has wrestled directly with the question of reconciling the goal of promoting human rights with that of preserving and enhancing the economic and social well-being of the nation. The case of China and the dilemma of whether to renew most-favored-nation (MFN) trade status brought human rights into direct conflict with Clinton's domestic-purpose orientation. The case of Haiti and the immigration, refugee, and economic pressures it placed on the state of Florida compelled Clinton to abandon a sanctions policy, which was never effectively implemented, and resort to a military option to relieve the economic pressures on the United States. In both cases, economic priorities ultimately prevailed, leading some Clinton watchers to claim that an underlying thread of consistency does exist in the president's foreign policy. Yet policy flip-flops throughout raise questions about whether Clinton even has the strength of these convictions.

In May 1994 Clinton renewed MFN status with China in a sharp departure from earlier policy statements and stances. During the 1992 presidential campaign, candidate Clinton had roundly criticized President Bush for his continued renewal of MFN status to China despite China's human rights violations. At the Democratic National Convention in July, Clinton promised that if he were elected, America would "not coddle tyrants, from Baghdad to Beijing." Clinton assured his supporters that he would not hesitate to use U.S. clout to force social change in nations where the United States conducts business.

Once in office, however, Clinton's position changed. In May 1993 the president signed an executive order conditionally renewing MFN. The executive order mandated that China must make "overall, significant progress" in human rights before MFN would be granted in the future.[53] In February 1994 Secretary Christopher traveled to China to demand compliance with the executive order. But the Chinese refused to budge. Instead, they accelerated the round-up of dissidents in defiance of U.S. demands, signaling they would not be forced into human rights concessions.[54]

Upon his return, Christopher began to soften the administration's policy of restricting trade on purely human rights grounds, stating that while "the character of our relationship with China depends significantly on how the Chinese government treats its people," the United States should integrate rather than isolate China. In Clinton's words, it "offers us the best opportunity to lay the basis for long-term sustainable progress in human rights and for the advancement of our other interests with China."[55] In April 1994 Assistant Secretary of State Winston Lord began to talk of "partial sanctions" if there were partial compliance with the May 1993 executive order. Then, on 26 May 1994, Clinton delinked trade from human rights and approved MFN status nearly unconditionally. For their part, the Chinese agreed to allow Voice of America to broadcast in China, but demonstrated little evidence of further compliance. The only sanction imposed by the administration, at the insistence of U.S. Trade Representative Mickey Kantor, was a ban on imports of assault weapons and ammunition, largely a symbolic gesture given that later enactment of a U.S. crime bill restricted imports of all assault weapons. Clinton's policy toward China had come full circle.

Clinton ultimately opted for the logic of "constructive engagement," totally separating human rights from trade. Asia specialist Robert Manning reasoned that "just as it took a conservative Republican president to open relations with China, maybe it takes a liberal Democratic president to delink trade from human rights."[56] But Clinton was sharply criticized for betrayal of the human rights cause. According to Sidney Jones, executive director of Human Rights Watch for Asia, the administration "looked vacillating and hypocritical," while the Chinese emerged "hard-nosed, uncompromising and victorious."[57] Clinton had backed down not only on his campaign promise but also on his executive order. Congresswoman Nancy Pelosi (D-Calif.)

pointed out that Clinton "went beyond Bush. He not only delinked trade and human rights but gave [the Chinese] credit for adherence to the Universal Declaration of Human Rights."[58] Most surprisingly, Clinton abandoned ideas for "partial revocation," for the creation of a human rights commission, and for a code of conduct for U.S. businesses in China similar to the Sullivan principles in apartheid-era South Africa.

Important strategic considerations were at stake, including China's leverage over North Korea and China's vote and veto power at the United Nations. Yet equally if not more salient were China's economy, at present the fastest growing in the world, China's 1.2 billion consumers, and the lucrative $40 billion U.S.–Chinese trade relationship. Beijing threatened to retaliate if the United States revoked MFN, jeopardizing the fortunes of nearly 550 U.S. companies operating in China.[59] Economic considerations, the one foreign policy priority Clinton has more or less consistently pursued, weighed in more heavily than enforcing significant progress on human rights. As in other arenas, Clinton was torn between his emotional responses and his domestic imperative, and the latter prevailed.

Haiti provides more insight into the primacy of domestic anchors in Clinton's foreign policy. Haiti, like China, was an issue in which the administration's human rights and domestic priorities collided. One month after the September 1991 military coup ousted democratically elected President Jean-Bertrand Aristide, over 6,000 Haitians fled the country. Numbers continued to rise through May 1992, reaching a monthly high of 13,053.[60] Watchdog groups, including Amnesty International and Human Rights Watch, as well as the U.S. State Department, documented serious human rights abuses from the time of the coup, including extrajudicial killings by security forces, disappearances, beatings, mistreatment of prisoners, and arbitrary arrests.[61] Candidate Clinton opposed the "direct return" policy established by President Bush on 24 May 1992, which ordered the Coast Guard to intercept at sea and forcibly repatriate Haitian boat people without conducting interviews to determine their risk of persecution. Clinton, persuaded by his future national security adviser, Anthony Lake, called the policy cruel, inhumane, and morally wrong, and promised to reverse it should he be elected.[62] Yet on 14 January 1993, with 200,000 Haitians poised to flee in anticipation of his inauguration, Clinton embraced Bush's policy.

Haiti was nowhere near the top of Clinton's agenda. The budget, the crime bill, and health care were foremost in the president's mind, while in the foreign policy arena, Bosnia loomed largest. But a small group of activists, headed by the congressional Black Caucus, cared greatly about Haiti. In June 1993, the caucus began "flexing real political muscle thanks to the precarious state of President Clinton's economic agenda on Capitol Hill."[63] By March 1994, they had made the restoration of Aristide a "litmus test" for the administration, threatening to withhold critical support for the president's domestic initiatives on health care, welfare reform, and crime. Allowing himself to be held captive to a "very narrow constituency of liberal groups," and to the dramatics of Randall Robinson, head of the lobbying group TransAfrica, who began a hunger strike to protest the repatriation policy, Clinton announced a critical shift in his Haiti policy on 8 May 1994.[64] As of 16 June 1994, the processing of refugees would commence on boats and in third countries, and victims of political repression would be offered asylum. Clinton also replaced Lawrence Pezzullo, the administration's special envoy to Haiti, with William Gray, a former chair of the congressional Black Caucus.

Not surprisingly, the announcement produced a new flood of boat people, but the numbers far exceeded anything the administration had predicted. Instead of the estimated 2,000 per week, by mid-June the Coast Guard was rescuing 2,000 to 3,000 per day. So on 5 July 1994, the administration changed its refugee policy again, this time announcing that fleeing Haitians, if it was determined that they faced persecution, would be sent to temporary "safe havens" in the Caribbean, such as Panama.[65] Three days later, the congressional Black Caucus denounced the policy as "inconsistent and confused," a policy of anarchy, "which changes by the moment."[66]

Human rights violations made the Bush policy untenable, particularly for "human rights firsters" like Lake. The question for Clinton was how simultaneously to reconcile his commitments to human rights and to his domestic agenda, particularly since one set of domestic pressures—the impact on Florida's economy of absorbing so many refugees—required denying Haitians asylum in the United States, while another set of domestic pressures emanating from leaders of the congressional Black Caucus supported the granting of asylum, branding any other policy racist. Clinton needed to resolve the Haiti problem and keep the refugees out of the United States, bearing in mind upcoming midterm elections and health-care legislation hanging in the balance. Clinton grasped the only alternative left to him, one being promoted by a small set of Aristide supporters and human rights activists but opposed by the general public and the Pentagon and certain to be challenged by Congress:[67] the military option. By this point, Haiti had become critical to the Clinton presidency, as much at home as abroad. Retreat was politically impossible, but a solution had to be orchestrated to accommodate a range of domestic pressures. Clinton backed into the military option for domestic, as distinct from strategic (i.e., enlargement) reasons. Haiti was not important as a case of democracy; certainly the democratic stakes were far higher in eastern Europe.

STEMMING PROLIFERATION

One of the key foreign priorities on Clinton's agenda has been to counter the proliferation of weapons of mass destruction. The record has been mixed. North Korea tops the list of proliferation challenges. It had refused to allow the International Atomic Energy Agency (IAEA) to inspect undeclared nuclear waste sites and repeatedly threatened to withdraw from the Nuclear Nonproliferation Treaty (NPT). But in a seeming foreign policy success, the Clinton administration ended an eighteen-month standoff on 18 October 1994 by signing an accord with North Korea whereby North Korea agreed to halt construction of two nuclear power plants in Yongbyong and permit the IAEA to inspect them.

North Korea instigated the "crisis" by refusing to allow IAEA inspectors into their nuclear facilities to determine compliance with the NPT. U.S. intelligence sources were convinced that the North Koreans were removing spent nuclear fuel and reprocessing it into plutonium at "undeclared" chemical storage facilities. But while North Korea had signed the NPT, it was not until 1992 that the government allowed the IAEA to inspect its seven "declared" nuclear facilities. From these inspections, the IAEA concluded that the North Koreans had reprocessed more plutonium than they were disclosing. Verification required inspection of two hidden nuclear waste sites, but the North Koreans refused to permit inspections. Then, on 12 March 1993, North Korea announced its intent to withdraw from the NPT in June.[68] The administration, hoping to avoid direct confrontation with North Korea, tried to use diplomacy to convince the North Koreans to submit to inspections. But diplomatic overtures proved fruitless.

In the early months of 1994 the Clinton administration began to take a more hard-line stance. U.S. intelligence sources had announced in January the possibility that North Korea already possessed one bomb.[69] The Department of Defense notified reservists to be ready to participate in joint military exercises with the South Koreans—"Team Spirit"—and Clinton threatened to send Patriot missile interceptors to South Korea to demonstrate further U.S. resolve. On 19 March 1994 Clinton asked the United Nations to lay the groundwork for economic sanctions, and on 22 March Patriot missiles were shipped to South Korea. They would take about a month to arrive. The administration sought to apply pressure gradually to convince the North Koreans to concede and to give the Chinese time to come on board. But by early May, the United States had still not succeeded in winning China's support for economic sanctions. Furthermore, Robert Gallucci, U.S. ambassador-at-large for North Korea, admitted that he was not confident a diplomatic solution could secure North Korean compliance with inspections. Then, on 14 May 1994, North Korea announced it had begun refueling one of its nuclear reactors at Yongbyong, which involves removing spent fuel rods. IAEA inspection of this process could determine whether plutonium was being diverted, but IAEA inspectors were again denied access. On 2 June the Clinton administration called for international economic sanctions against North

Korea.[70] The North Koreans responded that sanctions were tantamount to "an act of war."

To many observers, the United States and North Korea were at the brink of war in June. It was then that Jimmy Carter accepted an invitation from Kim Il Sung to visit Pyongyang to try to break the standoff. Carter, however, defied U.S. policy by asserting on 17 June, without consulting the president, that the United States would no longer pursue sanctions in the United Nations, which the United States had introduced in the General Assembly just two days earlier.[71] Furthermore, while Gallucci maintained the administration's position that North Korea must freeze nuclear production and allow IAEA inspections as a condition for further negotiations, Carter eased the demand for UN inspections. As one observer put it, Carter "was very effectively used by Kim Il Sung to dissipate the pressure for sanctions and split the coalition" Washington had been trying to build against North Korea.[72]

Carter's visit led to three rounds of high-level negotiations in Geneva in which the North Koreans succeeded in extracting significant concessions from the United States.[73] Under the Geneva Accord signed in October 1994, North Korea agreed to freeze and eventually dismantle its nuclear facilities. In return, North Korea will receive a host of benefits: $4 billion in economic and technological assistance to build two light water reactors; assurances that nuclear weapons will not be used against them; a U.S. commitment to take steps to establish full economic and diplomatic relations; U.S. commitment to lead efforts for an international consortium to provide 500,000 tons of heavy oil per year for several years as compensation for construction expenses and to provide citizens with energy while the reactors are being built; and U.S. agreement to urge the UN Security Council to grant North Korea special status that would delay IAEA inspections for undeclared nuclear facilities for three to five years.[74] Finally, North Korea refused at the last minute, and the United States conceded the point, to surrender 8,000 irradiated nuclear rods that could be used to produce nearly one dozen nuclear weapons, until after the construction of the light water reactors is under way.[75] The administration's initial goal was to prevent North Korea from developing nuclear weapons. In January U.S. policy subtly shifted to that of keeping North Korea from attaining a "significant" nuclear capability.[76] In short, Clinton was willing to live with one or two bombs if he could be assured that no further production would take place. But the last two provisions of the Geneva Accord fundamentally undermine even the administration's scaled-down goals. North Korea will be able to retain for years the nuclear weapons infrastructure it has developed.

The North Korean–U.S. nuclear weapons deal has ignited a great deal of debate. By one account, the deal sets a very dangerous precedent. As one editorial summed it up: "Sign the Nuclear NonProliferation Treaty. Cheat on it. Then the U.S. will give you billions of dollars worth of bribes to rejoin."[77] A Pentagon consultant added, "now you're going to have to give people lots of stuff just to live up to their treaty obligations."[78] Both supporters and critics, however, concede that the pact represents the least of all evils. True, the pact is vague, nonbinding, and may not be honored by the North Koreans, though IAEA inspectors confirm that the North Koreans have frozen their plutonium reprocessing and their construction of new nuclear facilities.[79] But the alternatives are even bleaker: the possibility of the United States, Japan, and South Korea pushed to the brink of war. As one reporter put it, "if it works, Bill Clinton will be the biggest winner, a master negotiator on a critical security issue. If it fails, no one will probably know for five years."[80]

The administration's counterproliferation policies in the former Soviet republics have been far less controversial and, in fact, a major foreign policy victory for the Clinton team. The Ukrainian parliament ratified the Nonproliferation Treaty on 16 November 1994. By offering security assurances and a package of aid to Ukraine, including $177 million to deactivate its nuclear missiles, the Clinton administration succeeded in convincing Kiev to relinquish its inherited arsenal of 1,800 nuclear warheads and 176 missiles, and its standing as the world's third-largest nuclear power, thereby clearing the way for Russia to implement the 1991 and 1993 Strategic Arms Reduction Treaties.[81] President Clinton's tenacity in promoting counterproliferation efforts and broader reform in the former-Soviet republics is particularly encouraging because it has been pursued despite opposition at home and in Europe.[82]

RECONFIGURING RELATIONS WITH TRADITIONAL ALLIES AND FORMER ADVERSARIES

The Clinton administration has not fared particularly well in managing the problems associated with alliance uncertainty as former enemies become friends and recipients of aid, while traditional allies become challengers. New fault lines have appeared with traditional allies in the absence of a common threat that compels a convergence of interests to prevail over collisions of interests. The administration, however, has been least adept at managing the formal dimension of alliance uncertainty, namely, whether to take the collective security route (to which Clinton is philosophically committed but on which he has failed to remain firm), to shore up traditional alliances (which the administration has bungled by neglect), or to embrace more forcefully a unilateral posture (to which the administration is least sympathetic but may be forced to by a Republican Congress).

Clinton initially embraced the United Nations and assertive multilateralism, only to switch tracks after the deaths of U.S. Army Rangers in Somalia. The president showed little interest in shoring up NATO early on, visiting Europe for the first time only in January 1994, though this was not as damaging to alliance relations as may appear at first blush. German Chancellor Helmut Kohl certainly recognized the domestic pressures on the new president, and Clinton succeeded at winning the confidence of the allies at the January 1994 NATO summit. Now, however, in Bosnia NATO faces its greatest crisis since Suez. In the meantime, midterm elections have ushered in a new Republican ascendancy eager to strengthen and expand NATO, by calling for the alliance's early expansion into eastern Europe, and committed to displacing the Clinton strategy—going along as merely the biggest member of a vague consensus—with a unilateralism making America "a maverick and a free agent: helping sometimes but often leaving its allies to sort their own messes out."[83]

On 5 May 1994, Clinton issued Presidential Decision Directive 25 (PDD 25) in a sharp departure from candidate Clinton's vision of the United Nations as the world's policeman.[84] Scuttled were the ideas laid out in PRD 13, drafted for Clinton's signature in August 1993, which had identified the United Nations as the prime peacekeeping vehicle and laid out a framework for placing U.S. soldiers under UN command.[85] PDD 25 set much more stringent criteria for U.S. participation in UN peacekeeping operations and for U.S. approval of any new peacekeeping operations, regardless of whether U.S. troops are involved. The Clinton administration also retracted its support for the creation of a UN standing army and for the contribution of any U.S. troops to such a force.[86] The president's vision of a United Nations that could keep the peace abroad while the United States turned its attention toward home was doomed once and for all by a Republican-led Congress intent on severely restricting future U.S. military commitments to UN missions.[87] The proposed National Security Revitalization Act seeks to prevent American units from serving under foreign officers *anywhere* in the chain of command. It would also count the costs of voluntary contributions to UN peacekeeping operations (ranging from contributions of special equipment donated, to the costs of UN-sanctioned operations like Haiti) against Washington's annual peacekeeping dues. The net effect could seriously cripple the United Nations if the United States were to end up paying nothing to the UN's annual peacekeeping budget.

It is in Europe, particularly over Bosnia, that U.S.–allied relations have been most severely damaged. The U.S. reluctance to commit ground forces in Bosnia never sat particularly well with the European allies. Christopher called Bosnia "an important moment for our nation's post–Cold War role in Europe and the world,"[88] but the administration's actions continually fell short of its rhetoric. Then, in May 1993, the administration floated its "lift and strike" policy to the European allies. The UN Security Council's arms embargo on the Bosnians would be lifted and U.S. air power would strike Serb positions in Bosnia.[89] The policy was characterized as a "least cost" approach that would minimize the possibility of derailing Clinton's domestic policy agenda while putting pressure on the Serbs to negotiate.[90] According to one reporter, "Clinton aides say that only by such a nuanced strategy can they hope to save Bosnia and the budget, Sarajevo and national service."[91]

Lift and strike did not sit any better with European leaders, who noted the tension between Clinton's reluctance to commit U.S. ground troops and support for a new arms flow into Bosnia coupled with air strikes that would place European soldiers on the ground at risk. Concerned with the safety of their troops, the Europeans preferred diplomatic means. Failing to persuade the Europeans to support lift and strike, the administration abandoned its policy only ten days after Christopher had traveled to Europe to promote it.[92] Christopher Gacek notes that, to skeptics, lift and strike, under Christopher's "limp diplomacy," was "a proposal designed for rejection. It was . . . a policy designed for American political constituencies expecting U.S. action in Bosnia but constructed in such manner as to meet with objections from Europe."[93] Drew concurs, noting that the British and French had warned the Americans not to present a fait accompli because they simply could not do lift and strike.[94] As Tucker and Hendrickson describe it, Clinton was always insistent "that help must be given but involvement avoided."[95] Bosnia, for this administration, was seen as a humanitarian crisis a long way from home, ultimately a problem *for* Europe rather than a problem *about* Europe, a problem not worth "steamrollering" the Europeans on and certainly not worth Americanizing.[96] The Clinton administration returned to a negotiating position to bridge the rift with its allies, only soon after to create an even greater rift that has sent new shock waves through the transatlantic alliance.

Forcing Clinton's hand over the arms embargo, Congress approved legislation on 5 October 1994 and the president announced, on 11 November, that the United States would unilaterally cease enforcing the UN-sponsored embargo on sea traffic to Bosnia and participating in related intelligence sharing. The move was roundly condemned by European leaders. The U.S. decision will have little practical effect for several reasons: only three of the eighteen NATO warships patrolling the Adriatic to enforce the embargo are U.S. vessels; most of the arms have been smuggled by air and over land through Croatia; over the past two years only three of the thousands of ships that have been monitored have been caught violating the embargo; and U.S. Navy personnel will still be permitted to board ships to search them for weapons that can be used against NATO forces.[97] Nevertheless, Congress is also pressuring the Clinton administration to lift the ban and supply weapons to Bosnia's Muslim-led government.

The political implications for U.S.–allied relations are far more serious than the effect on the ground in Bosnia might initially suggest, for, as NATO Secretary-General Willy Claes declared, the move sets a dangerous precedent that could cause major political damage to the alliance.[98] This is so because, with this decision, the United States unilaterally breached a policy adopted unanimously by NATO governments. Western European Union (WEU) Secretary-General Willem Van Eekelen called the move "divisive in NATO and in trans-Atlantic relations in general, because I don't know of any European country that wants to give up the arms embargo."[99] And Sir Dudley Smith, president of the WEU's parliamentary assembly, used this move to press the case that "Europe needs to be autonomous where intelligence gathering, satellite reconnaissance, and logistic support are concerned."[100] European allies interpret the move as yet another signal that the United States is seeking to extricate itself from Europe.

Recently, the Clinton administration has scrambled to limit the political damage, shuffling back to siding with the Europeans over a new peace plan while putting aside the threat of force to protect Bihac or pressure the Serbs into a peace settlement.[101] As divisions between Washington and its allies widen, perhaps Clinton is awakening to the fact that Bosnia is very much a problem about Europe, not just a regional problem for Europe. At risk is the failure of NATO unity and its military effectiveness, U.S. policy in Europe, and the United Nations. The challenge is, on the one hand, to decouple NATO's reputation from changing public and congressional attitudes toward peacekeeping and from association with these out-of-area activities. On the other hand, NATO's political glue must be stronger than ever if it is to survive. As *The Economist* reports: "In an attempt to adapt to a changed world, NATO has been rejigging its military workings. The idea is for it to continue to respond as an alliance politically, while letting 'coalitions of the willing'—sometimes Americans and Europeans together, sometimes Europeans alone—do the military jobs that need to be done. But Bosnia shows that, if anything, an arrangement where everyone has a say, but not everyone shares the same risks, will need even stronger political binding and more effective consultation if it is to work."[102] In this area, the Clinton administration has been farthest behind on the power curve.

On the other side of the fence, the Clinton administration has struggled to shape new relationships with former adversaries in the former Soviet Union and East-Central Europe that are struggling through varying degrees of political and economic transformation. U.S.–Russian relations have been one of Clinton's success stories, though at midterm those relations have sunk to their lowest level in years—since 1984, according to Russian expert Dimitri Simes.[103] From their first meeting in April 1993, Clinton and Boris Yeltsin developed a strong working relationship. One of Clinton's top priorities has been to enlarge the space for market democracies, and he successfully overcame congressional opposition to push through passage of a $2.5 billion aid program for Russia in September 1993. Clinton stayed the course on his Russia policy, supporting Yeltsin and his reforms when old-line conservatives launched an aborted coup against the Russian president and when ultranationalists secured major electoral victories in December 1993. Yet now, in light of the recent war in Chechnya, Clinton is being accused of misguided devotion to a "Yeltsin first" policy, tantamount to George Bush's "Gorbachev first" policy. Moreover, U.S.–Russian relations have recently foundered over the "Partnership for Peace" initiative—Clinton's premier instrument for building closer relationships between the NATO allies and the new democracies of the East—despite the president's willingness to make concessions to the Russians at the expense of East European democracies such as Poland, Hungary, the Czech Republic, and Slovakia, which are ready and eager to join NATO.

Partnership for Peace (PFP), a Clinton administration scheme, was adopted by NATO in January 1994 to deal with the thorny problem of NATO's eastward expansion. PFP bestows on all the former Warsaw Pact members, including Russia, the diluted status of "partners" rather than full members of NATO. It allows for combined military exercises and provides a mechanism through which NATO can share its experience and expertise in building democratically accountable defense institutions and military establishments. Critics, however, have dubbed PFP a "Policy for Postponement," a fundamentally flawed European policy on the part of a president who has eschewed U.S. leadership on the Continent. The problem has been how to embrace Russia's former East European satellites without offending Russia. In mid-1994, Mr. Yeltsin indicated that Russia might join if it received a special status reflecting its unique size and importance. Clinton signaled his willingness to grant Russia privileged status by establishing regular consultations, in effect giving Russia a veto.[104] But recently, Russia refused to sign on to PFP once NATO leaders began defining the conditions for NATO membership.[105] On 5 December 1994, at a fifty-two-nation summit meeting of the Conference on Security and Cooperation in Europe, Yeltsin seized the stage to denounce the Clinton administration's proposal to expand NATO. The *New York Times* reported that "in caustic tones reminiscent of the East-West tensions of the Cold War," Yeltsin "bluntly told other world leaders ... that NATO was trying to split Europe with its plans to admit new members from the former Warsaw Pact and that the United States should not be allowed to dominate the world."[106] Warning that "history demonstrates that it is a dangerous illusion to suppose that the destinies of continents and of the world community in general can somehow be managed from one single capital,"[107] Yelstin's charge of U.S. hegemonism was an amusing one to level at the Clinton administration.

Experts squabble over the cause of Yeltsin's bitter attack. Did it arise from attempts by the West to dictate Russia's economic policies through the IMF or the need to appease powerful anti-Western factions at home or anticipation of hostility from a Republican Congress or disagreement over air strikes and a tighter embargo against the Serbs? Neither can the worst-case scenario be dismissed, namely, that there is "a fundamental worsening of the relations, which reflects not domestic Russian circumstances, not the Republican congressional victory, not Bosnia, but trends in Russia that once again make it a serious power with nationalist interests and an increasingly assertive manner."[108] Chechnya does not augur well for the diagnosis. In defense of his foreign policy record, Clinton has heretofore been able to meet critics' charges with his record on Russia. That record may turn out to have more to do with events unfolding in Chechnya than in the White House.

The administration was once able to claim that it had done well enough on issues that affect the country's most vital interests: Russia, the future of NATO, and the Middle East. All three, however, now hang in the balance.

Foreign Policy Still in the Making

In the aftermath of the 1994 congressional elections, the president has started to refocus on foreign affairs, especially expanding trade and opening markets in the newly industrialized regions (as evidenced by his push for NAFTA and GATT). The president emerged from the APEC (Asian Pacific Economic Cooperation) summit with an announcement of a $40 billion joint-project deal with Indonesia to be implemented over the next decade. Still, President Clinton has been continually accused of making foreign policy decisions based on domestic political calculations. The irony is that Clinton's critics seem to disagree as to what those domestic political goals are, making Clinton seem inconsistent here as well. Before the Haitian invasion, Clinton was loudly criticized for "flip-flopping" in reaction to public opinion; then, with the invasion, he was criticized for not following it! *The Economist* reported that 73 percent of the U.S. public opposed an invasion of Haiti in early September. Similarly, many criticized Clinton for invading Haiti as preelection political maneuvering, but others view his decision as evidence of political obtuseness tantamount to political suicide. On Russia, Clinton has been simultaneously accused of dangerously coddling Yeltsin and of not providing enough proactive support (in terms of financial aid) to the democrat "reformers" there. The left sees Clinton as too restrained on U.S. interventionism (Bosnia), and the right sees him as too eager to intervene (Haiti).

In defending his administration's foreign policy, President Clinton said that there have been some mistakes; however, the world is more complicated today than it has ever been. "As we venture out in these new areas, we have to risk error. And when you do that, you get more criticism." As Joint Chiefs of Staff Chairman John Shalikashvili said in an address at Georgetown University, "the administration has sought to redefine the relationship between diplomacy and force in the post-Cold War era." The new "new world order" is one in which the United States has interests other than vital interests. It now faces security challenges that do not directly threaten U.S. survival but are nevertheless vital to U.S. global interests. Thus, military power will be used primarily for coercive purposes in support of diplomacy. In the words of Defense Secretary William Perry, "Oliver Cromwell once said that a man-of-war is the best ambassador. That's not really quite true. As the negotiations with North Korea proved, the best approach is a good ambassador backed up by a man-of-war."

President Clinton acknowledged his own learning curve. In an interview with *Time* on 31 October 1994, the president said regarding foreign policy, "I've completely stopped [talking on the fly] ... I think, tactically, we are making better moves. We're doing it better; we're making fewer mistakes. Part of that is, I think, just learning." The conventional wisdom is that President Clinton will have no choice other than "morphing" himself into a foreign policy president while redefining U.S. interests in the post-Cold War world. This evolution would be predicated on a "Clinton Doctrine"—an overriding set of principles to guide U.S. foreign policy. At this point, such a paradigm is still in the making.

Acknowledgments

We want to thank the following people for their helpful comments: Bruce Jentleson, Miroslav Nincic, Bertjan Verbeek, and the editors. We want also to thank our research assistant, Cyndi Boaz.

Notes

1. Larry Berman and Bruce W. Jentleson, "Bush and the Post–Cold War World: New Challenges for American Leadership," in *The Bush Presidency: First Appraisals,* ed. Colin Campbell and Bert A. Rockman (Chatham, N.J.: Chatham House, 1991): 93–94.

2. Ibid., 123.

3. See Eric Alterman, "So, Comeback Kid," *Mother Jones,* November/December 1994. See also Arthur Schlesinger, Jr, "Houdini in the White House," *Wall Street Journal,* 21 September 1994.

4. Quoted in "William Jefferson Bonaparte," *The Economist,* 17–23 September 1994, 25.

5. Bruce W. Jentleson, *With Friends Like These* (New York: Norton, 1994). See also Charles William Maynes, "Iraq Backs Down for Now," *New York Times,* 11 October 1994.

6. Fred Barnes, "Back Again," *New Republic,* 21 November 1994.

7. See Larry Berman, ed., *Looking Back on the Reagan Presidency* (Baltimore: Johns Hopkins University Press, 1990).

8. "Somali Showdown," *New York Times,* 11 August 1993, A2; "U.S. May Dispatch Commando Forces to Arrest Somali," *New York Times,* 11 August 1993, A1.

9. James A. Winnefeld, *The Post–Cold War Force Sizing Debate* (Santa Monica, Calif.: RAND/R-4243-JS, 1992), 32–34.

10. "William Jefferson Bonaparte"; see also Jim Hoagland, "Improvisational Foreign Policy," *Washington Post National Weekly Edition,* 3–9 October 1994, 22.

11. Elizabeth Drew, *On the Edge: The Clinton Presidency* (New York: Simon and Schuster, 1994), 58.

12. Berman, *Looking Back on the Reagan Presidency,* 7.

13. Arnold Wolfers, "The Pole of Power and the Pole of Indifference," *World Politics* 4 (October 1951).

14. Gaddis Smith, "After a Run of Bad Luck, It's Time to Discuss U.S. Foreign Policy," *Los Angeles Times,* 16 October 1994.

15. Colin Gray, "Off the Map: Defense Planning after the Soviet Threat," *Strategic Review* 22, no. 2 (Spring 1994): 34.

16. Adam Meyerson, "Ready, Fire, Aim: Clinton's Left-Footed Foreign Policy," *Policy Review,* Summer 1994, 4–5; Jim Hoagland, "Facilitator in Chief," *Washington Post,* 20 October 1994.

17. Fred C. Bergsten, "The Primacy of Economics," in *The Future of American Foreign Policy,* ed. Eugene R. Wittkopf (New York: St. Martin's Press, 1994), 96.

18. Dick Kirschten, "Martyr or Misfit?" *National Journal,* 29 October 1994, 2505.

19. Schlesinger, "Houdini in the White House."

20. Garry Wills, "Clinton's Troubles," *New York Review of Books,* 22 September 1994, 7.

21. Mary McGrory, "Exit William the Waffler," *Washington Post,* 20 September 1994.

22. Drew, *On The Edge,* 144.

23. Ibid.

24. On 20 September 1993 Secretary of State Christopher delivered a speech at Columbia University to a forum sponsored by the Council on Foreign Relations; on 21 September 1993 National Security Adviser Anthony Lake delivered a speech at Johns Hopkins University's School of Advanced International Studies entitled "From Containment to Enlargement"; on 23 September 1993 U.S. Ambassador to the United Nations Madeleine Albright addressed the National War College on the use of military force in the post–Cold War world; and on 27 September 1993 President Clinton addressed the General Assembly of the United Nations on the role of the United Nations after the Cold War, particularly regarding peacekeeping.

25. This insight was made by Professor Bruce Jentleson, a former Clinton State Department official.

26. Susumu Awanohara and Lincoln Kaye, "Full Circle," *Far Eastern Economic Review,* 9 June 1994, 14.

27. Drew, *On the Edge,* 326.

28. William Safire, "The UN Entraps Clinton," *New York Times,* 30 August 1993, A11.

29. "New Mission Perplexes NATO Chiefs," *Defense News,* 10–16 May 1993, 28.

30. Steven Erlanger, "Moscow Stepping In," *New York Times,* 20 May 1993, A12.

31. BUR II is under way because of recognition that BUR I is not affordable.

32. Winnefeld, *Post–Cold War Force Sizing Debate,* 5.

33. Ibid., 32.

34. William Clinton, *A National Security Strategy of Engagement and Enlargement,* The White House, 1994, 5.

35. Ibid., 6.

36. "U.S. Having Second Thoughts about Peacekeeping Missions," *San Jose Mercury News,* 26 November 1993, 18A.

37. Clinton, *A National Security Strategy,* i.

38. Ibid., 29.

39. Warren Strobel, "U.S. Had, but Lost the Chance to Lead," *Washington Times,* 9 May 1993, A9.

40. "Christopher's Remarks on Balkans," *New York Times,* 11 February 1993, A12; "Clinton Changes Balkans Strategy: President Rejects Use of Force, Accepts Process That Allows Gains by Serbs," *New York Times,* 11 February 1993.

41. Drew, *On the Edge,* 157.

42. Ibid., 273–79.

43. Ibid., 159.

44. Howard W. French, "Diplomats Flee Port to Escape Protesters," *New York Times,* 12 October 1993, A1, A12.

45. Elaine Sciolino, "Diplomatic Subcontracting's Fine If You Get Good Help," *New York Times,* 25 September 1994, E6.

46. Kirschten, "Martyr or Misfit?" 2504–5.

47. Drew, *On the Edge,* 151–53.

48. Ibid., 273–75.

49. Ibid., 411.

50. "This Time We Mean It," *Time,* 21 February 1994.

51. Elaine Sciolino, "The U.N.'s Glow Is Gone," *New York Times,* 9 October 1993, A1.

52. Thomas L. Friedman, "Clinton Reviews Policy in Somalia as Unease Grows—Seeking a Balance," *New York Times,* 6 October 1993, A1; Thomas L. Friedman, "U.S. Pays Dearly For an Education in Somalia," *New York Times,* 10 October 1993, sec. 4, p. 3; Michael R. Gordon and Thomas L. Friedman, "Disastrous U.S. Raid in Somalia Nearly Succeeded, Review Finds," *New York Times,* 25 October 1993, A1.

53. "Significant progress" had to be made in five areas: ending jamming of Voice of America radio broadcasts; accounting for political prisoners; allowing prisoners to be visited by the Red Cross; ending repression in, and pressure on, Tibet; and taking steps to adhere to the Universal Doctrine of Human Rights. Progress in two final areas, ending the export of prison-made products to the United States and allowing free emigration of dissidents previously barred from leaving China, was "mandatory." China had to meet these demands completely.

54. Susan V. Lawrence, "The China Syndrome," *U.S. News and World Report,* 21 March 1994, 40.

55. Awanohara and Kaye, "Full Circle," 15.

56. Ibid.

57. Ibid., 14.

58. Ibid., 15.

59. Lawrence, "China Syndrome," 39.

60. *Coast Guard Haitian Rescue Statistics,* compiled by Seventh Coast Guard District Public Affairs Office for House Subcommittee on International Law, Immigration, and Refugees, 15 June 1994.

61. State Department's 1992 Country Report on Haiti.

62. "Haitians' Plight Illuminates Volatile Nature of U.S. Policy," *Washington Post,* 29 June 1994, A8; Tom Masland, "How Did We Get Here?" *Newsweek,* 26 September 1994, 27.

63. Sam Fulwood III, "Congressional Black Caucus Turns up Heat on Clinton," *Los Angeles Times,* 11 June 1993, A1.

64. According to a Democratic Senate staffer, "Clinton was not going to watch Randall Robinson die and then have people criticize him at the funeral." Russell Watson et al., "Is This Invasion Necessary?" *Newsweek,* 19 September 1994, 41.

65. Ann Devroy and Bradley Graham, "U.S. to Bar Haitians Picked Up at Sea," *Washington Post,* 6 July 1994, A1.

66. John M. Goshko and Ruth Marcus, "U.S. Intensifies Effort to Set Up Haitian Havens," *Washington Post,* 9 July 1994, A1; Steven A. Holmes, "With Persuasion and Muscle, Black Caucus Reshapes Haiti Policy," *New York Times,* 14 July 1994, A10.

67. George Church, "Destination Haiti," *Time,* 26 September 1994, 24.

68. Young Whan Kihl, "Epilogue: Korean Conundrum in the Post–Cold War Era," in *Korea and the World: Beyond the Cold War,* ed. Young Whan Kihl (Boulder, Colo.: Westview Press, 1994), 329.

69. Bruce W. Nelan, "A Game of Nuclear Roulette," *Time,* 10 January 1994, 28–29.

70. The United States also began pressuring the Japanese to terminate illegal shipment of funds to North Korea, estimated as high as $600 million and the regime's only source of outside income. "Tensions Build over North Korea's Refusal to Allow Complete Nuclear-Site Inspections," *Facts on File,* 9 June 1994, 406.

71. Jeffrey Smith and Bradley Graham, "White House Disputes Carter on North Korea," *Washington Post,* 18 June 1994, A1.

72. Jeffrey Smith and Ann Devroy, "U.S. Debates Shift on North Korea: Carter's Visit Derails Sanction Drive," *Washington Post,* 21 June 1994, A1; "North Korean Nuclear Crisis Eases Following U.S. Ex-President Carter's Visit," *Facts on File,* 23 June 1994, 437.

73. J.F.O. McAllister, "Back to Square One: Clinton Could Face Another Showdown as Pyongyang Backtracks in Its Nuclear Negotiations," *Time,* 10 October 1994, 36.

74. Jeffrey Smith, "Clinton Approves Pact with North Korea," *Washington Post,* 19 October 1994, A1.

75. McAllister, "Back to Square One," 36.

76. Mark Thompson, "Well, Maybe a Nuke or Two," *Time,* 11 April 1994, 58.

77. Peter Grier, "N. Korea Pact Points Up Limits of Containment," *Christian Science Monitor,* 21 October 1994, 3.

78. Ibid.

79. "North Korean–U.S. Nuclear Weapon Deal Ignites Debate," *Defense News* 9, no. 48 (5–11 December 1994): 30.

80. David E. Sanger, "Who Won in the Korea Deal?" *New York Times*, 23 October 1994, E3.

81. "Aiding Peace," *Defense News*, 28 November–4 December 1994, 22; see also "U.S. Funds Ukraine Plan to Convert Munitions," *Defense News*, 28 November–4 December 1994, 4, 36.

82. "Marital Problems," *The Economist*, 3–9 December 1994, 15; "Europe Lags Again," *The Economist*, 26 November–2 December 1994, 27.

83. "Marital Problems," 15–16.

84. "Clinton Redirects Peacekeeping Policy," *Defense News*, 7–13 February 1994, 4; "U.S. to Limit Role in U.N. Peacekeeping: Conditions Set for Sending Troops," *San Jose Mercury News*, 6 May 1994, 19A.

85. "U.S. Having Second Thoughts about Peacekeeping Missions," 18A.

86. Elaine Sciolino, "New U.S. Peacekeeping Policy De-emphasizes Role of U.N.," *New York Times*, 6 May 1994, A1.

87. Jason Glashow and Theresa Hitchens, "GOP Eyes Cut in U.N. Activities," *Defense News*, 21–27 November 1994, 3, 28.

88. Drew, *On the Edge*, 148.

89. Thomas L. Friedman, "Bosnia Air Strikes Backed by Clinton, His Officials Say," *New York Times*, 2 May 1993, sec. 1, p. 1.

90. Christopher M. Gacek, *The Logic of Force: The Dilemma of Limited War in American Foreign Policy* (New York: Columbia University Press, 1994), 333.

91. Thomas L. Friedman, "Any War in Bosnia Would Carry a Domestic Price," *New York Times*, 2 May 1993, sec. 4, p. 1.

92. Richard C. Gross, "Christopher: Force Not an Option Now in Bosnia," *Washington Times*, 19 May 1993, A1.

93. Gacek, *Logic of Force*, 428, n. 87.

94. Drew, *On the Edge*, 155–56.

95. Robert W. Tucker and David C. Hendrickson, "America and Bosnia," *National Interest*, Fall 1993, 23.

96. Drew, *On the Edge*, 158.

97. These include weapons of mass destruction, air-to-air and air-to-ground missiles, and anti-ship missiles. "Europeans Make Case for Defense Autonomy," *Defense News*, 14–20 November 1994, 1, 37; "Mistake in the Adriatic," *Defense News*, 21–27 November 1994, 18.

98. "Claes: U.S. May Lose Much over Bosnia," *Defense News* 9 (21–27 November 1994): 1, 29.

99. "Europeans Make Case for Defense Autonomy," 37.

100. Ibid.

101. Michael R. Gordon, "U.S., in Shift, Gives Up Its Talk of Tough Action against Serbs," *New York Times*, 29 November 1994, A1.

102. "Patching Up NATO," *The Economist*, 19–25 November 1994, 19.

103. Steven Greenhouse, "U.S. Hopes to Lift Cloud over Ties with Russia," *New York Times*, 8 December 1994, A6.

104. "Pursued by a Bear," *National Review*, 13 June 1994, 19–20.

105. At this point, talk of NATO expansion is still just "talk." The U.S. government and NATO have designated 1995 as a year for studying the feasibility of early entry for new NATO members. And 1996 is an election year in both the United States and Russia. Furthermore, any change in the North Atlantic Treaty, such as NATO expansion, requires a two-thirds majority in the U.S. Senate to rat-

ify. In all probability, the chances of a state entering NATO before 1997 appear minimal. Dov Zakheim, "Expanded WEU May Offer Best Path to European Security," *Defense News* 10 (20–26 February 1995): 19–20.

106. Elaine Sciolino, "Yeltsin Says NATO Is Trying to Split Continent Again," *New York Times,* 6 December 1994, A1.

107. Ibid., A4.

108. "U.S. Hopes to Lift Cloud over Ties with Russia."

I I

Leadership Style and
the Clinton Presidency

BERT A. ROCKMAN

Leadership invites speculation. Precisely because leadership is about decision making under conditions of uncertainty, we can never be certain about what was the right decision to take or the right strategy to be applied. We can only guess with the benefit of hindsight. Sometimes hindsight clarifies the path that a decision maker could have taken to achieve an outcome that was more desirable or politically effective. Frequently hindsight merely illuminates the traps that lay in wait for the decision maker regardless of the direction in which he or she turned.

A leader's policy goals and political goals can come into conflict as well. A desirable policy outcome from the leader's perspective may prove to be incompatible with an outcome that also enhances the leader's political prospects. Perhaps more frequently, what leaders sometimes must do to sustain their political prospects precludes them from achieving their policy goals.

Nor do decisions and problems come as discrete packages to leaders. They are often entangled and interconnected, and they often arrive in ways that are unexpected. Choices about one affect the prospects of others, but the consequences of those choices can only be guessed about in advance; they cannot be known.

A leader deemed to be effective is one who keeps a steady ship while being buffeted around by forces he or she cannot directly control. Leadership is tough everywhere. American political institutions (which diffuse power) make it especially tough for those who come to the office of president. The decisions that presidents make are rarely decisive even when they are, as they almost always are, important. The problems presidents want to deal with are often sliced and diced and fragmented into pieces, weakening their ability to interconnect them when they think they need to. Almost always, a president has an influential voice; rarely does he have the last word.

There is no formula for successful leadership, partly because success lies to some measure in the eye of the beholder. Leadership, I suspect, has a lot to do with making good or even lucky guesses. It has something to do with instinct that cuts through the amber lights that intellect and analysis or simply political self-doubt place on the decisional pathway. It also has something to do with self-confidence and projection, perhaps even a dose or two of bravado. It has something to do also with resources to lead, a message to believe in, and huge gobs of good fortune. From this perspective, is it possible that persistence in the pursuit of simple dogmas is the key? Ronald Reagan and Margaret Thatcher suggest it might be, while their very success raises equally profound questions as to what effectiveness itself means.

Analyzing leadership inevitably leads eventually into one or the other (and sometimes both) of the following conundrums: (1) Can someone whose goals one objects to be regarded as an effective leader (alternatively, can a leader whose goals one agrees with ever be regarded as sufficient)? (2) How can one assess a leader's political strategy in the absence of being able to climb inside the leader's mind to discover the leader's priorities? The first of these problems is alluded to by Richard Rose, who notes that since Eisenhower most U.S. presidents have been Republicans, whereas most of those commenting about presidents are Democrats. This fact clearly distinguishes the commentators from the electors.[1]

Despite this inconvenient fact for those who cast judgments on leaders and the quality of their leadership, it is hardly unreasonable for substantive questions to be raised in assessing the effectiveness of leadership. A leader may be strategically successful on behalf of policies that are destructive. The problem is that one can rarely tell how destructive or constructive policies are in the long run without reference to the evaluator's own preferences. Certainly, the development of the social insurance state under Franklin Roosevelt and further refinements of it under Lyndon Johnson appear to its sympathizers as great accomplishments. Yet, the cost of these great accomplishments constitutes a major part of the budget deficit problems of the federal government. Equally, while Ronald Reagan's commitment to bankrupting the Soviet Union with extravagant defense expenditures may have helped end the Cold War, in the absence of a commensurate commitment to increasing revenues, it also contributed to the budgetary deficits of the federal government. In politics, someone's goods are someone else's bads, and, from this standpoint, judgments about leadership that focus on content are inevitably relative and contentious precisely because they are predicated on opinion.

Complications of this nature thus lead many analysts of leadership to forgo the temptation to make judgments about leadership based on its content. Whether or not this is justifiable, the notion that leadership can be assessed as a method or technique seems appealing because it leads the analyst to think of the problems of leadership as though they were engineering problems. Richard Neustadt's fascinating and highly nuanced book, *Presidential Power,* which first appeared in 1959, was often read as a "how to do it" book because it offered examples of three presidential styles of leadership that could be described as the good (Roosevelt), the not so good (Truman), and the bad (Eisenhower).[2] Putting aside the obvious influence of Neustadt's values (good presidents are activist presidents and activist presidents are liberal Democrats) on his assessment of presidential styles, readers of Neustadt could take from it the notion that there were ways for presidents to enhance their influence and many more ways for them to stumble badly.

Success, as Neustadt might think of it, however, is related to the policy goals of a president. (By inference at least, a president who had few or no policy interests must thereby be thought a failure.) Yet policy goals are remarkably unstable. They are likely to be affected in combination or singly by the flow of political events, the changing circumstances of policy problems, the differential capacity across issues and time to stitch together majorities for action, and the political need merely to stake out, if not act on, positions. If there is one thing that is constant about goals, it is that they frequently emerge from successive interactions as their product as much as their precipitant.[3] Treating leadership style, therefore, as simply a matter of mechanics in relation to a set of stable goals is a trickier business than it appears on the surface. Surely, we could hardly expect anyone other than an ideologically obsessed purist to be immune to changes in the environment. Nor should we expect any but the most densely committed to fail to adjust objectives accordingly.

An additional, if different, complication is added by the fact that while we tend to think of leadership in terms of an individual actor, effective leadership may involve a collective blending and conciliation of preferences. It may stem from a process of institutionalized norms and understandings through which mutual accommodations are reached.[4] From this perspective, the system works when leaders are in a repetitive game with other actors with whom they must establish mutual trust.[5] Institutionalized relations are important for cooperation to exist. Without such institutionalization, the costs of confrontation are low. While confrontation provides good theatrics, it rarely provides good governance. In the end, there must be some established community of interests willing to believe that they have a mutual stake in coming to agreements and some institutionalized ways of doing so. In the United States, the separation-of-powers system, among other institutional features, makes it incumbent on the different actors to find common ground if they are not merely to checkmate one another. It may well be, however, that norms of accommodation are waning in direct proportion to the growth of populist sentiments and ideological commitments within at least the most recent historical cycle. The large proportion of political neophytes at present residing in Congress have a lot invested in product and none in process. But process is almost always essential to getting a product.

The foregoing is a warning. The analysis of leadership style is not reducible to some rank order of quality based exclusively on a leader's attributes. How leaders fare mostly reflects their political circumstances and objectives. It is, in sum, least useful to analyze leadership from the standpoint of ranking leaders or casting summary judgments about them. Instead, analyzing leadership is a means to understanding the connection between desires and available latitude, between choices and options, between a leader's past and present, and, above all, between a leadership agenda and the capacity of a political system to absorb it.

With that in mind, my objective is to understand the uneasy presidency of Bill Clinton and how that is linked, if at all, to his style of leadership. I especially emphasize the political and policy conditions that have constrained and less frequently provided latitude for Clinton's presidency. It is wise, I think, to emphasize these conditions mainly because they shape the possible. How leaders react to these conditions certainly influences their future chances. Like investors, they are taking calculated risks that have a good opportunity to go bad. If they risk big, they may gain big, but they are more likely to fail big. If they choose safe strategies, there is no doubt that they will be criticized for not seeking greater yields. The great problem confronted by presidents in the contemporary United States is this: the governmental institutions are designed to lead presidents toward safe, low-yield strategies, but popular culture and the claims of direct democracy tend to direct presidents toward high risk but potentially high-yield strategies. Charles O. Jones has thus noted that expectations regarding the American presidency are dangerously out of whack with its legitimate institutional role in a system of separated powers.[6] Because Bill Clinton arrived in the White House on the heels of a 62 percent vote against the incumbent president, he arrived amid expectations of producing change and ending gridlock. And he arrived with an agenda of substantial ambition. He and the public were both destined to be disappointed.

Latitude and Constraint: The Case of the Clinton Presidency

In economics, the standard line is that there is no such thing as a free lunch. In politics, if there were a standard line, it should be that there is no such thing as a free agent. What does this mean? It means simply that no leader is free to carry on minus the weight of past commitments and obligations.

Who helped select the leader? Who helped elect him or her? Whose political support will the leader need to enable present and future majorities to be composed? Whose interests will need to be accommodated? To what extent, if at all, are these various constituencies compatible with a sustainable political strategy and a sustainable governing strategy?

  ● Clinton campaigned and came to office as a so-called New Democrat. Although filled with vagueness, the idea of a New Democrat was somehow to find a third way between the polarizing forces of the parties. From one perspective, of course, the idea was hardly new. Jimmy Carter was the original and true New Democrat whose ideas often were at odds with his party's majority in Congress. After Carter's presidency was lost, it was generally concluded that it was a good idea for presidential nominees to be in tune with their party faithful on the theory that if you could not bring along your friends, who could you bring along?

Although Ross Perot was neither "new" nor a "Democrat," he also appealed to many people during the 1992 election campaign as a more plausible proponent of a "third way" between the parties—or, perhaps, beyond them. Perot's independence of the parties and various interest groups and his willingness to spend big sums of his own fabulous fortune led many to believe that he could be a president who was truly a free agent, able to follow his own vision unimpeded by party or interest-group constituencies. The same thought that thrilled some chilled others. The notion of a leader unconstrained by political obligations raised at the least fears of an insoluble political crisis between such a president and other political institutions.

Clinton's embrace of the Democratic Leadership Council (DLC), which he served as president, was designed to solidify his status as a New Democrat. The DLC was created to attract constituencies of a presumed floating middle and offer policy options to appeal to them. Overwhelmingly, it attracted moderate to conservative Democratic politicians from southern and southwestern states. It took positions designed to eradicate the Democrats' vulnerabilities with the electorate, especially in regard to strengthening their identification with nationalist values and a more zestful defense posture, lessening the party's identification with the poor and strengthening it with the middle class, weakening its identification with traditional welfare state mechanisms and associating it with choice and incentives, and weakening the party's identification with the cultural avant-garde and strengthening it with the common person.

Whether Clinton's identification as a New Democrat was a matter of personal belief or merely cover for a political strategy cannot be known, but it is puzzling that if the electorate is clustered in the center, why a strategy designed to attract the center has nonetheless produced a presidency of persistent political weakness? The same, of course, could be said of Jimmy Carter. There are possible explanations. One, of course, was that in 1992,

Ross Perot took the votes in the center. The other is that there is, in fact, no real center—that the construct is a figment of an incorrectly constructed unidimensional space for articulating policy preferences. Put somewhat differently, there may be no majority to be had from the center; one can put together majorities only from minorities. In this sense, Robert Dahl's notion of American democracy as a system of minorities' rule is undoubtedly a better fit with reality than is Anthony Downs's notion of a normally distributed electorate across a single dimension in which two parties each seek to appeal to the median voter by looking more alike than different.[7] If Dahl's conception is the more accurate one, then advice to move to the center is feckless because there is no "there" there.

In addition, the growing polarization of the political parties makes it even harder for a president to find a third way and expect to find a core of support behind him. Recent presidents who for at least part of their administrations seemed either to want to find a third way or found themselves drifting toward one (Carter and, more arguably, Bush and Clinton) also usually found themselves having alienated their core support without attracting their opponents. Bush reread his lips, only to find his party in opposition, despite the fact that the budget deal he took part in cutting stabilized discretionary spending and produced real controls. Carter's early efforts to cut pork-barrel projects bought him no support within his party or among Republicans; all it brought was a reputation for clumsiness. Similarly, Clinton's effort to attack the budget deficit was bound to alienate some critical sets of interests regardless of what he did. The one thing he could hardly afford to do was to alienate his political supporters by treating them as roughly as the Republicans were inclined to do. It is possible and even plausible that in the polarized political climate existing over the better part of the past two decades of American politics, there is nothing a president can do to attract opposition support that will allow him to be credible with his own party. Bush's partisan credibility was endangered after he cut the budget deal with the Democrats in spite of the fact that the expenditure side of the agreement was advantageous to the Republicans. Clinton could survive NAFTA (an agreement made during the Bush administration) despite his party's lack of enthusiasm for it because of traditional deference to executive authority on trade issues, the regional connotations of the agreement, and the split it produced in the party's congressional leadership.

Clearly, Clinton arrived in office as a president with an immediate political dilemma, even if he did not immediately know it. Clinton's problem was that he had an uncertain political identity and that uncertainty created for him, just as it had for Jimmy Carter, numerous political obligations precisely because each part of his diverse base of support expected him to be unequivocally for them. He was a New Democrat but also an Old Democrat; he wanted to be an outsider but (unlike Carter) also an insider; he wanted boldness but also accommodation; he had full-loaf ideas but a political coalition unlikely to generate even a half loaf; he wanted to do good policy but was willing to accept good politics. His party, having rarely tasted executive power for a generation and having had its hopes dashed when it did, wanted a president to turn around the Reagan-Bush years by proposing (and acting on) new initiatives. Within the Democratic Party, power is concentrated in its liberal wing and among its new advocacy groups (women and minorities) and much less with the DLC. If Clinton was not to wind up being a dead duck, he would basically have to find some way of being attractive to each segment of his party.

Being attractive to all segments of his party was probably inherently impossible, however. By April 1993, according to Elizabeth Drew's account, the DLC was already expressing its disappointment at what its leaders perceived to be Clinton's left-hand turn.[8] Drew observes, as have other accounts of the Clinton presidency, that Clinton was continually conflicted as to what kind of Democrat he was, who his real constituency was, and how he ought to navigate among them.[9] The consequences of all these conflicting tendencies was that Clinton's words, to his listeners, carried very little commitment. Thus, when Clinton threatened to veto a Republican version of his 1994 crime bill if it stripped the bill of its provisions banning assault weapons, a Democratic congressional staffer commented that the Republican effort likely would fail because "when Bill Clinton is willing to take a stand on something, you know it's safe."[10] These same tendencies to want to please all his diverse constituencies and appeal to each of them may well be the cause of his loss of focus and of the tendency for his speeches to take on a rambling, inchoate quality. The journalist David Broder noted after Clinton's especially long-winded State of the Union address to the newly seated Republican Congress in January 1995 that his list of causes "was so long that ... no one other than the late Hubert Humphrey [a notorious stemwinder and passionate liberal] could have had his heart in all these fights. . . . That left little time—and less plausibility—for the evening's most important work, communicating a real sense of conviction and a clear agenda."[11]

Ultimately, Clinton's real dilemma was that he and even more his party and its most central constituencies wanted to act as though they were free agents not only in reversing most of what had been done in the previous twelve years but in pushing ahead policy reforms that had had to lie fallow during the Reagan-Bush years and even since the era of Lyndon Johnson's presidency. Regardless of what he wanted to do, Clinton knew that he was anything but a free agent to pursue a long-delayed Democratic wish list. Even within his own party, Clinton had to tread carefully between its DLC wing and its liberal mainstream. Should he reach beyond Congress to the populist sentiments welling in the country and alienate his party's congressional leadership, or should he deal with his congressional party and lose his outsider status in a political culture that increasingly despairs of insiders? Should he seek to generate majorities from within his own party or seek bipartisan coalitions? To do the latter meant that he might be able to solve some commonly defined problems, but could do so only at the cost of his broader policy agenda. Moreover, the policy world was now highly constrained. Budget deficits loomed, taxes were poisonous, and aversion to government was high (at least in the abstract). In short, this was not a great time for a Democrat with policy aspirations to assume the presidency. In addition to this, the electorate hardly had given Clinton or his party a ringing endorsement in 1992. From this standpoint, Clinton began with relatively modest political leverage that progressively deteriorated to the point that he has the unusual experience of being a Democratic president (a sufficiently unusual experience in itself) in a divided government. The only leverage he has left now is to say no—a word he does not often like to use and—what may be worse —a word not often taken seriously by those who hear it from him.

Like all presidents, Clinton had no tabula rasa on which to write. He has legacies left to him and personal baggage he brings with him. He has political circumstances that clearly shape, if not dictate, his range of behaviors. Such circumstances critically influence any leader's capacity to lead.

The Conditions of Clinton's Leadership

THE PERSONAL BAGGAGE

All presidents come to office with some personal and political baggage that helps identify them. Some are readily identified. Ronald Reagan had a vast reservoir of passionate support from his party's right wing and conservatives generally. People knew where Reagan was, which ironically gave him leeway to escape his ideological binds when necessary. Dwight Eisenhower, having been a wartime military leader, had different reservoirs of support to draw from. He was seen as a figure (much like the French president Charles de Gaulle) above political parties despite his Republican affiliation and conservative political beliefs. Eisenhower chose to govern minimally but did so by retaining an astonishingly high level of public confidence.[12] Others, such as Richard Nixon, arrive less trusted but with the expectation that they have some special competency or aptitude for the job. Still others, such as John F. Kennedy, bring a certain verve and style to the job and are forgiven much because of that. Yet others enter office under special circumstances and are welcomed for no other reason than that someone was there to take on the job. Lyndon Johnson and Gerald Ford were cut some slack because of the conditions under which they were ushered in. It is fair to say that, like Jimmy Carter, Clinton arrived in office as a question mark—a political personality with no Washington past and no clear identity.

In recent decades, as public confidence in government and political leaders has spiraled downward, presidents are granted less slack. And as media coverage has become more personalized and intimate, quite literally so, much more is known about the personalities who become presidential candidates and presidents, including in Clinton's case even his choice of underwear. There is a world of difference between 1960 and 1992. Then, popular confidence in government was high—roughly three-quarters of the public felt it could be trusted, whereas today only about a quarter of the public feels that way. Similarly, then, the news media were a great deal more tame in dealing with presidents and certainly far less intimate. The reputed extramarital affairs of Franklin Roosevelt, Eisenhower, and, particularly, Kennedy came to light only some time after their deaths. It is in this very different context that one has to consider public perceptions of Clinton as a candidate and subsequently elected president. The context generates skepticism about political leaders, and Clinton turned out to be highly vulnerable to a context of skepticism, featuring a media acquainted with far more intimate portrayals of would-be presidents than previously had been the case.

Clinton was vulnerable for a variety of reasons. One of them was his reputation for extramarital affairs. Not since Grover Cleveland has an American presidential candidate been pursued so relentlessly via sexual innuendo. The Gennifer Flowers case began during the New Hampshire primary campaign, and when that had died down along came the tales of ex-Arkansas state troopers who served as Clinton's escorts (presumably to liaisons) when he was governor. When that seemed to die down, Paula Jones emerged and filed a sexual harassment suit against Clinton. In all, Clinton was far more exposed (no pun intended) than was Kennedy because the media in Kennedy's time did not always blab publicly about what it knew privately and because the professional dirt diggers of Kennedy's day were more interested in knowing whether a candidate was in bed with communists than with women. It is not clear that the various sexual scandals that have been reputed have had any direct impact on Clinton's fortunes, but they have added to an aura of suspicion and distrust of Clinton.

A second part of Clinton's personal baggage is that by virtue of being the first of his generation to be a presidential candidate, he was also the first to face the charge of draft evasion during the Vietnam war, a period in which only a small segment of the current American political elite served in the military and an even smaller portion actually served in Vietnam. Clinton's generational peers either escaped service (Newt Gingrich, for example) or avoided being sent to Vietnam by using connections to join the otherwise difficult to join National Guard (Dan Quayle, for example). Clinton's letter to his draft board stating his hatred of the war and the military dripped with the kind of youthful sincerity that comes back to haunt one later in life. Newt Gingrich did not have to state his opposition to the war; he merely did what the fortunate others of his generation did, namely, keep his deferment and keep quiet. Unlike many of his contemporary political peers, Clinton did not keep quiet. He chose to elaborate his reasons for briefly allowing himself to be made draftable and for signaling his intention to enter the University of Arkansas Law School to do reserve officer training when he, instead, decided to enroll at Yale University Law School. His now infamous letter mixed youthful idealism and unconcealed political calculation.

This episode, suspicions about his sex life, and his tendency to explain his past with half-truths (smoking marijauna but not inhaling) earned him the sobriquet "slick Willie." There was a pervasive feeling that Clinton could not be trusted. That feeling was promoted by some of his bitterest political opponents even during his presidency, but it was often reluctantly accepted even among his putative supporters. It was certainly pervasive among the public. According to data organized by John Kessel from the National Election Study surveys, Clinton was the least trusted candidate winning or losing over the past five presidential elections. [13]

Unfortunately for Clinton, there was little positive change in these suspicions even after he became president. His honeymoon period was both shallow and brief. His problems with the military continued when the joint chiefs publicly opposed his proposal to end discrimination against gays in the military—a matter on which he eventually retreated nearly in full, while trying to cut his losses with both gays and the military. A young staffer, overly endowed with self-righteousness, contributed to Clinton's problems by refusing to return the greeting of a senior military officer, gratuitously commenting that she did not speak to the military. [14] By Memorial Day, Clinton gave an address at the Vietnam War Memorial that was met by a highly vocal and hostile crowd carrying placards accusing him of draft dodging and even of treason. General Colin Powell overtly saved Clinton from being shouted down by emphasizing to those jeering the president the respect due Clinton's role. It was clear from this who held the upper hand in public esteem.

While there had been murmurs about Hillary Clinton's law firm and the easy way of doing business in Arkansas, these all resurfaced, especially after the suicide death in July of Mrs. Clinton's former law partner, Vincent Foster, the White House deputy counsel. A brewing investigation of a complex set of business deals involving the Clintons was being referred to as the Whitewater affair—so named after the resort condos that the Clintons invested in with an Arkansas developer. It is not altogether clear what exactly Whitewater is about, if it is about anything, or the mysterious connections to Vincent Foster's death being imputed to it. Nevertheless, there was persistent smoke, as well as enough smokescreen coming from the Clinton White House, to make it appear that underneath there must be fire. For a presidency filled with unwelcome baggage, this was not what was needed. Inevitably, Whitewater not only fueled more suspicions about "slick Willie," it also brought back into play an image of Hillary Clinton as "calculator-in-chief."

Thus, a final but exceedingly important part of Bill Clinton's personal baggage was Hillary Clinton. For men of Bill Clinton's generation, the role of the professional spouse is now commonplace. But Mrs. Clinton was a novelty to the public, and as is often the case, a woman of considerable achievements and drive was stereotyped in unflattering ways. Her professional career and engagement in advocacy-group activities led some Republican orators and campaign strategists to depict her virtually as a wicked witch who would exercise great power within a Clinton presidency. Unlike previous First Ladies, Hillary Clinton had a public past with her business commitments and her investments in her policy interests. Despite efforts during the campaign to appeal to traditional conceptions of a First Lady's role, Mrs. Clinton had not come to the White House to serve tea and cookies. As a consequence, Bill Clinton inherited her legal and business dealings as his also (which, in fact, some were); he inherited her law partners (one of whom committed suicide, another of whom turned in a plea bargain on a felony indictment, and a third of whom resigned under fire); he inherited her friends and their policy commitments; and, above all, he inherited her expectation that she would be an important policy player in the Clintons' administration.

Although John Kennedy had hived off the Justice Department for his brother Robert to head in a move that arched a number of eyebrows, the thought of Clinton's wife as a sort of co-president raised even more doubts, some nonlegitimate and others serious. Among the fundamentalist Christian Right, a woman out of the house is out of order—so Mrs. Clinton, a strong-willed and independent woman, became a ready part of the religious right's demonology. But among serious students of government, as Colin Campbell observes in chapter 2, Mrs. Clinton's ascendancy as a formal policy adviser raises questions about the institution of the presidency and the proper relationship between advisees and advisers.

While many presidential spouses have advised their husbands and even carved out roles for themselves, none had heretofore been expected to be an official policy adviser. Obviously, one cannot so readily dismiss either the works or the person of a spouse or sibling. Indeed, one particular rendition of Hillary Clinton's policy role in the White House has this role being purchased through a kind of blackmail for her husband's purported marital indiscretions.[15] Whatever the case, there is no doubt that Mrs. Clinton's visible presence (as distinct from traditional free-ranging spousal advice of the sort given to their husbands by Mrs. Carter or Mrs. Reagan, for example) creates complications for how the Clinton presidency actually works. Her extremely high level of visibility also increases her, and therefore his, political vulnerability. Her hostile attitudes toward the press are deflected onto him; her friends' clumsy tactics become his liability, and so on. There is no doubt that future presidents, whether male or female, will have a problem defining the role of an intelligent policy-interested spouse. Much of this reflects the lack of institutionalization within the presidency as contrasted to parliamentary-cabinet systems. Nevertheless, the Clintons' problem, while a first, will not likely be a last.

THE STRATEGIC DILEMMA

Bill Clinton is a Democrat. That simple fact immediately defines a problem of political strategy for nomination and election to the presidency. Since 1968, Democrats have won only two presidential elections, and since 1940 only two Democrats have won popular majorities—Lyndon Johnson in 1964 and Jimmy Carter narrowly in 1976. These facts tell us that Democrats do not have an easy time in presidential races. They must struggle to put together coalitions of groups that are not readily mobilized, and they must appeal to people who are not necessarily sympathetic to core Democratic constituencies by emphasizing empathy and vague aspirations. When trying to get in, Democrats can talk about change in some amorphous fashion. When trying to stay in, they can talk about how unthinkably dangerous the opposing candidate is. Without therefore getting into a particularly nuanced discussion of whether or not there has been electoral realignment in the United States, it is clear from the outcomes that Republicans seem to have a natural advantage in presidential races.[16]

The past three Democratic presidents all hailed from the South: Johnson, Carter, and Clinton. Because Johnson's presidency was accidental (although his vice-presidential selection clearly was not), he had to connect himself to the party's main labor/liberal axis, which, of course, he proceeded to do in extraordinary ways. Because of Johnson's presidency, the American South was to change and so was the Democratic Party in it. New Democratic politicians in the South needed a coalition of both black and white votes to get elected. They needed big turnouts of blacks and their overwhelming support. But they also needed to get enough white votes to win. New Democrats in the South had to find ways of appealing to each set of interests, where the interests were often at odds. They had to appear to be both liberal and conservative. Southern Democratic politicians with national ambitions especially had to position themselves sufficiently carefully so that among the party's presidential candidates, they were not farthest to the right in a party that itself was moving farther to the left.

Thus, in 1976, the pacific if economically conservative Jimmy Carter was positioned to the left of the late Senator Henry ("Scoop") Jackson of Washington, a Cold War hawk. At the same time, the other Democratic contenders for the presidential nomination were in the party's mainstream —Senator Birch Bayh of Indiana, Representative Mo Udall of Arizona, and so on. Jimmy Carter could look liberal to potential liberal supporters, conservative to potential conservative supporters, and moderate to those looking for a central tendency—at least until he had to act as president, at which point he came to look too liberal to conservatives and too conservative to liberals. The trick for Carter in the 1976 election was to bring along much of the South and add it to the core Democratic strength, a feat he successfully achieved, yet in doing so he still only squeaked by.

In 1992, Clinton faced the same problem that Carter had, alleviated by the fact that the Democrats had run two northern liberals in a row (Walter Mondale and Michael Dukakis) with nothing to show for it. Unlike the even more unknown Jimmy Carter, Bill Clinton's appeal could not be predicated on "trust me," for the obvious reason that few did trust him. Clinton needed to call himself a New Democrat and connect himself to the party nationally while trying to emphasize his roots in the small-town South. Clinton's impressive intellect, his thoughtfulness about policy, and his interpersonal political skills wowed much of the policy intelligentsia. His connections to the DLC, his support of capital punishment and welfare reform, and his emphasis on communitarian values were designed to keep him in play with a different sort of crowd, however. In all, he could be to the right of such party stalwarts as Senator Tom Harkin of Iowa or of the new-wave candidate, former Governor Jerry Brown of California, while not so far right as the party's deficit hawk candidate, former Senator Paul Tsongas of Massachusetts.

In sum, a Democratic presidential hopeful with any eye toward winning the nomination *and* the election has to stitch together seemingly incompatible constituencies with seemingly compatible policy positions. Not many have been able to do it. Being from the South is at least not a disadvantage in trying to play this game. Being a politician without a national record is also a help. The rest can be left to the imagination of the public. What worked for Carter worked even better for Clinton. While he did less well in the South than Carter had done in 1976, he nevertheless held his own there and did substantially better in the West, where Carter had failed to gain electoral support.

The problem of governance after moving through all these hoops is apparent for Democratic presidents. Election is often achieved by an appeal to freshness and change that, by definition, must wear thin. On the whole, regardless of whether or not Democratic policy appeals are consonant with potential political majorities, they are often not consonant with the majorities that constitute the active electorate. Democrats tend to win by stealth—by being better service deliverers and caseworkers in Congress and emphasizing their local virtues. Of course, where the party's constituencies are densely concentrated, the party's political standard-bearers can play to party issues. But a presidential election does not exactly provide a natural majority for the Democratic Party's core constituencies. This puts a Democratic president in a strategic pickle. Such a president has to weave between various party constituencies while also needing to appear independent of them. When Clinton has put on his New Democrat hat, he has done so in a way that oozes artifice. His condemnation at the Reverend Jesse Jackson's Rainbow Coalition dinner of Sister Souljah (a black rap singer whose lyrics implied that black on black violence might more fruitfully be transferred to white victims) was intended clearly to make a political statement that Bill Clinton was a different candidate and that he was not in the Reverend Jackson's pocket. When Clinton returned to Arkansas during the nomination struggle to preside over the execution of a mentally retarded murderer, he wanted that also to make a statement that he was a Democrat who was tough on crime and criminals. Liberals cringed but figured this was one person the country could afford to waste on Clinton's behalf.

Governing involves making choices that will inevitably define a president. George Bush wanted to avoid making as many of those defining choices as he could. But after the glow of success in the Gulf War, Bush concluded he could not avoid them and marched to the beat of the party's growing right wing. His party's skepticism of him required Bush increasingly to play to its more extreme fringes. Clinton's decisions too would inevitably define him, and they did, ironically, by making him look too willing to cave in on the part of his partisans and too unwilling to seek compromises from the standpoint of the opposition. Some of this, I suggest, is clearly a matter of Clinton's personal style and the internal conflict between his policy beliefs and his desire for accommodation. Inevitably, though, much of this zigging and zagging and open-endedness is a matter of trying to find the narrowed path allowed by his political situation that, in turn, is partly created by the party banner he carries in the political time during which he carries it.[17]

POLITICAL WEAKNESS

After a long and personally bruising campaign, Bill Clinton arrived in the presidency under very limiting political conditions. Not only had he won by a lesser margin than the last polls had predicted (with Perot doing much better than expected), but his percentage of the popular vote was the lowest since Richard Nixon's first-term election in 1968, when George Wallace garnered over 13 percent of the vote as an independent candidate. Moreover, Clinton's election brought no particular glad tidings on the congressional front. There, his party lost ten seats in the House of Representatives and gained none in the Senate, not an auspicious beginning to his presidency. The Senate results left the Democrats three votes shy of the extraordinary (three-fifths) majority required to shut off debate in the chamber so as to allow a simple majority to work its will. It was clear that the electorate had been unhappy with the incumbent, President Bush. It was less clear what they wanted done. Yet, while the electorate had hardly produced an electoral mandate, Democratic Party elites and activists were anticipating coming in from the desert after twelve years. The prospect of discord between an uncertain public and a perhaps all too certain Democratic elite loomed. It was not that the public opposed Democratic policy objectives in the abstract, but that they might do so either when the shoe pinched or when they were told by opposition politicians and propagandists that it would pinch.

If the political legacy of the election failed to give Clinton much leverage, matters would soon get worse on the electoral front. Clinton lost one probable ally when Senator Wyche Fowler (D-Ga.) won a plurality but not a majority in a close senatorial race with his Republican opponent, Paul Coverdell. Georgia law had recently been rewritten to require runoffs in the absence of a majority. The timing of the law was bad news for both Fowler and Clinton. In the subsequent runoff election, conducted with a much reduced electorate, Coverdell won a majority by a small margin. One Senate seat was now lost. Through the appointment of Senator Lloyd Bentsen of Texas to the post of secretary of the treasury, another seat eventually would be lost. The popular governor of Texas, Ann Richards, refused to accept appointment to the Senate seat (she eventually lost her reelection bid for governor). In her place, Bob Kreuger, a former member of Congress and former failed hopeful for a Senate bid, was seated. A moderate-to-conservative Democrat, Kreuger went down to a landslide defeat in the special springtime election to Kay Bailey Hutchison, the Republican candidate. Now Clinton was down another Senate seat. So early in his term, no one could conclude with certainty that Clinton himself was responsible for these defeats, but they could conclude that being associated with Clinton was, at the least, no particular help.

The results of the fall elections of 1993 brought unrelieved bad news to the Democrats and thus to Clinton. A very conservative Republican, who had come from far behind early in the race, won the Virginia governorship. The Democratic incumbent governor of New Jersey, who had unpopularly raised taxes early in his term, was thought to have battled back to win, but in the end James Florio fell short, losing to the Republican challenger, Christine Todd Whitman, who ran on an antitax platform. (Clinton's budget proposal, which had passed exclusively on Democratic votes, was tarred as being merely a tax proposal.) Democrats lost to Republicans in mayoralty races in the two largest cities of the United States, each a Democratic bastion. Bill Clinton was not exactly a hot political ticket to follow. He was becoming more like a hot potato. Consequently, Clinton entered year two of his term with gaping political wounds. Even before the general election of 1994, there were further ominous portents for Clinton's presidency. Two Republicans of the Christian Coalition persuasion won House seats in special elections held by Democrats in Kentucky and Oklahoma.

The election of 1994, of course, changed Clinton's position completely. The Republicans, having won fifty-two seats in the House and eight in the

Senate, controlled both chambers. They were now best positioned to dictate the flow of proposals. By virtue of the House Republicans' preelection "Contract with America" (the brainstorm of the then-minority whip and now Speaker, Newt Gingrich), the House Republican majority came ready with a radical program in hand. It was fair to say that the Democrats were utterly discombobulated by the election result. Most of the remaining Democratic members of the House came from districts laden with core Democratic constituencies and found little reason to do other than what House Republicans had during their nearly forty years in the desert—go into opposition. But Clinton had no safe constituency to which to turn. If he is to return, he will have to navigate his way through rocky shoals, trying to look cooperative when he can and principled when he must. By sending out early feelers that he would seek areas of cooperation (the first a constitutional amendment on school prayer), Clinton only rankled those in his own corner, who concluded that he was untrustworthy and a weak bargainer even from a weakly leveraged position. By his expected supporters, Clinton often was seen as a politician too ready to give up a battle or accede to the terms of his opponents. Many of his personal inclinations clearly lead him to be a deal maker on terms that often seemed exceptionally weak. Still, it can hardly be denied that the political conditions bequeathed him and the political card he carries as a Democrat provide him with few options. The question is, does he know what he is willing to bargain for? That remains uncertain.

THE POLICY LEGACY

Deficits.—In real estate, location is the key; in policymaking, the budget is the key. Choices are heavily constrained by the budget deficit. The Reagan-Bush years ran up three-quarters of the present standing deficit, though who and what is to blame is not a matter I care to address here. The impact of big spending increases in defense, continued rises in entitlements such as Social Security, Medicare, and Medicaid, increased costs in managing the deficit, and the unwillingness to pay for it all through increased taxes add up to one result: increased deficits. Numerous efforts to deal with the deficit have floundered in the absence of a willingness to undertake politically risky efforts to rein in entitlement spending or substantially raise revenues through a general levy or rise in rates, or do both. Moreover, the political cost to politicians who have risked lesser efforts still seems substantial. Bush, for one, got little credit for cutting a deficit-reduction deal because it was claimed that the deal helped harden the recession, thus increasing the cyclical deficit.

Clinton came into office with the dual ideas of getting the deficit under control and investing federal resources into the human capital and technologies that he thought were at the cutting edge of twenty-first-century economic competition. Economically, if not politically, Clinton succeeded relatively well with the former (especially because, unlike poor Bush, Clinton has had a growing economy), but he did so unknowingly at the cost of the latter. Like many policy intellectuals in Washington, Clinton apparently argued that without deficit reduction nothing else he wanted to do could be done.[18] What he may not have realized is that deficit reduction was even more a political than a financial issue. To what extent the deficit should be reduced, how it should be reduced, and what priority it should be given were all political issues. Only the last of these issues had been taken off the table as a matter of debate, a decision that virtually assured that little else on Clinton's investments agenda would see the light of day.

While the 1990 budget plan produced caps and firewalls around spending categories, the 1993 budget bill wound up producing a hard limit on discretionary spending. Even had Clinton managed the political support for the investments he had in mind and for other proposals such as welfare reform that would entail significant up-front costs, he would have found it difficult to maneuver around the discretionary spending limit without damaging other programs favored by Democrats. Once again, this was not a cheerful time to be a Democratic president.

The Post–Cold War Blues.—A different kind of policy legacy inherited by Clinton was, unlike the budget, a liberating one rather than a constraining one. That is the end of the Cold War, which should have played to Clinton's advantage inasmuch as he wanted to concentrate on domestic policy initiatives. Unfortunately, however the world is structured, its problems do not go away when you are president of the United States. Because it is the world's remaining national superpower, its leader is supposed to have a position on everything, even when it clearly cannot have an interest in everything. Many of the world's problems, aside from the international economic issues that Clinton saw as part of his domestic policy portfolio, involve intranational rather than international conflicts. This makes them especially sticky and difficult to resolve. Big strategic military forces are irrelevant to solving such problems.

Bill Clinton did not want to be pinned down by conflicts such as those in the Balkans, Somalia, Haiti, and parts of the former Soviet Union. He did not want to be a captive of foreign policy. The idea, in fact, was to keep foreign policy from interfering with domestic business.[19] One way of dealing with some of these conflicts was to minimize the U.S. interest in them—either a form of neoisolationism or a particular form of Realpolitik (the two, of course, may be quite compatible). Another way of dealing with them is to moralize without putting one's money where one's mouth is. The former looks callous; the latter ridiculous. The Bush administration chose to suffer from perceptions of the first sort; the Clinton administration wound up suffering from perceptions of the second sort.

The moralizing may have had two causes. The most important of these,

I believe, lies at the heart of Democratic Party doctrines, namely, human rights. Democrats are drawn to a Wilsonian ardor for democracy and human rights, but they are not equally drawn to paying the often dreadful costs of seeing that commitment through. This makes for talk, which is cheap, except for the expectations and entanglements it creates among other actors. Bill Clinton, in this regard, appears to be a quintessential Democrat, morally disturbed by the frightful carnage of civil conflict in Bosnia and the predatory behavior of armed thugs in Somalia and Haiti. The second cause may be, as Elizabeth Drew suggests, that Clinton needed to reverse the Democrats' image of weakness on national security matters by outflanking Bush.[20] This meant talking tougher. Talking tough often makes for great campaign tactics but rarely for good policy unless there is a well-thought-out plan for the credible use of threat.

The end of the Cold War placed a premium on expressions of moral outrage because it both let loose nationalist forces that had once been constrained (or bought off) by a ruling Communist Party and seemingly created conditions for intervention by virtue of the absence of a Soviet retaliatory threat. At the same time, the end of the Cold War generated public expectations of peace and quiet and indifference to a world no longer threatened (or hyped to be) by the now-defunct Soviets. These expectations were rudely deflected by the Iraqi invasion of Kuwait in 1990 and the Desert Storm campaign that followed in 1991. The relative ease of military victory amid a powerful consensus to eliminate the Iraqi threat paradoxically limited future military options because they would have to be relatively costless, as was Desert Storm.

The end of the Cold War thus created new demands for policy and less political capability for responding. Clinton responded by flitting from one ad hoc formulation to another, seemingly unable to get his admirable moral sensitivities working in tandem with his equally admirable but often infirmly situated mind. In the end, former President Jimmy Carter twice saved Clinton's bacon by negotiating a deal with the North Koreans to assist and thus regulate their nuclear development and by cutting a deal for the departure of Haiti's military government. As in domestic politics and policy, Clinton too often thought out loud, too frequently seemed to promise things he either could not or chose not to deliver, and thus too frequently could not be taken at his word. As in the domestic arena, Clinton was seen as someone who would cave in (when he need not have escalated his position to begin with) and as someone whose word need not imply subsequent action.

Inasmuch as Clinton for the next two years can at best react to the Republican congressional agenda, or try to preempt pieces of it, he may find foreign policy more worthy of his attention. To get it right, he will have to learn a trait that seems to run counter to his very being, namely, to engage his considerable brainpower before, rather than during, the engagement of his always loquacious mouth. Rarely does Clinton seem to have an unsaid thought. Unfortunately, foreign policy often requires lots of thoughts to be left unsaid.

THE NEW PARTISANSHIP

One additional legacy requires at least brief discussion: the steady turn toward a more bitter and more ideological basis of partisanship among elites and activists in the United States. While Democrats and Republicans obviously had different median points, there was always some overlap between the parties in Congress. There was a hefty proportion of conservative Democrats, overwhelmingly from the South, and a fairly significant proportion of Republicans who could be regarded as liberal or moderate, mostly from the Northeast. For a variety of reasons, the overlap between the parties has diminished as the Democrats in general have fewer conservatives, while the Republicans especially have gravitated rightward.[21] Liberal Republican has become an oxymoron, and moderate Republican now virtually stands for anyone who has not fully bought into the Christian Coalition view of life.

There may be a spatial center but there is no political one among the elites and activists in spite of the fact that moderate positions seem to be populated by mass publics (who are, however, frequently indifferent or even confused) on most issues. For example, about a month after the midterm election of 1994, which produced a hyperconservative Republican majority in Congress, polls showed that spending more on programs for poor children had a plurality and was supported at least five times more than spending less on such programs. About two-thirds agreed that government has a responsibility to take care of the poor, and about 70 percent believed that welfare recipients should be able to receive benefits as long as they work, which nearly 90 percent of the public agreed they should be required to do.[22]

To be sure, one reason for the greater degree of partisanship has to do with the expansion of issues into the arena of partisan politics that had not previously been within the scope of party politics. Many such issues have had to do with sociocultural divisions based on attitudes toward restriction or choice on abortion, the role of women and minorities and preferential treatment in the labor market, the rights of homosexuals, gun control, and so on. Before the Supreme Court's *Roe v. Wade* decision (1973), pro-choice was not a viable political option; it was only a legal one. Soon enough, the issue found its way into the political arena and, for the most part, has come to divide along party lines. Although there are Republican politicians who are pro-choice, any of them would have an uphill struggle to get their party's presidential nomination. Even more so, a pro-life Democratic politician —and there are some—would have a nearly impossible task obtaining his or her party's presidential nomination.

Beyond the polarizing of party positions, there also has been another contribution to congressional partisanship, and that has had to do with the way in which the rules of each chamber have been put to partisan use. In the early to mid-1970s, especially, House Democrats sought in various ways to make the chamber more responsive to the party's majority. These efforts over time strengthened the Speaker and brought more action to the floor. Inevitably, procedures (including bringing legislation to the floor under a closed rule) that advantage the majority party's ability to conduct business weaken the influence of the minority party in the chamber and, ultimately, lead them toward oppositionist and confrontational tactics. That would likely increase their cohesion. Democrats came to see the Republican minority as wholly obstructionist. The Republicans came to view the Democratic majority as arrogant and dictatorial.

While the Senate remained a much more individualized body than the House, Senate Republicans had become increasingly conservative. While their House counterparts were often being steamrollered by the Democratic majority, the rules of the Senate, which allowed for substantial individual holds on legislation and for endless debate (the fabled filibuster), essentially required a supermajority (three-fifths) to shut off debate and consider moving legislation onto the floor. In view of the party polarization that was occurring, the filibuster was increasingly used as a minority-party technique to prevent the majority from getting its way. A party majority of less than three-fifths could not guarantee that debate would be brought to an end even if the majority party was cohesive, unless it could entice some members of the minority to join it. Much of Clinton's policy agenda, in fact, never reached the floor of the Senate.

Into this tempest of increased partisanship and even an increased coarseness of elite political etiquette stepped the newly elected Bill Clinton, seeking to promote his so-called third way. Whatever his way was, it seemed to make matters even worse.

The Leadership Style of Bill Clinton

It has taken a long time to set the table before focusing directly on Clinton's leadership style. That may be because the author suffers from Clinton's own reputed excesses of indiscipline and lack of focus, but it is mainly because the conditions of leadership so powerfully shape its possibilities. Normally, the system of American government frustrates those with large ambitions. Yet, appetites for change loomed large among the Democrats, who had unified government for the first time in more than a decade, and the public, which seemed to want change as long as it did not have a specific identification. The opportunity for frustration was great, and, unfortunately for Clinton, it was fulfilled. As a result, future opportunities have been seized from him, at least for now. The "change" candidate of 1992 is now ironically mostly in the position of defending the status quo from the new Republican congressional majorities.

I focus here on three aspects of Bill Clinton's political personality. The first is his policy style: How does he think about policy, and how does he mesh it with politics? How has that style served his purposes or failed to? The second is Clinton's political style: How does he relate to others, and how does that affect both his ability to do politics and to do policy? The third is Clinton's executive style: What are its characteristics, and how have they influenced his political and policy fortunes?

POLICY STYLE

Bill Clinton is a politician of extraordinary personal ambition—even for a politician. At the age of fifteen, as a member of a youth group, Bill Clinton was photographed shaking the hand of the then president, John F. Kennedy. The photograph makes sense retrospectively once we have had the benefit of knowing Clinton's subsequent career. Clinton has spent all his adult life but one year (that teaching law) in politics. It might well be that he spent much of his adolescence figuring out how to get where he is. By his mid-twenties, his girl friend and future wife, Hillary Rodham, a junior staffer on the Senate Watergate Committee, was reputed to have told Bernard Nussbaum, a more senior staffer and future White House counsel, that he should meet her boy friend because he was going to be president one day. Unlike, say, John F. Kennedy, who had family legacies to live up to, or Ronald Reagan, who had ideological commitments to fulfill, Clinton's ambition was all self-propelled.

Clinton's ambition, however, was not purely or perhaps even mostly of the ego-stroking sort. It was not the office as such that he seemed to crave, but what he could do in the office.[23] Still, he was not a candidate to fulfill an ideological mission, either his or that of his backers. Instead, Clinton's conclusion seemed to be that he had a facility for thinking about policy and an instinct for politics that in combination would augur well in the presidency. He was hooked on political life because he liked doing both politics and policy—a not-so-frequent combination, ironically, among recent U.S. presidents. A Republican politician and former colleague of Clinton's from the National Conference of Governors, Thomas Kean, the former governor of New Jersey, said of Clinton that "he has a first-class intellect as well as a sensitivity to the needs of others. You'll often find politicians with one or the other, but not both. It's quite a combination."[24]

As governor of Arkansas, one of the country's smaller and poorest states, Clinton developed a reputation as a policy innovator, with specific interests in human-capital development such as education and skill training for a more flexible labor market. He also developed a reputation for getting along with the Arkansas business establishment (in a state with weak labor unions, of course). His policy ambitions seem largely to have been contoured around problems of the future rather than debates of the past. He was not a New Deal Democrat with an unbounded faith in the capacity of government to run programs. He seemed certainly to understand that Americans had lost confidence in government and, whether correct or not, that they believed government more often failed than worked. He was not necessarily for more government, which, in any event, was made unlikely by budgetary restrictions. But he was inclined to look to government and to public policy to stimulate other mechanisms to achieve his policy objectives. Thus, the immensely complicated health-care plan developed through the Ira Magaziner and Hillary Clinton task force came about because the president believed that a straightforward extension of a single-payer system such as Medicare would be seen as more government, would have to be financed by new or increased taxes, would lack cost controls (other than those directly imposed), and had little chance of stitching together a majority.

All these reasons for going the route he did on health care say a great deal about Clinton's policy style and his blend of Old Democratic policy preferences with New Democratic methods, symbols, and rhetoric. The first thing it says is that in an age of skepticism about government, Clinton did not want to use traditional federally administered mechanisms to run the program. The second thing it says is that in an era of budget constraint, Clinton was trying to avoid projects that did not seem ("seem" is a crucial word here) to contain self-financing. The third thing it says is that in an era of antitax fervor (despite the U.S. having nearly the lowest taxes among all the highly developed economies), Clinton wanted to avoid general or direct tax increases. A fourth thing it says is that Clinton did not like to tilt at windmills. He wanted to put together proposals that had a chance to gain a majority. Yet a fifth thing it says, paradoxically, is that Clinton prefers comprehensive to incremental solutions. Sixth, it says that Clinton was in accord with the principal tenets of his party in believing that people's social security (health care, pensions, unemployment, etc.) was essential to their ability to function in society and that such needs should be cared for universally. But seventh, it suggests also that for Clinton's vision of the future to work—a society of adaptable citizens with sophisticated labor market skills and labor portability—citizens in the society had to feel secure.[25]

Clinton is a quick study and has a perceptive grasp of how problems and proposed policies link to one another. Unlike Jimmy Carter, who also had an addiction for grappling with big problems in big ways, Clinton understood that the American political system rarely digests wholly comprehensive policy proposals. Clinton's presidential ambitions, one suspects, were stoked by his belief that knowledge and vision were essential ingredients to leadership and that he came fueled with both, minus dogmas. In this regard, it is possible to interpret his ambition as idealistic in the sense that he believed he could make a difference for America's future and its preparation to cope with the problems of the twenty-first century. At the same time, Clinton may well have thought also that he could work the system better than most recent presidents—that he had powers of persuasion and relentless energy to expend on behalf of a policy agenda he hoped could find its way across the deepening ideological divides of American politics.

Bill Clinton is the rare combination of a complex policy thinker and a sophisticated thinker about politics—perhaps too complex and too sophisticated for his own good. Clinton's policy complexity often resists being boiled down to a succinct and memorable position or slogan. The public has had a hard time figuring out what he is about. By seeing so many angles to problems and by seeing that varying solutions have both costs and benefits of different sorts, Clinton often suffers from that which afflicted his equally brainy, if less sophisticated, predecessor Jimmy Carter, namely, paralysis by analysis. Bob Woodward's description of how Alan Greenspan, the Federal Reserve Board chair, perceived Clinton after their first lengthy discussion is indicative. According to Woodward's account:

> The chairman was quite surprised at the level of abstraction of their conversation. Yet he also knew that intellectuals, himself included, tended to know too much on both sides of an issue and sometimes found it hard to make decisions. He wondered if Clinton would be like Hamlet, afflicted with the problems of the thoughtful. Was he too thoughtful for his own good? Too thoughtful for politics?[26]

In politics, Clinton has understood that the American system is not a presidency-centric one and that, in the absence of supermajorities, the system works on compromise. When to compromise without disappointing one's followers is what is hard to decide. A key problem that has stalked the Clinton presidency is when to give in and to whom. The standard critique of Clinton is that he is remarkably infirm and gives away too much too early. The accounts of Bob Woodward and Elizabeth Drew, among others, frequently note that Clinton "made it too desirable for congressmen to hold out."[27] As a consequence, "everybody knew there was no real price for opposing Clinton."[28] Most of the giving and taking has been with his own party's members in Congress. In part, this is because every president has to start somewhere—and that somewhere invariably begins with his own party.

In reality, Clinton was confronted with three political options, only one of which—the one he chose—had any chance of working. One option was to play to the diffuse populism welling in the country, stoked by the agitprop talk show hosts on the AM dial, and the discontent with Washington's political institutions and the government. Another possibility was to try to create bipartisan majorities. A third was to try to create the majority from within his own party's then majority in Congress, a course of action urged on him by his party's congressional leaders and elders and by his own closest political adviser, George Stephanopoulos.

The third course is the norm and, for the most part, Clinton followed the norm, allowing room for compromise as he moved toward the end game. Ratification of NAFTA could readily be done across party lines, mainly because it was supported more by Republicans than Democrats. Few other issues were so amenable. On health care and the budget and numerous other issues, the then Republican minority moved farther away from Clinton's efforts to compromise rather than toward them. The Republican leaders and rank and file sensed Clinton's political vulnerability and found it advantageous to their cause to oppose him implacably regardless of what he was willing to deal. Putting forth proposals designed at the outset to attract Republican support would have mortally wounded him within his own party. Moreover, to put it kindly, the prospects of actually creating bipartisan coalitions ranged from faint to nonexistent. Going around Congress to arouse popular instincts also is tricky business. And when it fails, as Carter discovered, it can have lasting effects. In sum, Clinton, during his first two years, was going to have to go through his own party if he was to get anywhere, and that left him in a position to be picked apart. Elizabeth Drew observes keenly that "the truth was that the modern presidency didn't have a lot of leverage. And Clinton could not deliver strong grassroots support, since he had won only 43 percent of the vote and had no passionate following."[29] The only real question left was not by which route Clinton had to try to gain his majority, but whether gaining a majority at any price would be worth the price. At what point was it wiser—if it was wise at all—to have taken Nancy Reagan's advice, to just say no? As noted earlier, no is not a word that Bill Clinton likes to utter, but by virtue of that fact, it is a word he often hears.

POLITICAL STYLE

Bill Clinton is a politician to his bones. Because he has been in public life for virtually his entire adult life, Clinton's habits are those of a politician. Politicians normally succeed in getting reelected, not by saying no, but by saying yes or, more frequently, simply by not saying no and appearing to agree with the claimant. This is a syndrome that Clinton has as well, if perhaps even deeper than most politicians do.

Like most politicians—indeed, like most people—Clinton likes to be liked. By all accounts, he has a remarkably accessible personality and an easy way around people.[30] This is no brooding, vengeful Richard Nixon or mean-spirited Lyndon Johnson (who, story has it, on asking the curmudgeonly former secretary of state, Dean Acheson, why he was not more beloved, was told by Acheson that the reason was he was not a likable man). Nor is

Clinton an ideologue who sees things in black and white. He is pliable, perhaps excessively so. The pliability may make him look like a soft touch.[31] One description of Clinton's political style as governor was that "he was known as a big carrot/small stick governor [who] may complain, even rage, to his staff, but ... does not punish his enemies. Instead, he strokes them, often deftly. Sometimes this brings them around, but sometimes it just emboldens them to cross him again."[32] This style appears to have persisted into his presidency. That could be because of Clinton's nonconfrontational temperament and his desire to be liked. But it also could be an entirely rational (and eminently political) response to the stark realization as both governor and president just how limited one's ability to threaten is. After all, one may have to look past today's alignments and opponents to tomorrow's problems and whatever coalitions will be needed then. The problem for Clinton as an executive is that those with whom he is dealing and to whom he may be yielding will be making similar calculations about him.

Clinton does not have the John Wayne or Ronald Reagan swagger. Like Jimmy Carter, who invited the "outs" back in by granting amnesty to those who had left the country to avoid serving in the Vietnam war, Bill Clinton invited the air controllers whom Ronald Reagan had fired to reapply for their jobs. Clinton is not a man of hardened heart or enemies lists, or depressive moods. In fact, by all accounts he is an extraordinarily ebullient man with an overriding sense of optimism—a kind of latter-day Hubert Humphrey without his defining political pitch.

Clinton seems to fall just across the fine line between a willingness to give and a propensity to give in. Some of this has to do with ideological identity or lack thereof. Ronald Reagan gave when he had to, but everybody knew where he was coming from. Bill Clinton may give in no more than he has to either, but others expect he will because they do not know where he is coming from and, above all, what he intends to settle for. Mainly, the ambiguity derives from his delicate political situation and his position of dependence.

But the ambiguity is supplemented from two additional sources. One is his own level of information—the problem alluded to previously as knowing too much for his own good. As Elizabeth Drew observed, "Clinton carried a lot of information in his head, something that didn't always work to his advantage. Reagan, being underinformed, could be utterly clear about simple goals. Clinton, being exceedingly informed, sometimes got lost in his facts."[33] The consequence of being open-minded and subject to policy facts (as Carter often was) and sensitive to their interplay with political facts (as Carter rarely was) is indecision, uncertainty, and delay. These features of Clinton's endless process of making up his mind certainly had an impact on his executive style in managing—if that is the right word—the White House.[34]

The second source of Clinton's ambiguity derives from a combination of his political line, which might best be described as squiggly, and his personal style, which can best be described as an effort to be encompassingly endearing. What is so especially fascinating about each characteristic is that this man who seeks to find policy possibilities within acceptable political parameters and who invites the perception that he is all things to all people is, in fact, a persistently unpopular president. Clinton has only rarely risen above his minimalist level of electoral support. Frequently, he has fallen below it.

It is staggering to realize from this perspective precisely how politically adept Bill Clinton was perceived to be when he entered the White House in January 1993. Note carefully the words of the journalist Joe Klein (who later became far more critical of Clinton), shortly after Clinton's election:

> Clinton's greatest strength is his understanding that policy and politics are intertwined, not separate universes, as George Bush imagined. . . . Bill Clinton's challenge is to bring the same sort of "laserlike" attention—and virtuosity—to domestic policy, especially the economy, that George Bush gave to foreign affairs. Domestic problems are too complicated, intractable—and boring—to summon the sort of public support necessary for real change. But no president has really tried since . . . Richard Nixon, and Clinton has political skills that neither Nixon nor Carter could summon. . . . Having a president who believes in government activism (within limits) and really cares about domestic policy is something of a novelty in recent American history. . . . Bill Clinton may not be able to solve all—or even many—of our problems, but his inclination will be to resolve disputes rather than incite them, to negotiate rather than preach or condemn. That sort of leadership may not prove stirring, but it will be persistent, responsible, sunny—and perhaps even dependable."[35]

Yet another account just after Clinton's inauguration may help explain why the perception of Clinton's leadership is so sour. The answer may be expectations. In this account, it is argued that

> to be a great president, it's not enough to pass a modest deficit-reduction bill that allows everyone to say, "See, we broke the gridlock." Clinton and Congress must pass a health bill and a deficit-reduction bill (and other bills) that genuinely transform the landscape. That will require Clinton to move beyond the cooperation he loves to the confrontation he loathes. . . .[36]

Yet another journalistic guru, David Broder, commenting on Clinton's political style, observed that he frequently behaved like a governor but needed to act like a presidential tiger. When Clinton indicated flexibility in cutting a deal with Congress on his health-care plan, Broder wrote:

His instinct is to approach health care the same way [defining common goals and indicating flexibility on the means for reaching them]. But in partisan Washington, where House leaders are struggling to line up every Democratic vote in anticipation of expected near-unanimous Republican opposition, Clinton's nostalgic evocation of the spirit of gubernatorial accommodation sounded suspiciously like an untimely retreat.[37]

Is it plausible that Clinton lost all his instincts in Washington? Or is it, as I believe, more likely that Clinton's policy goals, and his party's, collided massively with his political possibilities? Indeed, at virtually no point did it appear that Clinton was unwilling to deal; nor did he seem spectacularly unprincipled—at least no more than one must be in politics. On health care, he enunciated a few simple goals, stuck to one, produced an overly complicated plan (but one he hoped would not be saddled with the political stigma of single payer), and showed himself willing to deal, alas, from a position of political weakness. Had there been a majority in Congress to cut a deal, one would have been had. The fact is that all but a tiny handful of Republican senators in Congress were fleeing persistently from any cooperation with the White House on health care, and most other issues as well, heeding their party's advisers and their own political instincts.[38] If there had been any instincts on the part of Republicans for interparty cooperation (as there had been on NAFTA), it could have been achieved. But there were none. They knew Clinton was politically vulnerable and gave him no berth at all.

Indeed, the great irony of Clinton's presidency is that he came into office with a set of attributes that many political scientists would have anticipated to be ideally suited to being a successful president in the American political system. First, he had a vision of what he wanted to achieve, even if blurred in its specific contents and its message; second, he was an eminently political personality, empathizing with others and seeing their points of view; third, he understood that it is better to get something that improves matters than to get nothing at all, but that in order to get something, one must ask for more than one is likely to get; fourth, he understood that the president could not command other actors in the system, but could only persuade them, deal with them, and negotiate. If this picture is correct, and obviously I think it is, and if the conventional wisdom is that somehow Clinton has failed deeply (a view that I think must yet remain open), it may well be that we need to look to the political system rather than the political personality for answers. Or, at the least, we may need to reappraise our theories as to what kind of political personality works in the presidency—if any can. The notable exception to the failed presidency thesis in recent years, after all, was Ronald Reagan, a man of unstinting, even dogmatic, convictions, frequently untempered by facts and certainly unadorned with complexity. Reagan was notably not out to cut any deals with anyone.

EXECUTIVE STYLE

There is no doubt that one of Bill Clinton's deepest weaknesses as president is his unwillingness to think about organization and staffing (or to have someone think about these matters for him). Much of the dishevelment in White House advisory and decision-making processes owes to the principal himself. Clinton is given to prolixity and indiscipline and is a notoriously gregarious individual. And like other gregarious individuals, he does not carefully calculate how organizational systems might influence what he can do. Jimmy Carter, by contrast, was a president who paid profound attention to what often appeared as the apolitical reorganizing of boxes on organizational charts. Unlike Clinton, Carter was a highly disciplined individual. But like Clinton, he wanted things to come to him and not be filtered through a chief of staff. By wanting to be on top of everything, Democratic presidents seem to love a system of White House organization that virtually ensures that they will be on top of nothing until deadlines force a level of intense (and often unvetted) engagement.

Bill Clinton, by his nature, wants to be involved with everything, but, of course, he cannot be. A system that brings everything to him will assure a greater than average number of foul-ups that are purely a function of the inability of the White House to work properly. Too frequently decisions are left unmade, guidelines unspecified, and responsibilities vague.[39] Personnel decisions were often left hanging, partly, as Joel Aberbach notes in chapter 5, because positions were preconceived, thus limiting the range of choice, and frequently because they were inadequately vetted, such as the Zoë Baird and Lani Guinier nominations for attorney general and assistant attorney general for civil rights, respectively. It is clear that Clinton has an aversion to organizational and process thinking. Thus the problems of the White House's management of decision making stem most directly from Clinton himself and the extent to which Clinton's decision-making style is predicated on indecision and disorganization. Clinton likes to chew the fat and explore a variety of perspectives. He gave no indication that he wanted otherwise or, above all, did he empower anyone on his staff to do otherwise. As a consequence, Clinton's unwillingness to put someone or some set of people in a position to see certain tasks through and fix responsibility on them to do so added to his burdens and narrowed his choices. However vast were Ronald Reagan's limitations as a president, one of his great assets was that he knew what he did not know (which was most everything) and, to that extent, empowered a set of people to organize decision-making processes and, equally important, image-making processes. There is not much that Bill Clinton does not know or that he does not care about, but one of the things that he seems neither to know nor to care about is the importance of staffing and organization.

Staffing and organization will not solve all problems or perhaps even many of them. The political coalitions a president has to work with and the nature of the problems to which he has chosen to respond will largely determine his success. But an effectively run White House can lead to an effectively run government and can minimize what tennis buffs would call unforced errors. As in tennis, a good serve puts the server at an advantage. A weak serve places the server at a disadvantage. White House staffing and organization, when it is good, can put the president in the position of initiating the flow of events. There will be much that a president cannot control, but this is one thing he can—and Clinton hasn't controlled it.

Republican presidents seem to have a more developed sense of organization about them. This may be because hierarchy and fixed responsibilities and meetings with defined and limited agendas are a more natural part of their world. It also may have to do with the more limited goals and generally unambitious policy agendas that Republicans typically have brought to the office. Of late, it also may have to do with the fact that Republicans can dig deeper into a well of experienced staff personnel, advisers, and White House managers. Democratic presidents, by virtue of their greater policy ambitions and their personal desire to be involved with them, produce ambiguously structured systems of advice and decision making. In Clinton's case, precisely because there are so many sides to him and precisely because he tends to see so many sides to an issue and so many different feasible political (but not simultaneously consistent) strategies, he is in desperate need of being reined in and having decisions forced. Otherwise, he will avoid doing what needs to be done. Because Clinton is a politician of either extraordinary adaptability or, less charitably, extraordinary indecisiveness, he is "more than capable of seeing and feeling different things at different times."[40] Nothing about Clinton is set in stone.

One of the keys to leadership is the capacity to give off clear and consistent signals. Ronald Reagan left no one in doubt as to where he stood. Ironically, Bill Clinton seems to leave everyone in doubt when he is greatly engaged, as he has been in most matters of domestic policy, or minimally engaged, as he has been in most matters of foreign policy. When he is highly engaged, he often leaves it unclear as to where he has drawn his line and whether that will prove to be changeable or not. When he is disengaged, those acting in his name are left unsure as to what he wants or at least will settle for.[41] Clinton has vision but lacks the capacity for structuring decision making. George Bush's White House, conversely, could make decisions (though they often were to do nothing) despite Bush's own lack of vision.

In the end, an American president is responsible for organizing his own White House and his own administration. As has become fashionable these days in all organizations, Bill Clinton organized his administration around genetic and chromosomal diversity and his (and Mrs. Clinton's) friends, rather than around what would be required to make the administration work. The consequence has been, as Aberbach called it, "directionless diversity." Certainly, much of this reflects the fact that Clinton remained innocent of what it would take to make it work. Some is due to the fact that Clinton had difficulty tuning his political pitch—deciding just who he was and what it was that was most important to him. A lot is attributable to his own, mostly desirable, intellectual habits of open-mindedness (which risks the danger of open-endedness) and adaptability (which risks the danger of seeming to lack conviction).

Although the White House has lots of complex organizations, it is most distinctly *not* an institution. It has routines but no independent advisory or organizational capacity across administrations. There is no White House civil service as such. Too frequently, the White House becomes a mere extension of the president's campaign team. A president brings along his team or, frequently, his assortment. Not many of these assistants know the place or even the town. Many reinforce their principal in his own worst habits. This may well be the price for a political culture that takes politics seriously without taking government equally seriously. Clinton, in the tennis metaphor, has been a weak server. He has not used his opportunity to organize his administration or his office effectively. It has cost him, as it does most presidents. And like most presidents, learning how it needs to be done comes, but it often comes after a presidency has been damaged.

To put matters in perspective, however, this failing pales by comparison with his deeper problems, which had been, until the midterm election, how to create a coalition on behalf of his agenda. His own party both pressured and deserted him when it came to the actual pursuit of that agenda. Despite the expression of concern among Democrats about not wasting their opportunity, they proceeded to do just that, so much so that they lost their majorities in both chambers of Congress. Even were Clinton to have had the firmness of Ronald Reagan, he did not have Reagan's simplicity of agenda or his far more cohesive and ideologically driven party. He therefore could not have had Reagan's perceived success, even had he borrowed James Baker (as he did David Gergen) from the Reagan administration. In sum, Clinton failed to deliver the good serve but even had he done so, his opposition had too many other tools and he himself had resort to few others. His White House mess was debilitating but not fatal. Instead, his inability to expand his political base, both popularly and in Washington, was his more fundamental problem.

Looking Back and Ahead

Bill Clinton is a leader of large virtues and flaws. He brings intellectual agility, political sensitivity, and policy commitment (without dogma) to the office of president. By the same token, he has substantial flaws, some of which he brought to the office as part of his personal baggage. As a function of his past, he is primed to be mistrusted. But that also primes perceptions of his behavior. His frequent adjustments of position, his tendency to leave nominees hanging, and his tendency to dramatize positions or rhetoric for political effect are easily interpreted as the behavior of a guileful, calculating, and insincere politician. (In the present state of affairs in the United States, the term *politician* implies all of these modifiers in any event.)

Beyond these considerations, however, Clinton, simply put, is an indecisive person partly because he has the capacity to look at matters from a variety of angles and partly because he cannot, in the end, decide exactly what his political identity is and what he is willing to fight for. In the absence of decisions, others fill in the available space. They wind up interpreting him, defining him, or pinning him down. In the process, procrastination leads to default options and the arts of compromise lead simply to crass deal cutting. Clinton is made to look as though he stands for nothing and is willing to concede everything. He is viewed, in sum, as an easy mark.

By the same token, he is often seen as too willing to push an agenda larger than his political base will allow (see especially chapters 1 and 8) when he might have been more successful at taking incremental bites. And clearly, as George Bush was from domestic policy, Bill Clinton has been disengaged from foreign policy, with results that have contributed to making him look weak and inconstant on foreign policy matters. Finally, but hardly least, Clinton's mishandling of staffing and organizational matters is now legendary. That which was most in his capacity to control, he squandered.

All of this said and done, one question is, could the first two years have been done differently? The answer to that is safely yes. A second question is, could it have been done better (leaving, for the moment, "better" undefined)? Hindsight usually makes us wiser. So, probably it is safe to say that there was plenty of room for improvement in the Clinton operations of the first two years. Now comes the tricky question. Would doing it differently (and presumably better) have made a great deal of difference? We cannot know for sure, but I strongly doubt it. Hindsight illuminates our pathways, but it cannot tell us that going one way versus another would produce the desirable outcomes. Often, hindsight suggests only the different costs attached to going different routes, and it suggests them from a logic of reconstruction rather than the logic in use. (The observer gets to play back from the outcome, which remains unknown to the actor; in addition, the observer is often interested only in one outcome, while the actor is juggling several balls in the air.)

Suffice it to say, some options I do not believe were realistically open to Clinton (or virtually any president) without making matters worse for him. Even were a bipartisan coalition open to Clinton—a matter that is pure speculation—seeking it was not a possible move for him without earning the enmity of the Democratic Party's dominant wing. Clinton was elected for policy reasons much as, say, Ronald Reagan had been. This does not imply that a mandate existed for specific policies (which had not existed for Reagan either) but only that the public was unhappy with what they regarded as those of his predecessor. Clinton was not elected because of widespread public trust in him. In fact, he was elected in spite of widespread distrust of him. And as a matter of personal conviction, the idea of cutting social entitlements (or people's social security, in the larger sense) was not what he came to office to do. But that would have been necessary were he to have governed through bipartisan means.

Alternatively, should Clinton have impaled himself on his policy principles, seeming always ready to seek the full loaf and loathe to compromise? That would have made him look better to his partisans, but realistically the majorities simply were not there to do all that he would wish to do. Nor would past policy legacies so permit him. So Clinton tried to weave his way across a political and policy minefield, mostly succeeding on traditional Republican issues such as deficit reduction and spending cuts, or more recent ones such as free trade, and mostly failing on traditional Democratic issues such as universalizing health care, the stimulus package, and social investments. The consequence is reflected in an assessment by a once-favorable journalist half a year into the Clinton presidency:

> His concessions seem more vivid than his convictions. His natural curiosity and enthusiasm have been overwhelmed by his (equally natural, but less attractive) obeisance to authority, in this case to the Congress. He has replaced Bush's "Do No Harm" with "Do Not Offend." As a result, he seems in danger of replicating not just Bush's deficit-reduction package, but his remote, passionless, purposeless presidency.[42]

What can be concluded about this unusual presidency that seems endlessly to be in political trouble, despite an economy that has boomed without inflation during Clinton's incumbency and despite the incumbent's own centrist and deal-cutting tendencies?

First, and perhaps most important, Clinton was disadvantaged from the start by being a Democrat. If the presidency is still possible, it is so only asymmetrically. Republicans have a chance to govern, and Democrats do not. The simple reason has to do with political arithmetic. Democrats win presidential elections these days (on the rare occasions they do) through ambiguity. They need to appeal to the median voter, hold their own in the South, and appeal to their party's core constituencies, who are a declining force. Democratic members of Congress (at least when in the congressional majority) typically do better in their constituencies than their president has done. When push comes to shove, they do not always see it in their interest to follow their president. The range of variation among Democrats is greater than among Republicans, and they are, while increasingly cohesive, far less cohesive than the Republicans. Another way of putting that, if more starkly, is that Democrats jump ship because they think their president's specific proposals are politically unpopular at home, meaning, of course, that they are not likely commanding a majority in the country.

Second, the legacy of policy problems and the ambience of policy debate has not been favorable to Clinton's party. The policy possibilities now are not about what government can do or even do better; they are about what can be eliminated or cut back. It is hard for a Democratic president to find a center here and retain party support. Both Carter and Clinton tried. One met political disaster; the other is courting it.

Third, trying to find the political holy grail in the center, a strategy understandably pleasing to people of moderate temperament as well as to commentators who have run out of serious thoughts, is simply lazy rhetoric. The numerical majorities that so often make up the center are disproportionately indifferent, certainly compared to the far more opinionated mobilizable sectors at the extremes. The reason why the American political system seems to have so much difficulty generating majorities even when there actually appear to be some is that, in policymaking, intensity wins, unless it is offset by equally balanced intensity. Intense opinion is not, alas, located in the middle of opinion distributions. Robert Dahl's conception of democracy, which tells us that minorities rule (even while there is no minority rule), continues to be an accurate assessment of what produces meaningful issue majorities, namely, intensity. Each party has become a bastion of intense minorities of sharply differing worldviews and they exert a powerful gravitational pull on their nominees. The Republicans appear, however, to have a mobilizing advantage on most of these issues, and its members of Congress seem more firmly to have been recruited from sectors endowed with a powerful sense of mission. Not only is it unlikely that a Democratic president could expect to deal fruitfully with more than a modest group of Republicans without essentially operating on their priorities rather than his, but even Republican presidents who think that cutting deals might be good for the country (Bush's budget bill of 1990) are often hounded and opposed by the ardent and ample right wing of the Republican Party.

Fourth, therefore, a political figure who is seen to be committed to hard-and-fast policy principles may have a better chance of making things work at least politically for him or her than someone who lacks clear identity. My conclusion here, however, is again asymmetric. Democrats want to do things. Republicans more often want to stop things. Simplicity on behalf of the latter is easier to achieve. Reagan's achievements, if one wishes to think of them that way, continue to define the policy options of today. With clear identity, it becomes easier to move pragmatically toward compromise, which Reagan did when he had to. With clear identity, it is easier to buy credibility to do the occasional weaving that is necessary. Reagan had that capability. Clinton has not—but neither had Carter or Bush. Policy simplicity adds to a sense of constancy, and complexity detracts from it.

Fifth, presidents given to thinking in serious ways about public policy are doomed to fail. Why? Serious thinking about policy means relating pieces of the puzzle, how costs connect to benefits, what the incentives are for various actors to produce different sorts of goods, and so forth. Comprehensive thinking about public policy leads to frustration in the American system because the system inevitably fragments and often isolates policy choices.[43] Presidents with commitments to serious policy thinking inevitably will be ridiculed as technocrats when their grand schemes come crashing down to earth. The key to success is simplicity, not intellectual consistency or congruency. Some of this is politics wherever it takes place. A big part of it is the character of the American political system. Another part of it is what we expect presidents to do, which is to think big, despite knowing that big thoughts are likely to be pulverized in the political system. Somehow, but I don't know how, we need to realign expectations about presidential leadership with the realities of the American political system and the uncertainty endemic to it of creating and sustaining majorities. Or, less likely, we need to think about realigning the system to accord with the expectations that most often accompany changes in presidential leadership. In the meantime, the system will continue to chew up presidents and spit them out with considerable regularity. It is time to ask: if Clinton cannot succeed, who could?

Governing with a nominal Democratic majority for the first two years of his administration proved to be no picnic for Bill Clinton. When he was on the offensive, the game plan was uncertain and many of his teammates unreliable and cranky. Now that the midterm election has put Clinton on the defensive and given the Republicans joint responsibility for governance, what will Clinton do? So far, he seems still to be trying to answer that question. He has sought sometimes to preempt the Republican offensive (tax cuts and school prayer) by seeming to accept their election as a mandate. Other times, he has sought to draw a line in the sand (threatening to veto any repeal of the assault weapons ban or fixing on a budget-reduction level that does not essentially threaten entitlements). Clinton's instincts still seem uncertain as to whether to look reasonable and try to play ball to some extent with the new Republican majorities or to tough it out and try to renew voice and confidence in his message.

Bill Clinton is a reasonable man, who continues to believe that government can be a part of the solution and is not inherently a part of the problem. American politics, as it has evolved toward the end of the twentieth century, has made it difficult for a leader of his temperament and perspective to succeed.

It may be that Clinton's last and best hope is that the very radicalism of the Republicans' antigovernment agenda and the prospects of its coming to fruition will backfire. As Clinton becomes all that stands in the way of realizing that agenda, he has voiced newfound passion in opposition to it. As he has done so, his approval also has begun to rise and, thus, so have his electoral prospects for 1996. Should the Republican juggernaut be slowed or halted, however, the likely winner will be James Madison and not Bill Clinton. The tyranny of faction will have been prevented, along with the prospect of coherent action, however wrong- or clear-headed that may be.

Acknowledgment

I am grateful for the hospitality and support provided by the Centre for European Studies, Nuffield College, Oxford University, allowing me to complete this rather non-European project.

Notes

1. Richard Rose, "Evaluating Presidents," in *Researching the Presidency: Vital Questions, New Approaches,* ed. George C. Edwards III, John H. Kessel, and Bert A. Rockman (Pittsburgh: University of Pittsburgh Press, 1993), 453–84.

2. Richard Neustadt, *Presidential Power* (New York: Wiley, 1959). This book is now in its fifth edition, the most recent version published in 1990 as *Presidential Power and the Modern Presidents: The Politics of Leadership from Roosevelt to Reagan* (New York: Free Press, 1990).

3. See, for example, David Braybrooke and Charles Lindblom, *A Strategy of Decision* (New York: Free Press, 1963).

4. On the matter of institutionalizing norms, see James G. March and Johan Olsen, *Rediscovering Institutions: The Organizational Basis of Politics* (New York: Free Press, 1989); and Robert Axelrod, "An Evolutionary Approach to Norms," *American Political Science Review* 80 (December 1986): 1095–1111. The language of adaptive social processes may thus replace that of leadership because the emphasis is on the capacity to produce successful change as a result of norms based on reciprocal relationships. From this standpoint, reciprocity is wholly consistent with republican institutions but inconsistent with the logics either of command or of populist democracy. Despite the powerful emphasis by the American constitutional Framers on precisely the logic of reciprocity, current American trends often favor the paradoxical combination of populist democracy and forceful leadership.

5. Technically, this may be thought of as a repeated sequential equilibrium game. See Robert W. Axelrod, "The Emergence of Cooperation among Egoists," *American Political Science Review* 75 (June 1981): 306–18.

6. See Charles O. Jones, *The Presidency in a Separated System* (Washington, D.C.: Brookings Institution, 1994); and Charles O. Jones, *Separate But Equal Branches: Congress and the Presidency* (Chatham, N.J.: Chatham House, 1995).

7. See, for example, Robert A. Dahl, *A Preface to Democratic Theory* (Chi-

cago: University of Chicago Press, 1956); and Anthony Downs, *An Economic Theory of Democracy* (Princeton: Princeton University Press, 1957).

8. Elizabeth Drew, *On the Edge: The Clinton Presidency* (New York: Simon and Schuster, 1994), 128–29.

9. For example, see Bob Woodward, *The Agenda: Inside the Clinton White House* (New York: Simon and Schuster, 1994); and Michael Kelly, "Bill Clinton's Climb," *New York Times Magazine*, 31 July 1994.

10. As quoted in Katherine Q. Seelye, "House Weighs Bill to Repeal Law Banning Assault Guns," *New York Times* (national edition), 26 January 1995, A1, A8.

11. David Broder, "Clinton's Failure," *Pittsburgh Post-Gazette*, 26 January 1995, B3.

12. Fred I. Greenstein, *The Invisible Hand Presidency: Eisenhower as Leader* (New York: Basic Books, 1982).

13. One of the reasons that Clinton won the election was that trust was not an unusually salient issue in the 1992 campaign. There appears to be no strong relationship between trust and the electoral outcome. Barry Goldwater, for instance, held a large relative advantage over Lyndon Johnson on this score but lost massively. Similarly, while George McGovern had a moderate advantage over Richard Nixon on the matter of trustworthiness, he too lost overwhelmingly. There are other instances of this sort, including Gerald Ford, Michael Dukakis, and Jimmy Carter in his reelection bid, who were each more trusted but nonetheless lost. I am greatly indebted to John Kessel for sharing both his data and his insights with me. For the series from 1952 to 1988, see John H. Kessel, *Presidential Campaign Politics*, 4th ed. (Pacific Grove, Calif.: Brooks/Cole, 1992), 266–89.

14. As cited in Drew, *On the Edge*, 45.

15. See Connie Bruck, "Hillary the Pol," *New Yorker*, 30 May 1994. The author wonders in print after discussing the allegations of infidelity "how free the president is to deny his wife what she seeks . . . ." (p. 90).

16. For further evidence, see Michael Minkenberg, "The End of the Republican Era? Public Opinion and the American Electorate in the 1990s," in *The United States after the Cold War*, ed. Herbert Dittgen and Michael Minkenberg (Pittsburgh: University of Pittsburgh Press, 1996).

17. The concept of "political time" is suggested by Stephen Skowronek, who distinguishes it from chronological time. Political time encompasses the creation, maintenance, and exhaustion of political regimes. Clinton came into office, from this standpoint, either at the tail end of the exhaustion of the New Deal policy regime or toward the beginning of a conservative policy regime. See Stephen Skowronek, *The Politics Presidents Make: Leadership from John Adams to George Bush* (Cambridge, Mass.: Belknap Press, 1993).

18. Woodward, *The Agenda*, 298.

19. See Elizabeth Drew's account in *On the Edge*, 138–64, esp. 138 and 144. Also see Bert A. Rockman, "The Post–Cold War President," in Dittgen and Minkenberg, *United States after the Cold War*.

20. Drew, *On the Edge*, 138.

21. For example, see David W. Rohde, *Parties and Leaders in the Postreform House* (Chicago: University of Chicago Press, 1991). See also Stanley Berard, "Constituent Attitudes and Congressional Parties: Southern Democrats in the U.S. House, 1973–1993," Ph.D. dissertation, University of Pittsburgh, 1994.

22. Maureen Dowd, "Americans Like G.O.P. Agenda but Split on How to Reach Goals," *New York Times,* 15 December 1994, A1, A14.

23. Although this drive seems to be a constant in most accounts of Clinton's career, Michael Kelly tries to explain the odd combination of mistrust of Clinton and the public goods nature of his political ambition: "What has happened to Clinton has happened because he wanted, more than anything in life, to get to where he is today, and because he wanted this, at least in part, to do good—and because the great goal of doing good gave him license to indulge in the everyday acts of minor corruption and compromise and falsity that the business of politics demands." Kelly, "Bill Clinton's Climb," 24. Putting it a bit differently, Kelly argues that Clinton's ambitions were furthered by those who were convinced, as Kelly concludes Clinton himself was, "that he was ambitious for the right reasons—because he wanted power in order to do good" (p. 25).

24. Joe Klein, "Magic and Mystery," *Newsweek,* 16 November 1992, 35.

25. See, esp. Drew, *On the Edge,* 293–314.

26. Woodward, *The Agenda,* 70–71.

27. Ibid., 297.

28. Drew, *On the Edge,* 263.

29. Ibid., 266.

30. Elizabeth Drew quotes a source regarding Clinton's personality: "He's a very nice person, but he also works at it, so that it's a lot of effort, a lot of energy drained going into being so balanced." Accordingly, "he performed more than the political average of thoughtful gestures—making a considerate phone call, doing something special for someone who had been slighted" (ibid., 233).

31. An analysis offered by Leslie Gelb, a former journalist and national security official in the Carter administration, is that Clinton invites opposition by leaving it unclear as to where he stands, and by being willing to forsake what it was he was standing for, and by failing to threaten those who oppose him. According to Gelb, "If people think you really don't mean what you say, and they don't think you'll follow through on it, and if there's no cost in opposing you, then they'll do it every time." As quoted in Michael Wines, "Talk Often and Be a Soft Touch," *New York Times,* 17 July 1994, B1, B5.

32. Jonathan Alter, "Shooting the Moon—How Will Clinton Measure Up to His Predecessors in the White House?" *Newsweek,* 25 January 1993, 39.

33. Drew, *On the Edge,* 79.

34. One of Clinton's associates put it this way in attributing the source of indecisiveness in the Clinton White House: "Part of it is the Oval Office. You get in there and you get so overwhelmed you begin to lose your confidence and you begin to test your ideas with your aides and they all give you their thoughts. There's no system [in the Clinton White House]. He [Clinton] has a decision-making method that is a postponement process." Drew, *On the Edge,* 232.

35. Klein, "Magic and Mystery," 37–38.

36. Alter, "Shooting the Moon," 39.

37. David S. Broder, "Decoding Clinton," *Pittsburgh Post-Gazette,* 24 July 1994, F3.

38. Bert A. Rockman, "The Clinton Presidency and Health Care Reform—A Round Table on Health Care Reform," *Journal of Health Politics, Policy and Law,* forthcoming.

39. Elizabeth Drew noted accordingly that "a lot of people who dealt with

the Clinton White House complained about the difficulty of getting decisions from
it." *On the Edge,* 348. As a general matter, she noted that the amorphous structure of the Clinton White House encouraged staff freelancing, therefore a lack of
specific responsibility, and yielded a lack of coordination between policy groups, a
tendency to second-guess, a propensity for indulging in "friends of Bill's or
Hillary's" for positions requiring organizational and political mastery. Above all,
decisions did not get made, calendars got crowded, messages got lost. These are
among the few things a White House can control, and Clinton's hasn't. See, esp.,
ibid., 346–48.

40. Woodward, *The Agenda,* 185.

41. Drew, *On the Edge,* esp. 293–337.

42. Joe Klein, "Clinton's Bushed Presidency," *Newsweek,* 2 August 1993, 22.
This particular critique of Clinton as an inconstant leader searching aimlessly for
the median policy and the median voter is widespread. A.M. Rosenthal queried in
the *New York Times,* for example, after the disastrous (for the Democrats) midterm election that when Clinton tried to preempt a Republican tax cut with one of
his own: "Don't politicians appease all the time? Maybe—but when presidents
take the turnaround trail they gamble with the public's trust. And this president
does not seem to understand that he has already squandered any public assumption of his constancy; no free turnarounds left." A.M. Rosenthal, the *New York
Times,* 20 December 1994, A19. A few days earlier, R.W. Apple wrote in the *New
York Times:* "More than anything else ... Mr. Clinton has been damaged by the
widespread belief that he has no core beliefs, that he is a New Democrat one day,
an Old Democrat the next. As he has twisted and turned on viciously complicated
issues like Bosnia and health care, searching for consensus and finding none, he
has been denounced as a trimmer and a vacillator. In the process, he has received
astonishingly little credit for important achievements...." R.W. Apple, Jr., "Tight
Corner for Comeback Kid," *New York Times,* 15 December 1994, A12.

43. See, for example, R. Kent Weaver and Bert A. Rockman, eds., *Do Institutions Matter? Government Capabilities in the United States and Abroad* (Washington, D.C.: Brookings Institution, 1993), 467–68.

12

Realignment Lives: The 1994 Earthquake and Its Implications

WALTER DEAN BURNHAM

1994: A Seismic Event

After less than two years in office, Bill Clinton and his party suffered shattering defeat at the hands of the Republican opposition on 8 November 1994. Since then, the word *revolution* has been bandied about more than at any time in living memory, not only by jubilant Republicans but by many others. There are reasons for this, reasons that it is the task of this essay to explore. Technical though some of the following discussion must be, it is necessary to get below the surface of events, however dramatic the surface events are.[1] Our objective is to place the 1994 earthquake into a systemic context. This will take us back two hundred years before returning to the newspaper headlines on the day this essay was composed.

What kind of event was the 1994 election? Very probably the most consequential off-year election in (exactly) one hundred years. Remarkably, 1994 bears many characteristics of an old-style partisan critical realignment. Chief among these characteristics of realignment are the durability and comprehensiveness of the proposed new order of things. Since we cannot be certain about the future, it is possible only to offer informed speculation as to the meaning of the 1994 election for the future. There are, however, important reasons for believing that 1994 represents one of those rare elections from which bearings will have to be taken for a long time to come. Whoever wins or loses in and after 1996, the shape of American politics will very probably never be the same again.

We must go back a short distance in time to place this election in its proper context, for it is the latest stage in a politics of upheaval that became visible around 1990. This politics of disappointment, as some call it, ought more generally be deemed the politics of decline. It first became clearly if faintly visible in the 1990 congressional election. A vast and accelerating public discontent with government and governing political establishments then cascaded through the system in 1991 and 1992. In the latter year, this produced a crushing defeat for incumbent Republican president George Bush,[2] the largest support for a third presidential candidate since 1912, and a congressional election pattern perceptively described by Gary Jacobson as highly abnormal by contemporary standards.[3]

Since the 1992 election is in my view an integral part of the upheaval that was to shatter a great deal of the American political order two years later, a few further comments on it are in order before we proceed. For one thing, in 1992 remarkable Republican partisan robustness coexisted with Bush's slump to just 37.4 percent of the total presidential vote. This fact was reflected, but went well beyond, the GOP's gain of ten seats in the U.S. House of Representatives. Thus, for example, the Republican percentage of the 1992 congressional vote in the eleven former Confederate states (46.9 percent) was higher than in the nonsouthern states (45.4 percent) for the first time in history, including the period of Reconstruction.[4] Bill Clinton's 43 percent of the total vote reflected the narrowest base for a presidential winner since Woodrow Wilson's 41.8 percent in 1912, and the third smallest since 1828. In fact, Clinton's share of the total 1992 vote was precisely the same as the mean Democratic percentage of the presidential vote during the sixth electoral era (1972–88) following the critical realignment of the late 1960s.

For another thing, a key to all that has been happening since 1990 lies in the segment of the electorate that supported Ross Perot in 1992. This segment was disproportionately white and non-Jewish, very close to the core of the white middle class with whom politicians of both parties are now so desperately concerned. About three-quarters of Perot voters of 1992 who had voted in 1988 came from George Bush's electoral base, though a narrow plurality of them would have voted for Clinton had Perot not returned to the contest, as he did in October.

President Bush's campaign had no very clear message in an election dominated by domestic stress, beyond appealing to the voters to "stay the course" and pledging positively, absolutely no new taxes after having conceded some in 1990. Bill Clinton's campaign placed emphasis on the reality of economic stress on "people who work hard and play by the rules"; on state inputs for economic (re-)development of interest, in particular to high-tech and other export-oriented business elites; and on traditional Democratic arguments that the federal government continues to have an important, positive role in a complex political economy. Ross Perot's appeals, in contrast, stressed in general that the whole political system had broken down and needed fixing. This view had very strong resonance in the disturbed public opinion picture of 1992. More specifically, Perot concentrated on the debt-deficit morass that had grown up across the Reagan-Bush era from 1981. He secured pluralities among both partisan independents and those respondents identifying the budget-balancing problem as chief among their concerns. In 1994, 64 percent of 1992 Perot voters coming to the polls cast their ballots for Republican congressional candidates.[5]

Let us now turn to a preliminary overview of 1994. The first thing to note is that it involved Republican surges at all levels of election, state as well as federal. In the elections for the U.S. House of Representatives, Democrats lost 35 of 225 incumbents running for reelection and 21 of 31 open seats vacated by Democrats. Compensation for these losses was meager indeed and was confined to a pick-up of four open Republican seats (one each in Maine, Rhode Island, Pennsylvania, and Minnesota). Republicans also reelected all 157 of their incumbents running for reelection—an achievement not unprecedented but quite rare, having last occurred (to the benefit of the Democrats) in 1948.[6] As a result, the Republicans emerged with their first House majority since the 83rd Congress (1953–54), and the largest since 1946 (204 Democrats, 230 Republicans, and 1 independent).

The Senate election resulted in a Republican gain of eight seats and no losses. While not quite in the same league with the GOP gain of twelve Senate seats in 1980, this was still a noteworthy achievement. The election produced an immediate 52–48 distribution, a Republican majority of four. But perhaps equally worthy of note, since the election the Republicans have gained an additional two seats by conversion of sitting senators (Shelby of Alabama just after the election, long expected; and Campbell of Colorado in March 1995, very much a surprise to both parties). Moreover, in February 1995 twenty-three conservative House Democrats, preponderantly southerners, created a formal organization called The Coalition, ostensibly to gain leverage for a "middle way" policy alternative between the core House Democrats and the Republicans.[7] Is The Coalition perhaps a bridge to further realignment within the House? The sense of crumbling among congressional Democrats is certainly in the air as this is written, and the prospects for further Republican gains in 1996 are quite good.

Pursuing our review to the state level, we find a Republican surge with respect to governorships and state legislature outcomes. Table 12.1 reveals the magnitude of this event. There were many more vacancies among Democratic than Republican gubernatorial positions. Republicans lost no incumbents and only one open governorship (in Maine, which went to an independent, not a Democrat). Democrats lost three-eighths of their incumbents, including such famous names as Mario Cuomo of New York and Ann

TABLE 12.1
GUBERNATORIAL ELECTION OUTCOMES, 1994

Status at time of election

Outcome	Democratic Incumbents	Democratic Open	Democratic Total	Republican Incumbents	Republican Open	Republican Total	Independent Open	Total
Democratic	7	3	10	0	0	0	1	11
Republican	4	7	11	10	2	12	1	24
Independent	0	0	0	0	1	1	0	1
Total	11	10	21	10	3	13	2	36

Richards of Texas, and more than two-thirds of their open seats. The latter figure almost exactly parallels their huge losses among open seats in the House races. At the end of the day, the Democratic share of these open seats sagged from 58.3 percent before the election to 30.6 percent afterwards, while the Republican share swelled from 36.1 percent to 66.7 percent. If 38.4 percent of Americans had been living under Republican governors before the election, fully 71.8 percent were doing so following the 1994 upheaval. Not since 1867—before the readmission of ten of the eleven ex-Confederate states to the Union—had Republican gubernatorial candidates done this well. As we later see, this is by no means the only record-breaking feature of this order-shattering election.

It was not supposed to happen like this. Since the end of World War I, off-year electoral surges against the presidential party of the time have been not at all uncommon. We can find such cases in 1922, 1930, 1938, 1942, 1946, 1966, and 1974. But they have typically been associated not with the second but with the sixth or later year of a currently dominant partisan regime order. All but 1922 fall in this category, and that election immediately followed the greatest Republican landslide of all time (1920), which dug unusually deeply into normally Democratic territory. By the sixth year, after all, grievances have had ample time to accumulate, and the regime often takes on a shopworn look. The election of 1994 marks a break with this seventy-two-year past.

Nor is the fact that twenty years elapsed between the two most recent surge events, 1974 and 1994—instead of the four or eight years found earlier in this sequence—a matter of coincidence. A genuine critical electoral realignment (if not a conventionally partisan one) swept through the country between 1966 and 1972, giving us the contemporary partisan and regime order, what I have called "the interregnum state."[8] This particular order of things was chiefly notable for the partial dissolution of electoral coalitions across office-specific lines and the emergence of divided government as a *normal* condition for the first time in modern history. This condition also, it is important to note, materialized not only at the federal level but at the state level as well. Near-hegemonic at the presidential level, Republicans were unable for forty years to crack Democratic control of the House of Representatives, and only in six of the twenty-four years between 1968 and 1992 were they able to win control of the Senate. The underlying reason for this deadlocked state of affairs was a realignment of voting behavior increasingly favoring incumbents of both parties and declines in the number of open seats from already low previous levels.

A review of congressional election outcomes across the postwar period thus reveals a familiar pattern, one presented in table 12.2. This trend deepened still further across the 1980s, reaching a historic maximum of development in the 1986 and 1988 elections. Then came reversal. In 1990, for the

TABLE 12.2
TRENDS IN THE AGGREGATE STRUCTURE OF INCUMBENT SUCCESS IN CONGRESSIONAL ELECTIONS, SELECTED YEARS, 1940–94 [a]

	Democratic incumbents				Republican incumbents				Total incumbents [b]				
	N	N lost	Mean % two-party vote	−1 standard deviation	N	N lost	Mean % two-party vote	−1 standard deviation	N	N lost	Mean % two-party vote	Standard deviation	Variance
1940	175	14	63.8	51.2	143	23	57.5	50.2	318	40	54.1	14.82	219.57
1954	120	3	66.7	55.2	201	18	57.9	51.9	321	21	51.3	14.62	213.79
1962	172	8	63.8	56.6	149	4	60.7	54.7	321	12	52.4	14.51	210.51
1970	164	2	68.8	59.6	155	8	62.5	54.8	319	10	53.6	17.80	316.89
1978	207	14	66.2	54.9	107	4	66.6	57.6	314	18	55.0	18.78	352.67
1980	209	25	64.7	53.1	127	2	69.5	59.7	336	27	51.8	19.86	394.44
1982	164	1	69.0	59.2	159	21	60.9	51.8	323	22	54.2	17.69	312.85
1984	196	13	64.4	53.8	145	3	68.8	60.5	341	16	50.3	19.09	364.36
1986	176	1	70.9	61.6	145	6	65.8	57.6	321	7	54.3	20.46	418.52
1988	185	2	69.1	59.6	146	4	67.6	59.5	331	6	52.9	20.45	418.40
1990	199	7	65.6	56.4	122	8	62.3	54.3	321	15	55.1	16.35	267.33
1992	198	13	64.1	53.9	122	4	63.2	55.9	320	17	53.8	16.15	260.78
1994	215	35	61.2	50.0	124	0	68.6	61.6	339	35	50.4	17.61	310.05

a. Incumbents with major-party opposition only.
b. Democrats plus Republicans only (excluding third-party incumbents).

first time a quite symmetrically bipartisan decline in incumbents' mean share of the vote materialized, the two modes of this still highly uncompetitive distribution now converging toward each other. In 1992, Democratic incumbents' mean two-party percentage declined still further, while a faint rise on the GOP side was visible. The most obvious feature of this election—driven by the revelations in the House banking scandal, reapportionment, and other factors—was a high level of retirements yielding fully ninety-two open seats, the largest number in sixty years. Both parties, however, shared proportionately to their general strength in the House in the fruits of this open-seat bulge. On past form, "sophomore surge" should have protected the vast majority of the Democrats who first won in 1992. Instead, there was a modest sophomore slump, the first on record since the beginning (and indeed since well before the beginning) of the present electoral era. In 1994, the Democratic incumbent mean percentage fell to 61.2 percent, down 7.9 points from its 1988 level. Republicans, in contrast, triumphed at a level (68.6 percent of the two-party vote) that matched 1980, 1984, and 1988 showings in this category.

This latter asymmetry is one mark not of an incumbent-dominated election, but of an election with very strong *partisan* features. It is the culmination (thus far) of a very large marginal change over a six-year period. This partisan focus of the election, as one might expect, was particularly visible in the category of open seats. Here, as we have said, Democrats lost twenty-one of the thirty-one contested seats, while the Republicans yielded only four of their seventeen. Nationwide, this Democratic loss of 67.7 percent of the party's open seats also breaks a record of very long standing. Leaving aside the obvious case of the Whig Party in full dissolution in 1854–55, this is the largest proportionate loss of open seats held by *any* party in a file of 103 elections extending right back to 1790.

There is one further point to be made as far as these post-1920 off-year surge events are concerned. Down through 1974, it is very easy to identify clear signs of stress associated with the electoral context. These stress factors turn out to involve war and/or economic dislocation in the main, with occasional additional factors. Thus, stress factors were evident in 1922 (recession in the immediate "stabilization phase" following a major war); 1938 (sharp recession in already depression-level economic conditions); 1942 (major war); 1946 (reconversion turbulence and numerous shortages following a major war); 1958 (recession); 1966 (the Vietnam war and increasing racial backlash); and 1974 (recession plus intense negative fallout for Republicans from Watergate and President Nixon's forced resignation from office). But in 1994 there was no dog barking in the night. Not only was there no war, but both the Cold War and the Soviet Union had disappeared into the mists of history. As for the economy, it was into the second or perhaps third year of recovery from the recession that had done in George Bush two years earlier.

While Bill Clinton's problems with the "character issue" remained, there was no reason to think that these alone ought to have damaged his party. After all, Lyndon Johnson was not trusted either (even before Vietnam), but he did smartly through 1964 and 1965 until campus disturbances, the escalating war in Vietnam, and inflation overwhelmed his party in the 1966 elections.

It seems evident that mass discontent with government—a dominant theme of American politics since the beginning of the decade—was brilliantly tapped into by Republican strategists in 1994 and directed with devastating effect against a Democratic congressional establishment no longer protected by Republican presidents. Newt Gingrich's unprecedented innovation, a ten-point Contract with America promulgated in September 1994 and equivalent to a concise version of a party platform, was not all that visible to the American public at large. But it served admirably to give the kind of clear, focused, and integrated message that would energize and mobilize the Republican base—an important consideration in a context in which no more than two-fifths of the citizenry bothered to come to the polls. The Democratic side, in contrast, had very little to say. The Republican strategy concentrated on nationalizing this off-year election. The strategy succeeded, almost certainly beyond the GOP leadership's wildest dreams.

Thus, 1994 is a very big event indeed, both for what it was and for what it has made possible since. The closer I look at it and its unfolding ramifications, the bigger it looms. Conventional political science wisdom will in many respects have to be discarded and textbooks will have to be rewritten. The resumption of divided government in 1995–97 rests on electoral foundations that, in some respects, are the polar opposites of those dominating the classic 1969–93 version. Unlike that version, it may prove of very short duration. Those who have stressed partisan dealignment will now have to consider how this abrupt emergence of something remarkably like an old-fashioned partisan election fits their models. And those who have placed their bets on the argument that critical-realignment analysis is irrelevant to this modern candidate-driven electoral universe will have to reconsider their position. We now turn to a more detailed analysis of this election and its immediate aftermath on the basis of its being part of a genuinely realigning event sequence.

1790s to 1990s: The 1994 Election in Context

History both tempers and provides perspective. Consequently, my database is deeply historical. In addition to more generally accessible information, my data files include virtually complete information district by district on congressional elections from the 1st Congress through the 104th, stratified as well by incumbent-held versus open-seat status. They also include essentially complete information on the partisan distribution of seats in both houses of state legislatures holding partisan elections between 1834 and 1994. These files, along with an analysis of survey information on congressional elections from 1980 through 1994 conveniently provided by the *New York Times* shortly after the 1994 election, will form much of the empirical base for the argument that follows. First, however, it may be appropriate more generally to articulate once again what happens in critical-realignment sequences.

A very large part of the vast literature on these sequences has concentrated on them as partisan events being channeled through and in various ways redefining the institutionalized system of major parties in the United States. This is an understandable conceptualization in view of the fact that most initial work on the subject began at a time when partisan organization of the electoral market was taken for granted. But this approach has also been something of a straitjacket, leading us away from considering other reorganizations of the political landscape. In fact, these bursts of punctuated change have occurred at regular intervals, a long generation apart, beginning with the period of the American Revolution, which culminated in the ratification of the Constitution of 1788, up to the present day.[9]

Each realignment upheaval has very many specific, even unique, features that reflect the political conflicts of the particular historical moment in which it occurs. Two of these bursts of comprehensive change took place before the development of an institutionalized party system. One particularly controversial case—the critical realignment of the 1966–72 period—was centrally involved with the displacement of the old major parties from their previously dominant position in organizing American electoral politics. The election of 1994, on the other hand, bears many of the features of a partisan-centered event. Whether this is so in fact or is merely an optical illusion is a relevant question to be addressed toward the end of this essay. It is enough to say that thus far there have been six major bursts of large-scale punctuated change across the history of the United States.

These singular events have been spaced at remarkably regular time intervals. A good case can be made for suggesting peak years at about 1780, 1818, 1856, 1894, 1932, and 1970, or a thirty-eight-year spacing. This raises an immediate question about 1994 (or 1996), because the time interval from the last "peak" is now reduced to a quarter-century. Is the dialectic speeding up? Or are there other explanations? This timing issue, in any event, seems sufficiently singular to bear further reflection.

At the crudest and most general level, critical realignments are specialized sequences of events in which politically decisive minorities of the electorate abruptly stop what they have been doing, move to another political destination, and thereafter more or less stay there. But even if they are more proactive than usual, they do not act alone. Realignments more or less pro-

foundly alter things at all important levels of the political system. Comprehensive change thus unfolds at many levels, from the identity of the public
philosophy and dominant constitutional doctrine, to the identity and circu-
lation of political elites, and thence to the shape and content of dominant
public policy outputs. These are high-temperature, high-pressure events of
subrevolutionary sweep—America's surrogate for revolution, as I once
termed them. In such a pressure cooker, the ideological element of politics is
very greatly highlighted, and ideologically linked polarization reaches abnormal levels on all sides. In searching for the probabilities involved in identifying these exceptional events, it is usually possible to identify clusters of major policy innovations. These policy innovations are definable indicators of
what the incoming elites do with the victory that the electorate has given
them. Other aspects of the political universe are substantially modified as
well. These aspects include the institutional balance between the branches of
the federal government, between the federal and state governments, between
government and the socioeconomic world outside, as well as changes in
nonconstitutional political structures such as parties.

   The observation of change needs to focus on the extremely powerful element of cross-realignment continuity that links the present with the past.
There are elements of continuity that extend from the basic framework of
the constitutional order down to the voting behavior of the American electorate. The present is inherently anchored in the past. One of the leading defining characteristics of continuity is the American political culture—the
dominant liberal tradition that Louis Hartz depicted a generation ago.[10] This
weight of continuity, of repetitiveness, can, however, mislead. In their otherwise powerful account of how "policy monopolies" in American politics can
be obliterated, Frank Baumgartner and Bryan D. Jones dismiss the applica-
tion of their punctuated change model to electoral politics precisely because
they are so impressed with the repetitiveness of electoral behavior.[11] Granted
the existence of continuity, there is some similarity between political change
and the phenomenon of rapid, semidiscontinuous speciation in evolutionary
biology that first prompted Niles Eldredge and Stephen Jay Gould to develop the punctuated-equilibrium model nearly a quarter-century ago.[12]

   The processes by which relatively sudden bursts of speciation occur in
evolutionary biology may be even more appropriately applied to American
politics. As Baumgartner and Jones suggest, we may gain insight from an
important conclusion of William Riker that, in contrast to economics, no
such thing as a naturally occurring stable equilibrium exists in politics.[13]
What we normally see instead is equilibrium as an artifact of human action,
regardless of how well established interests, norms, and behaviors seem to
be. What humans create, they or other humans also can modify or destroy,
very often with little or no warning. Moreover, in the absence of natural-
equilibrium conditions, flipover processes are likely to be inherently unpre-

dictable. In principle, at least, almost anything can happen in politics at almost any time. Thus, for Riker, politics rather than economics is the true dismal science.

This is so both on analytic grounds (unpredictability) and substantive ones (democratic assaults on liberty and property). The rational choice in such circumstances, of course, is to build institutional barriers against the dangerous potential of democracy in motion. Pursuing just such a strategy is pretty clearly what the Founding Fathers at Philadelphia had in mind in 1787. This strategy is also central to the agenda of contemporary conservative economists known collectively as "the Virginians,"[14] who may well be regarded as the intellectual godparents of the 1994 Republican Contract with America. Building buffers against this Great Unknown of politics makes admirable strategic sense. Of course, if the underlying logic of the analysis is correct, such efforts themselves would in the end be consigned to failure, because they too are of human rather than natural origin.

Successive electoral and regime orders, unlike the situation of the policy monopolies described by Baumgartner and Jones, are, however, not overthrown and replaced from nowhere. Critical realignment is part of a specific dialectical process. Like other such processes, it arises from the maturation of contradictions embedded in an ongoing state of affairs.[15] Among the most important of these polarities is a constitutional order, loaded with artifacts designed to fragment political power and to buffer government from populist impulses, that stands in contrast to the world's most dynamic and politically autonomous socioeconomic system. The institutional constitutional "pole" conduces to stasis, deadlock, requirements for extraordinary majorities in and across separated institutions, and behavioral routines such as the complex brokerage skills that are the stock-in-trade of major-party politicians. Elements abound that make the political system extremely resistant to change in direct proportion to its comprehensiveness. The governing order is very strongly biased toward inertia, being therefore an inherently and extremely conservative type of regime.

The effects of the socioeconomic "pole" center on the strikingly dynamic properties of capitalism. We not only have the testimony of Karl Marx but of the business theorist Peter Drucker (and much of the business press more generally) that capitalism is a form of permanent revolution. Its development constantly overturns established structures, statuses, and the lives of communities and the people who live in them. It is doing so even as we speak; and in a large sense this is what the Republican "revolution" of 1994 and after is about. These upheavals produce cumulative stress. In a society with democratic practices and expectations, this stress prompts losers to gravitate to government for redress or amelioration. But the change pressures they generate pile up behind the inability to mobilize power through the barriers imposed by the political system and by its fragmentation of authority. Thus state and society progressively tend to grow out of phase with one another over time. An increasing volatility results that weakens the popular legitimacy and stability of a given political regime order. At some point, events push the system across the threshold into a punctuated upheaval. Realignment, being a form of controlled explosion, then takes over and runs its usually brief course en route to the construction of a new electoral/regime order. This flipover process historically has been a decisively important mechanism for reintegrating, at least for a time, a static political steering mechanism with a superdynamic socioeconomic system.

The processes involved are cyclical, dialectical, and yet constrained. So far, none of them have broken the system; instead, they have more or less profoundly reshaped it. The element of the weight of continuity at all levels of action across the system has so far acted as the ultimate buffer standing in the way of Riker's nightmare. When all these elements are combined and, as surely should be done, the role of leadership, political elites, and especially presidents is added, the setting has been laid for political cycles. The cycles not only include realignments but also midpoint crises within the lifetime of any given electoral and regime order. This gives the appearance at least of some regularity and predictability that is rare in other instances of punctuated equilibrium.

Looking for Change

Let us now move toward a concrete attempt to evaluate the 1994 election in these terms, beginning with the electoral data and placing it both in a very long-term historical and present-day context. The process dynamics discussed earlier are such as to prompt a search for election "moments" when unexpectedly large-scale shifts in voting behavior abruptly occur. Such elections are obvious candidates for inclusion in the realignment category. When socioeconomic pressures pass a critical political-electoral threshold, we may speak of a shearing-off effect in which the strength of the existing political regime order yields. Such shearing-off effects are manifested clearly enough in the late-1960s survey data that Aldrich and Niemi have analyzed.[16] But in that case, one must examine in the main other than partisan components of electoral change, given the kind of realignment that occurred at that time. For 1994, in contrast, shifts in partisan balance can bear much of the weight of analysis.

Obviously, it would be better to conduct the search for "moments" of relative discontinuity were we in a position to use t-tests, discriminant analysis, or other such statistical routines that can be used to look for breakpoints in an extended time series. But this requires knowledge of "after" as well as "before," and we unfortunately lack information about the outcomes of the next four or five congressional elections. Thus we have to fall back on the second-best substitute, with the future as always a blank wall before us. The indicator is an extremely simple one. A five-election mean and standard deviation (*sd*) are derived. The deviation (*d*) of the sixth election value from this mean is produced and then divided by the five-election standard deviation ($d/_{sd}$). The value thus generated can range positively or negatively from zero to 10, 15, or higher. The underlying phenomenon thus measured is the percentage Democratic of a two-party distribution (votes or seats in a legislative body as the case may be). While it is a heroic and misguided act of faith to believe that aggregates of election data can be assumed to correspond to normal-curve distributions, we can employ the usual tables to suggest the approximate values that would appear to reflect "significant" shearing-off change. A value of 3 would correspond (both tails) to 0.27 percent of the normal curve and can be used for our purposes here as a benchmark or cutoff point for significance.[17]

Two points can be added regarding this technique. First, it can theoretically happen that a high value will occur at a moment not usually considered to be one of realignment. Conversely, a genuine realignment could occur with a lower value than might be expected. In the latter case, with historical realignments, "before-and-after" techniques can help resolve the issue. As we shall see, insofar as 1994 is concerned, it is not easy to see how these values could be much higher than they already are. There has been discussion since the election that it may prove to be like 1946, followed in its turn by a Democratic bounceback in 1996, like that of 1948. All that can be said here is that the value of the discontinuity indicator $d/_{sd}$ for 1946 is not particularly large and certainly does not compare with that for 1994.

Second, as is true with all such techniques, the value is dependent not only on the absolute magnitude of the deviation but on the size of the denominator (the five-election standard deviation, *sd*). One will therefore sometimes encounter historic instances where larger absolute shifts occurred than in 1994 but, because of a larger denominator, lower values of the quotient $d/_{sd}$ were produced. This also reflects a substantive and politically important property of the shape of data in the immediate pre-1994 past. All the indicators presented in table 12.3 rest on 1984–92 change rates that were extremely sticky by historic standards. That is, net interelection movement in congressional elections had grown increasingly glacial by the late 1980s and early 1990s. The same is true for the survey-based data in table 12.4. This stickiness (slow movement) is rooted in modal electoral behavior patterns of the sixth electoral era discussed earlier. The shattering impact of the 1994 swing perhaps owes less to its absolute size—there was, after all, no Republican landslide nationally—than to its *unexpected* magnitude and impact, striking in its disruption of a previously stable, well-known, and long-lasting state of affairs.

Setting up this procedure, one then scans by iteration across the entire field from the first five (1788–96) and sixth (1798) observations until we hit the end in 1994; or, with state legislature data, from the first five (1834–42) and sixth (1844) observations to 1994. This gives us 99 observations for the U.S. House election series (votes and seats) and 76 for the state legislature series (here given for the non-South and the total United States). The House elections are reported here for the North and West only in order to give true and uninterrupted continuity across the Civil War period. The entire distribution of 99 or 76 values for the discontinuity indicator $d/_{sd}$ is provided in the appendix table.[18]

As is evident, the overwhelming majority of elections produce values considerably below 3. Yet elections registering 3 or higher occur on the whole rather less than one-tenth of the time, considerably more than normal-curve standards would presuppose (see table 12.3).

While I had some obvious things in mind when initiating this automatic search routine, I was not prepared for what I found. The values of the discontinuity indicator $d/_{sd}$ for 1994 are enormous in this context, and that places them in a very select company indeed. As the table indicates, 1994 ranks third of 99 observations for U.S. House votes, second for U.S. House seats, third of 76 observations for state legislature seats in the nonsouthern states, and a very clear first for state legislature seats in the United States as a whole. By this measure, this election is clearly consistent with such historic electoral mega-events as 1800, 1860, 1894, and 1932. Of the thirty elections in the four columns of this table, moreover, only 1818 (perhaps), 1840, and 1920 would not likely fall in either the category of realigning events or that of midpoint-crisis transformations, presumably representing a moderately acceptable level of background noise. An analyst totally insensitive to other symptoms of the critical-realignment syndrome certainly would have to regard 1994 on this showing as a strong candidate for inclusion in the mega-event category. But other symptoms serve to buttress this judgment.

Before turning to a further discussion of these, let us apply the same general technique to survey evidence covering the congressional elections sequence 1980–94. Here we concentrate on measuring the 1994 deviation from the 1984–92 mean and standard deviation. The focus, of course, is on the relative shearing-off magnitude across population groups that is found in this election. This kind of analysis is rather different from the usual survey-research variety. We treat each of 74 population groups—some demographic, some partisan-political, some ideological—as a discrete unit, even though there is plenty of overlap. Looking for intergroup difference in the value of the discontinuity indicator $d/_{sd}$, we note again that rank-ordering these groups produces a somewhat different array than one arranged in descending order of raw swing (see table 12.4).[19]

Perhaps the first observation to make is that 1994 was very clearly a *polarizing election*. Only the top thirteen groups shifting pro-Democratic in

TABLE 12.3
THE HISTORICAL PANORAMA: INCIDENCE OF d/sd^a VALUES OF 3 AND OVER BY OFFICE, 1790/1834–1994[b]

Office, Year, and Value

House of Rep.: Votes North and West (N = 99)		House of Rep.: Seats North and West (N = 99)		State legislature seats			
				Non-South (N = 76)		United States (N = 76)	
1894	−8.099	1932	+9.309	1932	+6.643	1994	−9.917
1932	+4.720	1994	−5.628	1894	−4.268	1860	−7.424
1994	−4.572	1800	+4.257	1994	−4.003	1932	+6.371
1818	+3.908	1874	+3.812	1958	+3.788	1958	+3.711
1874	+3.266	1910	+3.591	1910	+3.447	1894	−3.394
1912	+3.257	1840	−3.406	1920	−3.312	1910	+3.301
1802	+3.215	1958	+3.374			1920	−3.268
1800	+3.117	1854	−3.147				
1958	+3.072						
(9)		(8)		(6)		(7)	

a. See text, p. 375.

b. Based ultimately on percentage Democratic of two-party vote. Plus denotes shearing-off benefiting Democrats; minus denotes shearing-off benefiting Republicans.

TABLE 12.4
INTERGROUP SHEARING-OFF EFFECTS: VALUES OF $d/_{sd}$
OF 3 AND MORE (PRO-REPUBLICAN) AND TOP 13 PRO-
DEMOCRATIC DISPLACEMENTS, 1994 CONGRESSIONAL ELECTION

Pro-Republican (16)	Mean % Dem. 1984– 1992	% Dem. 1994	Swing	$d/_{sd}$	Percentage of 1994 elec-torate
Men, age 30–44	52	43	−9	−15.701	17
Whites, age 30–44	49	39	−10	−14.142	28
White born-again Christians	34	24	−10	−6.330	20
Total, age 30–44	53	48	−5	−6.213	35
Employed	51	48	−3	−6.208	55
Whites: South	48	35	−13	−6.128	24
White women	51	45	−6	−4.065	40
Whites, total	49	42	−7	−4.042	79
Independents, total	52	44	−8	−4.001	24
White men	47	38	−9	−3.859	40
Whites, age 45–59	48	41	−7	−3.743	23
Married, total	51	46	−5	−3.681	69
Conservatives, total	33	21	−12	−3.394	34
Married women	52	48	−4	−3.221	34
White Protestants	43	34	−9	−3.183	41
Whites: Midwest	49	40	−9	−3.183	22
Mean	48	40	−8	−5.693	37
Median	49	39.5	−9.5	−4.021	34
Pro-Democratic (13)					
Unmarried women	61	66	5	2.380	17
Women, education 0–11 yrs	62	70	8	2.215	2
Liberal Democrats	88	96	8	1.882	13
Total, education 0–11 yrs	61	68	7	1.745	5
Democrats, total	83	90	7	1.716	41
Moderates, total	57	58	1	1.414	48
Jews	72	78	6	1.395	4
Moderate Democrats	83	88	5	1.368	22
Liberals, total	76	82	6	1.344	18
Men, age 18–29	49	52	3	1.080	6
Conservative Democrats	76	80	4	0.987	6
Total, age 18–29	53	54	1	0.971	13
Women, age 45–59	55	56	1	0.464	14
Mean	67	72	5	1.459	9
Median	67	74	7	2.405	13

SOURCE: *New York Times,* 13 November 1994, B15.
Total number (N) of groups used in analysis: 74.
United States total: 1984–92; mean, 53; 1994 % Dem., 50; swing, −3; $d/_{sd} = -1.938$.

1994 from the 1984–92 mean are included here, but there are some others as well. On the pro-Republican side, sixteen groups show displacement values of 3 or above, and six of them values of 6 or above. Both the displacement values and, in most instances, the raw magnitude of shearing-off are of course extraordinary by any recent standards, with more than half the groups showing a raw shift of nine percentage points or more toward the Republicans from the 1984–92 mean. As a polarizing election, 1994 would seem to have more in common with so-called interactive realignments, such as those of the 1850s and 1890s, than with the across-the-board or surge realignment of the 1930s. On the pro-Republican side, the 1994 shearing-off effect is clearly concentrated within the white middle class, and most conspicuously among the 30–44 age group in general and men in that group in particular. Particularly intense consolidation occurred among the usual bases of modern Republican support (white born-again Christians, self-identified conservatives, and white Protestants).

Regionally, the greatest impact was registered among whites in the South and Midwest. The southern Republican surge of 1994 has gained a lot of quite justified attention in postelection commentary. But the Democratic debacle in the Midwest was noteworthy in its own right, and comprehensive across all levels of election. While none of the data presented here directly reveal it, the northeastern region in general swung the least to the Republicans (for example, three of the four open House seats to pass into Democratic hands were located in this region). It should finally be noted that raw swings of 8 or greater very often produce a shift from closely competitive to landslide conditions within the groups involved. To take only the case of white midwesterners, for example, a 1984–92 mean of 49 percent Democratic, 51 percent Republican is translated into a 40–60 ratio after the election, precisely the margin that Theodore Roosevelt registered in the epochal landslide of 1904, and very close to the national margin by which Ronald Reagan beat Walter Mondale in 1984.

None of the pro-Democratic values come close to our 3 level of "significance." Their inclusion is warranted, however, if only to underscore the polarizing character of this election. The core cluster of groups here tends to be female, poor (as indicated by low education levels), and Jewish in demography and tending to be moderate, liberal, and Democratic in ideology and partisanship. One notes a remarkably sharp break in the election's impact on men aged 18–29 on the one hand and men aged 30–44 on the other. It is also noteworthy that the top pro-Republican groups are overwhelmingly demographic in character and, in the aggregate, constitute very large segments of the American electorate. Nearly one-half of the top pro-Democratic groups, however, are partisan or ideological. Moreover, taken in the aggregate, the top pro-Democratic groups' share of the American electorate is outweighed on the pro-Republican side by a 4–1 margin.

This looks very much like the emergence of a new "core-periphery" pattern, which, while new for congressional elections, is a pattern similar to the post-1968 profile of presidential elections. The "core" here is basically the Great Protestant White Middle as a support base for much of the economic elite. The "periphery" is composed of much of the rest of American society, divided in detail as this periphery is along racial, religious and gender lines. Particularly if the three-fifths who did not vote at all in 1994 are included, its overall center of gravity lies in the lower reaches of the class structure. One cannot predict the long-term stability of this realigned pattern; all one can say is that to the extent that it persists, it will ensure Republican political hegemony.

Republicans, Realignment, and the Politics of Decline

What is the explanation for such an abrupt flipover in formerly very stable patterns of voting behavior? The puzzle becomes the greater when one considers that there was no obvious triggering event to compare with those that helped launch realignment in the past. Neither war nor economic downturn were in the 1994 picture. Here, as we have pointed out earlier, 1994 ought not to be seen in isolation from the whole pattern of voter discontent that began to become visible in 1990. Naturally, one can point to Bill Clinton's weaknesses as contributory to his and his party's repudiation. The "character issue," ruthlessly exploited by new right-wing talk-show impresarios such as Rush Limbaugh, continues to dog him. Clinton has been, or certainly has given the appearance of being, indecisive on most issues apart from those centering on free trade in the global economy. Further, his clarion call of 1992, centering on the impact of the economy on the ordinary American, abruptly disappeared once he entered the White House. Even White House circles concede that no message went forth from them in 1994. One wonders who President Clinton's really important constituents are in his own eyes. Yet one also wonders how much of this ambiguity of appeal is cause and how much is effect of the general situation accounting for his elevation to the presidency in the first place.

The whole post-1990 cycle, 1994 included, appears to be a case in which gradual but very persistent, unilinear deterioration in the conditions of life for the Great White Middle simply crossed a pain threshold less than five years ago, and in doing so propelled the political system into a new upheaval phase. This pain is centrally and obviously related to the politics of decline, the flattening or decreasing of economic horizons for the future of self and family, and of increasing fear of violence at home—on the streets and in the schools one's children attend—as the social order appears to rot away. Milestones along the way had included the stagflation of the 1970s, the pivotal realignment of interest-rate policy from 1979 under Paul Volcker, and the quadrupling of the national debt under Ronald Reagan and his successor. Even larger sea changes included the progressive deindustrialization of America and a concomitant and rapid decline in the membership and political clout of organized labor.[20] And most recently, capitalism's thrust toward creative destruction has speeded up through corporate downsizing, significantly affecting middle-management strata with the specter of large-scale unemployment for the first time.

Beyond even this, as the collapse of the Mexican peso and the U.S. dollar crisis of early 1995 have made increasingly clear, are stresses produced by the vast acceleration of the financialization of the global economy over the past decade. Increasingly, national governments, even of nations as large as the United States, have lost control of their financial destinies. The activities of credit markets subvert any effort to sustain domestic demand-side macroeconomic policy at least as efficiently as the pre-1914–33 gold standard had once done. Nor are politicians unaware of this. In 1993 James Carville, the mastermind behind Bill Clinton's election campaign, commented: "I used to think if there was reincarnation, I wanted to come back as the president or the pope or a .400 baseball hitter, but now I want to come back as the bond market. You can intimidate everybody." Clinton himself has been even more pungent on this subject.[21] In March 1995, the U.S. Senate failed by a single vote to muster the two-thirds necessary to send that centerpiece of the Republican Contract, the balanced-budget amendment, to the states for ratification. But at the same time, Felix Rohatyn of Lazard Frères & Co. observed that the emerging currency crisis leaves the United States with the choice of raising interest rates or cutting the deficit. Going the former route would put a straitjacket on the productive economy. Thus, he concludes, "The collapse of the currency will force us to balance our budget."[22] It would seem that largely uncontrollable forces have entered into the great balanced-budget debate.

Our basic argument at this point is not that far different from that advanced in Kevin Phillips's recent writings. As far as the voters were concerned, by the early 1990s a public "boiling point" had been reached.[23] This volatile situation was successfully directed by Republican strategists against the congressional Democratic establishment and the Democratic Party in general in 1994. The underlying macrocontext virtually ensures that the pressures involved will not recede in the foreseeable future. In this setting, Phillips and others have given some attention to the politics of decline in earlier imperial states, such as Spain in the seventeenth century and the Netherlands and Venice in the eighteenth. One striking feature of the Spanish case is that it produced a remarkable group of intellectuals, the *arbitristas,* who were capable not only of specifying the economic and social-structural factors impelling the country toward decline but of specifying policy changes that might arrest it. A veritable spate of similar *arbitrista* literature has poured forth from American presses in recent years. Contributors have included economists such as Benjamin Friedman and Paul Krugman, as well as publicists like Phillips and the authors of the (characteristically) titled *America: What Went Wrong?*[24]

As Phillips notes, these earlier cases of decline involved countries governed by absolute monarchs or narrow oligarchies. In America, however, a very large mass public expects to, and actually sometimes does, play a major role in what happens. In such a setting, crucial minorities of this public will be energized by a distressing present and prospects for an even worse future to attack the sources of trouble they can perceive and reach. In the United States, whose political culture always contains a powerful antigovernmental element, this will lead to support for those who identify outmoded central government and its expensive programs as a basic part of the problem. The international capital market is, after all, unreachable through democratic politics. It is, moreover, unfathomable to a mass public. Instead, it sets a kind of natural-law context to which everyone, including politicians of all stripes, must conform. Meanwhile, what an energized and enraged Great White Middle can reach is the political establishment, as it did in both 1992 and 1994.

By now, most of the necessary ingredients for political and governmental change of massive proportions have been put into place. Only the future can determine just how extensive this change will be, which parts of society will pay most of the bill, and whether the change will be guided exclusively by Republicans. In realignments that begin in off-years there is, after all, no substitute for victory in the next presidential election. Nevertheless, enough has already happened since the election to require some comment on the transformed situation in Washington and its implications. A chief reason for this is that this situation corresponds across the board with what we would expect in a critical-realignment upheaval—it is another set of symptoms nested within the overall syndrome of critical realignment.

The first point to stress is the extraordinarily high level of ideological, party and policy cohesion among Republican legislators intent on enacting the Contract with America into law. On most key votes in the House through March 1995, more than 200 Republicans voted in favor, with only a handful (ranging from two to eight or none) voting against. This majority was also often supported by up to one-third of House Democrats, so that the "true" policy balance in the House favors Speaker Gingrich and his party majority by margins of close to 2–1. One must go back to the nineteenth century, one supposes, to find roll-call cohesion for either party so nearly monolithic as for House Republicans in 1995. Moreover, of course, the Contract itself spells major, nonincremental policy change toward the right; and it should be read as just a downpayment on an even more comprehensive set of changes. In the words of Republican pollster Linda DiVall, the Contract with America has become nothing less than "the Republican way of governing."[25] It has, it seems, acquired a kind of sacrosanct aura.

The Contract itself contains ten items, some procedural or administrative but many with a profound substantive reach. It emerges from an integrated ideological program aimed at dismantling many of the domestic policy functions of the federal government that had been built up over the past sixty years. In part it is a "devolution revolution," based on sending welfare and other functions to the states with block grants. The balanced-budget amendment was at its pivot for a very practical reason, namely that it would insulate its authors from negative constituency pressure when favorite spending programs begin to disappear. With the amendment out to the states for ratification, the representative or senator voting for cuts to bring the federal budget into balance by 2002 could make the argument that matters were really out of his or her hands. Without it, budget cutting will be a decidedly risky enterprise for the legislators involved. Some compromises, such as agricultural subsidies, already have had to be made. Nevertheless, the overall scope of this effort, energized by a rock-hard ideology, is clearly to produce nonincremental, comprehensive policy transformation.

A number of abrupt and consequential institutional changes are also clearly in the making. The sleepy old House of Representatives has suddenly been catapulted into the forefront of political upheaval. The new Speaker, Newt Gingrich, is a self-described revolutionary. The new chairman of the House Appropriations Committee, Bob Livingston, commented after the election that "we are revolutionaries." Beyond the political hype inherent in such statements, there seems real sincerity in their self-presentation. The antitax Republican majority in the House created new rules to require a 60 percent vote before any measure to raise taxes can pass the House. Additionally, Gingrich's powers as Speaker have been enhanced by his majority to a point not seen since Joseph Cannon was stripped of many of his prerogatives in 1910.

Moving beyond Capitol Hill, one notes in particular a singular development with institution-changing implications. The states as units of government are suddenly now "in." This is natural enough, in view of the radical shift in the vertical balance within the constitutional order that Republican domestic policy not merely presupposes but demands. One even hears frequent approving references to the Tenth Amendment, once thought to have been put to sleep for good as a restraint on the exercise of federal power by the Supreme Court more than fifty years ago.[26]

None of this looks remotely like politics as usual. The intent of the Republican victors of 1994 is to produce a comprehensive ideological, structural, and policy transformation that goes to the foundations of the American political order. In doing so, they are once again acting out their roles in a very old realignment scenario, as their predecessors did before them. What they are doing reflects an integrated vision of what this particular realignment is all about. A simple enumeration of change in 1994–95 summarizes a full-scale realignment syndrome:

- boilover leading to punctuated, shearing-off change at the level of the voting population
- abnormal and still rising ideological salience impelled by escalating political temperature and pressure
- dramatic change in the identity of at least some key political elites, including the abrupt elevation of an ideological extremist from the fringes of power in the House to its controlling spirit
- significant procedural innovations starting with the Contract itself, unique in the history of off-year congressional campaigns
- unprecedented voting solidarity within the new majority party in Congress

This converges toward a single picture. That picture is made hard to draw by virtue of the current shape of the literature, which is largely disparaging of the prospect of critical realignments and realignment theory.

Yet one can hardly fail to appreciate the possibility that 1994-as-realignment may turn out at the end of the day to be something of an optical illusion. Honesty requires canvassing the elements that do not fit such a scenario quite so neatly. We have already referred to the timing problem and the absence of a clear triggering event. There is a third element that may not fit as well. Historically, realignments have often been associated with substantial increases in turnout.[27] The post-1990 sequence has seen some of this, but not very much. True, the participation rate in presidential elections rose from 52.2 percent in 1988 to 56.8 percent in 1992, but 1988 was a historic low point, and the 1992 turnout remained within the sixth-electoral-era trading range established in 1972. The 1994 turnout for House races was 38 percent—about a two-point increase from the abysmal levels reached in 1986 and 1990, but no vast mobilization either. The Republican "revolution" of 1995 rests on the support of one-fifth of the American adult citizenry. This reflects a prime reality of 1994, a political artifact of what E.E. Schattschneider long ago called the "mobilization of bias" within the American political system.[28] The bias still apparently dominates. In March 1995, the pollster Andrew Kohut remarked that Democratic Party supporters still appeared to be "asleep out there": only 16 percent of them are "paying close attention" to what is going on in Washington, compared with 26 percent of Republican supporters. The whole election was marked by very asymmetrical energizing and consolidation of the Republican, but not the Democratic, base. If countermobilization does develop in or after 1996, it will inevitably be reflected in a considerable jump in turnout. In any event, it has not happened yet.

Notwithstanding these elements of anomaly in the picture we have been painting, one is struck by change factors that may well portend a *deepening* Republican control of Congress in the immediate future. First, one should consider interested money and its possible effects on future campaigns. In his new book *Golden Rule,* Thomas Ferguson reports something quite unprecedented since the beginning of FEC financial accounting in the 1970s: a vast, last-minute shift of campaign contributions into Republican coffers.[29] One can interpret this in a variety of ways. The most parsimonious explanation, given most literature on campaign finance, is that it had become clear to the knowledgeable quite a few weeks in advance that a Republican electoral surge was in the making. What is sought is not ideological purity but what political scientists usually call "access"—custom-fitting public policy to particular clients, hitherto provided by Democrats for more than a generation. One could read this last-minute 1994 switch as simply a rational-choice exercise in placing bets and buying access with the other side in case it won the election. But a further point to consider is that access strategies are also linked to ideological congruence with the party of business.[30] The financial advantage of the Republicans was somewhat offset in the past by the Democrats' grip on congressional power and the money that seeming permanence of control attracted. The Democrats' loss of control, combined with the convergence of both interest-based and ideological contributions to the Republicans, could prove damaging to Democratic financial prospects. This alteration has received less attention in postelection commentary than it deserves.

The second point has to do with the South and its relationship to the national political balance in Congress. Regional secular realignment toward the Republicans has been under way in this region for decades. This has typically taken the form of bursts forward in such elections as those of 1972 and 1980, followed by little change for a number of elections thereafter. This has given Democrats a substantial if constantly diminishing regional advantage (29 seats by 1992) in their bid for control of the House. In 1994, a third burst converted a regional Democratic margin from 77–48 to a Republican one of 64–61 in the former Confederate states. There is every reason to suppose that secular realignment in this region has not run its course: an eventual *Republican* advantage from this region of twenty-five to thirty seats seems far from unlikely.

Two conclusions emerge from these considerations. First, in the future partisan control of the House is likely to change hands far more frequently than all but the very oldest of us can remember. Second, when Democrats win control of the House at all, their majorities are likely to be far smaller than they were across the forty-year period of ascendancy terminated in

1994. And, given the true policy balance among voting Democratic representatives, the prospects for extended conservative—if not necessarily always formally Republican—control of the House of Representatives in the years ahead seem very bright.

One further reasonable interpolation can be made from the scene immediately before us. Extreme ideological polarization will be the order of the day in Washington, including, increasingly, the Senate. The welfare-reform debate in the House on 24 March 1995 gives us more than a clue as to what to expect. Democratic Representative Cynthia McKinney, an African American from Georgia, read from a letter sent to her office by a Texas man, obviously white, referring to "Negro females who pop out bastard Negro children like monkeys in the jungle." Representative John Mica (R-Fla.) held up a sign on the House floor reading, "Don't feed the alligators." Though he was good enough to concede that people are not alligators, he insisted on the analogy to convey the point that the current welfare system also violated the natural order. Another Republican, from Wyoming, found parallels between wolves and welfare recipients.

For his part, thirty-four-year Democratic veteran Sam Gibbons of Florida called such remarks the most outrageous he had heard during his whole time on Capitol Hill, and added: "We have a millionaire from Florida comparing children to alligators, and a gentlewoman in red has compared children to wolves. That tops it all!" The newspaper from which this colloquy is taken carried the story on page one with a lead headline *Savage debate scars House's welfare vote,* and a subhead: "Rhetoric includes parallels between GOP and Nazis, aid recipients and animals."[31] When we academics speak in terms of abstractions such as escalated polarization, it helps to give concreteness to such terms from time to time. We are now evidently moving toward increased polarization. Nor is the above debate the only late-breaking development along these lines. In announcing his decision not to seek reelection in 1996, Senator James J. Exon (D-Neb.) gave as his main reason "the ever-increasing vicious polarization of the electorate, the us-against-them mentality." Exon went on to say:

> The traditional art of workable compromises for the ultimate good of all, the essence of democracy, has demonstrably eroded. The hate level fueled by attack ads has unfortunately become the measure of a successful campaign. As long as money and plenty of it continues to pour in, absent campaign spending limits, the deterioration will continue.[32]

At this juncture, one can only speculate regarding the prospects for Republicans' success in their bid to produce realignment across the political system. As much of their program amounts to undeclared—if hotly denied—class warfare, it is possible that countermobilization among the disfavored many who will bear the brunt of the pain will duly materialize. But this requires both entrepreneurial political elites and, as Professor Ferguson would insist, financial investors in our money-driven electoral system. It is anything but a foregone conclusion that such countermobilization will in fact emerge. If that fails to happen, then the new political order of Republican ascendancy may last for quite a while.

And yet, one cannot but be impressed with the extent to which the keen ideological edge among the Republican winners of 1994 has overridden so many conventional norms of American politics. If the Contract is "the Republican way of governing," it can only retain an adequate political base even in our shrunken active electorate if these norms among the Great White Middle remain overridden by their fears, their sense of threat, their existential crisis. Two of these norms may be mentioned. The first is that American voters as a whole usually have little taste for ideological politics or ideological politicians. Parties who temporarily forget this norm and offer such ideology to the voters are not acting as rational vote maximizers in Anthony Downs's sense, and—as with the Republicans in 1964 or the Democrats in 1972—have gone down to thundering defeat at the hands of the voters. The second point to bear in mind is that the American public as a whole sorts itself out in *two* liberal-conservative dimensions, not one. It tends modally to be ideologically conservative (against big government in general), but also operationally liberal (favoring concrete programs of benefits, programs that only an activist and sometimes even competent federal government can deliver). Can a Republican strategy that insists on fusing ideology and the operational dimension of policymaking into a single, consistent right-wing package prevail against these norms, and if so, for how long? One wonders whether the huge transfer of wealth and other resources upward that is embedded in the Republicans' grand design could be implemented in any other capitalist democracy short of bringing democracy itself to a more or less violent end. Granted the extreme American skew toward the well-off in the organization of effective political power across the class structure, such a spectacular outcome may not be necessary here.[33] But even in the American case, one rarely sees bet-the-bank politics on this grandiose scale. The earlier Reaganite effort to combat the growth of the state and its fiscal crisis foundered in part on its failure to crack Democratic control of the House of Representatives. It also was fifteen years earlier in the cycle of the politics of Democratic decline. Social harmony through public expenditures thus generally continued as it had since New Deal times. The price of these deadlocked conditions was an explosion in the size of the national debt. Now, granted the fact that one-fifth of this vastly expanded debt is owned today by foreigners and that international capital markets increasingly call the tune, that old game is over, probably for good.

Thus the Republicans see the future with crystal clarity within the limits of their own ideological analysis of the situation. But given their mentality and the constituent and investor interests that support them, their vision must inevitably appear to a great many other Americans as a one-sided, even brutal and heartless, exercise in class favoritism. They are playing "go for broke" politics on a scale beyond any historical precedent that readily comes to mind. The Democrats, for their part, as befits the party of operational liberalism, can be expected to stress the concrete, the specific human-interest impact of policy in its appeals to the electorate. In their turn, they are now and will continue framing the issues in terms of tax breaks for the rich versus school lunches for children.

At the loftiest level of contestation, the challenge the Republicans have launched against the preexisting order of things rests on their ideological conviction that there is no objective or legitimate reason for the existence of a domestically powerful or competent federal government. Many or most others not sharing that ideology would come to the opposite conclusion—and much of the history not only of this but of other advanced capitalist democracies over the past half-century would seem to support them. The present political struggle thus amounts to a colossal clinical experiment to decide this issue. The stakes in this experiment are as high as stakes have been in any realignment in American political history. For the foreseeable future, accordingly, we are condemned to live in what an old Chinese curse is said to have called "interesting times."

Conclusion: Realignment Leading to What?

One supposes that the most important reason for doubting that 1994 will inaugurate a classic partisan realignment at the end of the day is that it is difficult to imagine that the durability criterion can be met. Is it possible for a stable partisan regime order lasting a full generation to develop and flourish as in the past? The full integration of the United States into a world economy lessens the control that politicians of any party have over the nation's economic fate. This, in turn, raises substantial doubts as to whether a stable party regime order can emerge.

We may find, nonetheless, that substantial parts of the Republican agenda will be put into place even if Bill Clinton is reelected in 1996, and even if Republicans lose control of either or both houses of Congress. Some form of "devolution revolution," for example, is strongly implied by spokesmen on both sides of the aisle. Renewed and urgent effort to move toward balancing the budget will be impelled by the force of financial market-driven necessity. If so, and if the Republican solution is also rejected in its turn, some other budget restricting option will have to be sought. As moving in any such direction inevitably negates much of what the Democratic Party has stood for since the New Deal, it is not easy at the moment to see such budget-constraining solutions emerging from its ranks.

Both Newt Gingrich and other Republican leaders have claimed that if the Republican effort breaks down, terminal meltdown of the entire party system might ensue. Discounting for the obvious political motivations driving such arguments, the apprehension of the Republican leadership may be not only sincere but also accurately prophetic. Zero-sum conflicts often place powerful stresses on the system in which they arise. Democracies are not usually well suited to tolerate elite efforts to apportion pain to their constituents. With this in mind, it is entirely possible, if less likely, that 1994 may prove to be the gateway not to old-style realignment but to a wholly unprecedented breakdown of traditional political order.

Nevertheless, 1994 constitutes a sharp enough break with a previously stable state of affairs to imply the emergence of some sort of seventh electoral era and its affiliated regime order. This order, assuming that it emerges, will very likely have important similarities in policy orientation to the fourth era, the "system of 1896–1932." Moreover, the possibility should be raised, particularly in view of the thrust of the foregoing discussion, that an even greater turning point may be at hand. In his recent work in American constitutional history, the legal scholar Bruce Ackerman locates three supreme "constitutional moments" and three American republics chronologically defined and bounded by them.[34] These moments are the Creation in the 1780s, Reconstruction in the 1860s, and the New Deal in the 1930s. They are associated with critical realignments of exceptional transforming potency. (The other three are not canvassed, though it is evident that each of them had significant elements of constitutional transformation in the course of their development.) Might there not be the possibility that the present politics of upheaval may lead to a fourth American republic?

One could make a certain case for such a surmise, given the global and domestic context and the magnitude of the constitutional stakes involved in the current political struggle. One clue to this may arise from the apparent likelihood that these macrocontexts are rapidly closing the opportunity space for the continued existence of welfare states of the classic post-1932 pattern. A precondition for these states everywhere was the existence of a long historical interval between two world-integrated economic orders. The first such order dominated the world before 1933 and especially before 1914, and was enforced by the imperatives of the gold standard. The second of these orders has been very rapidly taking shape before our eyes and is linked to the processes and dynamics of a globalized economy. In the interval, national states and their leaders could have fundamental latitude to shape the national political economy, and they exercised their power and opportunity accordingly.

In that now vanishing world, leftist political forces could and did make decisive contributions to the building of welfare states. An essential precondition of this, to be sure, was a conjuncture that permitted sustained economic growth. With the lapse of these conditions and the reintegration of the world market, the opportunity space both for the left and for the welfare states it did so much to create has rapidly begun to close.[35] Moreover, as the eminent historian Eric Hobsbawm has recently emphasized, the war-filled and thus state-enhancing "short twentieth century" that began in 1914 and ended around 1991 is itself now a part of history.[36] On all planes, we move into a radically different twenty-first century a decade early. Considering the magnitude of reshaping forces now in play, and their implications as to what democratic politics can continue to be about, a view that we are en route to the fourth American republic does not seem far-fetched, nor does the possibility that 1994 might have had something important to do with this transition.

Our task here has been to attempt to site a manifestly important election into a broader context and to probe its meaning. Beyond that, we conclude with a very brief consideration of cyclical influences in politics. Cyclical theories usually presuppose a negation of the notion of unilinear progress commonplace in social science—a notion that also provides an important ingredient in American political culture. So much that was once thought unassailably achievable through politics and government is now called into doubt. The extent to which "progress" or "political development" in America is illusory can only be underscored. The mystery of how political cycles themselves break down and are replaced by other forces of change is too large a matter to be resolved here. It is enough to say that 1994 provides the most recent evidence that the electoral/political cycles of realignment are still alive and well.

APPENDIX TABLE

GENERAL DISTRIBUTION OF ELECTION OUTCOMES BY VALUE

(+ OR −) OF $d/_{sd}$, 1790/1834–1994

	Number of cases (N)			
	North and West		State legislature seats	
Value of $d/_{sd}$	House of Rep. votes	House of Rep. seats	Non-South	U.S.
0–0.99	54	59	41	40
1.00–1.99	27	20	21	22
2.00–2.49	4	7	6	4
2.50–2.99	5	5	2	3
3.00–3.49	5	3	2	4
3.50–3.99	1	2	1	0
4.00–4.49	0	1	2	0
4.50–4.99	2	0	0	0
5.00 and above	1	2	1	3
Total	99	99	76	76

NOTE: Another way of indicating how remarkable the 1994 values are is to note how many of the global total lie below them: 96 of 99 for House votes; 98 of 99 for House seats (both North and West only); 73 of 76 for nonsouthern state legislative seats; and 75 of 76 for U.S. state legislative seats.

It may be of interest to add election years for the next-lowest and still rather rare category (2.50–2.99) below the 3 cutoff (see table 12.3, p. 377, for higher values). They include the following, in descending order:

House votes: 1920, 1812, 1854, 1824, 1840.

House seats: 1912, 1824, 1802, 1894, 1890.

State legislative seats:

Non-South, 1854, 1864.

United States, 1870, 1888, 1912.

Notes

1. A spate of narrative accounts can be expected. The first to come to hand as this essay was being written is the useful contribution by Clyde Wilcox, *The Latest American Revolution? The 1994 Elections and Their Implications for Governance* (New York: St. Martin's Press, 1995). See also the often illuminating early survey report from the Roper Center: Everett C. Ladd, ed., *America at the Polls 1994* (Storrs, Conn.: Roper Center, 1995). It is noteworthy that also, shortly before the election, *Congressional Quarterly Weekly Report* explicitly canvassed the realignment questions, even including an 1896 cartoon of William Jennings Bryan and his Cross of Gold on the cover (5 November 1994, cover and pp. 3127–32). Their conclusions on the question are more negative than mine.

2. On the 1992 election, see Paul Abramson, John H. Aldrich, and David W. Rohde, *Change and Continuity in the 1992 Elections* (Washington, D.C.: CQ Press, 1994); Michael Nelson, ed., *The Elections of 1992* (Washington, D.C.: CQ Press, 1993); and Gerald M. Pomper, ed., *The Election of 1992* (Chatham, N.J.: Chatham House, 1993).

3. Gary C. Jacobson, "Congress: Unusual Year, Unusual Election," in Nelson, *Elections of 1992*, 156.

4. Another portent of things to come was also registered in the South in 1992. From 1982 to 1990, the mean number of Democratic representatives elected with no major-party opposition was 28 (36.8 percent of the delegation), compared with nine (22.1 percent) on the Republican side. In 1992, Democratic free rides suddenly and steeply declined, falling to six (7.8 percent) compared with eight Republicans (16.7 percent). Complete reversal then materialized in 1994. Only three of sixty-five Democratic incumbents in the South were without Republican challengers (4.9 percent), while fully twenty of the forty-four GOP incumbents won without Democratic opposition (45.4 percent).

5. Ladd, *America at the Polls 1994*, 156.

6. To be precise on the matter, since 1790 this has occurred in 13 of 103 elections, favoring the parties as follows: Democratic–Republican/Democratic: 1792, 1810, 1818, 1868, 1896, 1922, and 1948; Federalist/Whig/Republican: 1792, 1796, 1812, 1846, 1894, 1938, and 1994.

7. *Congressional Quarterly Weekly Report*, 18 February 1995, 496–97.

8. This is not my view alone. See John H. Aldrich and Richard C. Niemi, "The Sixth American Party System: Electoral Change, 1952–1992," in *Broken Contract: Changing Relationships between Americans and Their Government*, ed. Stephen C. Craig (Boulder, Colo.: Westview Press, 1996).

9. I have given my own most recent interpretation of these processes in two related essays: "Critical Realignment: Dead or Alive?" in *The End of Realignment?* ed. Byron E. Shafer (Madison: University of Wisconsin Press, 1991), 101–39; and "Pattern Recognition and 'Doing' Political History: Art, Science or Bootless Enterprise?" in *The Dynamics of American Politics*, ed. Lawrence Dodd and Calvin Jillson (Boulder, Colo.: Westview Press, 1994), 59–82.

10. Louis Hartz, *The Liberal Tradition in America* (New York: Harcourt, Brace, 1955).

11. Frank R. Baumgartner and Bryan D. Jones, *Agendas and Instability in American Politics* (Chicago: University of Chicago Press, 1993), esp. 1–24.

12. Niles Eldredge and Stephen Jay Gould, "Punctuated Equilibria: An Alternative to Phyletic Gradualism" (1972), conveniently reprinted in Niles Eldredge,

Time Frames: The Evolution of Punctuated Equilibria (Princeton: Princeton University Press, 1989), 193–223.

13. William F. Riker, Liberalism against Populism: A Confrontation between the Theory of Democracy and the Theory of Social Choice (Prospect Heights, Ill.: Waveland Press, 1982), esp. 170–96, 233–53.

14. A useful survey of this, the "Chicago School,"and other groupings of theorists is contained in William C. Mitchell and Michael C. Munger, "Economic Models of Interest Groups: An Introductory Survey," American Journal of Political Science 35 (1991): 512–46. "The Virginians" (Buchanan, Tullock, Tollison, et al.) appears on pp. 523–31. As the authors point out, much of their work (notably on rent seeking) closely parallels that of Mancur Olson, especially his The Rise and Decline of Nations (New Haven: Yale University Press, 1982). It strikes me that Riker and these other authors provide the social science theoretical rationale for the Contract with America and such countermajoritarian rules changes as the 60 percent requirement for passing tax increases, as well as a proposed similar "supermajority" provision in the budget-balance amendment. Conventional arguments involving the asserted intent of the Framers, the Tenth Amendment, "liberty against government,"and other such things buttress this deconstructive vision from the traditional political theory side.

15. See Kenneth Boulding's interesting discussion of dialectical processes, and their location in society's threat system, in his A Primer of Social Dynamics: History as Dialectics and Development (New York: Free Press, 1970), esp. 37–53. Rhetoric and debates in and surrounding Marxism have contributed to closing off social science analysis of this phenomenon. It deserves much more attention than it typically gets.

16. Aldrich and Niemi, Sixth American Party System.

17. A value of 4 (both tails) would cover 0.006 percent of the normal curve. Higher values, while they duly occur in the data we report here, are at the level of chemical traces in a normal-curve context.

18. As the appendix table shows, four-fifths of the observations in these four columns have values lower than 2 (81.8 percent, 79.8 percent, 81.6 percent, and 81.6 percent, respectively).

19. The only group that fits into the top sixteen of the seventy-four analyzed (maximum pro-Republican swing) in terms of its raw magnitude of swing, but not in terms of our quotient measure, $d \div sd$ (or d/sd), is the Republican-identifier group. The reason, of course, is that this particular group had a relatively large standard deviation around its 1984–92 mean, and indeed across the whole period from 1980 on. The 1994 swing of 12 percent (only 7 percent voting Democratic) is very large by any standard. Moreover, in this group unlike virtually all others, a strong movement toward GOP voting consolidation is already visible in the 1992 election: one more reason for including it in the whole sequence.

20. For a particularly grim and compelling account of deindustrialization and its social consequences, involving the near-obliteration of a once-thriving and now "throwaway" community, see William Serrin, Homestead: The Glory and Tragedy of an American Steel Town (New York: Times Books/Random House, 1992).

21. Kevin Phillips, Arrogant Capital: Washington, Wall Street and the Frustration of American Politics (Boston: Little, Brown, 1994), 77.

22. Business Week, 20 March 1965, 48. The whole article, "Hot Money," (46–50) repays reading, as does the editorial on p. 128. One should also note that

Mr. Rohatyn has also been an influential figure in Democratic Party politics over the past two decades.

23. Kevin Phillips, *Boiling Point: Democrats, Republicans and the Decline of Middle-Class Prosperity* (New York: Random House, 1993).

24. In addition to the works by Phillips cited above, see Benjamin N. Friedman, *Day of Reckoning: The Consequences of American Economic Policy under Reagan and After* (New York: Random House, 1988); Paul Krugman, *The Age of Diminished Expectations: U.S. Economic Policy in the 1990s* (Cambridge: MIT Press, 1990); Paul Krugman, *Peddling Prosperity: Economic Sense and Nonsense in the Age of Diminished Expectations* (New York: Norton, 1994); and Donald L. Bartlett and James B. Steele, *America: What Went Wrong?* (Kansas City, Mo.: Andrews & McMeel, 1992). This list could be extended a very long way indeed.

25. Remarks as a member of a panel of opinion analysts on *The MacNeil-Lehrer NewsHour*, 17 March 1995.

26. This euthanasia was supposedly permanently administered in *U.S. v. Darby*, 312 U.S. 100 (1941), overruling *Hammer v. Dagenhart*, 247 U.S. 251 (1918). Note, however, the temporary revival of the Tenth Amendment as a constitutional barrier to certain kinds of federal regulation of state-government activities in *National League of Cities v. Usery*, 426 U.S. 833 (Rehnquist, J., for the Court), which also overrules a case (from the Warren era) that stood in the way. The amendment then seemed to be reinterred again—along with the *Usery* case—in a 5–4 decision nine years later (*Garcia v. San Antonio Metropolitan Transit Authority*, 469 U.S. 528 [1985]); but Chief Justice Rehnquist, now in dissent, served notice that he regarded this as only a temporary setback. This is a particular area where "stay tuned" seems a good motto. It seems perfectly reasonable to suppose that Tenth Amendment jurisprudence may have a real future in the next political era, and the judicial rediscovery of other hitherto unsuspected virtues in the jurisprudence of the 1895–1936 era may also occur.

27. This generalization, of course, has its exceptions. The 1968–71 realignment was associated with *declining*, not rising, turnout; and the system that developed in its wake was singularly marked by subsequent and class-skewed declines that reached a historic trough between 1986 and 1990. This makes perfect sense in the context of a realignment that was fundamentally antipartisan in character—the first such in our history. By much the same token, the system that emerged from the very high turnout upheaval of the 1890s acquired profound antipartisan features not long after its implantation. Again characteristically, this was linked to the largest proportionate demobilization of the electorate in American history.

28. E.E. Schattschneider, *The Semisovereign People* (New York: Holt, Rinehart and Winston, 1960).

29. Thomas Ferguson, "Postscript: The 1994 Explosion," *Golden Rule: The Investment Theory of Party Competition and the Logic of Money-Driven Political Systems* (Chicago: University of Chicago Press, 1995), 359–95. Ferguson is careful to point out that only preliminary data were available at the time of writing.

30. Naturally, the Republicans are as aggressively proactive on this front as they have been on all others. See the story by Richard L. Berke in the *New York Times*, 20 March 1995, A1, A11, with its three-part headline summary: "Republicans Rule Lobbyists' World with Strong Arm / Past Slights Recalled / New Congressional Majority Seeks to Collect Donations and Change Allegiances."

31. *Austin American-Statesman,* 25 March 1995, A1, A8.

32. *Austin American-Statesman,* 18 March 1995, A3. It may also be useful to refer at this point to Chalmers Johnson, *Revolutionary Change* (Boston: Little, Brown, 1966), esp. 59–118. Johnson employs a cyclical model taken from the work of the anthropologist Anthony Wallace on the Seneca Indians. This is a five-stage process model, passing from homeostatic equilibrium to increased cultural stress and thence to cultural distortion, revolution (or disintegration), and thence, if surviving, to a new homeostatic equilibrium. This model has close analogies to that famously proposed for scientific research communities by Thomas R. Kuhn, *The Structure of Scientific Revolutions,* 2d ed. (Chicago: University of Chicago Press, 1970)—and, for that matter, to critical-realignment processes. One chief feature of the cultural-distortion phase immediately antecedent to revitalizing revolution is the emergence of ideologically polarized interest groups. In my own view, such a situation has clearly emerged in the United States.

33. Both points were first raised in the context of the first "right-turn" wave of around 1979–81 by Adam Przeworski and Michael Wallerstein in 1982. See their "Democratic Capitalism at the Crossroads," in *The Political Economy,* ed. Thomas Ferguson and Joel Rogers (Armonk, N.Y.: M.E. Sharpe, 1984), 335–48. The analysis, needless to say, rings true today.

34. Bruce Ackerman, *We the People: Foundations* (Cambridge: Harvard University Press, 1991).

35. This was the subject of a conference of German, British, and American scholars that I attended at the University of Göttingen in November 1994. My role was to deliver a keynote address that was to initiate discussion, the main theme of the conference being the diminishing prospects for various lefts and welfare states in the developed world. This presentation ("What Future for the Left?") will appear in a German-language work edited by Peter Lösche, tentatively entitled *What's Left for the Left?* in English paraphrase. The discussion here grows out of the analysis presented there, though in much truncated form.

36. Eric Hobsbawm, *The Age of Extremes: A History of the World, 1914–1991* (New York: Pantheon, 1994).

Index

in Confederate states, 364, 379
in Congress, 205, 263–64
congressional gains of, 365
and "Contract with America," 14, 44, 47, 197–98
and control of state legislatures, 192, 365–66
and health-care reform, 117–18
ideological bases of, 388
increase in campaign funds of, 385
increase in strength of, 11–12
interparty confrontation by, 267
and majority of governorships, 192
as majority in House, 192
and realignment, 380–88
regional secular realignment toward, 385
South tilts toward, 198
takeover of Congress, 282
Resolution Trust Company, 132
"Responsive competence," 53, 55
Responsiveness, vs. responsibility, 122
Richards, Ann, 339, 365–67
Richardson, Bill, 110
Riche, Martha, 170–71
Ridley Group, 227
Riker, William, 372–73, 374
Riley, Richard, 23, 147
Rivlin, Alice, 24, 28, 241
Robinson, Randall, 310
Rockman, Bert A., on Clinton/Congress relations, 4, 10, 11
Roe v. *Wade*, 146, 148–49, 150, 343
Rohatyn, Felix, 381
Roosevelt, Franklin D., 74–75, 326

Roosevelt, Theodore, 300, 379
Rose, Richard, 326
Rose law firm, 231
Rosin, Hanna, 220
Rubin, Robert E., 25, 27, 77–78
Rumsfeld, Donald, 79
Rushdie, Salman, 221
Russia, 291
Rust v. *Sullivan*, 152
Rwanda, 68, 301

Salokar, Rebecca Mae, 156
Sarajevo, 306
Sarokin, H. Lee, 141, 142
Scalia, Antonin, 148
Schattschneider, E.E., 384
Schlesinger, Arthur, Jr., 298
Schneider, William, 251
Schumer, Charles, 108
Scowcroft, Brent, 77, 291
Senate
  Democratic party influence in, 94–95
  majorities in, 16, 192
  party cohesion in, 93
  Republican gains in, 365
  Republican obstructionism in, 118
Senate Armed Services Committee, 101, 153, 223, 268
Senate Finance Committee, 114, 115, 248
Senate Judiciary Committee, 141, 143, 152
Senate Labor and Human Resources Committee, 114
Senatorial courtesy, 134, 135
Senior Executive Service (SES), 8, 167, 168, 182
Separated system
  Clinton and, 36–41
  presidency in, 16–18
Separation of powers, 4, 5
  and divided government, 54
Sessions, William, 131

Shalala, Donna, 39, 71, 114, 281
Shalikashvili, John, 67, 318
Shearing-off effect, 374
Shelby, Richard C., 44, 192, 365
Simpson, Alan K., 142
Sinclair, Barbara, 3, 5–6
"Single payer" plan, 276
Skinner, Samuel K., 79
Skowronek, Stephen, 213, 231
Smith, Dudley, 316
Smith, Gaddis, 296
Smith, Robert C., 149
Smith, William French, 129
Social Security Act of 1935, 258
Society of Manufacturing Engineers, 214
Solomon, Burt, 165, 168
Somalia, 42, 60, 67, 68, 247, 291, 294, 296, 301, 303, 304–5, 341–43
Souljah, Sister, 165, 338
Souter, David H., 150
South Korea, 311
Split-party government, 45
Sporadic engagement, as presidential style, 298
Srebrenica, 306
Stanley, David, 167
Stanley, Harold, 3, 8
Stark, Pete, 276
Stenholm, Charles W., 266
Stephanopoulos, George, 70, 79, 190, 220, 248, 348
Stevens, John Paul, 150
Stillwell, Lee, 226
Stockman, David, 272
Strategic Arms Reduction Treaties, 313
Strauss, Robert, 230
Sullivan, Michael J., 140
Sullivan principles, 309
Sundquist, James L., 20
Sununu, John, 53, 61, 70, 79
"Super 310," 77

About the Contributors

Joel D. Aberbach is professor of political science and policy studies and director of the Center for American Politics and Public Policy at the University of California, Los Angeles. His books include *Keeping a Watchful Eye: The Politics of Congressional Oversight*.

Larry Berman is professor and chair of the Department of Political Science at the University of California, Davis. He is the author of *Lyndon Johnson's War: The Road to Stalemate in Vietnam* and *Planning a Tragedy: The Americanization of the War in Vietnam*.

Walter Dean Burnham holds the Frank C. Erwin, Jr., Chair in government at the University of Texas at Austin. He is the author of *The Current Crisis in American Politics* and editor of *The American Prospect Reader in American Politics*.

Colin Campbell is University Professor of Public Policy at Georgetown University, where he heads the Graduate Public Policy Program. His books on executive leadership in Anglo-American democracies include *Managing the Presidency*, which won the American Political Science Association's Neustadt Prize for the best book on the presidency.

George C. Edwards III is Distinguished Professor of Political Science and the director of the Center for Presidential Studies at Texas A&M University. He is the author of *Presidential Approval* and *At the Margins: Presidential Influence in Congress*.

Emily O. Goldman is associate professor of political science, director of international relations, and codirector of the Joint Center for International and Security Studies at the University of California, Davis. She is also the author of *Sunken Treaties: Naval Arms Control between the Wars*.

Joseph Hinchliffe is an attorney and a Ph.D. candidate in political science at the University of Illinois at Urbana-Champaign.

Charles O. Jones is the Hawkins Professor of Political Science at the University of Wisconsin, Madison, and in 1994–95 is the Douglas Dillon Visiting Fellow at the Brookings Institution. He is the author of *Separate but Equal Branches: Congress and the Presidency* and *The Presidency in a Separated System.*

David M. O'Brien is professor in the Department of Government and Foreign Affairs at the University of Virginia. He is the author of *Storm Center: The Supreme Court in American Politics* and annual editions of *Supreme Court Watch.*

Paul J. Quirk is professor in the Department of Political Science and the Institute of Government and Public Affairs at the University of Illinois at Urbana-Champaign. He is the author of *Industry Influence in Federal Regulatory Agencies.*

Bert A. Rockman is University Professor at the University of Pittsburgh, where he teaches in the Department of Political Science and the Graduate School of Public and International Affairs. He is the author of *The Leadership Question: The Presidency and the American System.*

Barbara Sinclair is professor of political science at the University of California, Riverside. She is the author of *The Transformation of the U.S. Senate,* which won the American Political Science Association Fenno Prize in 1990.

Harold W. Stanley is associate professor of political science at Rochester University. He is the author of *Voter Mobilization and the Politics of Race* and coauthor with Richard Niemi of *Vital Statistics of American Politics,* 5th edition.

Graham K. Wilson is professor of political science at the University of Wisconsin–Madison. He is author of *Interest Groups* and *Business and Politics,* and coauthor with Colin Campbell of *The End of Whitehall.* Wilson is the editor of *Governance.*